Assessing Reading

THE CAMBRIDGE LANGUAGE ASSESSMENT SERIES

*Series editors:* J. Charles Alderson and Lyle F. Bachman

In this series:

**Assessing Languages for Specific Purposes** by Dan Douglas
**Assessing Vocabulary** by John Read

# Assessing Reading

*J. Charles Alderson*

PUBLISHED BY THE PRESS SYNDICATE OF THE UNIVERSITY OF CAMBRIDGE
The Pitt Building, Trumpington Street, Cambridge, United Kingdom

CAMBRIDGE UNIVERSITY PRESS
The Edinburgh Building, Cambridge CB2 2RU, UK   http://www.cup.cam.ac.uk
40 West 20th Street, New York, NY 10011–4211, USA   http://www.cup.org
10 Stamford Road, Oakleigh, Melbourne 3166, Australia
Ruiz de Alarcón 13, 28014 Madrid, Spain

First published 2000

Printed in the United Kingdom at the University Press, Cambridge

*Typeface* 9.5/13pt Utopia   [CE]

*A catalogue record for this book is available from the British Library*

*Library of Congress Cataloguing in Publication data applied for*

ISBN 0 521 59000 0 hardback
ISBN 0 521 59999 7 paperback

**To my parents, John and Rose Mary Alderson.**

I wish they had lived to see this book, for their support and encouragement to me throughout my education and beyond were of the utmost importance. I only hope they would not have been too disappointed that I did not become the Town Clerk of Burnley, as my mother hoped.

# Contents

# Series Editor's Preface

Reading, through which we can access worlds of ideas and feelings, as well as the knowledge of the ages and visions of the future, is at once the most extensively researched and the most enigmatic of the so-called language skills. Reading has been investigated from numerous perspectives – by linguists, psychologists, educators and second language researchers, and a huge volume of research is now available. Reading also plays a critical role in applied linguistics research and in the day-to-day professional life of the language teacher. Similarly, the assessment of reading ability is of critical importance in a wide range of educational and professional settings, and the need for expertise in this area is widespread. This book brings together what is known about reading and its assessment into one volume in order to provide practical guidance to teachers and others who need to develop tests of reading, be this for their own classes, for large-scale proficiency tests or for conducting research in applied linguistics.

The author of this book, Charles Alderson, has extensive experience in both teaching and testing reading, and has conducted considerable research himself in these areas. He is one of the world's leading authorities in language assessment in general, and in the assessment of reading in particular. Furthermore, his long experience as an educator, mentor and teacher trainer has enabled him to distill from the vastness of the reading research literature those concepts, ideas and frameworks that are most relevant to reading assessment, and to present an array of often complex information in a way that is readily accessible to practitioners.

This book guides the reader through a wealth of research in reading and assessment, with a clear focus on practical applications, and is illustrated throughout with examples from actual tests of reading. Alderson first surveys the theoretical and conceptual foundations of reading, clearly delineating the implications of these for reading assessment. He then draws on his own experience in assessment to discuss practical issues such as developing specifications for reading tests, designing and writing reading test tasks, and specifying the purposes for which reading tests are intended. The discussion draws on a variety of situations, including the classroom assessment of second-language reading and first-language literacy, large-scale assessments for high-stakes decisions in educational settings and assessment for professional certification and employment. The main points are illustrated with a range of examples, including multiple-choice items, cloze tests, as well as assessment techniques such as reading aloud, impressionistic judgements, miscue analysis, and self-assessments. The last two chapters explore areas that have to date been largely considered too difficult to assess: developmental stages or levels of reading ability, and the strategies and processes involved in reading.

Throughout the book, Alderson draws on both the theoretical insights from reading research and the fundamental requirements and demands of assessment, and describes how these can fruitfully inform reading assessment practice. In a nutshell, this book offers a principled approach to the design, development and use of reading tests, and thus exemplifies the purpose of this series to bring together theory and research in applied linguistics in a way that is useful to language testing practitioners.

Lyle F. Bachman

# Acknowledgements

The editors, author and publishers are grateful to the authors, publishers and others who have given permission for the use of copyright material identified in the text. It has not been possible to identify, or trace, sources of all the materials used and in such cases the publishers would welcome information from copyright owners.

*DIALANG Assessment Specifications for Reading Comprehension*, Version 6, 18 February 1998. Pages 8 and 9 © University of Jyväskylä: Finland; Council of Europe. 1996. *Modern Languages: learning teaching, assessment. A Common European Framework of Reference.* Strasbourg: Council for Cultural Co-operation, Education Committee. Page 175; Bachman, L. F. and A. S. Palmer. 1996. *Language Testing in Practice.* © Oxford University Press Page 49/50; Toney, T. 1984. © The British Council; *Certificate in Advanced English CAE handbook*, July 1998. Page 14. With permission of University of Cambridge Local Examinations Syndicate; *Key English Test KET Handbook.* January 1998. Pages 9 and 11 With permission of University of Cambridge Local Examinations Syndicate; *British Rail text, Times text*: The Oxford Delegacy Examinations in English as a Foreign Language © OCR; Kundera, M. 1996. *The Book of Laughter and Forgetting.* © Faber and Faber. Page 37. (translation by Aaron Asher); *International English Language Testing System, Specimen Material*, April 1997. Pages 10, 11, 12, 14, 15, 16, 17, 18, 19 and 20. With permission of University of Cambridge Local Examinations Syndicate, The British Council and IDP; *Cambridge Examination in English for Language Teachers Handbook.* December 1998. With permission of University of Cambridge Local Examinations Syndicate; de Witt, R. 1997. *How to prepare for IELTS.* Pages 63, 64 and 65. © The British Council; Chamot, A. U. 1982. *Read Right! Developing Survival Reading Skills.*

Minerva: New York, cited in Silberstein, S. 1994. *Techniques and Resources in Teaching Reading.* © Oxford University Press; Fordham, P., D. Holland and J. Millican. 1995. *Adult Literacy: A handbook for development workers.* Oxford: Oxfam/Voluntary Services Overseas. Page 116; Griffin, P., P. G. Smith, and L. E. Burrill. 1995. *The Literacy Profile Scales: towards effective assessment.* Belconnen, ACT: Australian Curriculum Studies Association, Inc. Pages 20, 21, 148 and 149; Urquhart, A. H. 1992. *Draft Band Descriptors for Reading.* Plymouth: College of St. Mark and St. John. Unpublished. Pages 34 and 35; *Certificates in Communicative Skills in English Handbook.* August 1999. Page 12. With permission of University of Cambridge Local Examinations Syndicate; Grellet, F. 1981. *Developing Reading Skills.* Cambridge: Cambridge University Press. Pages 12, 13, 32, 34, 60 and 62; Baudoin, E. M., E. S. Bober, M. A. Clarke, B. K. Dobson and S. Silberstein. 1988. *Reader's Choice.* (second edition). University of Michigan Press. Pages 82, 236, 237 and 238. Cited in Silberstein, S. 1994. *Techniques and Resources in Teaching Reading.* Oxford: Oxford University Press. Pages 45, 46, 47, 81, 82 and 83; Tomlinson, B., and R. Ellis. 1988. *Reading Advanced.* © Oxford University Press. Pages 2–6; Chang, F. R. 1983. *Mental Processes in Reading: a methodological review.* Reading Research Quarterly, 18 (2). International Reading Association. Page 218; Duffy, G. G., L. R. Roehler, E. Sivan, G. Rackcliffe, C. Book, M. S. Meloth, L. G. Vavrus, R. Wesselman, J. Putnam and D. Bassiri. 1987. *Effects of explaining the reasoning associated with using reading strategies.* Reading Research Quarterly. 22 (3). International Reading Association. Page 360.

# Abbreviations

| | |
|---|---|
| ACTFL | American Council for the Teaching of Foreign Languages |
| ALBSU | Adult Literacy Basic Skills Unit |
| ALTE | Association of Language Testers in Europe |
| ASLPR | Australian Secondary Language Proficiency Ratings |
| CAE | Certificate in Advanced English |
| CCSE | Certificate in Communicative Skills in English |
| CPE | Certificate of Proficiency in English |
| CUEFL | Communicative Use of English as a Foreign Language |
| EAP | English for Academic Purposes |
| EFL | English as a Foreign Language |
| ELTS | English Language Testing Service |
| EPTB | English Proficiency Test Battery |
| ESL | English as a Second Language |
| ETS | Educational Testing Service |
| FCE | First Certificate in English |
| GCSE | General Certificate of Secondary Education |
| IEA | International Association for the Evaluation of Educational Achievement |
| IELTS | International English Language Testing System |
| IRI | Informal Reading Inventory |
| JMB | Joint Matriculation Board of Northern Universities |
| KET | Key English Test |
| L1 | First Language |
| L2 | Second Language |
| NEA | Northern Examining Authorities |
| PET | Preliminary English Test |
| RSA | Royal Society of Arts |
| TEEP | Test in English for Educational Purposes |

| | |
|---|---|
| TLU | Target Language Use |
| TOEFL | Test of English as a Foreign Language |
| TOEIC | Test of English for International Communication |
| UCLES | University of Cambridge Local Examinations Syndicate |
| UETESOL | University Entrance Test in English for Speakers of Other Languages |

........................................................................................

# CHAPTER ONE

# The nature of reading

## Introduction

I am not the first person to say that an overview of the study of the nature of reading is impossible. The sheer volume of research on the topic belies any individual's ability to process, much less to synthesise, everything that is written. Similarly, the number of different theories of reading is simply overwhelming: what it is, how it is acquired and taught, how reading in a second language differs from reading in a first language, how reading relates to other cognitive and perceptual abilities, how it interfaces with memory. All these aspects of reading are important, but will probably never be brought together into a coherent and comprehensive account of what it is we do when we read. Added to this are the inevitable complications when we consider the complexities of analysing texts: since the nature of *what* we read must have some relation to *how* we read, then text analysis must be relevant to theories of reading and to research into reading. Yet the simple phrase 'text analysis' covers an enormous range of study within linguistics, which again no individual can hope to overview.

Any review, therefore, of 'the nature of reading' is bound to be somewhat pretentious, and this introductory chapter will inevitably be selective, rather than exhaustive. Yet consider the dilemma for anybody wishing to assess reading. In order to assess the **construct** – the ability we wish to test – we need to know what the construct is. In order to devise a test or assessment procedure for reading, we must surely appeal, if only intuitively, to some concept of what it means to read texts and to understand them. How can we possibly test whether somebody has understood a text if we do not know what we mean by 'understand'? How can we possibly diagnose somebody's 'reading problems' if we have no idea what might constitute a problem, and what the possible 'causes' might be? How can we possibly decide on what 'level' a reader is 'at' if we have no idea what 'levels of reading' might exist, and what it means to be 'reading at a particular level'? In short, those who need to test reading clearly need to develop some idea of what reading is, and yet that is an enormous task.

The fact is, however, that if we wait until we have a perfect understanding of our constructs before we begin to devise assessment instruments, then we will never begin test construction. Some might say: 'Good. Better not to start than to design something invalid that may do harm.' And we might have sympathy with such a position, yet the plain fact is that assessment of reading is necessary – we will look at the multitude of real-world needs for this throughout this book. To refuse to get involved in designing instruments would thus be irresponsible, and risk the danger that others, with a lesser understanding of what is involved in reading, might design the instruments instead, with more calamitous results. Thus, testers have to get involved in test construction even though they know in advance that their understanding of the phenomenon – the construct – is faulty, partial and possibly never perfectible.

The consolation, however, is that by designing admittedly imperfect tests, we are then enabled to study the nature of the tests and the abilities that appear to be being measured by those tests. This will in turn hopefully lead to a better understanding of what one has assessed, which should feed back into theory, and further research. Thus by doing testing, provided that we research what we design, we can contribute to a growing understanding of the construct.

This is a fundamental tenet of this volume and other books in the series: it is only by trying to operationalise our theories and our understandings of the constructs through our assessment instruments that we can explore and develop our understanding. The corollary is that we need to look to theory in order to have some idea of what it is we are trying to test. This is what I shall do shortly. Before I begin, however, I should acknowledge that another approach to test design seems possible, and indeed, potentially more practical, and that is, rather than starting with theory, to begin with **target situation language use**. In other words, to begin by determining the situations in which the persons to be assessed will need to 'read'; to analyse such situations; and then to devise assessment instruments which reflect reading in those target situations; and 'see' 'how well' our assessees can 'read'. Indeed, such approaches will be illustrated later in this book. Note, however, that even such an approach needs some crude notion of what we mean by the words in quotation marks: 'read', 'see' and 'how well'. 'How well' implies some sort of standard, at the very least some notion of comparison with how others read; 'see' implies that there are acceptable ways of externalising either how people are reading, or what they have understood of what they have read; 'read' implies that we know what it means to read, to process text meaning through some process of interaction with print.

Rather than continue in this vein indefinitely, we need to start somewhere, and I shall do so by considering the nature of reading.

## Process and product

It is commonplace to make a distinction between the **process** of reading, and the result of that process, the **product**. The process is what we mean by 'reading' proper: the interaction between a reader and the text. During that process, presumably, many things are happening. Not only is the reader looking at print, deciphering in some sense the marks on the page, 'deciding' what they 'mean' and how they relate to each other. The reader is presumably also 'thinking' about what he is reading: what it means to him, how it relates to other things he has read, to things he knows, to what he expects to come next in texts like this. He is presumably thinking about how useful, entertaining, boring, crazy, the text is. He may be consciously reflecting on the difficulties or ease he is experiencing when reading, and on ways of overcoming the difficulties or of continuing the pleasure. He may be completely unconscious of how he is reading, and of what is happening around him: he may be fully absorbed in 'reading'.

Evidently, many different things can be going on when a reader reads: the process is likely to be dynamic, variable, and different for the same reader on the same text at a different time or with a different purpose in reading. It is even more likely, then, that the process will be different for different readers on different texts at different times and with different purposes. Understanding the process of reading is presumably important to an understanding of the nature of reading, but at the same time it is evidently a difficult thing to do. The process is normally silent, internal, private.

Research has focused on examining the eye movements of readers, and interesting insights have been gained from eye movement photography. Watching what the eyes are doing, however, may not tell us what the brain is doing if, in Smith's (1971) terms, 'What the Brain Tells the Eye is More Important than What the Eye Tells the Brain.'

Asking the reader to read aloud is an alternative to eye movement photography as a means of externalising the reading process, and **miscue analysis** (which analyses the mistakes readers make when reading aloud – for details see Goodman, 1969) is one method of investigating the reading-aloud process. Yet reading aloud is not the 'normal' way in which people read, and the process of reading aloud may be very different from reading silently. Externalising the private process of reading may be the only way to inspect it, yet such externalising risks distorting and changing the nature of the process.

Introspection, through think-aloud protocols or verbal retrospection in interviews, is an increasingly frequently used method of investigating the reading process, and researchers have identified different strategies that good and poor readers appear to use when reading; they have investigated the parts of text that cause problems when reading; and they have also looked at the affective issues that arise when readers are processing particular texts. Introspective methodologies have their critics and are obviously limited in how much light they can throw on the process, but, equally obviously, such methodologies have their uses.

Other research methodologies are also possible and indeed used; it is not the purpose of this chapter to review research methodologies (see Chapter 9), but simply to indicate both the importance and possibilities of examining the reading process in order to understand it, and to understand the limitations that such research must, perhaps inevitably, have.

An alternative approach to examining the process of reading is to inspect the product of reading and, often, to compare that product with the text originally read. It is sometimes said that, although different readers may engage in very different reading processes, the understandings they end up with will be similar. Thus, although there may be many different ways of reaching a given understanding, what matters is not *how* you reach that understanding, but *the fact that* you reach it, or, to put it another way, what understanding you do reach.

The problem of potentially infinite variation in processes of inter-preting text is then supposedly reduced by a focus on what one has understood. Product approaches to reading have been unfashionable in recent years as research efforts have concentrated on under-standing the reading process, and as teachers of reading have endeav-oured to improve the way in which their students approach text. However, a great deal of research into reading earlier this century used essentially product approaches to reading, and much research into the effect of linguistic variables still concentrates on the product of reading. Both a growing realisation that processes of reading are more complex than originally assumed, and the inevitable pendulum swing in research and teaching fashions, have led to revived interest in the product of reading.

As mentioned above, earlier research into reading used a product approach. This means that researchers would typically design tests of understanding of particular texts, administer the tests to suitable informants, using particular research designs, and then inspect the relationship between the results of the tests and variables of interest.

For example, readability researchers would relate scores on reading tests to measures of the linguistic complexity of particular texts, in order to arrive at estimates of text difficulty. Researchers interested in understanding reading ability would devise text comprehension ques-tions at various 'levels of understanding' (see below) and would then see how readers fared on these different questions. Other researchers, wishing to understand what distinguished one type of reader from another (boys versus girls, first-language readers versus second-language readers, children taught by 'whole-word approaches' versus children taught by 'phonics' methods, and so on), might compare and contrast the summaries made by their subjects after reading parti-cular texts. What these studies have in common is that they take some measure of text understanding – test questions, summaries, even interviews – and relate that measure to other relevant variables.

There are at least two limitations to, or problems with, product approaches to reading: one is the variation in the product, the other is the method used to measure the product.

To take the matter of variation first. As we shall see in more detail in Chapter 2, it is clear that what readers understand from text varies. Obviously what people *remember* of what they have read will be affected by their ability to remember. Leaving aside variations in memory, however, and assuming that our measures of understanding do not depend upon readers' memories, it is still the case that different readers will develop somewhat different understandings of what a text 'means'. This is at least in part because a text does not 'contain' meaning which is waiting to be discovered by an able reader. Rather, meaning is created in the interaction between a reader and a text: the text has what Halliday (1979) and Widdowson (1979) call **meaning potential**, and the potential is realised – in the product of understanding – only by readers reading. Since, as we shall see in Chapter 2, readers' knowledge and experiences influence the realisation of this meaning potential, and since readers may differ in their knowledge and experiences, then the products of reading will also necessarily differ.

Given such differences in understanding – the products – the issue is: how are we to determine (if at all) which product, which understanding is 'correct', and which is 'incorrect'? One approach popular among post-modernists is to say that all products are possible and equally 'correct', or that none are correct, and that the notion of correctness is inappropriate, or theoretically misguided. Without wishing to take sides in this somewhat philosophical argument, which clearly has some force – how else can we account for the fact that people do have legitimately different interpretations of text? How else can we account for the existence of lawyers as a profession? – there must also be some acceptance at a common-sense level that some interpretations of text are simply 'wrong': they do not represent any plausible interpretation of an author's possible intentions. The problem remains, for researchers, theorists and test constructors alike: how to decide which interpretations are acceptable and which are not? Test constructors in particular will need to be able to answer that question, since it is surely not adequate to say that somebody has only understood a text when he agrees with the test constructor's interpretation. Yet this is all too often what happens.

The second problem alluded to above is the method by which one has assessed the product of understanding. This issue will be addressed in more detail in Chapter 7, since it is central to concerns in the testing of reading. It is mentioned here to show the inevitable limitations in theories as well as tests.

If the method of assessing reading product – comprehension – involves a reader recalling what he has read without further recourse to the text (as happens, for example, in the use of recall protocols and interviews, or in some kinds of summary test), then it will be difficult to distinguish understanding from remembering. If the method of testing is unfamiliar to readers (as happens in some cultures with multiple-choice tests, for example), then one risks a test-method effect. Similarly, if the method – as seems to happen in the case of cloze techniques and gap-filling – induces some readers to read in a particular way (paying close attention to individual words, for instance, or reading the text preceding the gap, but not the following text), then it will be difficult to generalise from a specific test performance to an ability to read, especially when assessed by other methods. It may be the case that some understandings can be assessed by some methods and not by others: can the cloze procedure, for instance, assess whether the reader has read a text critically, rather than passively? If not, obviously the view of understanding derived from the product assessed by such a method will be limited.

What is not always realised when building theories of reading upon the results of such research is that the theories do depend rather centrally on the validity of the measures of understanding used, and the 'accuracy' of the researcher's definition of 'adequate understanding'. This, incidentally, is a nice illustration both of the centrality of some means of assessing reading to the development of a theory (and the limitations therefore of such theories), and of the near circularity of using test results to build theories on which to base test construction. I shall return to this issue in later chapters.

To summarise thus far: it is possible to see reading as a process, or to examine the product of that process. Any theory of reading is likely to be affected by the emphasis that is placed on process or product. Product is easier to investigate than process, although this is not without its problems.

## Levels of understanding

It is commonplace in theories of reading as well as in everyday talk about reading to distinguish different **levels of understanding** of a text. Thus, some may distinguish between a literal understanding of text, an understanding of meanings that are not directly stated in text, or an understanding of the main implications of text. Similarly the distinction between understanding details and understanding the main idea of a text is familiar enough to teachers of reading, as is Gray's (1960) distinction between reading 'the lines', reading 'between the lines', and reading 'beyond the lines'. The first refers to the literal meaning of text, the second to inferred meanings, and the third to readers' critical evaluations of text.

Such distinctions clearly relate to the product of reading, and enable us to describe some of the observed differences in understanding among readers. They also enable the evaluation of such differences, since it is believed that inferred meanings are somehow 'deeper' than literal meanings, and that a critical understanding of a text is more highly valued by society than a 'mere' literal understanding. Such value judgements lead to an implicit (at times explicit) hierarchy of levels of understanding: the literal level being considered somehow 'lower' than critical understanding. This in turn leads to an assumption that it is more 'difficult' to reach a critical understanding of text than it is to infer meanings, and that both of these are more difficult than 'merely' understanding the literal meaning. Thus the notion of levels of understanding becomes overladen with an ordered hierarchy of increasingly valued and increasingly difficult 'meanings'. The next logical leap is from this ordered hierarchy of difficulty and value to a hierarchy of acquisition: it is very frequently assumed that readers first learn how to understand texts literally, then to infer meanings from text, and only later do they learn how to approach text critically, to evaluate text, and so on. Thus it is often asserted that the levels are ordered: i.e. one must understand the lines in order to read between them, and one had better understand both before adventuring beyond them. In fact, the empirical justification for such assumptions is very slim indeed, as we shall see in Chapter 2, but the theoretical notions are persuasive, especially to teachers of reading, and they are thus pervasive.

However, although intuitively appealing, such distinctions among 'levels of understanding' are not always easy to define. Since language is rarely completely explicit, normal language processing requires the reader to make inferences. As Bransford *et al.* (1984) show, readers of the sentence '*The floor was dirty because Sally used the mop*' will readily – some would say automatically – infer that '*the mop was dirty*', yet this statement was not made 'literally'. Similarly, writers must make assumptions about their readers' knowledge, since total explicitness would lead to enormously unwieldy use of language, and would probably make communication impossible. If readers do not possess the knowledge that writers assume, then difficulties in literal understanding will occur, even if inferences can be made.

In summary, a consideration of the nature of reading must include recognition of frequently made distinctions among levels of meaning and understanding in and from text. Test constructors, thus, must also consider the level of meaning that they believe readers ought to 'get out of' a particular text when assessing 'how well' they have understood the text in question.

## What does it mean to be able to read?

Discussions of 'levels of understanding' frequently merge into a discussion of a reader's ability to understand at certain levels. Kintsch and Yarbrough (1982), for instance, distinguish levels of comprehension: it is possible to comprehend the words but not the meaning of a sentence, and sentences but not the organisation of the text. Kintsch and van Dijk (1978) relate the former to 'microprocesses' and the latter to 'macroprocesses': microprocesses have to do with local, phrase-by-phrase understanding, macroprocesses with global understanding. In fact, as mentioned above, reading researchers have frequently attempted to identify reading skills or abilities by giving subjects a series of passages, and asking them questions intended to test different levels of understanding of the passages. Thus 'the ability to make inferences' becomes defined as 'the ability to answer a question relating to meanings not directly stated in text'. There is, of course, a degree of circularity in such definitions, but that has not stopped researchers and theorists from positing the existence of reading skills and subskills from the answers to such questions. It is common to factor-analyse the results of such answers, and then to state that questions that load on the same factor measure the same skill or subskill. In such a fashion, many different lists, taxonomies and even hierarchies of skills have been developed, as Alderson and Lukmani (1989) point out. The New York City Board of Education is cited by Lunzer and Gardner (1979) as identifying thirty-six different skills. Davis (1968) defines eight skills, as follows:

1 recalling word meanings
2 drawing inferences about the meaning of a word in context
3 finding answers to questions answered explicitly or in paraphrase
4 weaving together ideas in the content

5 drawing inferences from the content

6 recognising a writer's purpose, attitude, tone and mood

7 identifying a writer's technique

8 following the structure of a passage

As we shall see in Chapter 2, however, there is a considerable degree of controversy in the theory of reading over whether it is possible to identify and label separate skills of reading. Thus, it is unclear (a) whether separable skills exist, and (b) what such skills might consist of and how they might be classified (as well as acquired, taught and tested). Nevertheless, the notion of skills and subskills in reading is enormously pervasive and influential, despite the lack of clear empirical justification.

Bloom's 'Taxonomy of Educational Objectives in the Cognitive Domain' (Bloom *et al.* 1956) appeals to similar theorising about the components of educational achievement, and his taxonomy has been enormously influential in the devising of curricula, instructional material and tests. In second-language education, Munby's taxonomy of microskills has been influential in syllabus and materials design as well as the design of language tests. Munby (1978) distinguishes the following reading 'microskills':

- recognising the script of a language
- deducing the meaning and use of unfamiliar lexical items
- understanding explicitly stated information
- understanding information when not explicitly stated
- understanding conceptual meaning
- understanding the communicative value of sentences
- understanding relations within the sentence
- understanding relations between parts of text through lexical cohesion devices
- understanding cohesion between parts of a text through grammatical cohesion devices
- interpreting text by going outside it
- recognising indicators in discourse
- identifying the main point or important information in discourse
- distinguishing the main idea from supporting details

- extracting salient details to summarise (the text, an idea)
- extracting relevant points from a text selectively
- using basic reference skills
- skimming
- scanning to locate specifically required information
- transcoding information to diagrammatic display

Such lists or taxonomies are seductive because they offer an apparently theoretically justified means of devising test tasks or items, and of isolating reading skills to be tested. They also suggest the possibility of diagnosing a reader's problems, with a view to identifying remediation. They are potentially very powerful frameworks for test construction and will doubtless continue to be so used.

However, as has been suggested above, they need to be treated with care. Firstly, their origins are more frequently in the comfort of the theorist's armchair than they are the result of empirical observation. Secondly, they are frequently ill defined (or undefined) and give a misleading impression of being discrete when in fact they overlap enormously (see, for example, criticisms of Munby by Davies, 1981; Mead, 1982; Skehan, 1984; and the discussion in this book in Chapter 5; and of Bloom by Seddon, 1978). Thirdly, it is frequently difficult to get expert judges to agree on what skills are operationalised by which test item (Seddon, 1978; Alderson, 1990b), and finally, analysis of test performance does not reveal separability of skills, nor implicational scales, nor even a hierarchy of difficulty or discrimination (see Alderson and Lukmani, 1989; Alderson, 1990b; Alderson, 1990c). Despite all these problems, a skills approach to defining reading remains popular and influential and cannot be ignored in a treatment of the nature of reading (see Chapters 2, 3, 4 and 9).

Several alternative views are possible on this issue of reading skills. One, expressed by Lunzer *et al.* (1979), is that there is no evidence that distinct separate skills exist, and that, instead, reading consists of one single, global, integrated aptitude. The second view, to which Alderson (1990c) inclines, is that 'at least part of the reading process probably involves the simultaneous and variable use of different, and overlapping, "skills". The division of skills into "higher" and "lower" orders, however tempting, does not seem to be justified in practice' (1990c:478). A third view is represented by Matthews (1990) who states: 'the items in Munby-based taxonomies appear to be a slightly random and overlapping collection of strategies, skills and (chiefly) knowledge, and represent an impoverished account of the reading process.' She claims that most of what Munby calls 'skills' are, in fact, aspects of knowledge. Thus, 'understanding explicitly stated ideas' is just a more general statement of 'skills' like 'knowing the meaning of the word "tree"'. Matthews calls for a better understanding of what skills are required in reading, citing Eskey and Grabe's view (1988) of the importance of speed and automaticity in word recognition. She suggests that, if speed and flexibility are important, then they need to be tapped in tests of reading. It has been suggested that lists like Munby's are not processes, but products: they identify what is done, not how it is done. If this is so, it might explain why it is difficult to isolate skills of the Munby type. What needs to be isolated are the processes which lead to these outcomes.

An increasingly common view in the research literature is that reading is essentially divided into two components: decoding (word recognition) and comprehension. The latter is often described (e.g. in Gough *et al.*, 1992b) as consisting of parsing sentences, understanding sentences in discourse, building a discourse structure, and then integrating this understanding with what one already knows. This comprehension process, however, is not seen as unique to reading, but also describes the process of listening. In other words these are linguistic skills, not reading skills. The difference between listening and reading is suggested to be minimal: 'comprehension is largely a centrally-determined function operating independently of the mode of presentation of the material' (Larsen and Feder, 1940:251, cited in Gough *et al.*, *op. cit.*).

A further alternative is Carver's view that a 'simple view of reading' should be reanalysed into a three-part separability of word recognition skills, reading rate or reading fluency, and problem-solving comprehension abilities. In a number of publications (Carver, 1982, 1983, 1984, 1990, 1992a, 1992b), Carver distinguishes what he calls **rauding** ('typical' reading done under conditions wherein the individual has no difficulty comprehending each sentence) from memorising, studying, skimming and scanning. He claims that these are five different processes, and only one of these – rauding – is normal reading, where the reader is comprehending all or most of the thoughts the author intended to communicate. Carver has amassed a considerable amount of evidence to show that rate fluency abilities change as readers develop – in other words, that reading speeds increase with reading development.

Finally, in this illustrative set of alternatives, Grabe (1991) proposes the following six component elements in the fluent reading process:

- automatic recognition skills
- vocabulary and structural knowledge
- formal discourse structure knowledge
- content/world background knowledge
- synthesis and evaluation skills/strategies
- metacognitive knowledge and skills monitoring

Among the **metacognitive skills** he includes: recognising the more important information in text; adjusting reading rate; skimming; previewing; using context to resolve a misunderstanding; formulating questions about information; monitoring cognition, including recognising problems with information presented in text or an inability to understand text. Self-regulation strategies like planning ahead, testing one's own comprehension, and being aware of and revising the strategies being used are also said to be typical reading strategies of fluent readers. We will discuss the evidence for these views in more detail in Chapter 2 of this book.

## What do we do when we read?

If theorists are not (yet) agreed on what skills are involved in the reading process, is it at least possible to find some consensus on what happens when we read? What kinds of tasks characterise the activity involved in reading?

Clearly, reading involves perceiving the written form of language, either visually or kinaesthetically (using Braille). Here we already encounter the first problem: do readers then relate the printed form of language to the spoken form? If so, then once that translation has taken place, reading is the same sort of activity as listening, and the only specific aspect of reading that we need to concern ourselves with as testers is the process of transformation from print to speech. One argument, put forward by theorists like Smith (1971), is that readers proceed directly to meaning, and do not go via sound. They claim that readers can process print much faster than sounds, and so there would be an upper limit on the speed with which we read if we had to go from print to sound. Fluent reading is frequently done at speeds up to three times as fast as many people speak in everyday conversation.

However, research has consistently shown that listening comprehension does not break down with accelerated speech. Carver (1982), for example, shows that there are optimal rates of processing prose, and they are roughly equivalent for reading and listening, at 250 to 300 words per minute. The results of such studies challenge the views of Goodman (1969, 1982) and Smith (1971) and allow the question of whether we access meaning directly or via sound to be revisited.

We have all experienced the sensation of sounding out, possibly subvocally, difficult words, or parts of text where we have to concentrate. Does such subvocalisation constitute normal activity (which we are usually unaware of), or does it only occur when we encounter difficulties, when we need the extra support of the subvocally heard sounds? There is a growing consensus in the recent cognitive psychology research literature that all reading requires what is called 'early phonological activation': in other words, that readers typically identify the sound of words as part of the process of identifying their meaning. An issue frequently discussed is whether this phonological identification proceeds independently of and in parallel to the use of semantic and other cues (the 'modular' approach), or whether it is sequential, proceeding in stages – i.e. sound is recognised first, then meaning. Research is unclear on the matter, but the view one takes on this presumably affects what one considers essential to assess when looking at reading success or abilities.

Recent accounts of the fluent reading process tend to emphasise that it is rapid, purposeful, motivated, interactive (in terms of component skills as well as in the relation between knowledge and the printed word), it is comprehending (readers expect to understand), it is flexible, and it develops gradually (it is the product of long-term effort and gradual improvement).

When we are reading, we are clearly engaged in a great deal of mental activity, some of it automatic, some of it conscious. For example, we may consciously decide to skip a page or two in a rather boring text, we may decide just to focus on the headlines in a newspaper, or to read the end of the detective story first before reading the introduction. We may scan through a telephone directory ignoring all names except the one we are looking for; or we may read every letter and word of a memorandum we are writing to our boss, in which we want to be sure we have made no spelling mistakes, and have expressed ourselves diplomatically but clearly.

These conscious strategies involve a deliberate choice of process or task, each of which may involve different constellations of skill and knowledge (being able to spell words in English, for example, or knowing the order of the alphabet). Such strategies may be semiconscious, or at least recoverable to consciousness, as when we try to figure out the meaning of a word we have never met before by thinking about the context in which it comes, its form, the sort of word it is (noun, verb and so on) and the sort of meaning it is likely to have. We may consciously decide to look the word up in a dictionary, or not to worry about its 'exact meaning', since we have sufficient idea of what it must mean to be able to continue reading without disruption.

Other activities are not amenable to consciousness – hence the use of the term **automaticity**. We are not normally conscious of processing the distinctive features in each letter in English text, for example, yet word recognition for the normal reader must involve some process of discriminating visual shapes. When we are absorbed in a novel we are not normally conscious that we are visualising the setting – the faces, dress, voices of the characters, the location of the action, the surrounding scenery – yet evidence suggests that we do precisely this, and that what we visualise becomes part of our meaning for what we are reading. Researchers seek to identify and characterise these processes and strategies, and useful lists have been developed in recent years (see for example Harri-Augstein and Thomas, 1984; Nevo, 1989; Storey, 1994).

There are two broad approaches available for assessment for those who feel that the view of reading as a series of strategies and activities is correct, or at least relevant to their purposes. One is the analytic approach: to seek to test whether readers successfully engage in, or master, those aspects of the process which testers consider to be important. Thus one might seek to devise test items which explore whether a reader can successfully deduce the meaning of unknown words from context. One might devise tasks that require readers to scan rapidly through a number of headlines in order to identify the one(s) that are relevant to a particular need or topic. In other words, one seeks to isolate and identify components of the reading process relevant to the purpose for which one is testing (see Chapter 6 for more on testing purposes). Some aspects will, however, be easier to test than others: can one, for example, successfully test whether readers are visualising settings 'appropriately' when reading a short story? Can one assess whether readers are fully absorbed in a novel, with no sense of their surroundings, or are just pretending for the sake of the assessor?

The other broad approach is to recognise that the act of assessing itself risks disturbing parts of the process one is wishing to assess, and to acknowledge that individual readers may well not need to engage in a particular activity in order to read 'successfully' (they may already know the meaning of the word, they may find an irrelevant news story interesting). Such an approach would entail seeking to simulate as far as possible the conditions in which one is interested – reading newspapers in order to get an overview of the day's events, scanning TV guides in order to plan the evening's viewing – and then assess whether the reader had successfully completed the task. The assumption would be made that if the task was successfully completed, then either the reader would of necessity have engaged in the sorts of processes of interest or had not, and such processes were not necessary. We return to this difference of approach later in this volume, in Chapters 4, 5 and 6.

## Top-down and bottom-up processing

Much has been made in reading research over the last twenty years or so of an apparent dichotomy between two different approaches that may be taken by readers. One is the bottom-up approach, and the other is the top-down approach. The latter owes much to the work of Smith (1971) and Goodman (1969, 1982), who emphasise in their writings the importance of the contribution made by the reader to the reading process, and who downplay the importance traditionally ascribed to the printed word.

**Bottom-up** approaches are serial models, where the reader begins with the printed word, recognises graphic stimuli, decodes them to sound, recognises words and decodes meanings. Each component involves subprocesses which take place independently of each other, and build upon prior subprocesses. Subprocesses higher up the chain cannot, however, feed back into components lower down (identification of meaning does not lead to letter recognition, for example). This approach was typically associated with behaviourism in the 1940s and 1950s, and with 'phonics' approaches to the teaching of reading that argue that children need to learn to recognise letters before they can read words, and so on. In this traditional view, readers are passive decoders of sequential graphic–phonemic–syntactic–semantic systems, in that order.

On the other hand, as we shall see in Chapter 2, much research has emphasised the importance in reading of the knowledge that a reader brings to text. Models of reading that stress the centrality of this knowledge are known as **schema-theoretic models**. They are based upon schema theory, which accounts for the acquisition of knowledge and the interpretation of text through the activation of schemata: networks of information stored in the brain which act as filters for incoming information (for much more detail, see Bartlett, 1932; Ausubel, 1963; Hudson, 1982; Carrell, 1983a, Carrell *et al.*, 1988). In this view, readers activate what they consider to be relevant existing schemata and map incoming information onto them. To the extent that these schemata are relevant, reading is successful. **Top-down** approaches emphasise the importance of these schemata, and the reader's contribution, over the incoming text. Goodman (1982), for example, calls reading a 'psycholinguistic guessing game', in which readers guess or predict the text's meaning on the basis of minimal textual information, and maximum use of existing, activated, knowledge. Smith (1971) claims that non-visual information transcends the text, and includes the reader's experience with the reading process, knowledge of the context of the text, familiarity with the structures and patterns of the language and of specific text types, as well as generalised knowledge of the world and specific subject matter knowledge.

A typical statement of the top-down approach can be found in Schank (1978):

> We would claim that in natural language understanding a simple rule is followed. Analysis proceeds in a top-down predictive manner. Understanding is expectation based. It is only when the expectations are useless or wrong that bottom-up processing begins.　　　　　　　　　　　　　　　　　　(Schank, 1978:94)

However, many psychologists and psycholinguists now question the usefulness of schema theory to account for, rather than provide a metaphor of, comprehension processes. One issue is *how* prior knowledge is called up from memory, and how it is then used in understanding. The problem is that schema theory does not lead to explicit definitions or predictions of processes of understanding, although it has clearly provided a powerful incentive to research into the products of understanding for first- as well as second-language readers.

Partly as a result, recent research tends to emphasise the important contribution of bottom-up or data-driven processing to fluent reading. In particular, numerous studies of eye movements using sophisticated instruments have consistently shown the importance of rapid and automatic processing of most of the words on the page: one estimate is that fluent readers process some 80% of content words and 40% of function words (in English). What distinguishes good from poor readers is not the number of letters in a fixation, nor the number of words fixated per page, but the speed of the fixation – the automaticity of word recognition – and the processes that occur during fixation. It has been suggested that after initial word identification, but still during the fixation, good readers move onto higher-level prediction and monitoring, as well as planning of subsequent fixations. This is thought to be because they use less capacity to analyse the visual stimulus, and therefore have other resources available for other sorts of processing.

Not only are good readers rapid in their word recognition, they are precise as well. Readers take in letter features of short words simultaneously and appear to recognise all the letters in a word. The ability to recognise words rapidly and accurately is an important predictor of reading ability, especially with younger first-language readers, and even for college-level students.

In fact, however, neither the bottom-up nor the top-down approach is an adequate characterisation of the reading process, and more adequate models are known as **interactive models,** in which every component in the reading process can interact with any other component, be it 'higher up' or 'lower down'. Processing, in fact, is now thought to be **parallel** rather than **serial** (Grabe, 1991:384). Rumelhart's (1977) model, for example, incorporates feedback mechanisms that allow knowledge sources (linguistic as well as world knowledge) to interact with visual input. In his model, a final hypothesis about the text is synthesised from multiple knowledge sources interacting continuously and simultaneously. Stanovich (1980), on the other hand, has developed an **interactive compensatory model** in which the degree of interaction among components depends upon knowledge deficits in individual components, where interaction occurs to compensate for deficits. Thus, readers with poor word recognition skills may use top-down knowledge to compensate. (However, the evidence that such compensation does in fact occur is controversial, as we shall see in Chapter 2.)

Although Goodman's model is often characterised as a top-down model, and Smith's popularisations acted as useful correctives to excessively bottom-up approaches in the 1970s, Goodman himself (1982) rejected the label, and claimed that his model assumed that the goal of meaning is the construction of meaning which requires interactive use of grapho-phonic, syntactic and semantic cues to construct meaning. Readers are not passive identifiers of letters and words but active constructors of their own knowledge. He saw reading as a complex process of **sampling** the text for graphic clues, **predicting** grammatical structures and meaning, **confirming** the validity of the hypotheses advanced and **correcting** the hypotheses as necessary as text sampling proceeds.

Less proficient readers often appear 'word-bound'. Traditional psycholinguistic models such as Smith's claimed that such readers need to take more risks, but more current views suggest that these readers are not yet efficient in bottom-up processing. They do not recognise the words sufficiently rapidly and accurately (and for second-language readers there might well be graphic as well as lexical problems anyway – there are too many new forms for students to attend to). Guessing will not overcome this deficiency and lead to automatic recognition – there are no short-cuts to automaticity, although some research has attempted to improve automatic recognition.

More recent approaches to reading have begun to investigate the importance of the visual input once more. It is recognised that letters are not processed serially in order to identify words (Samuels and Kamil, 1988) – there are syntactic and semantic effects on word recognition, so that related pairs of words will be recognised more quickly than unrelated pairs, and in word recognition errors, substitutions are often of the same syntactic category as the word being substituted. It has been shown that good readers do not simply sample text – they do not skip over words in normal fluent reading: 'the single immutable and non-optional fact about skilful reading is that it involves relatively complete processing of the individual letters of print'

(Adams, 1991:105). What seems to matter is the speed of recognition, the automaticity of the process.

Poor readers are distinguished from good ones by: poor phonetic decoding; insensitivity to word structures; and poor encoding of syntactic properties (Vellutino and Scanlon, 1987). They see reading difficulties as a linguistic problem, involving a failure to recognise how particular structures encode information, and not as a problem of insufficient background knowledge or insufficient top-down strategies.

Thus, the pendulum swings. It is clear that both bottom-up and top-down information is important in reading, that the two interact in complex and poorly understood ways, and that the balance between the two approaches is likely to vary with text, reader and purpose (see Chapter 2). Given the emphasis placed by researchers and teachers alike on more top-down approaches in the 1970s and 1980s, it is likely that we will soon see some change of emphasis as the importance of text recognition receives more attention from research and pedagogy.

What are the implications for assessment? Clearly there are diagnostic issues: causes of poor reading can be hypothesised to be more bottom-up or more top-down, depending upon one's model and the data available, and diagnostic testers would do well to pay attention to both possibilities, rather than to concentrate on one. One can envisage situations where poor reading may be due to poor bottom-up strategies or inappropriate application of background knowledge, and knowledge of which approach has prevailed might be useful.

However, reading achievement and proficiency tests may well be less influenced by notions of the nature of the process and the strength of the arguments in the debate, since I would argue that, by their very nature and purpose, at least as presently conceived, such tests concentrate on product rather than process (but see Chapter 9). It is, moreover, difficult to envisage a reading test that would *require* students to adopt either a bottom-up or a top-down approach, since it may well be that either can result in a given understanding.

It might be useful for testers to ask themselves, when looking at test items they have devised: is this a top-down or a bottom-up item? Would top-down reading give a better chance of getting this item right or wrong? But it is highly unlikely that any test item involving meaning would involve only one or the other approaches. It is most likely that there will be an *interaction* between textual clues and the reader's knowledge.

## Reading and cognition

It will not have escaped the reader (note the appeal to critical approaches to reading!) that Goodman's characterisation of the reading
process as one of sampling, predicting, confirming and correcting
might describe a more general process than that of reading. It might
even be argued that such a process is fundamental to hypothesis generation and resolution in many sciences, and could thus be described
as part of a general problem-solving strategy. Indeed, there are those
who hold that many aspects of reading represent **problem-solving**,
and that problem-solving strategies are useful for the resolution of
many difficulties in reading, for example the deduction of the meaning
of unknown words. Indeed it was Thorndike who, as early as 1917,
characterised reading as **reasoning**. By this he meant that many of the
strategies by which readers resolve matters of meaning approximate to
a logical process of deduction and inference, and that good readers are
those who can think clearly. Since then, the metaphor has been taken
up, especially by those tending towards a top-down interpretation of
the nature of reading, and used to emphasise the importance of schemata and logical inferencing abilities in the reading process.

Indeed, recent interest in the development of **critical reading skills**
or abilities not only draws upon the study of reading and thinking – it
draws little if any distinction between the two. So-called subskills in
the ability to read critically presented in Abdullah (1994), for example,
include:

> the ability to evaluate deductive inferences
>
> the ability to evaluate inductive inferences
>
> the ability to evaluate the soundness of generalisation
>
> the ability to recognise hidden assumptions
>
> the ability to identify bias in statements
>
> the ability to recognise author's motives
>
> the ability to evaluate strength of arguments   (Abdullah, 1994:291)

The fact that tests based on such inventories showed considerable
overlap with tests of reading comprehension and language proficiency
variables underlines the closeness of 'critical reading' to reading more
generally. Those persuaded of the value of teaching critical reading
(see, for example, Benesch, 1993) will doubtless feel a need to test
such abilities also.

However, before rushing into the wholesale production of tests of critical reading, we must ask ourselves to what extent we wish to assess reading ability, and to what extent we wish to distinguish this from other cognitive abilities. It is at least intuitively possible to make a distinction between the ability to read and the ability to think critically. Carroll (1969, 1971, 1993) even makes what he considers to be a clear distinction between comprehension and inference. Whilst acknowledging that 'critical reading' blurs this common-sense distinction, we need to pause before deliberately confusing the two.

To the extent that we wish to gain a picture of somebody's reading abilities uncontaminated by other cognitive variables – and I accept that this desire is fraught with difficulties – then it seems to me that we should endeavour to keep 'reading' separate from 'reasoning'. For many purposes, it is possible to envisage wishing to identify 'good readers' who may or may not be 'good thinkers'. That this is not so easy can be seen from the desire of many teachers and testers to ensure that their tests assess 'higher-order' reading skills at least as much as 'lower-order' skills (Alderson, 1990b). The problems of so doing, however, especially where the language is the reader's second language, are highlighted in Alderson and Lukmani (1989). In any case, where one is dealing with second-language reading, i.e. in cross-cultural contexts, we need to be sure that we are not introducing unwanted cultural bias when testing 'critical reading abilities', which may or may not be appropriate in the context of a different language or culture (see Hill and Parry, 1992, for a view of the socially embedded nature of reading).

However, if one accepts an increasingly common view (see the discussion above) of reading as consisting of decoding/word recognition, and general comprehension or problem-solving skills, then the distinction between comprehension and 'critical thinking' becomes harder to draw and doubtless is more of a continuum than a dichotomy. I would nevertheless want to argue that it is important, in second-language contexts at least, to be clear what it is one wishes to test, especially in view of the debate surrounding the difference between first- and second-language reading, and to place one's test on that continuum accordingly.

## First-language reading, second-language reading

The mention of assessing reading in a second language inevitably brings us to the question of the nature of reading in a second or foreign language. The question is whether the ability to read transfers across languages: is a good first-language reader also a good second-language reader?

The issue usually poses itself somewhat differently, as an assertion: many second-language teachers believe that poor second-language reading is due to a lack of good reading abilities/skills/habits in the first language. Alderson (1984) addresses this issue, and reviews much of the research published at that time, to conclude that there is likely to be a **language threshold** beyond which second-language readers have to progress before their first-language reading abilities can transfer to the second-language situation. I shall review more recent research in Chapter 2, but the answer to Alderson's original (1984) question, 'Is second-language reading a reading problem or a language problem?', is ambiguous. The importance of both factors – language knowledge and reading knowledge – is clearly acknowledged, but the evidence is that, in second-language reading, knowledge of the second language is a more important factor than first-language reading abilities.

Cummins (1979, 1991) has advocated the hypothesis of linguistic interdependence, suggesting that linguistic proficiency has two basic components: basic interpersonal communication skills (BICS) and cognitive/academic language proficiency (CALP) – in more recent writings this has been formulated as conversational vs. academic language proficiency. He argues that, when asked to perform school reading tasks in two languages, bilingual pupils seem to be able to draw on the same knowledge base – academic language proficiency – which, he posits, underlies either language. This, he asserts, means that once reading ability has been acquired in the first language, it is available for use in the second or subsequent languages also. The implication is that no instruction in second-language reading is necessary – all that is required is sufficient second-language knowledge for the ability to transfer. If first-language reading abilities are poor, then the posited existence of the underlying academic language proficiency would suggest the wisdom of improving first-language reading, and then allowing that ability to transfer. One could of course argue the opposite: since reading abilities are assumed to transfer across languages, improving second-language reading will lead to improved reading in the first language also. However, as Cummins points out, the evidence shows that in practice transfer occurs from minority language to majority language, for sociolinguistic and sociopolitical reasons. Thus, if one wishes minority language pupils to learn to read in both the majority and minority languages, instruction should be given in the minority language, not the majority language.

It is important to note, however, that the distinction between conversational and academic language proficiency is not a simple dichotomy but must be seen within two intersecting continua. These are the context-embedded/context-reduced and the cognitively-undemanding/cognitively-demanding continua (Cummins, 1991). An important question arising from these distinctions is: when assessing second-language reading ability, how much of the observed performance is due to a knowledge of the second language *per se*, and how much is simply due to a transfer of reading ability from the first language base?

There may, however, be a big difference between second-language readers who have highly developed reading (and problem-solving) skills already through their first language, and second-language readers who, for whatever reason, have had little or no formal education. This is presumably important for interpreting the outcomes of second-language reading assessment. The implication for assessment is clearly that conversational language proficiency needs to be distinguished from academic language proficiency, and that measurement needs to take into account the range of cognitive demands and contextual support involved in particular language tasks or activities.

The notion that poor second-language reading is due to inadequate first-language reading receives little support from the research literature, as we shall see in Chapter 2. Results increasingly confirm the existence of a linguistic threshold, a threshold which will certainly vary for different texts being read for different purposes by readers with differing amounts of world knowledge (and, doubtless, other cognitive abilities). The implication for the assessment of second-language reading and the interpretation of results is that poor second-language reading performance is likely to be due to insufficient language knowledge, and any attempt at remediation might more profitably pay attention to the linguistic problem than to any supposed reading deficit.

## Reading as sociocultural practice

Despite the impression that may have been created in this chapter so far, reading is not an isolated activity that takes place in some vacuum. Reading is usually undertaken for some purpose, in a social context, and that social context itself contributes to a reader's notion of what it means to read, or, as recent thinkers tend to put it, to be literate. Street (1984) contrasts what he calls the **autonomous model of literacy** – which assumes that texts, readers and reading are autonomous entities – with his **ideological model of literacy**. He denies that texts are autonomous and sees readers as social beings rather than as isolated individuals. Reading, for him, is not merely a cognitive operation of meaning extraction (echoing the view of Widdowson and Halliday put forward earlier in this chapter that reading is meaning construction). Hill and Parry (1992) present a model similar to Street's, which they call a **pragmatic model of literacy**, in which texts are social in origin, intimately related to other texts, and reading is context-bound and socially embedded.

There is an increasing tendency to see reading as only one of a number of literacy practices. Recent research (e.g. Barton, 1994b) shows the richness of the social world within which literacy events take place: shopping lists are written and used, TV adverts processed, church magazines flipped through, telephone directories consulted, posters and signs in airports are noticed and acted upon. Moreover, reading may be the result of writing (for example, the use of shopping lists mentioned above) or may lead to some form of writing – taking notes whilst reading an academic textbook, writing an essay after re-reading the notes. Reading will often be accompanied by talking – reading aloud a snippet from a newspaper in order to discuss political bias or the performance of a football team – or by listening – reading the print in TV advertisements whilst hearing the voice-over read them aloud, listening to one's mother reading a bedtime book whilst following her in the text.

Moreover, what it means to be literate, how this literacy is valued, used and displayed, will vary from culture to culture. Some cultures have enormous respect for the printed word, such that it is implicitly accepted as authority, and cannot be questioned. Others fear the implications of putting any opinions in print, since the greater permanence accorded to opinions thereby makes the owner of the opinion more 'accountable'. These are doubtless crude over-generalisations of attitudes to literacy and reading, and the interested reader is referred to Barton (1994a) and Hamilton *et al.* (1994) for greater insights into what it means to be a reader within a given culture. The substantive point remains: to become literate is to be introduced into a new culture, or an extension of an existing one, and literacy in two or more languages may well have cultural implications also (see, for example, the advice in Fordham *et al.* 1995, to those teaching adult literacy in developing countries).

How does a view of reading as socioculturally transmitted and mediated literacy affect the assessment of reading? One obvious way is that the values implicit in the way reading is assessed – what questions are asked, the very idea implicit in testing that there are correct and less correct interpretations, that readers are being asked to critically question the text, to develop their own opinions and interpretations – all this may be culturally alien and therefore biased. Being aware of cultural bias is crucial in multicultural societies, especially when the interpretation of test results might have important consequences for those taking the test.

However, there are also implications for the treatment of reading as a distinct ability and as a skill. Firstly, a relatively discrete approach to the assessment of reading is frequently advocated: it is claimed that having candidates respond in writing to comprehension questions may contaminate the measurement of reading. 'Pure' measures of reading are often thought to be necessary, in diagnosis as well as in achievement. This is contradicted by the argument that such isolation and separation of reading from the uses to which reading is put, through other 'macro-skills', is itself a distortion which is inauthentic, and which biases measurement. Proponents (see, for example, Hill and Parry, 1992) advocate the use of integrated measures, where, for example, some reading input might lead to some writing, which might lead to a listening task, together with some further reading, which might then lead to a group discussion.

Such ideas are interesting, of course. The problem arises when communication is less than successful. How, if at all, is one to attribute breakdown, especially during performance on a test? Can it be the case that an integrated assessment of reading and other literacy 'events' might be more difficult, because more complex, than more discrete approaches?

The answer is that at present we have little idea what the effect might be of such isolation or integration, and research is urgently needed. Lewkowicz (1997) suggests that the assessment of writing may not be improved by the provision of written input. An important question is how in such integrated approaches the writing might be affected if the candidate is a poor reader, or how reading itself might be assessed, if the only output is in writing.

The second implication of this recent view of reading as part of literacy is a tendency to downplay the psycholinguistic 'skill' element in reading, and to emphasise the sociolinguistic aspects of literacy. Whilst accepting that a view of reading as a skill is a narrow and possibly limiting view of the nature of reading, it has not yet been worked through what an alternative view might mean in assessment terms. Hill and Parry (1992) are highly critical of reading tests, claiming that they derive from the autonomous model of reading mentioned earlier. Instead, they advocate what they call 'alternative assessment', based on their pragmatic model of literacy. Sadly they fail to illustrate what such assessment might look like.

Some, no doubt, would simply say that assessment itself is inappropriate, and indeed harmful in being prescriptive. Others, whilst not going so far, might consider that the very act of assessing changes the sociocultural nature of the event. When we read 'normally', we are not being assessed. Thus, knowing that we are being assessed when reading creates a different event, and it is difficult to extrapolate from 'performance' in one event to 'performance' in the other.

The riposte is partly empirical: let's see what difference it makes. But it is also partly philosophical: society needs assessment. Assessment is a different event from many other activities, but it is valued by society for its own sake, and is therefore justified. The ability to extrapolate from assessment to the real world is still important, but it is equally important not to confuse the assessed event with the 'real thing'. A similar argument has raged for decades in the arena of communicative language teaching and testing (see, for example, Alderson, 1981, and Widdowson, 1979), and is currently recurring in the context of performance assessment. It is unlikely to be resolved by argument or even evidence. The important thing is perhaps to be aware of the fact that there is an issue, and to decide where one stands on that issue.

Finally, we need to consider the limits of assessment. A constant theme of this chapter has been that the choice of the model of reading has implications for what and how one assesses reading. It has also been argued that there is no one correct view of what reading is: many different views are possible, and perhaps indeed inevitable. A view of *assessment* as a socioculturally determined practice, just as literacy is socioculturally determined, leads one to view assessment relatively. Some activities may be more appropriately assessed, some less so.

Reading is, for many people, an enjoyable, intense, private activity, from which much pleasure can be derived, and in which one can become totally absorbed. Such reading – sometimes called extensive reading in the teaching literature, sometimes called reading with intrinsic motivation in the psychological literature – is difficult if not impossible to replicate within an assessment setting. The intervention of questions, tasks, outcomes, between the reader and text is likely, for some at least, to be disruptive and to create a self-consciousness which destroys the very nature of the event. We need to acknowledge that in such settings, for some purposes, the assessment of reading may be both difficult and undesirable (but see also on this subject Brumfit, 1993, and Nuttall, 1996).

## Implications for test design

Throughout this chapter, I have argued that our view of reading has a crucial influence on how we might go about testing and assessing reading. In this final section I wish to illustrate this by reference to Grabe's thoughts on the implications, for the teaching of second-language reading, of recent research into reading. I then speculate on how these might be extended to testing and assessment.

Grabe (1991) derives a general set of guidelines for reading teaching and curricula from current reading research:

1 Reading should be taught in the context of a content-centred integrated skills curriculum, since content provides motivation and integration reinforces learning.

2 Individualised instruction should additionally be provided in a reading lab, including a range of skills and strategies (timed reading, vocabulary learning strategies etc.).

3 Sustained silent reading should be encouraged to develop automaticity, confidence and enjoyment.

4 Reading lessons should take account of background knowledge through pre-, during- and after-reading tasks.

5 Specific skills and strategies should be practised consistently: the nature of these will depend on the group and goals.

6 Group work and cooperative learning should promote discussions of the readings and explorations of different task solutions and textual interpretations.

7 Students need to read extensively: students need to learn by reading.

The parallel implications for testing and assessment might be characterised as follows:

1 Reading might be tested within a content-focused battery: texts that carry meaning for readers, that interest them, that relate to their academic background, leisure interests, intellectual level and so on, might motivate a deeper reading than the traditional, relatively anodyne or even contentless texts.

2 Students should be tested on a range of relevant skills and strategies, with the results possibly being provided in a diagnostic, profile-based format.

3 Students should be encouraged to read longer texts, rather than short snippets, and tasks should attempt to get at the degree of enjoyment experienced. Tasks should be do-able in the time available and not discourage students because of their difficulty level.

4 Background knowledge should be recognised as influencing all comprehension, and therefore every attempt should be made to allow background knowledge to facilitate performance, rather than allowing its absence to inhibit performance.

5 Tests should be open to the possibility of multiple interpretations. Test designers should be as open as possible in the range of different interpretations and understandings they accept.

6 Group tasks might be devised for a discussion of student interpretations of text. Teachers might keep a record of salient points brought out, and each student's reactions and interpretations. Such a procedure is more suitable to ongoing continuous assessment than to high-stakes testing situations.

7 Extensive reading should not be discouraged by the assessment procedures. Portfolios of texts read, and appreciations of the readings, might be one way of keeping a record, for evaluative purposes, of such reading.

8 The importance of identification skills needs to be explored, and means need to be found of testing them. Timed readings, especially in computer-based test settings, might provide useful diagnoses of developing automaticity, and thought needs to be given to measuring the rate at which readers read, as well as to their comprehension of the text. Speed should not be measured without reference to comprehension, but at present comprehension is all too often measured without reference to speed.

9 Inevitably, there will be settings and tests where it will be impossible to reduce extrinsic motivation to a minimum and to emphasise enjoyment. The results of such tests should be interpreted cautiously and where possible by reference to other measures of reading ability.

10 Similarly, there will be occasions when integrated testing, say of reading and writing skills, is not possible or desirable since a clear picture is required of a student's reading ability, in as uncontaminated a way as possible. The purposes for such measurement should be quite clear, however – often they may be diagnostic rather than selective. Similarly, the dangers of what Weir (1990) calls 'muddied measurement' (i.e. the contamination of the measurement of one skill by the involvement of other skills at the same time) should also be identified and, if important, guarded against.

11 Exploration is needed of ways in which synthesis and evaluation skills/strategies and metacognitive knowledge and skills monitoring can be tested or assessed. Often, it will be sufficient to test reading in as unitary or global a way as possible in the assumption or hope that these skills will thereby also be included. All too often, however, testers focus upon the assessment of vocabulary/syntactic skills, discourse skills, or the ability to understand the literal or at best inferred meaning from texts, and the other sorts of abilities – be they higher-order or just different – are neglected. Test designers, then, need to consider to what extent the tests they design cover Grabe's six components of the reading process, and to what extent this can be done in an integrated fashion or relatively discretely.

12 Above all, perhaps, test designers need to consider to what extent their tests reflect and build upon what recent research into reading suggests about the process, not just the product.

## Summary

In this chapter I have argued that an understanding of the nature of reading is crucial to the development of our assessment instruments. I have not merely presented a review of theory and research in reading: I have discussed the possible implications for testing and assessment of adopting a particular theory or model of reading, and I have by implication considered the validity of the relationship between the model and the test, the test and the use to which it will be put. I shall enlarge on these themes in later chapters. But first, in the next chapter, I will consider the influence on 'reading' of some of the more important factors that might affect test design.

# CHAPTER TWO

.................................................................................................

# Variables that affect the nature of reading

## Introduction

As explained in Chapter 1, the amount of empirical research into reading in the mother tongue is simply enormous and, although it is much smaller in quantity and scope, there is also a growing research literature on reading in a second or foreign language. But anybody who wishes to assess reading must have at least some idea of what reading is, and therefore of what the main findings of research are. The aim of this chapter is not to present an extensive, much less exhaustive, review of the literature, but rather to acquaint the reader with the main thrusts of research findings in so far as they are relevant to the design of tests or assessment procedures for reading. The interested reader will find an extensive bibliography for further reference at the end of the book.

It has become common practice to divide research into factors that affect reading into the two main constellations of variables that are typically investigated. This chapter follows that convention by presenting first the research that has looked at factors within the **reader**: aspects of the person doing the reading that have been thought or shown to have an effect on the reading process and the product of reading. The second major section will look at those aspects of the **text** to be read that are of significance.

Inevitably this division leads to a degree of distortion, both of the research in some cases, and of our overview of reading. What is key is the interaction between reader and text variables in the process of reading, and at appropriate points throughout the chapter I shall discuss such interactions.

## Reader variables

Research has looked at the way readers themselves affect the reading process and product, and has investigated a number of different variables. The state of the reader's *knowledge*, broadly speaking, constitutes one significant field of research, as does the reader's *motivation* to read, and the way this interacts with the *reasons* why a reader is reading a text at all. The *strategies* that readers use when processing text have received considerable recent scrutiny, to some extent superseding earlier attempts to establish what *skills* are required by good readers in order to process text efficiently. In addition, relatively *stable characteristics* of readers, like sex, age and personality, have been studied alongside *physical characteristics*, like eye movements, speed of word recognition, automaticity of processing and such like. I will now highlight the main findings of relevance to assessment.

### Schemata and background knowledge

Ever since the work of Bartlett in the 1930s, it has been clear that the nature of the knowledge that readers have will influence not only what they remember of text (the focus of Bartlett's own research), but the product – their understanding of the text – and the way they process it. The development of schema theory has attempted to account for the consistent finding that what readers know affects what they understand. Schemata are seen as interlocking mental structures representing readers' knowledge. When readers process text, they integrate the new information from the text into their preexisting schemata. More than that, their schemata influence how they recognise information as well as how they store it.

Slightly different theories have developed over the years to account for the influence of what is sometimes called background knowledge: some theorists refer to **scripts** for common events like eating in a restaurant or going to the laundry, and others write about **frames**, into which new knowledge is slotted. The differences between the theories are trivial compared with what they have in common: an insistence that the state of the reader's knowledge influences process, product and recall.

It is not unusual to distinguish different types of knowledge or schemata: Carrell (1983a), for example, distinguishes formal schemata from content schemata. By the former she means knowledge of language and linguistic conventions, including knowledge of how texts are organised, and what the main features of particular genres are. By the latter she means, essentially, knowledge of the world, including the subject matter of the text.

However, content schemata can also be divided into background knowledge – i.e. knowledge which may or may not be relevant to the content of a particular text – and subject-matter knowledge, which is directly relevant to text content and topic. Moreover, some researchers have focused upon certain aspects of background knowledge, in particular that knowledge which is common to a particular culture, or cultural knowledge. I shall deal with each of these different aspects of knowledge in turn.

### Formal schemata: knowledge of language

It may seem self-evident that, if readers do not know the language of the text, then they will have great difficulty in processing the text. And indeed in studies of first-language reading the language knowledge of the reader is often taken for granted. However, this implies that first-language readers are homogeneous with respect to their knowledge of their mother tongue, yet this is manifestly not the case. Not only do younger, beginning readers have a less developed knowledge of their language, they also have less awareness of the nature of that language and of their knowledge of it (what is known as metalinguistic knowledge, see below). A reader's linguistic knowledge continues to develop with age and experience: vocabulary size and depth develop, knowledge of the conventions associated with particular types of text develops well into adulthood, and the ability to process the more complex linguistic structures associated especially with written language must inevitably develop with increasing literacy. Thus, the ease with which the language of a particular text can be processed must depend upon the nature of the reader's linguistic knowledge.

A problem for theorists and test developers alike, however, is this: what sort of linguistic knowledge is needed, and how much of it?

Inevitably, the answer will in part depend upon the nature of the text and the outcomes of reading that are expected (for example, according to reading purpose), a fact which underlines the importance of the interaction between text and reader variables.

In first-language reading research, it is much more common to investigate the effect of linguistic features in text, than to measure directly the knowledge of such features that readers have. Such studies will be reviewed in the second main section of this chapter, alongside research by psycholinguists into syntactic processing: the so-called 'garden-path' studies.

In first-language reading, research into linguistic knowledge has concentrated on vocabulary size and metalinguistic knowledge: how much awareness is needed of the nature of language, and how this affects reading. It is commonly assumed that first-language readers already possess basic linguistic knowledge (syntactic and semantic, above all). Indeed, Gough *et al.* (1992b) assert precisely this when positing a two-component theory of reading (see Chapter 1), consisting of decoding and comprehension, where the latter is said to underlie all language use, not just reading.

> Preliterate children can already comprehend. They have internalized the phonology and syntax of their native language, they have acquired a vocabulary of thousands of words and they can understand stories and follow instructions. What they cannot do is read stories or follow instructions in print.     (Gough *et al.*, 1992b:36)

Nevertheless, structural knowledge has been shown to have a facilitative effect on reading (Perfetti, 1989; Rayner, 1990; Garnham, 1985). Vocabulary knowledge has long been recognised to be crucial in first-language reading: estimates of the vocabularies of fluent first-language readers vary from 10,000 to 100,000 words (see also Read's volume on assessing vocabulary, in this series – Read, 2000). Measures of readers' vocabulary knowledge routinely correlate highly with measures of reading comprehension, and are often, indeed, the single best predictor of text comprehension.

Having to struggle with reading because of unknown words will obviously affect comprehension and take the pleasure out of reading. Research by Laufer (1989) and Liu and Nation (1985) shows that readers need to know 95% of the words in text to gain adequate comprehension and to be able to guess unknown words from context. Hirsh and Nation (1992) estimate that in order to be familiar with 97%

of the words in text, a reader needs a vocabulary of roughly 5,000 words. Readers familiar with only the 2,000 most frequent words of English, as compiled by West in his (1953) *General Service List* (*GSL*), will only understand roughly 90% of the words in text. Hirsh and Nation show that around 40% of words in the novels they analysed were not in the *General Service List*. Moreover, three-quarters or more of these 'infrequent' (i.e. non-*GSL*) words only occurred once or twice in the novels.

Discourse strategies based on extralinguistic, syntactic and semantic cues of text are investigated by van Dijk and Kintsch (1983) and are shown to be related to reading performance, but such studies typically still do not measure readers' knowledge directly. Rather they infer it from the result of the manipulation of text variables – see the next main section.

On the other hand, not surprisingly, in second- and foreign-language reading studies, there was an early emphasis on the importance of syntactic as well as lexical knowledge, and only recently has rhetorical knowledge and metalinguistic knowledge been studied in any depth.

In second- and foreign-language reading, it has always been assumed that learners must first acquire language knowledge before they can read. Early (1970s) approaches to the teaching of English for Specific Purposes, for example, assumed that what learners needed to know in order to read texts in their subject disciplines was knowledge of the language of that discipline: initially lexis, and then later syntactic and rhetorical features. The earliest ESP textbooks (e.g. Mackin's *English Studies* series, with titles like 'Military Texts', 'Geography', 'Agriculture') presented learners with specialist texts to be read. Each section of the books followed the same pattern: Test Paper, Lexical Simplification, Structural Simplifications, followed by exercises like Vocabulary Exercises, Structure Exercises, Questions on the Text, and Summary of the Contents of the Text, and finally The Application of the Contents of the Text to the Student's Own Country or Experience. The clear aim of such series, as well as later textbooks and courses in the 1970s, was to concentrate on teaching the language of the discipline in order to ensure that readers had the necessary formal linguistic schemata.

However, not much of this pedagogy was supported by research findings. When, for example, researchers investigated how important a knowledge of the passive voice in English might be to enable readers to process scientific texts (typically said to contain many such structures), the results were ambiguous. It could not be shown that a knowledge of the passive was essential to process texts containing passives. What appears clear with hindsight is that a knowledge of the lexis of the text, as well as more general and specific content knowledge, might well compensate for lack of linguistic knowledge.

Nevertheless, at the risk of oversimplifying, research has shown the importance of a knowledge of particular syntactic structures, or the ability to process them, to some aspects of second-language reading. Berman (1984) showed that students had difficulty identifying the constituent structures in sentences with complex or unusual syntax, for example where material is preposed before the main verb, or adverbial phrases come before the main clause. The ability to parse sentences into their correct syntactic structure appears to be an important element in understanding text. Not surprisingly, her students found it harder to process syntactic structures in English that differed from structures in the mother tongue (in this case Hebrew).

She refers to perceptual factors like 'heaviness' and 'opacity', as well as physical discontinuities in interdependent elements. Opacity may be created by the use of certain cohesive devices like deletion and substitution, or by nominalisations rather than the corresponding simple verbs and adjectives. Heaviness is created by the use of constructions (embeddings, modifications) which increase the amount and depth of information that must be stored in memory when moving from one constituent to another. Successful readers, she suggests, are able to get at the core of more complicated sentences. Interestingly, however, she also suggests that the ability to process complex syntax may be more important for the understanding of detailed information in sentences than for the understanding of the gist of a text.

Cooper (1984) contrasted what he calls 'practised' readers (those who have been largely educated in the medium of English even though their mother tongue is not English) with 'unpractised' readers, and concluded that what distinguished the two groups was not so much weaknesses in a range of syntactic features (tense, aspect, modality and so on) and affixation – even the practised readers had weaknesses in these areas. Rather, unpractised readers were disadvantaged by a poor knowledge of vocabulary (especially sub-technical words) and a weak understanding of semantic relationships between words, as well as the meaning of common sentence connectors. They showed considerable inability to use linguistic cues in the larger context in order to deduce word meaning, to understand lexical relationships and meaning relationships between sentences. The superior lexical competence of practised readers, rather than a greater syntactic competence, was the key distinguishing feature.

Despite the common-sense assumptions of the importance of language knowledge, the belief has existed for some time that, if students cannot read well in their first language, they will be unable to read well in the second/foreign language (see Chapter 1 and Alderson, 1984, for a discussion of this belief). From such a belief developed a pedagogical approach that concentrated on teaching students reading strategies in their first language as well as in the second language, at the expense of the imparting of L2 linguistic knowledge (see for example, the Brazilian ESP project reported in Celani *et al.*, 1988, and elsewhere).

Research to investigate or resolve the question whether second-language reading is a *language* problem or a *reading* problem has suggested the notion of a threshold of linguistic knowledge, without which readers cannot expect any first-language reading ability to transfer to the second language. Clarke's **short-circuit hypothesis** posits that inadequate knowledge of the second language short-circuits or prevents successful first-language readers from reading well in the second language.

Bernhardt and Kamil (1995) survey a number of studies and claim that first-language literacy is a strong predictor of L2 reading ability (upwards of 20% of variance – the variability in test-takers' scores – was accounted for). But L2 linguistic knowledge is a consistently more powerful predictor, accounting for more than 30% of the variance. They conclude that the second-language reading problem should be reformulated, not as an Either/Or question, but as a question of the interaction between the two abilities/knowledge sources. 'How L1 literate does a second-language reader have to be to make the second-language knowledge work? How much second-language knowledge does a second-language reader have to have in order to make the L1 literacy knowledge work?' This is essentially, of course, the question form of the short-circuit hypothesis, positing an interaction between L2 knowledge and L1 reading ability. Bernhardt and Kamil also point out that most studies leave 50% of the variance in L2 reading ability unexplained.

Bossers (1992) shows that while both second-language knowledge and first-language reading ability were related to reading ability in the second language, the former was more closely related (and especially vocabulary knowledge, rather than knowledge of grammar) at lower levels of linguistic proficiency. Only at relatively advanced levels of L2 proficiency did first-language reading ability prove to be the sole predictor of second-language reading. Hacquebord (1989) tested young Turks living in the Netherlands in a longitudinal study and showed a declining influence over time of L1 reading on L2 reading. However, this can be accounted for by a declining ability to read in the mother tongue (not the medium of instruction) and a growing ability to read in the second language. Carrell (1991) also shows that both first-language reading and second-language knowledge are important. A somewhat surprising result was that for Spanish speakers their first-language reading was more related to second-language reading than L2 knowledge, compared with native English speakers reading in Spanish, where L2 knowledge had more influence. However, this is potentially accounted for by the superior second-language proficiency of the Spanish speakers in that study over the foreign-language proficiency of the English speakers.

The clear conclusion of such studies is that second-language knowledge is more important than first-language reading abilities, and that a linguistic threshold exists which must be crossed before first-language reading ability can transfer to the second-language reading context. However, it is clear that this linguistic threshold is not absolute but must vary by task: the more demanding the task, the higher the linguistic threshold. What makes a task demanding will relate to issues like text topic, text language, background knowledge and task type. As Bossers (1992) suggests, future research should use tasks that vary in the demands they place on readers. This is highly relevant to those who wish to test reading ability: since the validity of a reading test might be conceptualised to depend in part on whether it taps first- or second-language reading ability, it is important to know what variables allow or inhibit such transfer. Similarly, however, in first-language reading, it is important to know whether the measurement of reading ability is unduly influenced by the difficulty of the language of the text, the difficulty of the task, or the state of the reader's language knowledge.

## Knowledge of genre/text type

Knowing how texts are organised – what sort of information to expect in what place – as well as knowing how information is signalled, and how changes of content might be marked – has long been thought to be of importance in facilitating reading. For example, knowing where to look for the main idea in a paragraph, and being able to identify how subsidiary ideas are marked, ought in principle to help a reader process information. However, there has been surprisingly little empirical research into readers' knowledge of the text features of particular genres, and its relationship to reading process or product. Most research has tended to concentrate on the textual features themselves, and how they contribute to text readability, rather than on the state of the readers' knowledge of such features. This is particularly true of reading research on native speakers of English, as we have seen. We will discuss such text-based research in the next major section of this chapter.

A study typical of such text-based research is Mandler (1978), who showed that when the text content was kept constant but the rhetorical structure varied (a simple story schema as contrasted with a deliberate violation of such a schema), first-language readers found the text harder to understand. I cite this study here, although it is clearly a study of text rather than schemata, because it was replicated in a much-quoted study by Carrell, with second-language speakers (1981). Carrell's results showed that when stories violating the formal story schema were processed by learners of English as a second language, both the quantity of recall and the temporal sequences of recall were affected.

Carrell (1983a) discusses the relationship between content schemata and formal schemata, and points out that much research has confounded the effects of the two. There is a need for research which separates the two sorts of schemata, and examines their interaction, especially in cross-cultural and cross-linguistic contexts.

It is perhaps difficult to distinguish between a reader's knowledge of how texts are organised, and their metalinguistic textual knowledge. In other words, readers might 'know' – in the sense in which they 'know' the syntax of their mother tongue – how texts are organised, and yet be unaware of this knowledge, and be unable to state it explicitly. Whereas research into the more traditional aspects of linguistic knowledge – syntax, lexis, morphology, semantics – is able to distinguish between knowing how to *use* and knowing what one *knows*, researchers have been less successful in distinguishing these two types of knowledge at text level. Thus one might argue that much of the research reported in this section was in fact not investigating linguistic proficiency, but metalinguistic knowledge. Obviously much depends upon how the knowledge was tapped: what sort of instruments were used.

This then leads us naturally to the topic of explicit versus implicit knowledge of language, what I have called here metalinguistic knowledge and metacognition.

## Metalinguistic knowledge and metacognition

As noted above, studies of first-language readers have investigated directly the effect of metacognition on reading. Research has revealed the relationship between metacognition and reading performance. Poor readers do not possess knowledge of strategies, and are often not aware of how or when to apply the knowledge they do have. They often cannot infer meaning from surface-level information, have poorly developed knowledge about how the reading system works, and find it difficult to evaluate text for clarity, consistency and plausibility. Instead they often believe that the purpose of reading is errorless word pronunciation, and that good reading includes nothing more than *verbatim* recall.

Block (1992) provides a useful review of metacognition and its relation to reading. Metalinguistic awareness plays a part in learning to read; bilinguals profit from sensitivity to metalinguistic information. With first-language readers, evidence suggests that comprehension monitoring operates rather automatically, and is not readily observable until some failure to comprehend occurs. Older and more proficient readers have more control over this monitoring process than younger and less proficient readers; good readers are more aware of how they control their reading and more able to verbalise this awareness. They also appear more sensitive to inconsistencies in text, although even good readers do not always notice or report all inconsistencies, perhaps because they are intent on making text coherent. Good readers tend to use meaning-based cues to evaluate whether they have understood what they read whereas poor readers tend to use or over-rely on word-level cues, and to focus on intrasentential rather than intersentential consistency.

A typical study is provided by Duffy *et al.* (1987) who show how low-group 3rd grade readers can be made aware of the mental processing involved in using reading skills as strategies (metacognitive awareness), and how such students then become more aware of the content of reading lessons, and of the need to be strategic when reading. They also score better on measures of reading achievement.

Pressley *et al.* (1987) examined students' perceptions of their readiness to take a test of reading (PREP), before reading target passages, after reading the passages and after being tested. Although the trend was for an increase in the accuracy of the perception as compared with their actual test performance, only the differences between perceptions before reading and after testing were significant. They make the suggestion that taking a test may be the best way of enhancing students' accuracy of PREP. However, when students were given adjunct questions (questions which accompanied the text – see below for a discussion of the effect of adjunct questions more generally) to answer whilst reading the texts, their PREP increased significantly after reading, as well as after testing. The authors thus suggest the value of adjunct questions in enhancing students' metacognitive awareness of their understanding of text.

Block (1992) compared proficient native and ESL readers with less proficient native and ESL readers, in a US college. She gathered verbal protocols and investigated in particular how they dealt with a referent problem and a vocabulary problem. She examined the monitoring process involved and concluded that control of the various stages of this monitoring process seemed to depend more on reading ability than on whether the reader was a first- or second-language reader of English. Proficient readers used the process completely and explicitly, less proficient readers were not as adept at recognising that a problem existed, or in identifying its source, and usually lacked the resources even to attempt to solve the problem, especially the referent problem. The less proficient readers, including the native readers, were frequently defeated by word problems. Whereas less proficient readers noticed and emphasised word problems, more proficient readers appeared not to worry so much if they did not understand a word: 'Strategic resources . . . seem more important than specific linguistic knowledge for these readers' (p. 336). Part of their strength lies in being able to decide which problems they can ignore and which they have to solve.

Alderson *et al.* (1997) investigated the metalinguistic knowledge of university learners of French in the UK. They looked at students' ability to identify parts of speech and linguistic functions, and to identify errors and describe what rules have been contravened, as well as the (non-metalinguistic) ability to identify similarities in structure without the requirement to describe such similarities. They found that there was little relationship between both types of knowledge and students' reading proficiency in French (as well as with other linguistic variables like the ability to do well on grammar and cloze tests). They conclude that metalinguistic knowledge is separate from linguistic ability, and that teaching students the rules of a language is unlikely to enhance their ability to use that language, however desirable such knowledge may be for other reasons. The obvious consequence for the testing of reading is that the ability to talk about (or answer questions about) the language of a text is unlikely to relate to the ability to understand the text – the latter is likely to be possible without the former.

## Content schemata

Psychologists, applied linguists and educationists alike have long been interested in exploring content schemata, as discussed in the introduction to this chapter. The classic studies are by Rumelhart (1980, 1985) and Bransford and his associates (for example, Bransford *et al.*, 1984) which show clearly that readers need knowledge about the content of the passage to be able to understand it. Moreover, and arguably more importantly, such knowledge does not simply need to be available – it needs to be activated by the reader, or the text, if it is to be used in accurate understanding. Studies have shown how readers can learn how to activate their own schemata, and performance on reading tasks can improve as a result of such training.

The background-knowledge effect is very strong; it has been shown that even across passages on the same general theme, which had identical structure and syntax and very similar vocabulary, the more familiar version was better recalled. Laboratory studies have manipulated the information available to readers (and listeners, in some of the Bransford studies), for example by removing relevant visual support, or titles and headlines which might activate the knowledge needed to understand the passage. Such studies typically involve information directly relevant to the text content. Other studies have looked at more general knowledge.

## Knowledge of subject matter/topic

Whilst it would seem obvious that, if one knows absolutely nothing about the topic of a text, one will find it difficult to process, such a common-sense approach cannot explain how readers can learn new information, and indeed understand texts in unfamiliar areas. The value of schema theory (see Chapter 1) is that it attempts to explain such integration of new information with old, but it has difficulty handling the integration of new information with non-existent information. The argument is, of course, that no information is completely new – similarities can be seen with something one already knows, which can then be used to process the new, but this does not explain how the similarities are noticed in the first place, nor how readers can misunderstand text on the basis of false similarities and comparisons/parallels.

Similarly it would appear obvious that readers will find it easier to read texts in areas they are familiar with, for example those they have studied, than those which they are not or have not, even if their knowledge is more general than, or different from, the exact content of the text. Thus, subject matter familiarity might be expected to have a facilitating effect. Curiously little research had been done in this area, certainly in second or foreign languages, until recently. Alderson and Urquhart (1985) were able to show that reading tests on texts in subject disciplines that students were studying or had studied were sometimes easier to process than those which were not, but not always. Some texts outside their subject disciplines proved easier to understand than texts within the disciplines, despite being of roughly equivalent difficulty. Other studies have provided evidence that superior linguistic proficiency can compensate for lack of subject knowledge, and that familiarity with subject matter can compensate for inferior linguistic proficiency. I shall return to this topic in Chapter 3.

## Knowledge of the world

The specificity of content knowledge varies. We have already seen how knowledge related to but not contained in a text, as in subject discipline, may or may not have an impact on text processing. Background knowledge, or knowledge of how the world works, also has an effect. The classic example is cited by Rumelhart:

*The policeman held up his hand and the car stopped.*
(Rumelhart, 1985:267)

Normal language users or readers have no difficulty understanding such a sentence, yet to do so it is necessary to know or to infer that the car has a driver, that a policeman holding up his hand is a signal to the driver to stop the car, and so on. None of this is stated, but it is part of our knowledge of how the world works. Imagine the following scenario where the cars have been parked on a hill, and their owners have departed. Suddenly, there is an earthquake, and the cars begin to roll down the hill. Then appears the sentence: '*The policeman held up his hand and the cars stopped.*' To make sense of this readers now have to revise their schemata and conclude that some magical agency has intervened.

All language processing requires world knowledge. The activation of such knowledge is fast and automatic, and without such processes, language comprehension would be slow and laborious, if it could take place at all. Thus, world knowledge is essential to reading, too.

## Cultural knowledge

However, world knowledge typically refers to *your* world – the way your world works. And such knowledge may be limited, that is, other people's worlds may work differently. Such worlds may be idiosyncratic – because of personal history, experiences unique to one person – and thus difficult to predict or control, but they may also be held in common with other people. To the extent that those other people are conventionally said to share a culture, then cultural knowledge is also crucial to text understanding.

The classic study is Bartlett's (1932), which showed how British informants, when reading a North American Indian folktale, consistently altered it to conform to their own cultural assumptions about the world. Since then, numerous studies with first-language readers have examined cultural differences among groups of readers, including children: religious group membership, black vs. white, inner city vs. rural, members of different dialect groups, and so on. Effects of cultural differences on reading recall, test scores and reading miscues have been consistently found in such studies. Interestingly, they have also found that this cultural group difference increases with age, supporting the notion that cultural knowledge develops as we progress from child to adult.

In a classic and much quoted study, Steffensen *et al.* (1984) explored differences in cultural knowledge between Indians from the subcontinent and North Americans, by having both groups read an account of weddings, one in a cultural setting familiar to them, and one in an unfamiliar setting. Subjects were able to recall more, and more accurately, from the familiar setting than the unfamiliar one, and they reported greater difficulty in processing the unfamiliar cultural setting. In addition, whereas in the unfamiliar setting their recalls of the text showed distortions of the information in the text – distortions towards their own cultural expectations – even in the familiar texts they made mistakes: they elaborated information not actually contained in the text, in line with their own cultural knowledge. Thus reading texts in unfamiliar cultural settings can result in difficulty of processing and recalling, but reading texts in familiar settings can also result in misunderstanding, or at least in factually inaccurate recall.

One problem that studies of content and cultural knowledge face is distinguishing between knowledge of the content/culture and knowledge of vocabulary. Much more research is needed to tease out whether empirical effects are due to lexical (i.e. formal) knowledge, or content/cultural knowledge. This is of course crucial for testers of reading in a second language, who may wish to avoid bias by content knowledge, yet may be prepared to accept that lack of relevant vocabulary has caused lower reading test scores.

### Criticisms of schema theory

As stated above, the value of schema theory is that it attempts to explain how new information is integrated with old, but it does not explain how completely new information is handled. Although similarities may be perceived with related information (schema theory is after all a prototype theory), it does not explain how the similarities are noticed in the first place, nor how readers can misunderstand text on the basis of false similarities and comparisons/parallels.

Critics of schema theory point out that it does not lead to explicit definitions or predictions of comprehension processes, although it has stimulated a considerable amount of research into the products of understanding. Carver (1992a) is critical of many schema-theory–based studies for failing to measure general reading ability, the time allowed to read, the 'rauding rate' of the individual and the relative difficulty of the material, since reading speed is known to be an important indicator of reading comprehension.

Carver argues that schema theory in fact applies not to normal reading (rauding) but to study reading and memorising. He claims therefore that schema theory applies only when materials are relatively difficult. Schema-theory variables are thus likely to be applicable to college-level students who study relatively hard materials, but not to elementary school children because asking them to read such materials is not normal practice.

He reviews two classic studies that claim to support effects which schema theory predicts (Valencia and Stallman, 1989, and Johnston, 1984) and shows that the claims of the studies are untenable. There was no effect for prediction activities on performance on tests after reading, and the effect of prior knowledge was much less than the effect of general reading ability.

Yet it appears that many school boards in the United States have adopted tests based on schema theory, which often include prediction activities, measures of prior knowledge and questions on a single lengthy passage. Attempts have apparently been made to eliminate standardised reading comprehension tests, in part because such tests are said to have no theoretical basis in schema theory, and because it is thought that the tests are substantially biased because they include no measure of prior knowledge. Carver is critical of such prejudice, and also criticises school boards for introducing instructional practice that appears to have no effect empirically, simply because it is fashionable.

> The direct evidence that activating prior knowledge facilitates comprehension during typical or normal reading is highly questionable. The direct evidence that standardised reading comprehension tests are biased because they contain no measure of prior knowledge is highly questionable. Finally the direct evidence that text type affects comprehension in normal or ordinary reading is highly questionable.
>
> If instructional ideas derived from schema theory are in fact mostly irrelevant in normal reading situations (i.e. not involving relatively hard materials that require studying), then we need to be concerned about the possibility of wasting a great deal of

valuable time on instructional techniques that are fashionable but have no more effect than large doses of chicken soup.

(Carver, 1992a:173)

## Reader skills and abilities

So far, the discussion has been of knowledge that readers have. However, readers not only have knowledge, they have abilities: abilities not only to learn new knowledge, but also abilities to process information. Researchers have long been concerned that readers may have relevant knowledge but that they may not possess, or have learned, the ability or skill to process text. Here I use the terms ability and skill interchangeably.

It is possible that what distinguishes good readers from poor readers, or poor understanding from good understanding, is not so much the existence of relevant schemata or even the ability to activate them, but a more general cognitive ability, what some researchers have called Schematic Concept Formation. This may be verbal or non-verbal. Perkins (1987) showed a very close relationship for second-language readers between proficiency in finding the common set of features which constitute a single graphic pattern or multiple patterns in a set of stimuli, and the ability to understand text and especially the story structure of texts. He suggests that the operations of detecting the conventional structure of stories and performing a non-verbal schematic concept formation task might be similar. This provides some support for the argument put forward in Chapter 1 that much of reading is a general cognitive, problem-solving ability, which underlies all language processing, including listening, and is not specific to reading.

Nevertheless, researchers have long tried to establish what verbal skills are essential to text comprehension, what is involved in being a good reader. Typically this has involved two approaches: either identifying readers known to be good and contrasting their understandings – process and product – with readers known to be poor. Or it has involved identifying *a priori* what skills are thought to be needed, and then devising tests aimed at measuring such skills. Typically the relationship between the items testing the different skills is then analysed, to see to what extent they can be empirically isolated (and therefore presumably tested and taught).

Much controversy surrounds such research. There is contradictory evidence as to whether these 'skills' are separately identifiable. Different analyses of the same databases of skills have resulted in more or fewer factors that appear to underlie adequate understanding. Davis claimed that the skills 1, 3, 5, 6 and 8 cited in Chapter 1 were empirically distinguishable, whereas Thorndike (1974), who re-analysed the data, claimed that only the first skill (word knowledge) could be distinguished from the others. Spearitt (1972) also did a re-analysis, and claimed there were four separate factors: recalling word meanings, drawing inferences from the content; recognising a writer's purpose, tone and mood; following the structure of the passage. The latter three skills were highly correlated, however, and he concluded that 'present types of reading tests, as distinct from word knowledge tests, largely measure one basic ability, which may well correspond to the label of "reasoning in reading"'.

When judges are asked to identify which skills the items are measuring, they are often unable to do so with any convincing degree of agreement. It is frequently difficult to get expert judges to agree on what skills are operationalised by which test item. Moreover, as pointed out in Chapter 1, analyses of test performance do not reveal separability of skills, nor implicational scales nor even a hierarchy of skill difficulty. Thus there are statistical and judgemental reasons for doubting whether skills can be measured separately, or whether sub-skills of reading can be shown to exist and be related to the ability to answer particular sorts of test questions. Indeed whether test questions can unambiguously be said to be testing particular skills is quite unclear, as we shall see in more detail in Chapter 3.

Alderson concludes: 'Answering a test question is likely to involve a variety of interrelated skills, rather than one skill only or even mainly. Even if there are separate skills in the reading process which one could identify by a rational process of analysis of one's own reading behaviour, it appears to be extremely difficult if not impossible to isolate them for the sake of testing or research' (1990b:436).

This issue is crucial to the assessment of reading: if we are not able to define what we mean by the 'ability to read', it will be difficult to devise means of assessing such abilities. Yet our very operationalisations of such abilities may be imperfect, however plausible our theoretical constructs. And the very act of analysing skills might falsify the real world, where such 'skills', even if they exist, might operate dynamically, in parallel, or in compensatory fashion. And, of course, they might do so differently for different learners on the same text and for the same learner on different texts or the same text on different occasions.

One of the causes of the variation we have noted in readers and readings might be that readers have different amounts of knowledge relevant to the text in hand, as discussed above. Such differences might result in some readers having to call upon certain skills, e.g. lexical inferencing, whereas readers with the necessary knowledge do not need to use such skills. However, lack of knowledge or skill in one area might be compensated by abilities or knowledge in other areas. This is known as the compensation hypothesis.

Stanovich's (1980) interactive–compensatory hypothesis is similar to the compensation hypothesis and is intended to account for differences between good and poor readers:

> A deficit in any knowledge source results in heavier reliance on other knowledge sources, regardless of their level in the processing hierarchy. Thus, according to the interactive compensatory model, the poor reader who has deficient word analysis skills might possibly show greater reliance on contextual factors.
>
> (Stanovich, 1980:63)

This has not been borne out in empirical studies: for example, a high degree of cohesion in text has not been shown to compensate for difficulty in vocabulary (see next main section for further discussion). The nature of any possible interaction among skills thus remains obscure at present.

### Reader purpose in reading

Another possible cause of the variation between readers and readings which we need to consider is that different readers read texts with different purposes. If all you wish to do is get a general idea of text content, you will pay less attention to the detail of the text, and you may well read in very different ways than if you are studying a text in order to identify key information. And so you may well need different skills suited to these different purposes. Thus it has become almost a platitude to say that the reason you are reading a text will influence the way you read it, the skills you require or use, and the ultimate understanding and recall you have of that text. Reading a short story

for pleasure at bedtime is likely to be different in all three aspects –
process, product and recall – from reading a history text for an examination the next morning.

One of the problems with much research in this area is that the
reasons the informants are reading texts is because the researcher is
paying them, or because they have to take a test. Their purposes may
not be their own, but somebody else's. The process and product may
be very different if the reader reads for self-generated reasons.

Studies have attempted to manipulate reader purpose (what some
call 'reader intent') by a variety of means. Readers have been given
the objectives of reading particular passages, and their subsequent
performance on tests is inspected. Effects have been mixed, but in
general, objectives that direct students' attention to aspects of text
they would otherwise ignore have been shown to be somewhat effective in enhancing comprehension. Other studies have inserted
adjunct questions in the text, both before the information relevant to
the question, and after (what are called pre- and post-questions). In
some cases answers are then provided to the questions alongside the
question, and in other cases they are not. The content of the questions is varied according to whether they were higher- or lower-level
in terms of the information-processing required. Researchers have
also examined the information in student recalls to see whether they
only recall information directly related to the questions asked or
objectives described, or whether they also contain information incidental to such questions and objectives (referred to as **intentional**
versus **incidental** learning).

Results show that inserting post-questions has a greater effect than
pre-questions, and supplying answers depresses the students' performance, presumably because they need to make less effort with the
text. Post-questions of a higher order result in incidental as well as
intentional learning, and, unlike lower-level pre-questions, result in
retention of both factual and higher-order information over time. It
would appear then that to improve student learning from text (not
necessarily the same thing as reading) higher-order post-questions
without answers would be desirable. The implication for testing might
be that students should not be encouraged to read the questions
before they process text. However, the only purpose students often
have in taking a reading test is to answer somebody else's questions,
and therefore to deny them access to the questions might encourage
purposeless reading. It would certainly result in less efficient reading.

It is often noted, however, that although significant results are achieved in laboratory settings, it is arguable whether the effects could be replicated in the real world outside the laboratory, as they are typically fairly small.

Thus empirical support for the effect of purpose on reading process and product is available, but perhaps not meaningful, or even relevant to assessment. Nevertheless, little research has been done to see what effect the simulation of real reading purposes might have on reading performance – see Chapter 3.

However, Carver (1984) shows that changing the purpose for typical reading (what he calls 'rauding') has no effect on what students understand, or their reading rate. (The two purposes used were to decide which would be the best title for the passage – a gist question, and to detect missing verbs – a detail question.) Carver concludes that his data provide no support for those who would contend that purpose for reading has a large effect upon comprehension in relatively normal or typical reading situations.

Carver (1990) also provides evidence from many researchers which indicates that the goals associated with each of what he considers to be the five basic reading processes (scanning, skimming, rauding, learning and memorising) are quite different, and that the research results involving one of these reading processes will not necesarily generalise to another. This would seem to argue in favour of gross distinctions among what we might call macro-purposes, as evidenced by these five reading types, at the very least, and therefore testers of reading should be clear which of the five purposes they intend to simulate or measure.

Despite the lack of firm evidence of a substantial effect of varying readers' purposes, I would argue that test developers need to consider carefully the tasks they set readers, or the purposes with which their test-takers read, in case there might be undetected but important biasing effects – I discuss this further in Chapters 5, 6 and 7.

## Real world versus test taking

It is important to remember that even if research results have been gathered in ways that reflect real-world real-reader purposes, when we ask readers to take a test of reading, we are rarely doing this for the reader's own reason – other than the extrinsic motivation involved in taking any test – but we are imposing, with greater or lesser force, our own purposes. And even if we try to simulate real-world purposes for reading a given text, as I discuss in Chapter 5, the fact remains that the ultimate purpose of the event is to evaluate the readers' ability to read. This is rarely the purpose for which real readers read real texts.

However, I accept the argument that reading for a test is as real as any other reading. The point is not how *real* it is but how *different*, and thus how generalisable our conclusions can be from one setting to another. When assessing reading ability we are not interested in how well a person can perform in a reading test but how well that performance approximates to or predicts how they will read in other settings, or (in the case of diagnostic tests) how well that performance can explain reading in other settings.

### Reader motivation/interest

Studies of poor first and second-language readers have consistently shown that poor readers (Cooper's 1984 'unpractised' readers) lack motivation to read or to spend time improving their ability to read. Of course, this is as likely to be the effect of poor reading as the cause of it, but once established, poor motivation doubtless compounds the problem ('success breeds success, failure breeds failure'). The problem is how to improve reader motivation.

The dilemma touched upon above, of needing to avoid imposing a purpose on the reader, has long been recognised in studies of motivation. A distinction is frequently made between extrinsic and intrinsic motivation, and the latter, generated internally by the individual, is generally thought to be superior to extrinsic motivation. Reader motivation has been shown to relate to the quality of the outcome of reading, in that extrinsically motivated students seem to read at a surface level, paying attention to facts and details rather than to the main ideas, to what the text is about, to how ideas in the text relate to each other, and to how the text relates to other texts, or to what the reader knows about the subject or the world. These latter types of understanding, often called higher-order levels, are held to be educationally desirable – more so than the simple ability to remember and regurgitate facts – and so there is considerable interest in how higher levels of understanding can be achieved. If intrinsic motivation leads to higher levels of understanding, and the research suggests that it does, then can intrinsic motivation be induced?

Fransson (1984) attempted to do so, by using texts which he thought particular groups of students would be interested in, and others not. However, he subsequently discovered that students he had predicted would be interested in the text were not, and vice versa. When he analysed his results according to reported levels of interest (which he interprets as intrinsic motivation) he found the expected results: higher levels of processing and recall. He concludes that it is very difficult to induce intrinsic motivation – it has to come from the readers, undisturbed by an externally imposed task, who are reading for their own enjoyment or satisfaction.

Fransson was able to show that those students who expected a test after their reading read for facts rather than for higher levels of information. Those who perceived the situation as threatening (some were told they would be asked to summarise orally their under-standing of the text after reading it, in front of colleagues, and the summary would be audio-recorded) reported paying much more at-tention to detail than to the main idea or to connections, or the general sense and value of the text. Again, insofar as students find test situations threatening, we risk inducing an understanding of the text which is 'lower' than the same individuals might be able to achieve in other settings. In this regard, it may be that informal assessment procedures might result in qualitatively better performances than test-based assessments.

What test designers can do about this will be discussed in later chapters, but at least those who interpret test scores should bear in mind that the score may well be an underestimate of unpressured, intrinsically motivated reading.

## Reader affect

One of the reasons why informal assessments might result in better performances is the emotional state of the reader induced by the test. Fransson (1984) compared readers who reported state anxiety – i.e. who were anxious during the experience – with those who reported trait anxiety – i.e. who are habitually anxious people. He found that high trait anxiety led to readers ignoring the expressed purpose of the reading, and expecting threats – tests – never intended by the experimenter. In other words, habitually anxious readers might expect threatening conditions, for example during study reading, regardless of expressed intentions. In addition, he found an interaction between intrinsic motivation and state anxiety: students who reported being anxious during the reading showed weak intrinsic motivation. State anxiety interfered with intrinsic motivation and depressed factual test scores for those with strong intrinsic motivation. Students who have low trait anxiety tend to read at a deeper level, whereas highly state-anxious students tend to be surface processors. He concludes:

> Conditions provoking adaptation to expected test demands and high state anxiety are closely related to surface-level processing and high intensity of reading. In contrast all subjects not adapting to an expected test and low in state anxiety reported deep level processing and in most cases a low intensity of reading.
>
> (Fransson, 1984:112)

Clearly these findings are highly relevant to those who design high-stakes tests which might be expected to induce adaptation to test demands and high state anxiety.

Emotional responses in reading literature have long been the subject of research, at least for first-language readers. Miall (1989) has argued that conventional schema theory and other cognitive models which neglect affect are inadequate for explaining literary response. In fact, Bartlett himself emphasised that the organisation and activation of knowledge was crucially affected by factors such as emotion, interest and attitudes. Goetz *et al.* (1992) report a number of studies that have used either qualitative or quantitative means to investigate readers' responses, including affective responses. They also report their own study of readers' self-reports of emotions experienced while reading a literary text. Unsurprisingly, different story episodes evoked different emotional responses. Although they do not report the degree of agreement among readers in their emotional response, their results showed great complexity in the readers' emotional responses to stories and story episodes.

It is clearly important to understand in greater depth the constructive and imaginative processes necessary to bring a text to life, in order to contribute to a more complete understanding of the reading process and the literary experience in particular. Given the likelihood that different readers will have at least partially different emotional responses, understanding affective responses during the process and their effect on the product has important implications for the testing and assessment of reading.

## Other, stable, reader characteristics

The distinction made above between state and trait anxiety leads us to consider the effect of reader variables that might be considered to be stable over time. Personality is one such, and the difference between trait and state anxiety is normally related to personality differences among individuals. We have already discussed the influence of variables like knowledge, which may or may not be stable, but other reader factors have also been of interest in reading research, among them sex, social class, occupation, intelligence and so on. It is beyond the scope of this chapter to report all the results, and in any case it is unclear how much would be of interest to those concerned with language assessment.

Nevertheless, it is important to know, for example, that girls generally are thought to perform better on first-language reading tests than boys, and Bügel and Buunk (1996) show a similar effect for foreign-language reading. Test designers cannot change the sex of the test-takers, but they can take care not to bias their tests unduly towards either sex, they can check for such possible biases in their analyses of results, and they can issue cautions in the interpretation of results of males and females respectively.

One set of reader characteristics that has received considerable attention relates to physical and cognitive aspects: the speed at which readers can recognise words or sentences, their processing capacity in both short- and medium- to long-term memory, their eye movements and fixations, and their reading speed and cognitive strategies.

Numerous studies of eye movements have shown the importance of rapid and automatic processing of most of the words on the page: one estimate is that fluent readers process some 80% of content words and 40% of functions (in English) (Grabe, 1991). The visual span in eye fixations has been demonstrated to be very limited: first-language readers are capable of seeing no more than 15–16 letters in a fixation – typically 3–4 letters to the left of a fixation and 10–12 to the right (Rayner and Pollatsek, 1989). What distinguishes good from poor readers is not the number of letters in a fixation, nor the number of words fixated per page, but the speed of the fixation – the automaticity of word recognition – and the processes that occur during fixation. Rayner and Pollatsek (1989) report that words are identified quickly: the rate for skilled readers exceeds the recognition of five words per second.

It has been suggested that after initial word identification, but still during the fixation, good readers move onto higher-level prediction and monitoring, as well as planning of subsequent fixations. This is thought to be because good readers use less capacity to analyse the visual stimulus, and therefore have other resources available for other sorts of processing.

Not only are good readers rapid in their word recognition, they are precise as well. Readers take in letter features of short words simultaneously and appear to recognise all the letters in a word. The ability to recognise words rapidly and accurately (encoding time) is an important predictor of reading ability, especially with younger first-language readers, and even for college-level students. This interestingly suggests the use of encoding time as a possible diagnostic tool.

Carver (1982) shows that there are optimal rates of processing prose, and they are roughly equivalent for reading and listening, at 300 words per minute (wpm). This optimal processing rate is known as the rauding rate in Rauding Theory. Earlier research had suggested a linear relationship between speed and comprehension: an almost linear loss in comprehension as speed is increased. It had also been suggested that the optimal rate for listening was 200 wpm, much lower than that for reading at 300 wpm.

The work of Carver challenges such assumptions. It also challenges the Goodman and Smith view that individuals are quite flexible in their rate because it varies with the nature of the information: the more redundant or predictable the letters, words or sentences, the faster the individual supposedly reads. It used to be claimed that individuals adjust their rate during reading so as to keep efficiency at a constantly high level across a wide range of rates. Carver's results show that this is simply not true.

> The data suggest that there is nothing inherent in the reading mode which makes it more efficient for comprehending sentences in passages than the auding mode. Any superiority there might be either be artifactual – a result of distortion in compressing the speech – or because individuals are simply not used to listening at rates much higher than 150–175 wpm, and auding rate is beyond their control. (Carver, 1982:73)

Moreover, the optimal rate tends to be constant across a wide range of difficulty levels (for college students) and this contradicts the hypothesis-testing view. If good readers did hypothesise what lies ahead and adjust rate to match changes in difficulty, reading rates would adjust to suit materials. Carver's results show that approx 300 wpm is the most efficient rate for typical college students, whether they are reading Grade 4 or Grade 5 materials. It 'would not seem appropriate for good readers to adjust their rate as materials decrease in difficulty, because it would be inefficient to do so' (1982:85). Rauding Theory contends that individuals maximise their efficiency of reading prose by keeping their rate constant at the optimal rate. Interestingly the rauding rate is a threshold rate: when rate increases beyond it, efficiency drops 'precipitously'. Carver therefore concludes that future theory regarding the detailed cognitive processes during reading should make a hard distinction between typical prose reading, at rates around 300 wpm, and skimming, at rates around 1000 wpm. This is important for understanding what skimming is and suggests it is qualitatively different from reading.

> Theories about the cognitive processes involved in reading need to account for a) the optimal rate b) the equivalences of reading and auding and c) the constancy of the optimal rate across varying difficulties of prose materials.          (Carver, 1982:87)

Some research has also been conducted with second-language readers. Segalowitz *et al.* (1991) show that even advanced second-language learners do not read as easily or quickly in their second language as in their first, not because they do not have an absolute deficiency in vocabulary knowledge but because they exhibit poorer processing 'in lower mechanisms that may be involved in basic word recognition' (1991:20). Lower-level processes are not automatised to the same extent as they are in the native language and thus consume resources needed for higher-level processes such as linking propositions, making inferences, resolving ambiguities and integrating new information with existing knowledge. What appears to matter is massive overlearning of words and much recognition practice in transferable and interesting contexts, in order to ensure quick access during reading.

The question for test developers is how they can take account of such findings in their assessment procedures. One obvious way is consciously to measure reading speed in addition to comprehension.

Another is to pay attention to both the length of texts to be read and to the time allowed for reading them. A further possibility is to consider the diagnostic value of assessing lower-level processing abilities (see the work of Koda, 1987 and 1996, for example). It may be the case that computer-controlled reading tasks might offer interesting opportunities for innovation and measurement in this area also – see the discussion at the end of this chapter and in Chapter 9.

We should note that many of the variables discussed in this section almost certainly interact with those described in previous sections: with knowledge, interest, affect and so on. They are also highly likely to be conditioned by and interact with text variables, such as text topic, topicality, layout and so on. This latter area is the topic of the next major section of this chapter. However, before moving on to consider text variables, there remains one major area of research that we need briefly to consider, and that is young children who are learning to read.

## Beginning readers and fluent readers

The interest of research into the difference between beginning readers and fluent readers is in how beginning learners actually become fluent readers, what variables affect their progress and how educators in particular might intervene in order to improve the teaching of reading.

This is of obvious interest to testers, since, if we can characterise what differentiates successful from unsuccessful readers, we can focus on those differences if we wish to diagnose reading ability, or to predict reading proficiency. Similarly, a knowledge of what beginning readers have to do in order to become better readers would influence instruction, placement in suitable classes or schemes of instruction, and the assessment of achievement. Equally, what distinguishes those children who eventually become good readers from those who show less rapid, or no, development, has implications for both diagnosis and placement, and for the assessment of reading readiness.

Research into first-language reading development is extensive, and some has been referred to above under the heading of processing capacity and other cognitive and physical characteristics. However, much of the research with young children is of very limited relevance to the assessment of reading in a second or foreign language, and is much more relevant to the diagnosis and assessment of dyslexia, for example, which is too specialised a topic to be treated in this book.

Clearly, for second-language readers, an important component in a developing reading ability must be increasing language proficiency. We have already, in Chapter 1 and above, come across the notion of a language threshold which a reader must cross before the reading ability acquired in the first language can transfer, and thus one major difference between beginning and fluent second-language readers must be their differential language proficiency. However, as already discussed, the ability to use metacognitive skills effectively and to monitor reading is also an important component of skilled reading. Good readers are more effective in using metacognitive skills than less fluent readers, and older readers are better than younger readers. Among such metacognitive skills are:

- recognising the more important information in text
- adjusting reading rate
- skimming
- previewing
- using context to resolve a misunderstanding
- formulating questions about information
- monitoring cognition, including recognising problems with information presented in text or an inability to understand text

Self-regulation strategies like planning ahead, testing one's own comprehension, and being aware of and revising the strategies being used are also said to be typical reading strategies of fluent readers.

What distinguishes good from poor second-language readers will be a recurring theme in this volume, but specifically in Chapter 8 I will discuss in some detail how reading development has been operationalised in reading tests and scales of reading ability.

## Text variables

The other side of the coin in the reader–text interaction is the text itself. Many aspects of text that might facilitate or make difficult the reading process have been studied, from a variety of different disciplines. Although linguistics is the obvious major source of insight into the language of text, texts have often been studied from a linguistic perspective without concern for the reader. It has all too often been assumed that the analyst represents a typical reader, and that what results from the analysis can therefore be assumed to be true of any language processor.

The simplistic nature of such an assumption will be clear from the previous section, where I examined at some length those aspects of readers that impinge on the reading process. As a result of this neglect of the reader, therefore, much linguistic study is strictly irrelevant to this chapter. However, some linguists and particularly applied linguists have indeed been concerned with the impact of linguistic variables on the process of understanding texts.

In addition, text analysts from other backgrounds, including education, psychology, the study of rhetoric, sociology and even journalism and communication studies, have contributed to our understanding of those factors in text that influence the process. These factors range from aspects of text content, to text types or genres, text organisation, sentence structure, lexis, text typography, layout, the relationship between verbal and non-verbal text, and the medium in which the text is presented.

## Text topic and content

Just as it is commonly assumed that what readers know will affect what they understand when reading, so too it is commonly assumed that text content will affect how readers process text. Yet curiously no theory has emerged analogous to schema theory to account for the difficulty of text content.

Information theory was one such attempt, where researchers attempted to compute indices of information density in text, but this theory has not made any significant contribution to the field. Content analysis, popular particularly among sociologists in the 1970s, was an approach to the quantification of propositions in a text in such a way as to enable both objective measures of what a given text was 'about' and estimations of text difficulty, but, again, little was achieved. It might be significant that there has been a recent revival of interest in content analysis with the wider availability of cheap and powerful computers, but as yet such research has been limited in its relevance to the study of reading.

It is generally assumed (and has long been established) that abstract texts will be harder to understand than texts describing real objects, events or activities. The more concrete, imaginable and interesting, the more readable the text. Texts on arcane topics are likely to be harder to process (although what is arcane for one person may well be familiar to another – an illustration, if one were needed, of the intimate and complex interrelationship between text content and reader knowledge). Texts located in familiar settings, on everyday topics, are likely to be easier to process than those that are not.

The quantity of information in a text affects understanding and recall, as does the density of propositions. The extent to which information is stated explicitly in the text, requiring less inferencing, has an effect on recall, but there is also some evidence that texts which seek to spell out all the presuppositions they imply are harder to process: legal texts are notoriously difficult to follow precisely because they seek to avoid all possible ambiguities and alternative interpretations. It would appear that texts that appeal to commonly held assumptions will be easier to process, but ironically only for those who share those assumptions: they will be harder to process for those who do not.

Despite such findings, it is interesting to note that all too often research studies make the assumption that findings based on one set of texts will generalise to other texts. Clapham's work (see Chapter 3) shows very clearly that such assumptions are quite unjustified, since she found test difficulty to vary unpredictably, largely, as far as can be seen, as a result of text content. Alderson and Urquhart (1985) draw similar conclusions from their apparently contradictory results.

Given the nature of general Western education, it does appear to be the case from empirical studies that, on the whole, non-specialist texts in the arts and humanities, and to some extent in the social sciences, will be easier to process for more people of equivalent educational background than scientific texts. This is presumably because, in that culture at least, more people will have read fiction, popular journalism, advertisements and simple expository texts, than will have read technical or scientific texts. It is after all part of most people's education to read the literature and contemporary journalism of their mother tongue. It is less certain that most people will have read scientific or technical texts. However, it may be, with a growing emphasis in the West on science education and the increasing role of technology in society generally, that future generations will be more familiar with broadly scientific texts than current generations.

As we shall see in the next chapter, one conclusion that test designers have drawn from all this is that it is more appropriate to take texts from popular fiction and non-fiction on the grounds that they are likely to be less biased in terms of difficulty, and therefore more suitable for tests of reading.

An alternative procedure is to select or construct texts on topics which are so arcane that nobody will be familiar with them. This used to be the approach of the JMB Test of English (now the NEA's UETESOL), where texts were often used on subjects such as medieval armour, ships' riggings or the hallmarks of silverware, on the assumption that these would be equally difficult for all test-takers. Hill and Parry (1992) make the erroneous assumption that this is common practice in test design. However, if we accept Swain's principle of Biasing for Best (Swain, 1985), such practice would seem to be unnecessary and possibly unethical, faced with the alternative of selecting texts that most or all of the test-takers could be expected to be familiar with in some sense.

Whichever approach one takes, and whether or not one accepts the universality of certain topics or text content, the test designer would be well advised to be aware that variation in text content might be expected to lead to different test results, and to sample accordingly. Good tests of reading and good assessment procedures in general will ensure that readers have been assessed for their ability to understand texts in a range of different topics. Bachman and Palmer (1996:120–127) argue that the approach one takes must take into consideration the presupposed background knowledge (BGK – what they call topical knowledge) of the test-takers, and suggest three general options for deciding on which approach is most appropriate to a given testing situation: excluding BGK from the construct; including both BGK and language ability in the construct; and defining BGK and language ability as separate constructs.

## Text type and genre

It may be that certain topics are associated with certain types of text. For example, descriptions of how things work are more likely to be found in expository texts than in narrative texts. It could be that what causes difficulty in texts is less the actual content than the way the text is written: its style, or the features that make one text different from another, and that give rise to a number of different classifications of text type.

There is a long tradition of research into the differences between expository and narrative texts. The general conclusion is that expository texts are harder to process than narrative texts, perhaps because of the greater variety of relationships among text units, possibly due to greater variety of content. Certainly the conventionalised macro-structures associated with stories (story grammars) seem to facilitate comprehension by allowing readers to quickly construct a model of the text. And simpler story grammars are easier to follow than more complex ones, or ones that violate expectations.

One interesting feature of narrative texts in particular is that they appear to induce visualisation in the reader as part of the reading process (Denis, 1982) – readers report 'seeing' scenes in their head when they read such texts. What is interesting about this process is that different readers are likely to visualise different scenes, depending upon their prior experience and expectations. However, the visualisation appears to become part of the emerging understanding, and subsequent summaries or recall protocols of texts where much visualisation is either possible or has been reported often incorporate information that has been visualised, but was not in the original text. This could be an extension of the normal inferencing process that underlies all language understanding, and it could be analogous to the elaboration and distortion that Steffensen *et al.* (1984) discuss with respect to the recall of texts from familiar and unfamiliar cultures (see previous section). It would certainly be interesting to see if it is harder to get agreement on what texts that are easily visualised actually contain, or whether it is harder to recall such texts accurately because of the contamination from the visualisation process.

The study of text types has received recent impetus from the pioneering work of Swales (1990). His studies of the abstracts to scientific articles is a landmark in such work, clearly presenting the way in which the structure of article abstracts derives from the function of the abstract and from the purposes of the writer. Although empirical studies of the relationship between genre and reader processing are rare, it has been shown by Salager-Meyer (1991) that there is an interaction between text structure and familiarity with the topic of a passage. When subjects reading medical abstracts were familiar with the topic of the passage, changes to text structure intended to make the text more difficult did not have the expected effect. In moderately familiar texts, deficient structuring had a negative effect only on less skilled readers. And in unfamiliar texts, the highly structured format did not enhance the reading performance of either skilled or less skilled readers. Thus text variables only have a crucial role when materials are conceptually more difficult or unfamiliar and when readers are relatively less able.

## Literary and non-literary texts

Any discussion of text types is incomplete without at least some consideration of the distinction popularly made between literary and non-literary texts. Apart from the supposed intrinsic worth of literary over non-literary texts, it is sometimes assumed that literary texts are somehow harder to process, either because of the multiple layers of meaning they are held to contain, or because of the wider and more complex range of language they exhibit. Certainly many of my students refuse to read poetry because they say they find poems 'hard to understand', although this may simply be because they are less familiar with poetic conventions than they are with those of prose or drama. Clearly, however, not all literary texts are of the same order of difficulty, and what causes difficulty is certain to be a complex matter.

It has long been suggested that literature uses formal devices like deviation to increase the difficulty for the reader, in order to defamiliarise language and cause the reader to reflect and to process differently. However, it is well established that the devices that produce deviations are also used outside literature. Van Peer (1986) concludes that the processing of poems with regard to phonological, linguistic and semantic deviations is very similar to the processing of nursery rhymes, jokes, riddles, advertisements and even election slogans.

Thus, whether there are significant differences between literary and non-literary texts that can be identified and which cause different sorts of processing problems, is controversial. Even to talk of literary texts assumes that they represent a homogeneous whole, whereas in fact, there are many different sorts of genres, including non-fiction as well as fiction, within what is popularly thought of as literature. What work has been done suggests that the division of texts into these two gross categories is difficult to justify: rather there might be a cline of 'literariness' on which texts might be placed, and whose features might be identifiable empirically.

Van Dijk (1977) claims that literary and non-literary discourse comprehension proceed in similar ways, but Zwaan (1993) tries to distinguish literariness in terms of the strategies readers use. Steen (1994) makes a distinction between literary and non-literary in terms of metaphor and reader response, based on careful empirical work. Halasz (1991) showed that the literary text he studied exerted a strong influence on readers because it evoked multiple, and often idiosyncratic, cues and meanings. He found that readers made more personal associations with the literary text than the non-literary, the literary text aroused more suspense and curiosity, greater interest and empathy than the non-literary. Although he concedes that there is no absolute divide between literary and non-literary texts, he suggests that when processing literary texts, the reader is not only reminded of personally significant events and emotions but also of other literary texts he may have read.

Some literary critics (see, for instance, Culler, 1975) assume that readers need a special literary competence to understand literary texts: that, after all, is what many purport to be teaching. Such beliefs are largely lacking in empirical verification, however. Furthermore, little work has been done to examine what skills might be necessary to process certain sorts of literary texts, and it is unlikely that separate skills exist, even if the way in which literary texts are processed is different.

Given the reported difficulty of many texts of a literary nature, test designers would be wise to consider carefully whether to test students' ability to read literary texts alone. Certainly I would advise testers to include non-literary texts as well in any battery of tests, and to examine carefully the relationships between the ability to understand the various types of text. Of course, if the relationships are not close, that might be an argument for the position which claims that the way we understand literary texts is indeed different and therefore also needs to be tested. However, given that many literary texts are often culturally specific, it may be that any differential difficulty is due more to the content of such texts than to their style. And if it is the case that readers respond to literary texts in personally meaningful, often idiosyncratic ways, it is hard to see what sort of 'meaning' one could test in order to say that a reader had actually understood a literary text.

## Text organisation

One thing that distinguishes one text type or genre from another is the way the text is organised, as Swales' work has shown. Text organisation – how the paragraphs relate to each other, how the relationships between ideas are signalled or not signalled – has long been an object of study. Even within one genre, researchers have been concerned to show how different organisations might lead to different outcomes or processes.

Rhetoricians often advocate particular forms of text organisation, to make texts easier to read. Yet, as Urquhart (1984) points out, there is surprisingly little empirical evidence to show that such advice is justified. He explored the effects of chronological and spatial ordering in text, and was able to show that for both native and non-native readers of English, texts organised according to the sequence of events could be read faster and were easier to understand than texts whose temporal sequencing was disturbed (as often happens, for example, in newspaper accounts of events). He also showed that texts with a consistent spatial organisation, e.g. descriptions of objects that followed a clear logical sequence, from outside in, or left to right, were easier to understand and recall.

Meyer (1975) distinguishes five different types of expository text, representing different ways in which writers organise (and readers understand) topics: collection (lists), causation (cause and effect), response (problem–solution), comparison (compare and contrast) and description (attribution). She embedded the same paragraph in two different texts. When appearing as a solution, the paragraph was recalled better than when appearing as one of a number of items in a list. It is thus suggested that the organisation of texts may make some texts easier to follow and more memorable than others.

Text that is coherent is much easier to comprehend than less coherent text: for example, texts that present facts with little explanation of relationships between them, forcing readers to make many connecting inferences (Beck *et al.*, 1991). Text written in such a way as to expose the reasoning that connects a cause to an event, and an event to a consequence, is easier to understand than text that fails to make causal sequences clear, for first-language readers as well as second-language readers.

When texts are manipulated into good and bad rhetorical organisation, comprehension is affected by poor rhetorical organisation

(Kintsch and Yarbrough, 1982 – the rhetorical structures they tested were classification, illustration, comparison and contrast, procedural description and definitions). The results obtained by Mandler with first-language readers and Carrell with second-language readers, have already been referred to in the previous main section.

Text coherence best facilitates comprehension when the content is moderately unfamiliar, but coherent text also enables readers with relevant background knowledge to understand text better (McKeown *et al.*, 1992).

The effects of cohesion on understanding and recall are weak (Free-body and Anderson, 1983, and Hagerup-Neilsen, 1977). Lack of connectives does not seriously damage comprehension. It may be that the effects of cohesion are weak because readers can make bridging inferences: cohesion is not a key variable in readability. However, conjunctions do facilitate discourse processing for average-ability readers when the topic is less familiar. Thus cohesion interacts with text topic to create an effect, although cohesion effects may in fact not be as strong as linguistic theory might predict.

### Traditional linguistic variables

Much research has been concerned with the issue of whether the language of the text affects readers. In a classic study, Schlesinger (1968) tested the hypothesis that syntactic complexity caused processing difficulties for first-language readers. However, his results indicated that syntax was not a significant factor. He showed that, at least for first-language readers, syntax only becomes a problem when it interacts with other factors in the utterance.

The effect of syntax on language processing has been more intensively studied in so-called garden-path studies. The prediction, crudely, is that sentences which induce readers to make one syntactic parse and then confound it will be harder to process than sentences for which a syntactic structure can be umabiguously assigned: Sentences like 2 below are garden-path versions of sentence 1 and an unambiguous, non-garden-path version of sentence 2 is illustrated by sentence 3:

1 *The experienced soldiers warned about the dangers before the midnight raid.*

2 *The experienced soldiers warned about the dangers conducted the midnight raid.*

3 *The experienced soldiers who were told about the dangers conducted the midnight raid.*

Although psycholinguists have done much research into the processing of such sentences and structures, the relevance to theories of reading and to the processing of syntax embedded in texts in the real world is very difficult to establish, and such research will therefore not be referred to in this chapter.

Berman (1984) discusses a number of linguistic variables that made text harder to process for second-language readers. These included the opacity and heaviness of the constituent structure of sentences which make it difficult for readers to parse sentences – to recognise the basic constituents of subject–verb–object, noun–verb–noun relations, and so on. It is, however, unduly simplistic to believe that particular syntactic structures will *always* cause difficulty, as Schlesinger showed.

However, syntactic and discourse differences might have an effect on word identification: German readers appear to focus more attention on function words than do English readers, who appear to pay more attention to content words (Bernhardt, 1987, cited in Grabe, 1991). There are also suggestions that syntactic parsing strategies may differ across languages (Flores d'Arcais, 1990; Mitchell *et al.*, 1990)

Vocabulary difficulty has consistently been shown to have an effect on understanding for first-language readers as well as for second-language readers (for example, Freebody and Anderson, 1983). It has also been shown, however, that topic (un)familiarity cannot be compensated for by easy vocabulary: both difficult vocabulary and low familiarity reduce comprehension, but texts with difficult vocabulary do not become easier if more familiar topics are used, and vice versa. Vocabulary difficulty, especially the meanings of idiomatic expressions, make study texts hard to read for second-language readers too (Williams and Dallas, 1984). Homonyms are especially hard to process, as readers seem to fix on one meaning, but do not detect lack of fit in the context, recalling Cooper's (1984) study cited earlier, in which practised readers showed much greater ability to use linguistic cues in the larger context in order to disambiguate homonyms.

It is important, however, to be clear what we mean by vocabulary difficulty and how knowledge is measured. Carver (1992b) points out that vocabulary tests for first and second graders are very different from vocabulary tests for fourth or fifth graders, yet they are often given the same label. Vocabulary tests for young readers have distractors which may look and sound different from the right answer and be unrelated in meaning. In harder questions, the distractors represent perceptual confusions, thus if the correct word is 'house', distractors might be 'horse' or 'mouse'. The vocabulary items get harder as they use words less likely to be known as sight words, or words that include more difficult letter combinations. Later vocabulary tests, on the other hand, are more concerned with whether children understand a variety of words they find in written material. The reading vocabulary test has evolved into a test that is nearly indistinguishable from the vocabulary section of many group intelligence tests.

Context is often held to influence text comprehension. Although readers are often exhorted to guess the meaning of unfamiliar words from context, Deighton (1959) suggests that context reveals meaning far less frequently than may be supposed. Although context determines the meaning of an unknown word, it may not reveal it: revelation is limited not only by the explicitness of the connection between context and the unknown word, but also by the experience and skill of the reader. Whilst it is believed that context has little effect on the automaticity of word recognition, many studies have investigated the extent to which different sorts of contextual information aid getting the meaning of unknown words from context. Carnine *et al.* (1984) study this with 4th, 5th and 6th grade first-language readers, for example. Explicitness of clue (synonyms, contrasts [by antonym plus 'not'], inference relationships and the closeness or distance of the clue from the unknown word) were investigated. Determining the meaning of unfamiliar words proved to be easier when they were presented in context (same words in isolation vs. in passages). Deriving meaning from context is easier when the contextual information is closer to the unknown word, and when it is in synonym form rather than in inference form.

The language of texts would seem, *prima facie*, highly relevant to the testing and assessment of reading. The interesting thing about much of the research is that a common-sense assumption proves too simplistic, and that identifying text variables which consistently cause difficulty is a complex task. Clearly at some level the syntax and lexis of texts will contribute to text and thus test difficulty, but the interaction among syntactic, lexical, discourse and topic variables is such that no one variable can be shown to be paramount. Moreover, even the ability to guess words from context has to be seen in context: the context of the reader, and other variables in the text. It is to readability research that we must now turn to see whether it is possible to understand what makes a text difficult.

## Text readability

Researchers have long been concerned to identify what features make text readable, in order to adjust text difficulty to the intended readership. This has been especially important in educational contexts. Many attempts have been made to develop formulae, or other simple procedures, which could be used to estimate text readability, based upon empirical research into difficulty. For a useful survey of methods and their applicability to ESL, see Carrell (1987).

Since syntax and lexis can cause problems in text, as we have seen in the previous section, estimates of the syntactic complexity and lexical density of text are commonly used. However, it is clearly not very practical to have to analyse texts for such features, and so indices have been developed to allow rough estimates.

One way of estimating lexical load is to check how many words in a sample of the target text appear in a word frequency list like the Thorndike and Lorge list (1944), the West list (1953), the Carroll *et al.* list (1971) or the Dale-Chall list (Dale, 1965). Cruder indices use word length, since word length, in English, is very roughly related to word frequency: the more frequent words tend to be shorter. One index of word length is the number of syllables a word contains: the FOG index (Alderson and Urquhart, 1984:xxii) only counts the number of words in text containing three or more syllables. Another frequently used readability formula is the Flesch, first used in 1948 and still in use today. The formula produces a reading-ease score:

$$RE = 206.835 - (0.846 \times NSYLL) - (1.015 \times W/S)$$

where NSYLL is the average number of syllables per 100 words and W/S is the average number of words per sentence (Davies, 1984:188).

A crude index of syntactic complexity is how many T-Units are contained in the text (Hunt, 1965, cited in Carrell, 1987). An even cruder measure sometimes used is how many words there are on average per sentence. Short sentences tend to be syntactically simpler than long sentences, although there is considerable research which shows that to make sentences easier to understand, words may have to be added, not deleted. Some research has shown that a simple count of the number of letters in text of a given length will provide a rough estimate of readability (being an index of both lexical and syntactic load).

Cloze techniques (the random or pseudo-random deletion of words from text) were first developed (by Taylor, 1953) to measure text readability, and many studies have established high correlations between readability as measured by formulae, and readability measured by cloze. Taylor's point was that cloze could provide a more accurate estimate of readability since it involved real readers processing texts. Bormuth has written extensively on the use of cloze tests as measures of readability, and has suggested that a score of at least 44% is required for reading ease, or rather for a text not to be frustratingly difficult for the reader. A cloze score of 57% is said to be required before a text can be considered to be capable of being read by a reader independently of any support. These cloze levels correspond to multiple-choice test scores of 75% and 90% respectively (Bormuth, 1968; Rankin and Culhane, 1969) – ignoring for the moment the inconvenient fact that it is possible to write easy multiple-choice questions on difficult text and difficult questions on easy text. It should be noted that these normative levels were obtained from native-speaking readers of English: second- or foreign-language learners may perform somewhat differently.

However, Alderson (1978) and Harrison (1979) caution against uncritical acceptance of cloze test results. Harrison claims that the best measure of text difficulty is combined expert judgement, and when that is not available, readability formulae. Davies (1984) suggests that what experts take into account over and above linguistic variables are things like potential interest and availability of text for its intended readers.

Readability research has been complemented and paralleled by research into text simplification: how to simplify texts if they are found to be too difficult for the intended readership. Different methods of text simplification have been studied for their effects on readers and textual understanding. Davies (1984) and Widdowson (1978) make a distinction between 'simplification' and 'simple': a simple account is an authentic piece of discourse, a simplified account may or may not be authentic, and is usually pedagogic in intent. It may, however, not be simple. As many researchers have established, making a text less syntactically complex may have the effect of distorting the message, or increasing difficulties in other text features. Mountford (1975) showed, for example, how simplification of a scientific article might change the illocutionary force of the text. Nevertheless, Davies (1984) was able to show that simplifying a text can indeed make it simpler as measured by readability formulae and cloze tests.

However, although it might be naively assumed that a simplification of the syntax of texts will make the text more readable, Strother and Ulijn (1987) compared reading comprehension scores of native and non-native subjects reading original texts and texts that had been simplified syntactically but not lexically. They discovered no differences, and so they concluded that simplifying syntax does not necessarily make texts more readable, since a thorough syntactic analysis of text may be unnecessary. They suggest that a conceptual rather than a syntactic strategy is used, which involves processing content words, and thus requires lexical and content knowledge. Indeed, it has long been known that vocabulary load is the most significant predictor of text difficulty. 'Once a vocabulary measure is included in a prediction formula, sentence structure does not add very much to the prediction' (Chall, 1958:157).

A rather more sophisticated approach to simplifying text in second-language educational contexts is illustrated by Williams and Dallas (1984), who advocate considering how the book will actually be used at home and in class. They discovered that their Hong Kong readers used dictionaries at home to identify Chinese equivalents of unknown English words, and then wrote these translations in the text. They therefore advocate improving text readability by providing in-text Chinese translations of new vocabulary. They suggest the need for a range of different methods of helping readers cope with new words, by glossaries, key word sections, vocabulary revision checks, and by presenting, defining, illustrating, providing clearer context in a variety of ways to help second-language readers cope with the vocabulary load of texts from which they are expected to learn content matter.

The clear relevance of research into text readability and simplification to test developers is that they need to consider the readability of the texts used for testing comprehension, and should only use texts that are appropriate in difficulty for the population being tested. However, readability formulae give only crude measures of text difficulty, and are rarely suitable for second- or foreign-language readers, even of English texts. Moreoever, cloze techniques are themselves a testing procedure, and so will give a biased estimate of text difficulty.

Given the range of variables that affect text difficulty – topic, syntactic complexity, cohesion, coherence, vocabulary and readability – language testers should beware a simplistic approach to language difficulty when selecting texts. One solution is to attempt to control text difficulty, by simplifying or transforming texts, especially for lower-level learners. In such cases, however, testers need to be aware that tampering with genuine texts in order to make them 'easier', or more amenable to test questions or assessment tasks, might have the unwanted effect of actually making them harder to process, as text simplification research shows. In many circumstances, text difficulty will not be definable in absolute terms, and instead testers will prefer to identify a range of authentic texts that might have to be read in the test-taker's target language use situation (see Chapters 5 and 6).

## Typographical features

Much early research in reading was concerned with the perception of print, and how readers could turn it into sound. Later scholars tended to downplay the importance of the print itself – Smith's classic statement 'What the brain tells the eye is more important than what the eye tells the brain' has already been cited in Chapter 1. However, more recent research has shown that perceptual features influence how rapidly readers can recognise print and thus process meaning. Researchers remain interested in what features of print, fonts and layout might be important in causing reading ease or difficulty.

For English, it is clear that the top half of normally mixed-case print is more informative than the bottom half: a simple proof is to photocopy a line of print obscuring first the top half and then the bottom half, and give each distorted text to readers to read aloud. This is so because there is more information in the upper half of normal English printed words: there is more variation in the shape of the upper part of words. It is also the case that in English, and in other languages like Arabic and Hebrew, the vowels convey much less information than do the consonants: again, partly because there are fewer vowels anyway. Thus it is easier to restore vowels in distorted words than the consonants:

-n -ngl-sh, th- c-ns-n-nts -r- m-r- -nf-rm-t-v- th-n v-w-ls.
-a- -e - -i- i- -e-au-e - -e -o-e- - a-e -a- -e-y -e-u- -a- -.

It is also the case that the first half of English words is more informative than the second half: C-tests (where the second half of every
second word is deleted, and the candidate's task is to restore the
missing letters) are relatively easy for educated native speakers to
complete (see Chapter 7 for a discussion of C-tests), but they would
be much harder if the first half of each word were deleted:

–ch early —earch in —ding was ——erned with -he perception -f
print, -nd how —ders could –rn it –to sound.

Much less research in this area appears to have been done with other
languages, and especially with other scripts: what is redundant in one
language and script is likely to vary across languages. The relevance of
this to language testing, of course, is that whilst cloze techniques and
the C-test might work for a language like English, they may have to be
modified considerably to take account of the different features and
redundancies of other languages.

Since difficulty in processing letters is related to automaticity of
word identification, and since speed of word recognition affects speed
and efficiency of reading, one might expect that second-language
readers processing different orthographies or scripts might experience
greater difficulty. For example, in English upper-case letters are
harder to process than lower-case, or than a mixture of upper-case
and lower-case. In Russian and other languages that use the Cyrillic
script, this may be quite different, and therefore native English
speakers learning to read Russian may find the script particularly
difficult because they are not used to attending to the same features
of what to them appear to be upper-case letters (see Carrell, 1987;
Suarez and Meara, 1989; and the review in Koda, 1996).

However, it appears that for advanced readers of English at least,
direction of reading differences creates few problems, and differences
in punctuation and spacing of written forms appear to cause little
difficulty either (Rayner and Pollatsek, 1989). Languages with regular
sound–letter correspondences (so-called 'orthographic transparency')
might be expected to be easier to read than those, like English, with
many irregular sound–letter correspondences, but there is much discussion of whether speakers of the former languages access words via
sound, or whether in both cases it is more efficient to access the

lexicon directly rather than via sound. Orthographic transparency differences do not appear to lead to different fluent-reading strategies, although they might very well be different at lower levels of second-language proficiency. Readers of logographic writing systems like Japanese or Chinese do appear to access words directly through recognition of word forms, but phonological activation is nevertheless important for fluent readers of such languages, and the same appears to be true of syllabic writing systems like Hebrew or Arabic. The research evidence appears to show that, whilst preferred routes for lexical access may vary across languages, fluent readers in different languages read equally rapidly and combine direct access with phonological activation (Rayner and Pollatsek, 1989).

The layout of print on the page is considered especially important for beginning readers: partly for perceptual reasons, and partly in order not to overwhelm readers with too much information. The pages of beginners' textbooks and readers often contain very few words, in large fonts, for ease of processing, and to allow more illustrations to accompany and contextualise the language. Interestingly, it also appears to be the case that when complex sentences are presented to children graphically laid out in segments that conform to the phrase structure, they are easier to read than text graphically presented in segments that violate phrase structure (Wood, 1974). Wood concludes that 'parsing sentences into their natural surface structure constituents clearly facilitates the speed at which sentences can be processed regardless of the grade or skill of the reader' (1974:21), and so visual presentation that facilitates such parsing has an effect on understanding.

Although research is not entirely clear cut on the effect of such variables in reading in a second or foreign language, test developers would be well advised to ensure that texts are suitably presented, and are at least as legible as 'normal' texts of any given genre in the target language. It is clearly undesirable for readers to be penalised because of poor or untypical text layout or reproduction.

## Verbal and non-verbal information

The mention of the use of illustrations in beginning readers leads me naturally to the use of non-verbal or graphic information in text. Text that contains only verbal information, especially in small print, will be not only intimidating but also more dense and therefore much more difficult to process.

Research into the relationship between verbal and non-verbal or graphic information has particularly concentrated on advertisements. Typically, there is a disjunction between text and illustration in many advertisements, such that one or the other appears surprising, contradictory or humorous, thereby attracting the readers' attention and becoming more memorable.

However, applied linguists have tended to analyse the advertisements themselves rather than real readers doing readings of them. Marketing companies, and especially advertising agencies, have done more empirical research in this area, although many of their findings are unpublished.

Many genres use tables, diagrams and other forms of presentation of data, partly to offer an alternative and complementary way of processing information. However, information presented in tabular and other forms often provides support for the processing of the verbal information. Readers of journal articles often need to read both the tables and the text in order to understand fully, and especially in order to read the data critically. The text often describes and interprets the data in the tables in a partial rather than complete manner, and a different view of results can often be gleaned from a critical and close inspection of the tables.

Often, moreover, the text cannot be understood without the non-verbal, graphic data. This is more usually the case with diagrammatic and other illustrations than with tables of data. One UK examination board used to devise tests of reading by systematically separating the non-verbal information in texts from the verbal, and then deleting information from the illustrations (often labels). These labels then had to be restored by reading the text, in a so-called information-transfer exercise. The problem was that the separation of the two forms of presentation, and the deletion of the labels from the diagrams, made the reader heavily and unnaturally dependent on the text: the task became much harder than the original text plus labelled diagrams were.

The implications for testing are clear: not only must the normal relationship between the verbal and the non-verbal in text be maintained in test texts, but testers should consider assessing a reader's ability to understand that relationship, as well as their ability to use the graphic information to understand the verbal, and vice versa. Any test task that disturbs such a verbal–graphic relationship is to be avoided, however superficially attractive it may appear, as in many information-transfer techniques (see also Chapter 7).

## The medium of text presentation

Finally in this discussion of the effect of text variables on reading, and especially relevant to the late 20th century, is the medium by which the text is presented. In academic settings information is often presented on overhead slides or on TV screens, especially in distance-learning contexts. I once devised a test of speed reading in which I needed to have complete control over the exposure of test-takers to text, and so I projected the text on OHP slides, and the test-takers read the questions and answered them in printed booklets. I had, and still have, no idea whether that form of presentation influenced the students' reading (although I observed that they found it difficult to have to look up to a screen to read and then down to a not very well-lit desk to process the task). Clearly research is needed into how people process information presented via OHP slides, TV screens, films or other media.

More and more information is now available on computer screens, especially with the development of the Internet and the World Wide Web, and the use of computer-based self-instructional materials. Interestingly, many readers prefer to print out texts and process it at leisure, but much information is still simply processed on screen. One significant limitation of this medium is that readers can only process one screen at a time, and scrolling forward and backwards is more time-consuming and less efficient than turning pages.

More and more tests are being delivered by computer – a computer-based version of the TOEFL test was introduced in 1998. At present the only research into computer-based testing has looked at the effect of computer literacy on TOEFL scores (Taylor et al., 1998). But it is important to know whether processing text on screen is different from processing print – not only because of the potential fatigue effect due to screen glare, but also because generalisations from screen-based reading to print-based reading may not be justified (and vice versa).

Oltman (1990) reviews a large number of studies of user interface characteristics, including display characteristics and features of user control. Aspects of the display on screen, such as text fonts, colour and line spacing, have been the subject of much research. Screen fonts and character types can have a marked effect on ease of reading – proportionally-spaced screen fonts are easier to read, and mixed upper- and lower-case characters are generally better for continuous reading. Regular line-spaced text, and right-justified text are harder to read; double spacing makes screen reading faster. High contrast between characters and background is helpful, and muted palettes are less tiring. High screen resolution involves less eye strain, and both perceptible flicker and glare cause stress. Reading from paper is generally faster, more accurate and less fatiguing. In terms of user control, blocks of text should be scrolled rather than individual lines, and much research has gone into the optimal design for menus.

Many test developers recommend that test-takers should not be asked to process text of more than a single screen in length – research needs to be undertaken into whether this recommendation is justified or not. In the meantime, the best source of advice for designers of computer-based tests is the recommendations given to designers of computer-based instructional material. These typically recommend many more blank spaces on screen than on the equivalent printed page, fewer words, shorter paragraphs, the avoidance of certain colours and colour combinations, and so on.

Once again, there are clear implications for computer-based testing, and test developers must beware assuming that it is possible simply to transfer texts from paper to computer screen. Ideally, computer-based tests of reading would concentrate on testing the ability to read texts that have been designed for reading from monitor screens (as, for example, texts put up on the Internet). If a wider range of texts is required, as in the computer-based TOEFL, then it is crucial that close attention be paid to interface and screen design features – and that is likely to include the relationship between verbally and graphically presented information.

## Summary

In this chapter, I have reviewed a range of studies that have investigated aspects of reading which might conceivably affect how we conceptualise the construct of reading, what we might assess and how we might assess it, as well as having a number of other implications for assessment. I have considered both reader and text variables, whilst admitting that the distinction between the two is not as clear cut as one might wish.

Aspects of readers that affect both the process and product of reading include the readers' background and subject/topic knowledge, their cultural knowledge and their knowledge of the language in which the target texts are written. This linguistic knowledge includes phonological, orthographic, morphological, syntactic and semantic information, but it also includes discourse-level knowledge, including that of text organisation and cohesion, text types and associated conventions, as well as metalinguistic knowledge. If reading is taking place in a second or foreign language, then linguistic knowledge includes that of the first language, and the relationship between the first and target languages at all linguistic levels. The role of second-language knowledge and first-language reading ability was also considered in the context of reading in a second language. In general, it proved difficult in practice to separate the reader's internal knowledge from the features of the texts being read: one is clearly a mirror image of the other.

The reader's ability to process printed information is clearly also crucial, and indeed might be said to be the main object of any assessment procedure or test. Research is unclear as to the exact nature of many of these reading 'skills', and to what extent they are to be considered as part of 'reading' or as part of general language understanding processes. Nevertheless, it is clear that word recognition, and especially the automaticity with which this proceeds, is central to fluent reading, and readers' ability rapidly to identify words and meanings at 'lower levels' is likely to be key to any diagnosis of reading problems or abilities. In addition, however, the purpose for which a reader is processing text is important, and the readers' motivation and emotional state generally are likely to impact on how deeply they read, and what information they pay attention to.

Linguistic features of text clearly affect readability of text and readers' comprehension, and text type, organisation, genre and so on as well as text topic clearly influence how well readers can process meaning. Finally, many features of text layout and presentation have been shown to impact on how readers read, and need to be considered in the design of tests of reading.

I have throughout the chapter touched upon the possible implications of research for test design and development. In these final few paragraphs I wish to pull together some of these considerations. However, this discussion is far from exhaustive. The reader may well have identified implications of the research that are not discussed here, and in subsequent chapters I shall have occasion to refer back to variables identified in this chapter, even where they are not explicitly presented in the summary below.

The obvious major point is that any variable that has been shown to have an impact on either reading process or product needs to be taken into account during test design or validation. If reading process or product varies according to such influences, and if such influences occur in our test or assessment procedures, then this is a risk to the validity of test scores, to the generalisability of results, or to the interpretation of performances. A simple, if not simplistic implication is that test designers should seek to sample as many different texts, tasks, topics, test methods and so on as possible, in as varied a set of situations as possible. Inevitably, however, any test is limited in what it can sample and measure, and therefore test designers need to sample and design in as principled a manner as possible, bearing in mind the likely effects of the relevant text, reader and task variables.

The importance of background, cultural, subject and topic knowledge in comprehension means that test designers must be aware that such knowledge may well influence test scores or measures of reading. Normally we are not interested in measuring such knowledge in reading tests: this would represent a reduction in the validity of our measure. One precaution, then, can be to select texts on topics which are known to be equally familiar or unfamiliar to all candidates. The obvious problem is finding such topics.

An alternative, as apparently happens in some states in the USA, is to include a measure of topic knowledge in the test battery, and then to estimate the impact of such knowledge on the reading score – and indeed to adjust the reading score in the light of high (or low) scores on the knowledge test. An obvious objection to this method is the time such a procedure would take; a second problem is that the knowledge test itself is likely to measure reading ability, and so pure estimates are unlikely anyway.

Given the (not very strong) evidence for the impact of linguistic variables, like knowledge of syntax, on first-language reading, test designers should examine carefully the language of questions, rubrics and texts to ensure that they fall within the test population's likely ability range. Although one possible strategy, if texts are found to be too difficult for a given group of learners, is to simplify the texts, not only does this disauthenticate the text, it also risks making the text harder to understand. In addition, an ability to read simplified texts is unlikely to generalise to an ability to read genuine texts. A more appropriate way to adjust for text difficulty might be to develop easier tasks or test questions.

The importance of vocabulary in reading suggests the need for careful control or at least inspection of tests for extraneous lexical difficulty. However, it is clearly important to comprehend the vocabulary in a text: perhaps the simplest advice is to guard against *only* testing lexical knowledge when attempting to measure reading ability. If estimates of vocabulary size or quality are available, one might be able to estimate vocabulary effects in the final reading score. But testers and test users should probably simply realise that measuring vocabulary knowledge in a reading test is inevitable, and interpret test results cautiously.

The association of metacognition and metalinguistic knowledge with a developing reading ability means that one must be careful not to confuse the one with the other. The ability to talk about (or answer questions about) the language of a text is different from the ability to understand the text: the latter is likely to be possible without the former, especially in a second language. However, tests of metacognitive strategies, or even of metalinguistic knowledge, might prove useful for diagnostic purposes.

The existence of a linguistic threshold which must be crossed before first-language reading ability can transfer to the second-language reading context receives considerable support from the literature. However, it is clear that this linguistic threshold is not absolute but must vary by task: the more demanding the task, the higher the linguistic threshold. What makes a task demanding will relate to variables like text topic, text language, background knowledge and task type. Since the validity of a reading test depends in part on whether it taps first- or second-language reading ability, it is important to know what variables allow or inhibit such transfer. In both first- and second-language reading, we need to know whether the measurement of reading ability is unduly influenced by the difficulty of the language of the text, the difficulty of the task, or the state of the reader's language knowledge.

The influence of purpose on text processing and understanding suggests that testers need to think of their test questions/tasks as reading purposes. The closer they can come to real-life purposes, within the obvious limits of the testing situation, the more likely we are to get test results that will generalise and present a valid picture of that particular type of reading.

The evidence that there are five or so different types of reading, with distinct processes, goals and outcomes, means that testers of reading should be clear which of the five purposes they intend to simulate or measure.

The influence of motivation on reading is important for test interpretation. Inevitably, the anxiety created by testing settings will result in a different performance than under other conditions, and scores need to be interpreted accordingly. It may be that informal assessment procedures in non-threatening environments might result in qualitatively better performances than test-based assessments.

Given the likelihood that different readers will have at least partially different emotional responses, understanding affective responses during the process and their effect on the product has important implications for the testing and assessment of reading. One approach is to try to select texts and contexts that will promote positive rather than negative affective responses: advice to item writers to avoid distressing topics in texts is clearly relevant here.

To the extent that research enables us to characterise what differentiates successful from unsuccessful readers, test designers may wish to focus on those differences if they wish to diagnose reading ability, or to predict reading proficiency. In particular, definitions of reading-ability levels should be informed by what is known about reading development.

Test designers need to be aware of the features of text that contribute to readability. Since text difficulty is intimately connected with the outcome of a reading test, testers need to ensure that the texts they choose are of an appropriate level of difficulty, as estimated by a variety of readability formulae or other estimates.

Similarly, the effect of text content, text type/genre, text organisation, and so on is such that the test designer should be aware that variation in texts might be expected to lead to different test results, and should sample accordingly. Good tests of reading and good assessment procedures in general will ensure that readers have been assessed on their ability to understand a variety of texts in a range of different topics. If it is the case that readers respond to literary texts in personally meaningful, often idiosyncratic ways, it is hard to see what sort of 'meaning' one could test in order to say that a reader had understood a literary text. However, in an assessment context it might be feasible at least to establish that readers have actually read texts assigned to them, through a portfolio of readings and responses.

Given that more and more tests are being delivered by computer it is important to know whether processing text on screen is different from processing print: not only because of the potential fatigue, but also because generalisations from screen-based reading to print-based reading may not be justified.

These are some of the considerations that test designers need to have in mind when developing test specifications and constructing instruments, and I shall refer to others in the course of the next few chapters. However, perhaps the most important thing testers need to be aware of is that their test represents their view of reading. What they believe reading to be influences what they test, and how they test it. Their model of reading ability will determine, for example, whether they try to test separate reading skills, whether they simply estimate an overall reading ability, or whether they attempt to diagnose components of reading in order to help learners become better readers. Their view of the nature of reading, and their knowledge of the variables that can influence the reading process and the reading product, are intimately linked to the validity of their reading tests.

In subsequent chapters, I shall be discussing how tests and assessment procedures might derive from the above considerations. But first, in the next chapter, I need to summarise what the research literature has established with respect to the testing and assessment of reading, in order to identify what variables affect our assessment, and what remains to be investigated.

CHAPTER THREE

..................................................................................................................

# Research into the assessment of reading

In this chapter, I present a summary of the main research findings that have focused on language tests, and the variables that might affect their construction or interpretation. Many studies have used language tests as their elicitation instrument, as discussed in Chapter 1. Some of these have already been reviewed in Chapter 2, and inevitably, there will be a degree of overlap between that chapter and the current one. However, the main focus of this chapter is on the direct implications of language-testing research for test design and for the development of assessment procedures. Not surprisingly, research *into* assessment, rather than research *using* assessment tools, has focused upon assessment issues rather than sought directly to apply models of reading. Assessment, after all, has its own purposes and needs for research.

This chapter will address the question: how do we know what affects the assessment of reading? I concentrate on variables with demonstrated relevance to assessing reading.

One major area for language-testing research has been test methods: their validity, reliability and factors affecting their use. As this is such a large field, I shall present the main findings of relevance separately in Chapter 7, when I discuss testing techniques.

It has long been recognised that the difficulty of a reading test is at the very least a function of both passage difficulty and **item difficulty** (an item is a test question or test task; the difficulty of an item is very simply measured by the proportion of candidates getting the answer correct compared with those getting it wrong). It is clearly possible to ask easy questions of difficult texts, and difficult questions of easy texts. A reading score may be high or low because of item difficulty rather than text difficulty and vice versa. An important area for testing research has thus been to estimate what contributes to item difficulty – to complement much text readability research which seeks to establish causes of text difficulty (see Chapter 2 for a more extended discussion of this issue). Inevitably, however, it is difficult to distinguish between item effects and passage effects, as the two interact. However, I shall first attempt to emphasise variables that affect test items, and then examine factors that affect passage difficulty.

## Factors affecting the difficulty of reading test items

### Language of questions

Fairly obviously, if the language of the questions is harder to understand than the passages themselves, the reader is presented with an additional layer of difficulty, and we cannot tell whether poor performance is due to the passage difficulty or to that of the questions. The usual advice to test writers is to ensure that the language of the questions is simple, and certainly easier than the passage. This is often difficult for tests for beginning first-language readers.

However, for second-language readers, there is a further issue: should the questions be in the target language – the language of the passage – or in the first language of the reader? If the test population has a number of different first languages, the only practical solution is to have simply-worded questions in the target language, as happens, for example, with TOEFL. However, when test-takers share a first language, might it be better to ask questions in that language?

Shohamy (1984) found that multiple-choice questions in L1 were easier than the same questions translated into the L2, and, similarly, open-ended questions in L1 were easier than open-ended questions in L2. She speculates that this fact is possibly explained by reduced anxiety, especially among low-level learners. It is also possible that the L1 wording gave clues to the general meaning of the text, thereby helping students guess the correct answer, especially for multiple-choice items. Presenting questions in the L2 may also add a degree of difficulty due to unfamiliar vocabulary. This supposition was supported by item analysis which showed differential difficulty of distractors in the two languages. Shohamy suggests that the use of questions in the L1 may also be more 'authentic' in that students are likely to ask themselves questions of L2 text in their first language. However, all these speculations have yet to be confirmed by research.

## Types of questions

It is fairly commonplace to distinguish items that focus explicitly on one part of a text from those that cover more of a passage. Pearson and Johnson (1978) identify three different types of questions and suggest that they might vary in their difficulty. **Textually explicit** questions are those where both the question information and the correct answer are found in the same sentence. **Textually implicit** questions, on the other hand, require respondents to combine information across sentences. **Script-based** questions (sometimes called **scriptally implicit** questions) require readers to integrate text information with their background knowledge since correct responses to the questions cannot be found in the text itself. (One might ask whether such questions are comprehension questions at all since they rely on information outside the text.) It has yet to be shown that these three question types vary consistently in difficulty, although Davey and Lasasso (1984) found, as expected, that their textually explicit items were significantly easier than the textually implicit ones.

Anderson *et al.* (1991) also used this classification scheme but do not report relationships with item difficulty or discrimination (**item discrimation** is the ability of an item to distinguish between good and poor students; an item with good discrimation will be responded to correctly by many more good students than poor students, most of whom will get the item wrong). However, Anderson *et al.* failed to find any relationship between question type and the strategies used by candidates to answer the questions. This is somewhat surprising, given that the classification is designed to account for differences in the relationship between question and passage. One would hypothesise that differences in passage–question relationships would indeed affect the way readers approached questions and related them to passages. Quite what is involved in processing these three different types of questions remains unanswered.

Another way of categorising test questions is to distinguish between **local** and **global** comprehension (a distinction that is related to

Pearson and Johnson's textually explicit and textually implicit questions). Bensoussan *et al.* (1984) concluded that local questions are easier than global ones, and that local questions are more affected by changes in the language of the items.

Other classifications of comprehension questions have been attempted. Freedle and Kostin (1993) investigated TOEFL reading item difficulty and found that seven categories of item characteristics predicted 58% of the variance in item difficulty (**variance** is a statistic which indicates the variability of scores, i.e. the extent to which candidates are spread out on a scale of ability). These were: lexical overlap between the text and the key; sentence length; passage length; paragraph length; rhetorical organisation; the use of negation; the use of referentials and passage length.

Davey (1988) assessed the contribution of passage variables, question and format types on reading performance. The question-type variables were location of information and inference type, and the multiple-choice format variables were things like **stem** length (stem is the first part of a multiple-choice question, appearing before the optional choices), stem content words, stem-unique content words (unique content words are those nouns, verbs and modifiers that appear in the question but not the passage), correct choice length, incorrect choice plausibility, and so on.

The location of the information required for the response, and the length of the stem of a multiple-choice item, contributed most to item difficulty. Because of the relationship between inference type and location of information, Davey suggests that an item's difficulty can at least be partially accounted for by the degree of inferential processing required. In addition, however, items tapping implied information tended to have more words than did items expressing explicitly stated information. Moreover, the degree of plausibility of an item's incorrect options had an effect: when the correct response is not explicitly stated in the passage, the number of plausible options tends to increase. The suggestion is that correct responding to such items might involve better test-taking strategies, or greater problem-solving abilities.

Anderson *et al.* (1991) report the use of multiple methods for examining reading comprehension items. They used think-aloud techniques to identify the strategies that readers taking tests used, test content analyses based on the test developers' claims of what was being tested, together with the Pearson and Johnson categorisation system referred to above, as well as test performance statistics.

Unfortunately, despite the triangulation of their methodology, their conclusions do not lead to any particularly meaningful insights into which features of reading-test items bring about the use of particular reading or test-taking strategies or which features relate to item difficulty. For example, they report the unsurprising fact that students report guessing strategies on difficult items. However, their methodology offers considerable promise for test developers, both of large-scale tests and of classroom-based tests.

Bachman *et al.* (1996) review a number of studies that have attempted to relate characteristics of test items to item statistics, i.e. to difficulty and discrimination. However, results have been mixed.

> On the one hand they suggest that very few of the content characteristics that have been identified by test developers, EFL 'experts', experimental research or theoretical models are actually related to item statistics. On the other hand, three of the studies found that a significant amount of variation in item difficulty could be explained by a relatively small number of content characteristics. . . . In balance, many of the features that are most frequently cited as a basis for language test design . . . may, in fact, not be related to actual test performance.
>
> (Bachman *et al.*, 1996:129)

In fact, using specially designed rating instruments based on Bachman's 1990 frameworks, the authors analysed six different versions of the reading comprehension paper of UCLES' FCE examination (see Chapter 4). They were able to achieve high degrees of inter-rater reliability (the amount of agreement amongst raters) – something that has eluded other studies – across five raters who were rating test method characteristics both for passages and individual items associated with the passages. However, ratings for components of communicative language ability (i.e. content characteristics) were much less reliable: the overall trend was for only three of the five raters to agree on any characteristic. Although the authors are optimistic that the use of a properly trialled rating instrument such as the one they developed is helpful and enhances agreement amongst raters, they acknowledge that further work is needed to refine the definition of communicative language ability.

They discovered that relationships between item characteristics and item statistics varied enormously. The amount of variance in the difficulty of items that could be predicted from the characteristics of those items ranged from zero to a substantial 66%. Very few characteristics, however, proved capable of predicting difficulty for more than one of the six parallel test forms examined, suggesting that differences among tests in the passages used and the actual nature of the items have a strong influence on what item characteristics may emerge as important. Thus, to provide reliable, believable insights into the characteristics of items that affect the difficulty of tests, a rather large number of tests will need to be examined.

Recent research by Tatsuoka and colleagues, using a new statistical technique known as 'rule space analysis', has suggested that it may indeed be possible to identify what individual items actually test, by combining judgements of 'domain experts', introspections of test-takers, and a statistical classification procedure. Buck *et al.* (1996) analysed a multiple-choice test of reading in a second language (part seven of the Test Of English for International Communication – TOEIC) in terms of the 'cognitive performance attributes' believed to be needed to respond correctly to items. They report agreement between two raters on two-thirds of the items, and all disagreements in categorisation were resolved by discussion. After attributes had been deleted which were not working (essentially, which did not predict difficulty), 16 attributes and 8 interactions among attributes were able to account for the performance of 91% of the subjects taking the test, and virtually all of the variance in total test scores.

The attributes identified are, in effect, item and text characteristics. One item characteristic, for example, is: 'The necessary information is not in one continuous text, but is scattered across more than one place'; another is: 'The item is a "main idea" item.' Others include: 'The necessary information occurs out of order of the items', 'The item requires special background knowledge not provided in the text' and 'It is possible to delete two distractors using background knowledge.'

Interactions between characteristics were also significant, for example: 'The ability to hold information in memory and use it to make an inference, when the text is laid out in dense continuous formatting' and 'The ability to understand the gist when the paragraph or segment is longer, and the text is laid out in dense continuous formatting.'

Some of these characteristics might be desirable, but others might be irrelevant to what is supposedly being tested, since many relate to the method effect of multiple-choice items (for example: 'The correct option has low-frequency vocabulary', or 'the incorrect options tend to be long'). It would be useful to see which attributes proved not to be significant, but unfortunately the authors do not supply this. I hope they were not characteristics that the test designers intended to include! Buck *et al.* claim:

> The research indicates exactly what makes items difficult, and what characteristics of each item were relevant to its perform-ance; either in terms of the total test population, or in relation to particular ability levels. This is a mine of information that has not been available to item writers before, and suggests the possibility of writing items to far more precise specifications than has been possible. (Buck *et al.*, 1996:38)

Their methodology is very promising for identifying characteristics of items that contribute to difficulty, and we may expect new insights in the near future.

Davey and Lasasso (1984) report an interesting study into item and reader variables which also suggests future directions for research. Selected response items (i.e. mutiple-choice questions) were easier than constructed response items (short-answer questions – see Chapter 7); being allowed to look back at the text resulted in better performances than not being so allowed, and so on. No differences were found between readers who were field independent and those who were field dependent. However, when the interactions among variables were examined, they found interesting differences. When subjects were allowed to look back at the text, there were no signifi-cant differences between selected response and constructed response items. However, when subjects were not allowed to look back at the text, selected response items were easier than constructed response items. Interestingly, this was true for both textually explicit and tex-tually implicit items, whereas one might have predicted that con-structed response items that were textually explicit would be harder if students were not allowed to look back, since the item would lack the clues present in multiple-choice distractors, and memory would be affected to a greater extent than for textually implicit items.

This study shows that more complex research designs might reveal greater complexity among the variables that affect test performance. The interactions between such variables, be they text, item or reader variables, need to be examined much more carefully before we can say with confidence what influences item or test difficulty.

The implication for test design and use, apart from the need for further research, is that simple advice on item writing needs to be replaced by guidance that recognises the complexity of the test-taking process. Multiple-choice items might be easier than constructed response items under some conditions and not under others. Certain types of test-taker might respond differently than other types. This sort of complex interaction might also argue for different sorts of tests for different sorts of readers (different cognitive styles, preferences for different reading strategies) or different test methods for different readers. Certainly, the possibility of such interactions emphasises the complexity of the measurement of reading, and the difficulty of interpreting reading test scores.

It is important to remember, in accounting for the difficulty of test items, that there is an interaction between text and task variables (as well as among task variables). Kintsch and Yarbrough (1982) illustrate this point. They distinguish two levels of comprehension processes: macro-processes which have to do with global understanding, and micro-processes which have to do with local, phrase-by-phrase understanding.

The macro-level questions they asked were 'what is this text about?' and 'what are the x main ideas the author wanted to get across?' The micro-level tasks were every-fifth-word cloze tests. As reported in Chapter 2, their aim was to investigate the strategies required to process rhetorical structures like classification, illustration, comparison and contrast, procedural description and definitions. They manipulated texts containing such structures into good and bad rhetorical organisation.

They found that although performance on macro-level tasks was always affected by poor rhetorical organisation, performance on micro-level tasks was not affected by rhetorical organisation. In other words, they found an interaction with task type. Test-takers were better able to answer topic and main idea questions for texts that were clearly organised according to a familiar rhetorical structure than for texts with identical content but without such an organisation. But performance on cloze tests was not affected by poor rhetorical structure. Rhetorical structure was effective only when a comprehension test designed to be sensitive to macro-processes was used. They suggest that performance on the cloze test is determined by local processes that are fairly independent of global organisational processes, a debate which we shall examine in more detail in Chapter 7.

Kintsch and Yarbrough point out that 'comprehension' covers a complex of psychological processes and conclude that each of these must be evaluated separately:

This disassociation of macro and microprocesses in comprehension has important implications for comprehension testing . . . Only a collection of tests, each attuned to some specific aspect of the total process, will provide adequate results.

(Kintsch and Yarbrough, 1982:828 and 834)

This implies the need to consider whether such processes can indeed be tested separately, and which methods might be most appropriate to test which process. In the next section I consider the first issue, and the second issue in Chapter 7.

## Testing skills

We have already discussed in Chapters 1 and 2 the issue of the so-called skills of reading: the notion that the act of reading consists of the deployment of a range of separate skills, abilities or strategies – the literature does not clearly distinguish these terms. If reading has a number of different components, then these components might be differentially developed in particular readers. Thus readers may be able to get the literal meaning of sentences but be unable to infer unstated assumptions made by the writer, for example, or beginning readers might not have developed word recognition skills, despite their general ability to understand language in spoken contexts. Especially in the study of beginning readers, there has been much interest in identifying such component skills, in order to help children learn to read with more understanding, faster or more efficiently. Tests that could diagnose the state of development of a learner's skills would thus be very valuable. However, as we have already seen, the existence of such skills is in some doubt, at least as far as it is possible separately to identify and test them. Whilst many so-called skills tests have been developed for children at the early stages of learning to read in their first language, as well as for more advanced readers, the evidence that the skills were indeed being tested has proved elusive.

A number of issues related to the testing of skills have been investigated: how many underlying factors, or empirically separable skills, are there? Is reading simply one unitary skill? Can judges distinguish which skills the items are testing? Which skills contribute most to performance on reading tests? Which skills are easiest to test? Which skills is it most important to test? Which skills, especially higher-order skills, are not language skills, but more cognitive skills related to intelligence, for example?

The number of skills that have been theorised, or speculated upon, is very variable. Almost every armchair speculator seems to come up with a somewhat different list. Some of them, like the Munby list in Chapter 1, seem to relate more to the product of reading (i.e. 'has processed this level of meaning'), rather than to some aspect of *how* the reader processes meaning. But even those that are more clearly related to the process (i.e. 'is able to search the context in order to deduce the meaning of unknown words') vary in number. It has often been argued that the key thing is not how many skills we can dream up, but how many can be shown to exist on tests. However, there has been considerable disagreement about how many factors can be identified, depending upon the nature of the statistical technique used to analyse the data, and the nature of the test items used in the various measures.

In a classic article in 1962, Lennon asked the question: 'what can be measured?' He looks back over half a century of published output on reading, including countless tests, and says that if the labels of tests are to be believed, then we can test some seventy or eighty reading skills and abilities. He reviews numerous studies going as far back as the 1940s, which show very high correlations (i.e. statistical indicators of relationships) among test components supposedly measuring separate skills. Most of the studies reported conclude that there is only one ability common to all the measures, and that is a general reading ability. He summarises:

> It remains true that we still have little experimental evidence about the reality of the distinctions that are made among the various reading abilities and about the validity of supposed diagnostic profiles of reading skills.
> (Lennon, 1962:332)

He concludes that it is only possible to measure reliably at most the following components of reading ability:

a  a general verbal factor – in effect, word knowledge

b  comprehension of explicitly stated material – what most tests measure

c  comprehension of implicit or latent meaning – which he terms 'reasoning in reading'. Interestingly Lennon considers it 'inconceivable that a good test of reading as reasoning should not also be a valid measure of some aspects of the complex we term intelligence'. (Lennon, 1962:334).

d an element that he terms appreciation, for which there is less evidence, but Lennon thinks that this is the fault of test-makers who rarely attempt to measure such an ability.

What is at least as important for Lennon as what *can* be measured is what *cannot*. He points out that individual interpretations of text vary in relation to readers' backgrounds, experiences and interests, and says it is difficult to imagine a test of the quality or richness or correctness of each person's interpretation. It is equally difficult to imagine measures of the wisdom with which people choose what to read, or the extent to which they profit from their reading.

More recently, Rost (1993) found only one broad factor, 'general reading competence', for German first-language readers, or, at most, using a different statistical technique, two factors, 'inferential reading comprehension' and 'vocabulary'. He concludes that, as found in studies using other reading tests, the test he used 'cannot measure several clearly distinguishable components of reading comprehension. A reliable and valid diagnosis of typical L1 reading comprehension profiles is not possible' (Rost, 1993:80).

Carroll (1993) re-analyses over 30 factor-analytic studies and identifies four common factors in reading: (general) reading comprehension, special reading comprehension, reading decoding and reading speed.

Other studies, using a different statistical technique (multiple regression) have had more success in identifying separate subskills. Drum *et al.* (1981) found ten subskill variables accounting for up to 94% of the variance in a number of first-language reading tests. Pollitt *et al.* (1985) found 22 variables able to predict 61% of the variance, and Davey (1988) found two variables accounting for 29% of the variance for successful readers, and 41% of the variance for unsuccessful readers (all cited in Buck *et al.*, 1996).

However, there is still no consensus on the question of divisibility of skills. As discussed in Chapter 1, three positions are common:

- the first is that reading is a unitary skill;
- the second is that reading is multidivisible, even though there is no agreement on how many skills might be empirically distinguishable;
- the third is that there is a two-way split.

Weir (1994), after reviewing the testing literature, reanalysing the results of Alderson (1990b) and analysing some test-based results of his own for EFL reading tests, considers that there is clear evidence that vocabulary should be seen as a component separate from reading comprehension in general. He says that if vocabulary is to be considered part of reading, then a bi-divisible approach might be more appropriate. However, he then goes on to suggest three 'operations in reading', the third of which he says has little to do with general reading ability. These are:

a skimming: going through a text quickly;

b reading carefully to understand main ideas and important detail;

c using a knowledge of more specifically linguistic contributory skills: understanding grammatical notions (such as cause, result, purpose), syntactic structure, discourse markers, lexical and or grammatical cohesion, lexis.

This latter 'operation' contributes to operations (a) and (b), he claims, but admits that the degree to which these are necessary or indeed can be compensated for, is unknown and probably difficult to quantify. He calls such operations 'microlinguistic' and concludes:

> The evidence from the literature . . . and our own initial investigations throw some doubt on the value of including any items which focus on specific linguistic elements in tests which purport to make direct statements about a candidate's reading ability . . . some candidates might be seriously disadvantaged by the inclusion of such discrete linguistic items in tests of reading comprehension.
>
> (Weir, 1994:8)

The research of Alderson (1990b and c) and Alderson and Lukmani (1989) (see Chapter 1) called into question the ability of 'expert' judges to decide which skills were being tested on particular items. This research has been criticised for having failed to train the judges to make reliable distinctions, although I have argued that such training would amount to cloning. I believe that any agreement among cloned raters would simply indicate the success of the cloning process. However, others have reported greater agreement among judges. Bachman *et al.* (1996) devised and trialled a rating instrument for test content which includes the skills being tested by items. They were able to achieve a fairly high level of agreement among the raters (although less agreement for aspects of communicative language ability than for test method effects). Lumley (1993) reports high levels of agreement among raters of test items, after extensive discussion, exemplification and recategorisation of the skills being tested.

Unfortunately, such judges are not usually the people for whom the test was intended, and they might thus be expected to process the test items somewhat differently from target test-takers. Studies using test-taker introspections show that answering test questions is highly complex, and the process varies from reader to reader. Thus for one person an item might indeed be said to be measuring mainly one skill, but for another it might be measuring a number of interacting skills. The validity of a test relates to the interpretation of the correct responses to items, so what matters is not what test constructors believe an item to be testing, but which responses are considered correct, and what process underlies them. If different test-takers respond differently to an item, and yet get the item correct, there is a real problem in determining what the item, and the test, is testing.

Anderson *et al.* (1991) investigated reader strategies by analysing protocols of readers taking a reading test. However, they found no relationship between strategies used and item types, nor any relationship between item difficulty and readers' ability to understand main ideas, direct statements and inferences.

It might be the case that subskills are more readily identifiable in tests for beginning, weak or dyslexic readers. Certainly much of the beginning first-language reading literature suggests that such skills are identifiable: Carr and Levy (1990) discuss case studies at length. However, a review by Rost (1993) suggests otherwise. Studies reported showed very high correlations among supposedly different tests and subtests. It may be the case that once basic word recognition skills have been acquired, and children are able to understand connected text, the whole reading process becomes so very integrated that, although a variety of skills might be needed, they cannot be separately identified empirically during the reading process. Thus, the relevance (or validity) of a skills approach to testing reading might depend on the developmental stage at which the reader is being tested. Component skills approaches may be valid and justified for beginning, weak, dyslexic or low-level second-language readers, but not for more advanced readers.

## Role of grammar in reading tests

An issue for many developers of second-language reading tests is whether their tests test linguistic competence, and particularly grammatical competence as well as, or indeed more than, reading comprehension.

Bachman *et al.* (1989) found that almost 70% of the variance in item difficulties on the TOEFL reading subtest could be accounted for by aspects of test content related to grammar and to the academic and topical content of reading items – which is much more than would be expected of a test of academic reading ability.

In a research study conducted as part of the development of the IELTS test, Alderson (1993) reports worrisomely high correlations between a communicative grammar test and tests of academic reading ability. It appeared that sometimes the 'grammar' test was more closely related to a test of academic reading than the reading test was related to another parallel reading test. The result could be interpreted to imply a close relationship between the ability to use grammar and the ability to read for academic purposes. I have already discussed the common-sense assumption that language ability is needed in order to be able to read in a second or foreign language. But many tests of academic reading ability assume that they are testing something different from linguistic ability – hence the widespread reporting of scores on reading tests separately from scores on other sorts of tests. If grammar and reading tests overlap to a large extent, why bother testing 'reading' (although others might say, 'grammar')? The validity of a reading test might well be undermined if it were shown to measure little more than grammar, *if* one believes that reading involves much more than the use of linguistic knowledge.

However, from a test development point of view, the research was useful because it showed that a grammar test added little extra information to a battery of tests of linguistic proficiency for academic purposes (and reliability was not adversely affected by dropping the grammar test from the battery). This argues against the need to test grammar separately from reading in a battery of proficiency tests.

## Role of vocabulary in reading tests

As reported in Chapter 2, factor analytic studies of reading have consistently found a word knowledge factor on which vocabulary tests load highly. Tests of vocabulary are highly predictive of performance on tests of reading comprehension. In studies of readability, most indices of vocabulary difficulty account for about 80% of the predicted variance. In short, vocabulary plays a very important role in reading tests.

Johnston's (1984) study used content-specific vocabulary tests to estimate test bias due to prior knowledge, suggesting that what vocabulary tests measure might be prior knowledge as well as or rather than lexical knowledge. The average correlation between the prior knowledge/vocabulary test and the reading comprehension tests was a moderate .35. Johnston was able to divide his vocabulary test into specific vocabulary and general vocabulary – the latter was less related to the content of the passages he used. The correlation of specific vocabulary with performance on the reading tests was .39, but general vocabulary correlated lower, at .33. Interestingly, however, whilst the specific vocabulary only correlated with an IQ test at .25 on average, the general vocabulary correlated higher, at .32. The correlation of the whole vocabulary test with IQ was higher (.37) than with reading comprehension (.35).

Such correlations imply that vocabulary tests may not simply be measures of lexical knowledge, or even of subject matter knowledge. Clearly vocabulary is important to text comprehension, and thus to test performance. However, more subtle and informed definitions of 'vocabulary' are needed – a much better idea of what it means to know and use a word – and more carefully constructed tests of such constructs are necessary before we can derive useful insights for test development from such research (see Read, 2000, in this series, for an up-to-date view).

## Use of dictionaries in reading tests

To reduce the effect of vocabulary knowledge on measures of reading comprehension, it might be wise to allow students to compensate for lack of vocabulary by consulting dictionaries. However, some have argued that allowing students to use dictionaries during a reading test invalidates the test since the dictionaries provide some of what is being tested. It is also argued that students would waste time looking up words that would be better spent on reading the text. Bensoussan *et al.* (1984) investigated the effect of dictionary usage on EFL test performance and concluded that the use of dictionaries had no effect on students' test scores, regardless of whether the dictionary was bilingual or monolingual (although students showed a clear preference for using bilingual dictionaries). Interestingly there was a difference between the words that students said they would like to look up in a dictionary, and those that they actually did look up, and in fact relatively few words were looked up anyway. There was little relation between whether students used dictionaries and the time taken to complete the tests, but it appeared that more proficient students used the dictionary less. However, there is little data on how well students could use the dictionaries and how that ability related to test performance. They conclude that it is still an open question as to whether or not to allow students to use dictionaries during a reading test.

Nesi and Meara (1991) partially replicated Bensoussan *et al.* and confirmed the finding that the use of dictionaries did not significantly affect test scores, but they did find that students using dictionaries took significantly longer to complete the reading tests. However, students who had dictionaries available for use, but who did not actually use them, took the same amount of time to complete the test as those who did use the dictionary.

They explain their inability to show an effect on test scores by pointing out that very few of their test items actually 'depended to any degree on the comprehension of individual words . . . Tests which contain a large number of items where knowledge of individual words is crucial may be more affected by the availability of a dictionary than tests with few items of this type' (Nesi and Meara, 1991:639 and 641).

They also showed that the dictionaries used did not provide the meaning of the words in the passages used anyway; in other words, even for those items that required word knowledge, the dictionaries were unlikely to be of any use. Finally, they showed that many test-takers did not look up the key words needed to answer certain items and looked up less relevant words.

We can conclude that a much more detailed and sensitive study, like that of Nesi and Meara, is needed before we can safely say that using dictionaries does not help readers on reading tests. It is important to study the relationship between the actual words looked up and the demands of the test questions, the adequacy of the dictionary with respect to the words looked up and the success of dictionary use in relation to the correct answers.

## Reading and intelligence

A vexed question is whether aspects of reading tests, especially the so-called higher-order skills questions, are related to cognitive variables like intelligence, rather than language *per se*, as we have discussed in Chapters 1 and 2. Reading tests for first-language readers are often shown to correlate moderately with measures of intelligence, and that may not matter. But when designing tests of reading in a second language the aim is normally to test language-related abilities, not intelligence, and thus any correlation between second-language reading and intelligence is worrying. Berman (1991), for example, reports a concern in Israel at the moderately high (average .60) correlation between English reading comprehension tests and Hebrew reasoning tests. Interestingly, even when she selected reading items that might be said to be operating at Weir's level (c) – discrete linguistic knowledge – she found moderate correlations with the reasoning test. In other words, if we believe that there is a difference between the two groups of items, even linguistic knowledge items might be testing 'reasoning' to some degree.

It has long been held that 'reading is reasoning' (Thorndike, 1917). Carver (1974) is, however, critical of the Thorndike research. Carver distinguishes four different levels of reading: word, sentence, paragraph or above, and no particular unit. The latter two levels clearly involve reasoning, he says, but he maintains that the former two – word and sentence – do not. Thus the issue of whether reading involves reasoning is a definitional one, according to Carver. He criticises Thorndike for using very difficult passages and asking questions that clearly require reasoning. He argues that 'Reading is not primarily reasoning, but most standardised reading tests are actually standardised reasoning tests' (Carver, 1974:51).

As an example, he cites the following item (taken from Farr, 1971):

> The sheep were playing in the woods and eating grass. The wolf came to the woods. Then the sheep
> 1 went on eating
> 2 ran to the barn
> 3 ran to the wolf                   (Carver, quoted in Farr, 1971:50)

Carver sees high correlations between reading tests and intelligence tests (sometimes above .80) as artefacts of the way the tests are developed. When a distractor does not draw any responses, it is replaced by ones that do. He argues that the process of selecting among distractors may require various degrees of reasoning. Similarly, if all readers get an item correct on a reading passage, variance will be minimal and the item will be changed. Yet it is possible that all the readers have simply understood that aspect of the passage. Replacing it with an item that does discriminate may actually introduce irrelevant variance – based on reasoning – into the measure.

He argues that intelligence tests should seek to measure reasoning, and that reading tests should measure reading, not reasoning, if the real relationship between reading and reasoning is to be investigated.

> What is needed at this time is more attention directed toward the measurement of absolute levels of the ability to read sentences that make up paragraphs, not the ability to answer reasoning-type questions on paragraphs. What is needed is an investigation of the relationship between absolute levels of reading and absolute levels of reasoning. Hopefully the next fifty years will not find reading researchers in the same embarrassing situation of concluding from reading test data that the ability to answer reasoning-type questions on paragraphs mainly involves the ability to reason.                                      (Carver, 1974:55)

## Factors affecting the difficulty of reading test texts

### Background knowledge versus text content

Most studies of reading tests show that the choice of text has a marked effect. To cite but one example, Shohamy (1984) showed that the text had a significant effect on test scores, whether these were based on multiple-choice or open-ended questions, and whether the questions were presented in the L1 or the L2. Obviously this might be due to greater or lesser readability of the texts used, or it may be a content effect, or it may result from variable background knowledge in the candidates taking the tests.

Whilst one might claim that background knowledge in the content area of a reading text can enable students to perform to the best of their ability, tests based on texts which are too specialised might test subject matter knowledge rather than reading ability. Subject-related texts might also discriminate against individuals who happen to possess less background knowledge in a particular field. And if different specialised texts are used to test students – as happened in the British Council ELTS test and the first version of the IELTS (UCLES, 1989) – then the problem of comparable difficulty of texts and tests must be faced.

The development of tests of reading for specific purposes, usually subject-related, is an area where text and background knowledge effects might be thought to be crucial. Sadly, not a great deal of research has been done in this area, but what there is suggests that assumptions of the facilitating effect of having texts in relevant subject areas might be too simplistic.

Both Erickson and Molloy (1983) and Brown (1984) showed that specific-purpose tests designed for engineering students were indeed easier for non-native speaker engineers than non-engineers. Interestingly, in the Erickson and Molloy study, native-speaking engineering majors scored better than native-speaking non-engineering majors on language items (questions testing knowledge of non-technical vocabulary and text cohesion) as well as on questions with specific engineering content. This suggests that the facilitating effect of content familiarity may extend to enabling linguistic skills to be better deployed and displayed.

However, Carrell (1983a) found that her non-native students showed virtually no effect of background knowledge compared with native speakers of English. She suggests that, unlike native readers, non-native readers may not readily activate content schemata, failing to connect the content of the text with the appropriate background knowledge – perhaps because of a linguistic short-circuit (see Chapters 1 and 2).

Studies by Moy (1975), Koh (1985) and Peretz and Shoham (1990) show contradictory results: the highest performance on a given text was often not obtained by the group that was expected to be favoured by that text. Students do not necessarily do better on materials in their own academic field. This may be due to a superior linguistic proficiency compensating for ignorance of the subject matter.

Hock (1990) examined whether familiarity with test content or level of language proficiency was the best predictor of ability in reading comprehension. In all subject areas under study – Medicine, Law and Economics – she found that comprehension of a discipline-related text could be predicted by both knowledge of the subject area and by language level, but that language level was the better predictor.

Alderson and Urquhart (1985) argue that their own somewhat contradictory results can be accounted for in terms of an interaction between background knowledge and linguistic proficiency. On relatively easy texts, linguistic proficiency might be sufficient to answer test questions adequately, whereas more difficult texts might require more subject matter knowledge, or higher linguistic proficiency.

Clapham's study (1996) is especially relevant to this issue. As part of a study of the effect of content, specifically subject matter knowledge, she investigated the relationship between the language ability of students taking the IELTS test of reading for academic purposes, and their ability to understand texts in and out of their own subject discipline. She discovered two linguistic thresholds, not one.

The first one, at a score of roughly 60% on her grammar test, represented a level of linguistic knowledge below which students were unable to understand texts even in their own subject discipline. The second, at a score of roughly 80% on the same test, represented a level of linguistic knowledge above which students had little difficulty reading texts outside their own discipline.

The crucial area in which subject knowledge could facilitate understanding of texts within one's own subject area, was 60–80% on the test. In this case, knowledge could only facilitate comprehension once a minimum had been reached. The same may well be true of first-language reading ability. For reading ability to transfer to a second or foreign language, a certain minimum linguistic knowledge may be required, but a lack of reading ability in the first language might also be compensated for by a high level of linguistic competence in the second language.

Needless to say, Clapham's results need replication and extension. Nevertheless, they suggest that language testers might some day be able to define text difficulty in terms of what level of language ability a reader must have in order to understand that particular text, and vice versa, what sort of text a learner of a given level of language ability might be expected to be able to read. This might finally provide some empirical justification for the sorts of levels of reading ability contained in scales like the ACTFL and ASLPR, which have to date been arrived at only intuitively (see Chapter 8).

Hale (1988) examined performance on TOEFL reading tests and established that students in the humanities/social sciences and in the biological/physical sciences performed better on passages related to their own groups than on other passages. However, although significant, the effect was relatively small as expressed in points on the TOEFL scale and had little practical significance. It is suggested that this is because the reading passages used in TOEFL are taken from general readings rather than specialised textbooks, which are intended to be relatively nontechnical and understandable by a general audience.

Hale concludes that TOEFL test developers are justified in seeking to maintain a balance of reading passages across the humanities/ social sciences and the biological/physical sciences, in order to counter any possible bias. However, the consequences of not maintaining a balance in any one test form are unlikely to be substantial, given the relatively small effect.

Defining 'general' or 'generalised' knowledge is, however, highly problematic, as Clapham (*op. cit.*) showed. In her study of texts used in the IELTS tests, she found that some texts were too specific for the intended test-takers, in terms of their empirical difficulty (and thus resulted in lower scores than expected for some of the test-takers), whereas other texts were too general, and did not allow background knowledge to have the expected facilitating effect.

Whilst one might expect text effects in specific-purpose testing, especially in an academic context, are such effects to be expected on general texts in non-academic contexts?

Chihara *et al.* (1989) made minor adjustments to two English texts to make them conform to the expectations of Japanese readers: the names of persons and places were changed, and in one case 'kissing' was changed to 'hugging'. Despite such minor differences, students performed significantly better on cloze tests based on the modified passages than on the originals, and the authors conclude that even apparently minor differences in text in terms of their cultural location or content might have an important effect on reading comprehension during tests.

The study by Johnston (1984) reported earlier addresses the problem of the effect of prior knowledge as relating to bias in reading tests, for first-language readers. Poor performance may be due to deficits in an individual's reading ability or that person's prior knowledge, and test scores may then be subject to misinterpretation. He claims to have achieved the removal of bias for two groups of first-language 8th-grade students – urban and rural – by using a content-specific vocabulary test to estimate prior knowledge.

This study is important because it seems to have led to the situation described in Chapter 2, where those who use standardised first-language reading comprehension tests routinely try to control for prior knowledge effects by also administering tests of prior knowledge. In addition, it also appears to have encouraged the practice of testing lengthy single passages, rather than a number of shorter passages on a variety of topics.

However, Carver (1992a) is critical of this study. He points out that the prior knowledge effect was very small, accounting for a mere 3.5% of the within-subject variance (differential performance by an individual across different tests). He says that a better estimate of the prior-knowledge effect would have been to control for general reading ability rather than IQ, and he suggests that the between-subject variance (differential performance across subjects) uniquely explained by prior knowledge would have been much smaller had that analysis been conducted. He also notes that Johnston's data shows the reading task to have been difficult, and suggests that students were not reading normally – 'rauding' – but in effect reading for study purposes – learning or even memorising. As noted in Chapter 2, it is likely that such reading is untypical of most reading situations, although it may well be typical of reading during a test, where, especially if the stakes are high, one might expect readers to be paying very careful attention to test questions and to the text – i.e. not to be rauding. Of course, to the extent that this distinction is valid, then any test of reading does not measure rauding, but some other sort of reading, possibly unique to the testing situation.

### Presence of text while answering questions

An issue often discussed in connection with reading tests is whether to allow students to look back at the passage when answering questions, or whether to remove the text before allowing students to respond. A common-sense assumption is that removing the text increases the role of memory in the responding, although not in the comprehending, process.

The Davey and Lasasso (1984) study already cited found an interaction between question type and the removal of text before questions were answered. When subjects were allowed to look back at the text, they performed better than when not allowed, but also there was an interaction with item type. When subjects were allowed to look back at the text there were no significant differences between selected response and constructed response items. However, when subjects were not allowed to look back at the text, selected response items were easier than constructed response items.

In the study cited in the previous section, Johnston (1984) found that the availability of the text when students answered the questions influenced performance on some item types. Items peripheral to a central understanding of the text were most sensitive to such influence whilst questions central to an understanding of the text and scriptally implicit questions (which *required* background knowledge for successful completion) were least sensitive. In fact, performance on central questions actually improved when readers could not refer back to the text. He hypothesises that when the text is available, the question-answering process involves search-and-match strategies rather than 'actual comprehension', and he suggests that readers with greater general abilities may be the readers who can best use such strategies. Correlations between IQ and text comprehension dropped, the longer the delay between reading the text and answering the questions. The implication is that the separation of comprehension and intelligence is best achieved by only allowing students to answer comprehension questions after removing the text and introducing some delay.

Removing the text before the questions are being answered raises the issue of the effect of memory on test scores. Since Johnston investigated questions both peripheral and central to an understanding of the passage, he could explore the interaction between question type and text removal. When the text was available, peripheral questions were very easy, but when removed they were very difficult: peripheral information is easily obtained from searches of the text, but less readily stored or recalled. Central questions, on the other hand, were easier to answer without the text, and Johnston speculates that this is because, when the text is available, the reader uses search strategies even for central items, and may be distracted by less relevant textual information; whereas without the text, such strategies cannot be used and the answers must be retrieved from memory, which presumably have been more successfully integrated into schemata for the text, i.e. better comprehended.

Inevitably, when readers do not have access to the text when answering questions, items that are textually explicit (i.e. which require information from one sentence) become much more difficult to answer. Scriptal questions become somewhat easier when the text is absent, presumably because readers are more reluctant to use their prior knowledge when the text is available, whereas without the text they are more reliant on that prior knowledge.

One would expect that when the text is removed, readers would depend more on their prior knowledge. Johnston (*op. cit.*) found that text removal increased the role of prior knowledge in comprehension. When the text was available, the correlation of prior knowledge with comprehension was .23; with the text removed and when students answered the questions immediately, the correlation remained steady, at .24; when the text was removed but students were only allowed to answer after a delay, the correlation increased to .33.

In short, it appears that there are advantages and disadvantages to removing the text. Central questions are easier to answer with the text removed, perhaps because main ideas are incorporated into schemata and reinterpreted on retrieval, whereas peripheral questions are easier with the text because readers can use matching or search-and-retrieval strategies. This might argue for removing the text. However, prior knowledge becomes more important if the text is removed, which would seem to argue for not removing the text.

The implication of this research depends upon what one wishes to measure. If one is interested in knowing whether candidates can answer relatively low-level, linguistically oriented, explicit questions, then they should be allowed to refer to the text. If, on the other hand, one is interested in knowing whether candidates can understand the main idea of the text, it might be better to remove the text before allowing them to answer the question. However, it is important to acknowledge the risk that in such a procedure one might also be testing memory as well as understanding.

## Text length

A problem all reading-test developers face is how long the texts should be on which they base their tests. Text length is a surprisingly underresearched area.

Engineer (1977) found that when texts longer than 1,000 words were used, the abilities that could be measured changed. The suggestion is that longer texts allow testers to assess more study-related abilities and to reduce reliance on sentential processing abilities that might tap syntactic and lexical knowledge more than discourse-processing abilities. Similarly, the ability to identify the main idea of long texts might be thought to be qualitatively different from the ability to identify the main idea in shorter texts. It is also likely to be much easier to measure reading speed using longer texts (as for example in the speed reading test of the Davies Test [EPTB: see the review in Alderson *et al.*, 1985]) than with a number of short passages with associated questions.

A common argument in favour of the use of longer texts in, for example, testing for academic purposes, is that this practice reflects more closely the situation where students have to read and study long texts. Thus, even if research has yet to show that certain abilities can only be assessed using longer texts, the authenticity argument runs in favour of using longer texts, a practice followed by IELTS, for example, in contrast with that of TOEFL, where short passages are used. The reason the TOEFL programme gives for using a number of short passages is that it allows a wider range of topics to be covered, thus hopefully reducing the potential bias from a restricted range of topic areas. This points up the sort of compromise one is often presented with in testing, in this case between maximising authenticity by using the sort of long texts that students might have to read in their studies, on the one hand, and minimising content bias by using several shorter passages, on the other hand.

## Testlets

Many reading tests, like the TOEFL, are characterised by a number of (usually short) passages, each accompanied by comprehension questions. Since the questions all relate to the same text, they are often regarded as a subtest and are referred to increasingly as 'testlets'.

One important issue in the use of such testlets is whether items are independent of each other. Whilst the items are obviously all related to the same passage of text and are in that sense related to each other, a stricter definition of item interdependence is whether the response to one item influences or determines the response to any other item. Research has not yet been able to show conclusively that such strict interdependence does indeed occur in testlets, although it is always a danger.

In **computer-adaptive testing** (in which the difficulty of questions is adjusted to the developing measure of the ability of the candidate to answer previous questions correctly), one issue is whether one should wait until a candidate has responded to all the items in a testlet before deciding what level to pitch the next testlet at. If items are truly independent, then perhaps performance on one item should call up another, easier or more difficult item on the same text. Given the difficulty of writing many items for short passages, this is likely to be impractical. An alternative is to present a more difficult/easier item based on a different passage. Such practice is inefficient, however, in that one only gathers one response – to the item presented – despite the reader having processed a full passage. It would appear to be more efficient to require readers to answer several questions on each passage.

If a computerised test does not allow reviewing and revising answers, then its comparability with a paper-based test will be limited. This is especially a problem with computer-adaptive tests, since they cannot usually provide an opportunity to review answers, as item selection algorithms depend on previous responses. And since different examinees take different items in computer-adaptive tests, it is crucial that the closest possible fit exist between test specifications and test content (Oltman, 1990).

## The relationship between research into reading, research into reading assessment and the nature of reading assessment

It may be felt that there is something of a disjunction between research into reading, as reviewed in the previous chapter, and research into the testing of reading. Indeed, some scholars (see, for example, Grabe, 2000) believe that, although our understanding of reading has advanced considerably over the past 15 years, this has not affected the assessment of reading. It is often asserted that reading assessment has been dominated by concerns with reliability and psychometric validity:

> Simple and straightforward measures of main idea and detail comprehension questions on passages, combined with sections on vocabulary, provide strong reliability and at least arguable validity for these testing approaches. The traditional approaches are also popular because they are easy to administer, to score, and to scale, and they are economical.          (Grabe, 1991:21)

However, I question the assumption that reading research must necessarily impact on research into the assessment of reading, and I doubt whether we have any alternative to being concerned with the 'traditional' values of reliability and validity. Let me take these issues in turn.

Much of this book has already suggested that the relationship between reading research and research into assessment should be two-way, not one-way: much research is based upon the gathering of data from assessment instruments. Validation is central to testing concerns, and the identification of a suitable construct or constructs is central to such validation. Therefore it would appear only logical for reading assessment to base itself on the best constructs available. Unfortunately, as Chapters 1 and 2 show, there is no agreement on what such a construct might be. There are major disagreements about higher-level processing, about the nature and contribution of inferencing, the role of other cognitive processes and abilities in reading. Even with respect to the lower levels of text processing, there are disagreements about what exactly the phenomena to be tested are. So one not unreasonable way for test developers to be impacted by the confusing state of research is to wait and see what consensus eventually emerges.

Nevertheless, I believe that it is *not* true that reading assessment in general pays no attention to recent research into automaticity, word recognition skills and the like. Indeed, much of first-language reading assessment is concerned with the identification of such components, and many test batteries specifically claim to measure diagnostically. The problem is, as I have shown, that it is difficult to prove the separate existence of such skills. Is that the fault of the test constructors or the model builders? It seems unduly judgemental to blame test constructors for poor tests when theory itself is divided. Perhaps the problem is that the model builders are less than explicit about what these skills actually 'look like' (as we shall discuss in Chapter 9).

Moreover, many test batteries claim to be based explicitly on schema-theoretic approaches to reading – see the Johnston (1984) study and Carver's ridicule of the practice cited in Chapter 2. Whilst I acknowledge that schema theory is problematic, it was once considered by many to be 'state of the art', which is doubtlessly why reading test developers jumped onto the bandwaggon. Perhaps we ought, with hindsight, to be critical of test developers for having been impacted by current reading research? This may be more of an issue for second-language reading assessment, since the vast majority of reading research takes place into first-language, especially beginning, reading, and this may be of less relevance to second-language assessors.

However, it is not clear that second-language reading research provides satisfactory answers to many assessment questions. To revisit the issue raised in the previous two chapters, is second-language reading a reading problem or a language problem? The consensus of the research is fairly clear: second-language readers need to pass a language threshold before their first-language reading skills can be engaged. It also fairly consistently shows that this threshold interacts with background knowledge and text, so that on some texts with some topics, less linguistic proficiency is needed – the threshold is lower – than on other texts and topics. One obvious implication of such research is that low-level second-language readers need to improve, and therefore be assessed on, their language proficiency before 'true' reading ability can be estimated.

A second issue, that has little to do with traditional psychometric values, is whether a second-language reading test should measure language ability more than reading ability, reading ability more than intelligence, or any other construct which might be implicated in taking a reading test. The answer has to do with equity and justice as much as with reliability: if we say our test measures reading in a second language, then we need to be sure that it does. And that means that we need to know what the difference is between reading in a second language and knowing the language, and reading in a second language and first-language reading ability. Recent research and recent models do not provide adequately clear guidance on this matter, so why should second-language reading assessment be impacted?

Should we continue to use traditional criteria for assessing test validity and reliability when exploring future reading assessment procedures? Of course, the extent to which such criteria apply depends upon the purpose of the test, and whether it is high stakes or low stakes. I cannot imagine candidates for TOEFL being happy with the knowledge that the new techniques used to measure their reading ability on the computer-based TOEFL might have low reliability: surely they need to be certain that the assessment of their abilities is accurate? Would candidates be happy to take a test that was based on current reading models, yet was unreliable? Surely not. The point is that many tests are used in high-stakes settings. For many children, even being placed into or out of remedial reading programmes can be very high stakes, or can have a great deal of impact. We need to be sure that it is acceptable for any test or result to have low reliability before we can relax the criteria.

If there is indeed a disjunction between research into reading and research into reading assessment, this may be because the aims of the two types of research are different, because their methods may be different, and because the way in which results can be interpreted, and used – or misused – is certainly different. And methods used in reading research, and even in reading assessment research, may be radically different from what is practically feasible in many reading assessment settings, where issues of practicality, impact and other aspects of consequences (resources, personnel etc.) may weigh more heavily than in the research laboratory, or in specially designed assessment research settings. Nevertheless, I hope that research into reading assessment might have an influence on our understanding of reading, and not only on the development of better tests and assessment procedures.

## Summary

In this chapter I have explored the research that has examined which variables affect the assessment of reading in a first and in a second language. The influence of both the questions set and the passages on which comprehension is assessed is equally important, and the difficulty of a reading test depends also upon the relationship between text and items.

Many characteristics of items have been shown to affect question difficulty and the interaction of these different characteristics also contributes to difficulty. The language of the questions, their wording and the frequency of the vocabulary used in items and options are all important. The level of information being required by a question – local or global – and the relationship between the question and the required information in the text are clearly crucial. Textually explicit questions are likely to be easier than textually implicit questions; questions requiring the synthesis of information from various locations in text are harder than questions referring to information in one location only; questions that require candidates to engage in inferential processes are likely to be harder than those that require simple matching of question and text, and those that require background knowledge will be different from those that only require information contained in the text. Multiple-choice questions with plausible options will be harder than those without, and those where there is lexical overlap between the text and the question will require a different sort of processing depending upon the nature of that overlap and whether it leads to correct or incorrect options.

A macro-level of understanding may be most appropriately assessed using some test formats rather than others. However, it is difficult to demonstrate that items can test different reading skills – and for judges to reliably identify the skill(s) being tested. The relationship between items testing 'reading' and those testing what might be called 'linguistic skills' is something to be borne in mind when designing reading tests. The possibility of test bias by testing intelligence or reasoning rather than reading, or testing background knowledge rather than information gained from an understanding of the text, is also a potentially contaminating variable, depending on one's view of what reading involves in the first place. Similarly, whether vocabulary knowledge is felt to be a relevant or a contaminating variable in reading assessment is an important consideration. This will affect one's view of the desirability of using dictionaries during reading tests, although research suggests that the use of dictionaries may not be as productive (or contaminating) as one might have predicted.

Being allowed to look back at the passage that is being tested appears to have a number of interesting effects, not all of them necessarily negative. Strategies of searching and matching might be more prevalent if students are allowed to access the text whilst processing the questions, whereas only seeing and answering the questions once the text has been removed might engage students in more use of background knowledge, or may require greater synthesising abilities, rather than mere matching. Text topic clearly has an important effect on comprehension, and especially in the extent to which it engages background knowledge. Text length is also an important variable, as are aspects of text structure, text wording, and the number of questions asked on a text. Whether the understanding of several short passages is tested or a single lengthy passage may reduce or increase the possible biasing effect of background knowledge.

Finally, the very act of taking a test may require different sorts of reading from non-test-based reading, and may therefore limit the sorts of abilities or comprehensions that can be tested. It may simply

be the case that certain aspects of reading – like appreciation, enjoyment, individual interpretation – simply cannot be measured, and
need to be assessed, or reported, in different ways.

Even if it is true that testers are limited in what they can actually
test, it is clearly important that what tests measure is as little contaminated as possible by the test method, and that the results of a
reading test can be generalised to non-testing situations, as far as is
possible. Thus it is important to be able to relate test-based performance to real-world reading – the subject of the next three chapters –
and to avoid, where possible, test method effects – which I will deal
with in Chapter 7.

.........................................................................................................................

# CHAPTER FOUR

# The reader: defining the construct of reading ability

## Introduction

In the past three chapters I have reviewed a considerable amount of research into and theories about the nature of reading and the assessment of reading. I have also commented at the end of each chapter on the relevance of findings or opinions for testing and assessment procedures. I now need to pull the various threads together and discuss issues of test design and the relationship between theories of reading, reading in the real world and the assessment of reading.

At this point in the book, the reader is likely to feel somewhat overwhelmed, both by the mass of detail that emerges from any survey of theory or research into reading, and by the lack of an organising framework. True, I have presented a three-fold organising principle: of reader, text and interaction, but this is itself rather too broad for the purposes of test design. After all, in tests the focus is necessarily on the reader – their ability to read – since that is what we try to measure, to infer from test performance.

In this chapter I shall discuss test constructs and constructs of reading, and I shall illustrate how they have been operationalised. In Chapter 5 I shall consider the relationship between test tasks and real-world reading at some length. This will be partly in order to bring into a coherent and fairly comprehensive framework those aspects of reading that have been shown to be of importance for an understanding of the construct. It is also in order to begin to relate real-world reading to test-based reading and the interpretation of test performance.

Then, in Chapter 7, I shall consider a further issue: that of test method and the extent to which our testing method influences – contaminates or enhances – our measurement of reading. We are not interested in knowing whether a reader can do a multiple-choice test or write a summary – we are interested in knowing how well they read, and beyond that, how well they read some thing for some purpose with what degree of effectiveness, if not pleasure. Thus our test methods are a source of potential bias in our measurement. However, since what we actually measure on a test is the result of an interaction between ability and test method, the use of appropriate test methods can enhance the validity of our inferences, provided they are appropriately chosen and explicitly related to our constructs.

What matters in the end is the extent to which we can generalise from our assessment procedure or test to reading performance in the real world. We are not interested in knowing how well a reader can do our test, we want to know something about their reading ability or reading behaviour beyond the test situation – what is often referred to as the generalisability of our test results.

One way of addressing the issue of generalisability, which I shall shortly illustrate, is to take an abstract notion of reading ability, in effect a theory of reading, and then to seek to operationalise this theory in our tests. Constructs come from a theory of reading, and they are realised through the texts we select, the tasks we require readers to perform, the understandings they exhibit and the inferences we make from those understandings, typically as reflected in scores. This approach seeks generalisability by appeal to theory. Our test is generalisable to the extent that it adequately reflects theory and the extent to which that theory is 'correct' – an adequate account of what is involved in reading. This tradition has a long, respected and influential history, as we have seen in previous chapters.

In test development, we may begin with an attempt at defining a construct *for a given purpose*, or *a given setting*, but will then move fairly quickly into seeking to operationalise in test tasks the characteristics I shall discuss in more detail in the next chapter. We must then consider how an individual might, or indeed better does, process the test tasks we have designed, in order to see whether the performance we wish to elicit does indeed suggest that we have succeeded in measuring our construct. Our constructs are all pervasive when going about task design. Making them explicit is an iterative process, as test specifications and test tasks evolve mutually.

As a result of focusing in this chapter upon the constructs of reading, I shall necessarily concentrate upon aspects of readers and their mental abilities and processes, rather than upon features of texts, although as we have repeatedly seen, these are intimately intermingled.

In what follows, then, I shall discuss what is meant by a construct, and review our conclusions to date, and then I shall proceed to illustrate and discuss possible constructs of reading by inspecting test specifications and descriptions of reading ability contained in scales of language proficiency.

## Construct

Every test is intended to measure one or more constructs. A construct is a psychological concept, which derives from a theory of the ability to be tested. Constructs are the main components of the theory, and the relationship between these components is also specified by the theory. For example, 'Some theories of reading state that there are many different constructs involved in reading (skimming, scanning, etc.) and that the constructs are different from one another' (Alderson *et al.*, 1995:17).

Thus we would seek to design tests which would assess such skills either separately or in some integrated fashion – however assessed, they would form part of our theoretical construct of reading, but they would be operationalised differently.

To take another example, synthesis and evaluation skills may form part of our theoretical construct of reading. However, how these are realised in our tests will depend very much on the purpose for which the test is being used. Such a construct may be more narrowly defined as the ability to identify, distinguish, compare and evaluate evidence and opinions. But it may well be operationalised as the ability to distinguish between correct and incorrect inferences in a multiple-choice item based on one short passage about the history of astronomy, or it may be operationalised as the ability to read three different, fairly long texts presenting competing accounts of the history of astronomy, which the candidate has to summarise in a short synthesis.

It is important to emphasise that constructs are not psychologically real entities that exist in our heads. Rather, they are abstractions that we define for a specific assessment purpose. In designing a test, we do not so much pick the 'psychological entity' we want to measure, as attempt to define that entity in such a way that it can eventually be operationalised in a test. What I have called a 'theoretical definition' of the construct that we use for a particular testing purpose may be a definition which focuses on an aspect of the ability that is of particular relevance to our testing purpose, or it may be a definition that we adopt wholesale from previous research or practice. Of course, the construct that we define for a particular testing purpose needs to be grounded in research and theory, but it may depart from that theory in its focus or level of detail.

Thus, for assessing 'skimming' with beginning first-language readers, we may construct one definition and yet operationalise it quite differently from how we might operationalise it if our purpose is to assess this in adult second-language speakers reading texts for specfic purposes. The construct of 'skimming' thus may vary from one assessment situation to another, and this, as we have seen, is often one of the problems in trying to make sense of research – the researchers do not say precisely how they have defined the construct.

In earlier chapters, I have discussed theories of reading at length, and we have seen how many different constructs there might be for the ability to read, be it in the first language or a second or foreign language. Messick (1996) reminds us that the validity of tests is affected by an inadequate or incomplete sampling of the construct (what he calls 'construct-underrepresentation') and the measurement of 'things' that are simply not relevant to our construct (what he calls 'construct-irrelevant variance'):

> Invalidly low scores should not occur because the assessment is missing something relevant to the focal construct that, if present, would have permitted the affected persons to display their competence. Moreover, invalidly low scores should not occur because the measurement contains something irrelevant that interferes with the affected persons' demonstration of competence . . . Invalidly high scores may be attained by students well-prepared on the represented skills but ill-prepared on the underrepresented ones . . . Invalidly high scores may also be obtained by testwise students who are facile in dealing with construct-irrelevant difficulty.                                              (Messick, 1996:252)

Although constructs derive from a theory of the ability being measured, there are practical as well as theoretical reasons why we need to be concerned about the constructs that underly our tests:

> If important constructs or aspects of constructs are underrepre-
> sented on the test, teachers might come to overemphasize those
> constructs that are well-represented and downplay those that are
> not.                                      (Messick, 1996:252)

In other words, inadequate constructs may result in negative washback from the test to the teaching and learning, because teachers will
ignore important constructs if they are not included in the test.

In sum, we should test the range of constructs we wish to test, and
we should avoid test-method effects and other contributors to construct irrelevant variance. To repeat the conclusion from Chapter 2:
test designers should be aware that their tests reflect their model of
the nature of reading, and they should thus seek to ensure that they
reflect and build upon what recent research suggests about the
process and the product of reading.

## Constructs of reading

Constructs of reading are based upon a model of reading and the
factors that affect reading insofar as these are relevant to the assessment of the construct.

In previous chapters, I have argued that an understanding of
reading is crucial to the development of our assessment instruments
and I have discussed the possible implications for testing and assessment of adopting a particular model of reading. We have considered
both reader and text variables, whilst admitting that the distinction
between the two is not as clear cut as one might wish. In this chapter,
however, we will concentrate on matters relating to readers. Whilst it
may be theoretically possible to include text variables in our construct,
no model of reading that we have discussed explicitly distinguishes
the ability to process one sort of text from the ability to process other
sorts of text. Certainly, the different linguistic features of text have
implications for the sorts of knowledge and abilities that readers need,
but it would, I suggest, be perverse to include all possible linguistic
variables in our constructs. Rather, I propose to deal with such features in the next two chapters, when we consider task and text characteristics in the context of target language use situations.

Nevertheless, it is obvious that any variable that has an impact on
either the reading process or its product needs to be taken into
account during test design or validation. If the reading process or

product varies according to such influences, and if such influences occur in our test or assessment procedures, then this is a risk to the validity of our tests.

We have seen the importance of the readers' background and subject/topic knowledge, their cultural knowledge and their knowledge of the language in which the target texts are written. Whilst the latter (linguistic knowledge, at all linguistic and metalinguistic levels) is clearly relevant to our constructs, the former is much less relevant. We do not normally wish to incorporate background knowledge into the construct to be assessed, even though we acknowledge its importance in influencing reading process and product. Background knowledge should be recognised as influencing all comprehension. It is therefore a candidate for the sort of variable we would wish to control or neutralise and every attempt should be made to allow background knowledge to facilitate performance rather than its absence to inhibit. However, Douglas (2000), in a companion volume to this on assessing languages for specific purposes, does include background knowledge in his construct definition of specific purpose ability. There may indeed be situations, such as in assessing academic reading, where it might be appropriate to include subject matter knowledge as part of the construct.

If we are assessing the ability to read in a second or foreign language, then linguistic knowledge includes that of the first language. However, we would again not normally be interested in assessing readers' first-language knowledge, or even their ability to read in that first language. Rather, we would define our construct to focus upon relevant abilities in the second language.

The research evidence we have considered strongly suggests the existence of a linguistic threshold which must be crossed before first-language reading ability can transfer to second-language reading. Moreover, this linguistic threshold clearly varies by task: the more demanding the task, the higher the linguistic threshold. What makes a task demanding will relate to variables like text topic, text language, background knowledge and task type. The difficulty for the test designer is to take account of such variables in a way that will exclude irrelevant constructs. A strict definition of the second-language reading construct might exclude linguistic knowledge *per se*, as well as first-language reading ability. Given the linguistic threshold, however, targeting such an exclusive construct will be well-nigh impossible: go below the threshold and you test linguistic knowledge; go above it and you risk contamination from first-language reading ability. A more liberal and practical construct (if that is not an oxymoron) would be to acknowledge the contribution of both linguistic knowledge and first-language reading ability to second-language reading, but to seek to avoid the dominance of either by careful targeting of difficulty of text and task.

Most models of reading make reference to numerous skills or subprocesses that occur in reading. At the very least, therefore, students should be tested on a range of relevant skills and strategies, with the results possibly being provided in diagnostic, profile-based format.

However, as we have seen, research is unclear as to the exact nature of many of these reading 'skills', and to what extent they are to be considered as part of 'reading' or as part of general language-understanding processes. Word recognition, and the automaticity with which this happens, is clearly central to fluent reading, and a reader's ability rapidly to identify words and meanings is likely to be important in the diagnosis of reading abilities. Thus identification skills need to be tested and we need to develop diagnoses of developing automaticity and reading rate.

Synthesis and evaluation skills are an important component of many models of reading, and thus need to be added to our construct. Metacognitive knowledge and monitoring are also considered crucial to good reading, and so test designers need to consider to what extent the tests they design cover such components of the reading construct, and to what extent this should be done in an integrated fashion or relatively discretely.

In many settings it will be sufficient to test reading in as unitary or global a way as possible in the belief that all relevant skills will be included. Unfortunately, though, a 'unitary' approach may result in a concentration upon the assessment of vocabulary/syntactic skills, discourse skills or the ability to understand the literal meaning from texts, and other relevant abilities are neglected – construct underrepresentation.

The relationship between items testing 'reading' and those testing what might be called 'linguistic skills' is something to be borne in mind when designing reading tests. Depending on our view of what reading involves, we may well feel that tests should not test 'linguistic skills' rather than reading – construct-irrelevant variance.

Although metacognition and metalinguistic knowledge are seen to be associated with a developing reading ability, we must be careful not to confuse the one with the other. The ability to discuss or analyse the language of a text is different from the ability to understand the text. One is likely to be possible without the other. Again, therefore, we need to define carefully what our construct is, and to what extent it includes, or should exclude, metalinguistic or metacognitive abilities. This, of course, will relate to the purpose for which we are designing our test: tests of metacognitive strategies, or even of metalinguistic knowledge, might prove useful for diagnostic purposes.

In addition, the purpose for which a reader is reading is important, and the readers' motivation and emotional state generally are likely to impact on how deeply or superficially they read, and what information they attend to.

Given the likelihood that different readers will have different emotional responses, understanding affective responses during reading and their effect on comprehension and interpretation has important implications for the testing and assessment of reading. To what extent we wish to include effect in our reading construct is, however, debatable.

Inevitably, the anxiety created by many testing settings will result in a different performance than under other conditions, and scores need to be interpreted accordingly. It may be that informal assessment procedures in non-threatening environments might result in qualitatively better performances than test-based assessments, and involve less construct-irrelevant variance.

Nevertheless, there will be settings and tests where it will be impossible to remove the influence of extrinsic motivation. The results of such tests should be interpreted with caution and where possible reference should be made to other measures of reading ability as well.

The very act of taking a test may require different sorts of reading from non-test-based reading, and may therefore limit the sorts of abilities or comprehensions that can be tested. Certain aspects of reading – like appreciation, enjoyment and individual response – may not be measurable and need to be assessed, or reported, in different ways. This does not mean that they do not belong in our constructs, but that we need to be aware that the tests we produce will inevitably underrepresent those constructs.

Even if it is true that testers are limited in what they can actually test, it is clearly important that what tests measure is as little contaminated as possible by the test method, and that the results of a reading test can be generalised to non-testing situations, as far as is possible. Thus it is important to establish and, where possible to avoid, test-method effects: construct-irrelevant variance (see Chapter 7 on testing techniques).

## Constructs and test specifications

Test specifications should make explicit the theoretical framework underlying the test, in other words, they should spell out what the test's constructs are, and what the relationships between the con- structs are, or should be. However, in considering test specifications we move from theoretical, or conceptual, definitions of constructs to operational definitions. Test specifications provide the link between theoretical and operational definitions, since the test specifications provide guidance to the test writers, as well as to test users (see Alderson *et al.* 1995, for a discusson of the various audiences for test specifications). Thus, test specifications also describe test tasks, which entails a consideration of task characteristics.

Alderson *et al.* (1995:17/18) exemplify one theoretical framework of communicative language ability that might form the basis of test specifications: that developed by Lyle Bachman. This framework is divided into Organisational (grammatical and textual) and Pragmatic (illocutionary and sociolinguistic) Competences, and includes a state- ment of Test Method Facets. In general, however, this framework has not been used to construct reading tests (although see the discussion later in this chapter of North's attempt to do so). Alderson *et al.* point out that other theoretical frameworks are possible and have indeed been used as the basis for the development of test specifications, including the Council of Europe Common European Framework (Council of Europe, 1996), the Munby model (Munby, 1978) and so on. They also make the point that since researchers are still uncertain which variables affect construct validity, then test specifications should be more rather than less complete. And thus it is not always clear which aspects of a test's specifications do belong to the opera- tionalised construct and which do not.

For example, many of the facets of test tasks, which I shall discuss in Chapter 5 when describing target language use situations, might be essential components of a construct as well. Although time and place of testing cannot be said to form part of a theoretical construct, they may well affect the measurement of the construct, and so need specifying. Facets of input and expected response are, however, much more clearly relevant to a specification of the ability to be measured, and can thus be considered to affect the measurement of the construct even though a theory of reading might not explicitly make distinctions among constructs according to, say, text type, linguistic or pragmatic characteristics of the text, and so on. For instance, since most theories of reading make reference to, or explicit statements about, the role of background knowledge in reading, then any test facet which impinges on background knowledge must clearly be relevant to the construct, since it will affect the measurement of the reading ability.

## Test specifications exemplified: DIALANG

Test specifications are not always easy to get hold of: detailed descriptions of tests are frequently considered proprietary information. However, one project (DIALANG) to develop diagnostic tests of language ability, funded by the European Commission, has given me the right to draw on what it calls its Assessment Specifications and I shall quote extensively from these in this chapter, in order to illustrate how specifications and constructs inter-relate. Note that these specifications are not being held up as a model: far from it, as they are clearly still evolving and are subject to further testing and revision.

DIALANG aims to assess the four skills plus structures and vocabulary separately and also includes a self-assessment component. Each test component has its own set of Specifications, and I concentrate here on reading. In addition, DIALANG consciously bases itself on, and makes frequent reference to, the Council of Europe's Common European Framework, since it is intended to allow for the comparable assessment of proficiency in 14 different European languages. The Assessment Specifications themselves merely refer to the Common European Framework, the use of which is detailed in a separate document, the DIALANG Assessment Framework (DAF) – see the DIALANG website for more details: www.jyu.fi/DIALANG.

DIALANG defines what it calls a domain of reading (which I consider to be to all intents and purposes synonymous with the theoretical construct, in this context). However, the characterisation of the domain is not directly used for categorising tasks. Rather it is presented as background information for item writers.

DIALANG's main focus is reading for information (first two rows of Fig. 4.1), but also covers purposes like the reflective: 'to learn, to cultivate the mind'; the critical: 'to analyse, judge/improve text'; and the aesthetic: 'to relax, enjoy'. Cognitive processes include 'comprehending', 'comprehending + transforming or restructuring knowlege', and 'comprehending + reasoning/inferencing/interpreting/inventing/generating/discovering'. The resulting matrix identifies text types which correspond to these purposes and processes.

| Cognitive Processing / Dominant intention/ Purpose | Comprehending | | Comprehending + transforming or restructuring knowledge / creating connections | | Comprehending + reasoning/ inferencing/ interpreting/ inventing/generating/discovering | |
|---|---|---|---|---|---|---|
| | Events | Facts | Events | Visual images, facts, mental states, ideas | Ideas, mental states alternative worlds | |
| To locate information (functional) | Timetables TV/radio guides X This week guides | Environmental print: signs, adverts Telephone directories Figures | E.g. make an itinerary using several information sources | Utilise lists of contents Read/Check minutes for specific points | | |
| To acquire new information (referential/ efferent) | News, travelogue, report of activities, recipes, instruc- tions directions, biographies | Descriptions, definitions | News, narrative report, instruction, telegram, announcement, circular, summary of activities | Directions, description, tech- nical description, science report/ summary | expository texts, academic, essays/ article, book review, commentary | The traditional literary genres and modes can be placed under one or more of these four purposes |
| To learn, to extend one's world view, to cultivate the mind (reflective) | | | Popular science articles, professional journal articles, popularised 'how-to-books' | | | |
| To analyse/ judge/ assess/ evaluate/ improve text (critical) | | | Critical articles and reports State-of-the-art reviews | | Argumentative/ persuasive texts, editorials, critical essays / articles | |
| To relax, enjoy vicarious experiences, to enjoy language, (aesthetic, recreational) | Rhymes, jokes, anecdotes, popular magazines | | Occasional poetry | | causeries, columns | |

Fig. 4.1  Domains of Reading. DIALANG Assessment Specifications for Reading Comprehension, Version 6, 18 February 1998

| Text forms: | | Examples (text types): |
|---|---|---|
| Descriptive | • impressionistic descriptions | eg. travel accounts |
| | • technical descriptions | eg. reference books |
| Narrative | • stories, jokes | |
| | • reports: biographical notes, news, historical accounts | |
| Expository | • definitions | brief, one-line dictionary definitions |
| | • explications | broader accounts of esp. abstract phenomena, eg. newspaper articles, educational materials |
| | • outlines | eg. initial abstract, introductory paragraph |
| | • summaries | ... of phenomena, eg. in an encyclopaedia |
| | • text interpretations | eg. book review |
| Argumentative | • comments | eg. newspaper leader, letter-to-the-editor, column, book/film review... |
| | • formal argumentation | eg. scientific articles |
| Instructive | • personal instructions | eg. signs, notes |
| | • practical instructions | eg. signs, recipes, technical instructions |
| | • statutory instructions | eg. directions, rules, regulations, law text |

Fig. 4.2  Text forms. DIALANG Assessment Specifications for Reading Comprehension, Version 6, 18 February 1988

Item writers are required, for guidance on the selection of texts, to consider a second classification of text forms (based on that of Werlich, 1976, 1988). This divides texts into descriptive, narrative, expository, argumentative and instructive types as shown in Fig. 4.2 above.

Item writers are required to sample a range of different text types, and, in addition, they are requested to take into account the writer's point of view, i.e. whether it is 'a fact (objective) or an opinion, attitude, mood, wish (subjective)' (Werlich, 1998:10).

Reading tasks are said to vary in their difficulty according to the texts, the tasks, the reader and their interaction. Texts vary by content (level of abstraction, information density, theme, text form or type, contextualisation and cultural conventions) and writer's style (use of vocabulary and structures, cohesion and coherence and the use of redundancy).

The readers vary by shared background knowledge, language skills, strategies (both undefined) and 'other personal characteristics'.

Questions or tasks vary from easy to demanding, such that 'questions asking for specific facts are usually easier than questions requiring synthesis, analysis or inference' (*loc. cit.*). It is pointed out that the same text can be used with easier and as well as with more demanding items.

The test is divided into 'overall' and 'analytic' sections. The overall section includes items which 'tap overall reading' – presumably meaning main ideas, gist or the like – but can also include items which tap one or more of the three 'skills' focused on in the analytic section. These are: 'identifying main idea(s)/information/purpose'; 'reading for specific detail/information'; and 'inferencing/going beyond the literal meaning (including lexical inferencing)' (*op. cit.*:11).

It is emphasised that this list of skills is a reduced list, which will hopefully be expanded in future phases of the project. It is suggested that future items might include a focus on 'other skills, for example textual cohesion and coherence'. The DAF stresses that 'the performance data from the (test) trials will be analysed to assess the adequacy of the categorisation'.

Clearly here we have a fairly minimal construct. Stress is laid on text type, and potential sources of difficulty of text, and little allegiance is shown to a complex view of reading, or to a position that asserts that it is possible to test specific skills by individual items. The notion of an 'overall' estimate of reading comprehension reflects a unitary view of reading (Chapter 2), but hedges its bets by allowing both items which tap more than one reading skill and even items which focus on only one of the three skills, to be included in this section.

## The First Certificate in English (FCE)

The FCE examination, produced by the University of Cambridge Local Examinations Syndicate (UCLES), is the most widely taken EFL test produced in Britain. It includes a separate test of reading, and since this examination was revised as recently as 1996, it is reasonable to expect that it should reflect up-to-date views of the construct of reading in a foreign language. Although the detailed specifications are not available, a published Handbook gives quite a lot of detail on the test and its rationale. Whilst not labelled explicitly as the test's construct, it seems reasonable to consider the description of the test in the Handbook to represent what the test developers consider to be the operationalised test construct.

Until 1996, the FCE reading test was at least arguably as much a test of language as of reading. Paper 1 was entitled Reading Comprehension but Section A simply contained discrete sentences, with 25 discrete four-option multiple-choice questions relating to the sentence stem. Only Section B tested reading as it might traditionally be understood, namely using three or four written texts, with 15 four-option multiple-choice comprehension items relating to the texts.

From 1996 onwards, however, the reading test no longer contained discrete grammar items. There are now four sections to Paper 1, with a total of four long texts or three long and two short texts and 35 'reading comprehension questions':

- Part 1 has a text preceded by 6–7 multiple matching questions.

- Part 2 has a text followed by 6–7 four-option multiple-choice questions.

- Part 3 contains a text from which six or seven paragraphs or sentences have been removed and placed in jumbled order after the text (the task is to decide from where in the text the paragraphs or sentences have been removed).

- Part 4 has 13–15 multiple matching questions, based on one text.

FCE is aimed at Level Three of the ALTE Framework (see Chapter 8), which is labelled 'An Independent User'. The 1997 FCE Handbook says that learners at this level 'are expected to be able to handle the main structures of the language with some confidence and demonstrate knowledge of a wide range of vocabulary'. Their understanding of written texts 'should go beyond being able to pick out items of factual information, and they should be able to distinguish between main and subsidiary points and between the gist of a text and specific detail . . . Learners at this level can be assumed to have sufficient ability to operate effectively in English in many clerical, secretarial and managerial posts' (FCE Handbook, 1997:6).

The description of the reading test is as follows: 'Candidates are expected to be able to read semi-authentic texts of various kinds (informative and general interest) and to show understanding of gist, detail and text structure and to deduce meaning' (FCE Handbook, 1997:7).

Texts vary in length from 350–700 words per text, giving 1,900–2,300 words overall. Text types include: 'advertisements, correspondence, fiction, informational material (e.g. brochures, guides, manuals, etc.), messages, newspaper and magazine articles, reports'. The whole paper takes 75 minutes, and candidates have to answer 35 questions, including multiple-choice, multiple-matching and gapped texts (where paragraphs or sentences have been removed – see above).

According to the Handbook, Part 1 tests main ideas, Part 2 tests a detailed understanding as well as global understanding, the ability to infer meaning and lexical reference, Part 3 tests the understanding of how texts are structured, and Part 4 requires the location of information in sections of text.

It is claimed that the different tasks are designed to encourage different reading styles ('for example, reading for gist or reading to locate specific information') and, in a section on test preparation, it is suggested that candidates might be encouraged to decide on appropriate strategies to adopt depending on whether questions are placed before or after text. They might also be encouraged to use signals such as the layout of the text to help predict its nature and source' (FCE Handbook, 1997:10).

## The International English Language Testing System (IELTS)

It is interesting to contrast the FCE construct of reading with that of the IELTS test, also produced by UCLES. IELTS is intended to fulfil English-language requirements for entry to English-medium universities, for non-native speakers of English.

In the IELTS, reading is tested quite separately from linguistic competence (which is not explicitly tested). The test is based on some analysis of target language use situations (in particular the work of Munby, 1978, and Weir, 1983), and texts are intended to reflect in general terms what academic readers are expected to do:

> Texts are taken from magazines, journals, books, and newspapers. Texts have been written for a non-specialist audience. All the topics are of general interest. They deal with issues which are interesting, recognisably appropriate and accessible to candidates entering postgraduate or undergraduate courses. At least one text contains detailed logical argument.
>
> (IELTS Handbook, 1999:6)

The test seeks to sample candidates' ability to perform a number of tasks, although it is not implied that these can be tested in isolation or independently of each other. Such abilities amount to the construct that at least the original version of IELTS attempted to measure:

i   identifying structure, content, sequence of events and procedures

ii  following instructions

iii finding main ideas which the writer has attempted to make salient

iv  identifying the underlying theme or concept

v   identifying ideas in the text, and relationships between them, e.g. probability, solution, cause, effect

vi  identifying, distinguishing and comparing facts, evidence, opinions, implications, definitions and hypotheses

vii evaluating and challenging evidence

viii formulating an hypothesis from underlying theme, concept and evidence

ix  reaching a conclusion by relating supporting evidence to the main idea

x   drawing logical inferences          (IELTS Specifications, December 1989)

Further information about the construct thought to be underlying IELTS can be gleaned from de Witt (1997). The author claims that the major skills students need to know, and the things they need to do are: '(Know) how to understand main ideas and how to find specific information; (Do) survey the text; analyse the questions; go back to the text to find answers; check your answers.'

This account of the IELTS construct is amplified in the text of this test preparation book, where students are told that the IELTS does not test their ability to read for pleasure, but to find information quickly and accurately. Therefore they need to develop ways of reading quickly and efficiently, by surveying the passage, not reading every word, reading the instructions carefully, then finding the specific information needed, allowing time for checking their answers and looking back at answers they are not sure of. They need to analyse the question to discover exactly what is being requested, notice which questions require general information and which require specific information, and they need to know when to look for specific information and how to find it.

The comparison of IELTS and FCE shows clearly that it is possible to have quite different constructs of reading. Such different constructs may, however, not be mutually exclusive – they may be equally valid for their purpose, given the fact that any test is necessarily a sample of the underlying construct.

## Descriptors of reading ability, in scales of language proficiency

Test specifications are not the only source of information on the construct that underlies an assessment procedure. There is a long history of attempts to define the construct of language proficiency by designing scales of proficiency, which divide proficiency into stages of development. Detailed descriptions may be provided at each point or stage on the continuum of proficiency.

In devising such scales, as North and Schneider (1998) show, developers draw upon theory as well as the experience of other scale developers. The resulting scales and their associated descriptors represent the developers' best view of what the ability being described actually 'is'. Most scales are of the productive skills of speaking and writing, for the obvious reason that such scales can then be used to assess performance. However, another reason scales of productive skills are more common is that they can relate to actual performances: learners' interlanguage can be recorded and analysed for salient features, and related to stages of interlanguage development. For both reading and listening ability, any product of comprehension is at least partly an artefact of the elicitation procedure, and thus there are fewer examples of such scales. Such scales as exist are largely derived intuitively: from the designer's own view of how reading ability develops. (I shall deal with the topic of developing reading ability in more detail in Chapter 8.)

The work of North for the Council of Europe and for the Swiss Language Portfolio is therefore notable because it takes us beyond the speculations of many scales and represents a thorough attempt to provide empirical verification of a set of scales of reading. In order to develop a scale of reading ability, he explores the construct of reading, both by studying many different scales of reading ability, and by attempting to get at teachers' own constructs for reading.

The empirical work took place in two steps. Firstly in a series of workshops, experienced teachers were asked to judge what aspects of reading were being described by descriptors of reading ability taken from many different scales, and what level of difficulty the descriptors represented. They were also asked to reject descriptors they found verbose, ambiguous or difficult to understand.

Secondly, those descriptors which were interpreted most consistently by teachers with regard to subject and level were then put on questionnaires (together with descriptors for listening and speaking). The questionnaires were subsequently used by teachers to assess their students as part of the assessment procedure at the end of the academic year. This data was then analysed and the resulting descriptors were put onto a common scale.

Analysis of the results showed that Reading did not fit the dimension of the scales of Listening and Speaking, and so Reading had to be scaled separately, and then the two sets of scales were equated – this provides some reassurance that Reading as a construct is somewhat different from Listening or Speaking.

As reported in North and Schneider (1998), teachers found these scales very useful, and the measurement they provided of reading ability corresponded fairly closely to objective measures of reading.

The scales themselves represent an interesting perspective on the construct of reading. They are divided into an overall scale, and then several subscales for reading correspondence, reading for orientation, reading for information and argument, and reading instructions (earlier drafts also contained scales for reading fiction for pleasure, and reading and processing, which were subsequently dropped).

The subscales differentiate reading ability by text – correspondence (faxes, letters of various kinds, postcards); instructions (e.g. of a new machine or procedure, regulations) – and by purpose – for information and argument or for orientation. However, the purposes relate rather closely to text types. For example, the purposes of information and argument refer to social, professional or academic texts, texts of a specialist nature, or newspaper articles, and the purpose of orientation refers to news items, letters, brochures, official documents, advertisements, everyday signs and notices and the like, rather than to purposes as such.

The overall scale (Fig. 4.3 overleaf) also differentiates reading levels by the nature of the text that can be read: the difficulty of the language contained, the degree of familiarity of the subject matter of the text, and the length and complexity of the text. In addition, the

| | OVERALL READING COMPREHENSION |
|---|---|
| C2 | Can understand and interpret critically virtually all forms of the written language including abstract, structurally complex, or highly colloquial literary and non-literary writings. |
| | Can understand a wide range of long and complex texts, appreciating subtle distinctions of style and implicit as well as explicit meaning. |
| C1 | Can understand in detail lengthy, complex texts, whether or not they relate to his/her own area of speciality, provided he/she can reread difficult sections. |
| B2 | Can read with a large degree of independence, adapting style and speed of reading to different texts and purposes, and using appropriate reference sources selectively. Has a broad active reading vocabulary, but may experience some difficulty with low-frequency idioms. |
| B1 | Can read straightforward factual texts on subjects related to his/her field and interest with a satisfactory level of comprehension. |
| A2 | Can understand short, simple texts on familar matters of a concrete type which consist of high frequency everyday or job-related language |
| | Can understand short, simple texts containing the highest frequency vocabulary, including a proportion of shared international vocabulary items. |
| A1 | Can understand very short, simple texts a single phrase at a time, picking up familiar names, words and basic phrases and rereading as required. |

Fig. 4.3 A scale of reading development. From Council of Europe Common European Framework

degree of independence – the flexibility of the reader in approaching the text – is important for the higher levels of ability, and the extent to which readers can read critically, understanding subtle shades of meaning, as well as the extent to which they need to re-read the text in order to understand it satisfactorily, are seen as important elements in the construct. Skills of reading as such are not mentioned explicitly, although some of the above notions – critical reading, appreciation, understand in detail – are included.

## Constructs of reading and constructs of communicative language ability

In addition, North went beyond traditional scales of reading by considering how the construct of reading might relate to a construct of communicative language ability more generally, such as that developed by Bachman (1990) and discussed earlier in this chapter.

Although North's teacher–judges were critical of his attempt to integrate notions of strategic, linguistic, discourse and sociolinguistic competence into the construct of reading, the drafts of these scales (remember, taken from various and disparate scales of reading) are interesting from the point of view of construct. The following extracts illustrate North's attempt:

**Strategic competence** in reading:
(Mastery Level)
Can adapt style and speed of reading to different texts and purposes.

(Effectiveness Level)
Can read with a large degree of independence, using appropriate reference sources selectively.

**Linguistic competence** in reading:
(Mastery Plus Level)
Can understand texts which contain complex and unfamiliar language.

(Effectiveness Level)
Has a broad active reading vocabulary, but may experience some difficulty with low-frequency idioms. Can understand grammatical patterns and vocabulary ordinarily encountered in academic/professional reading.

**Discourse competence** in reading:
(Mastery Level)
Can distinguish in detail the various parts of the treatment of a theme and understand their interrelations.

(Effectiveness Level)
Can separate the main ideas and details from lesser ones. Can recognise the line of argument in the treatment of the issue presented, though not necessarily in detail.

**Sociolinguistic competence** in reading:
(Mastery Plus Level)
Can understand a wide variety of slang and pertinent cultural references. Can appreciate humour and subtle or culture-dependent nuances of meaning or style.

(Effectiveness Level)
Can understand many socio-linguistic and cultural references.

These descriptors are an attempt to classify descriptions of reading ability as contained in various proficiency scales in terms of constructs of general language proficiency, namely, in broad terms, the Canale–Swain and Bachman family of models. That family of models is essentially skill independent (although there are arguments for saying that in fact the model relates rather closely to the proficiency needed for oral interaction, and was not developed with reading ability in mind). What North and colleagues have provided us with is a first approximation at adjusting a model of reading ability to a model of communicative language ability.

The next step would be the reverse: to start with each of the broad competences in turn (strategic, discourse, linguistic and sociolinguistic), and to attempt to describe, for any given level of ability, what that would mean in terms of reading ability. A set of statements based on the family of models of communicative language ability would then provide a linguistically oriented, theoretically justified model. However, such an endeavour is beyond the scope of this book.

## Summary

In this chapter I have discussed what is meant by the notion of 'construct' and I have illustrated how constructs of reading, derived from theory, can be and have been incorporated into test specifications and scales for the assessment or description of reading ability. Chapter 8 complements the description of the construct of reading ability given in this chapter by presenting a number of descriptions of levels of reading development which are essentially related to a theory of reading ability.

The approach I have illustrated in this chapter – that of construct definition and operationalisation through test specifications and scales – has a long and venerable history. It is generally accepted as important to be explicit about one's test construct, not only for the purposes of test validation, but also in order to show how our test methods are separate from, or related to, the construct that our test attempts to measure.

However, test development based on the definition of the underlying construct has its problems, largely because of two factors. One is the extent to which it really is possible to operationalise the theory (as in the case of the notion of component reading skills, for example) and the other is the extent to which the theory is adequate. This is a problem I have addressed in previous chapters, where we have examined various competing theories. The problem for a test developer is both which theory to espouse and how best to operationalise it. If a test is adequately based on theory, but the theory is subsequently shown to be wrong, then logically the test is inadequate, and the uses that have been made of the resulting scores are in some sense invalid, at least theoretically, if not necessarily in practice.

Clearly, however, it is unlikely that in any given testing situation we will want to test every component in the theory. Instead, we focus on those parts of the theory that are relevant to our testing purpose and then define these, both theoretically and operationally, in ways that are appropriate for this purpose. Indeed, since the competing theories are seldom mutually exclusive, test developers may adopt parts of different theories (hopefully on some principled basis) for test development. This pragmatism provides test developers with a way of developing tests in the face of inadequate or competing theories.

In the next chapter I shall illustrate an approach which attempts to characterise what readers actually do in real-world settings, and then attempts to replicate this in the test setting. I have argued in the introduction to this chapter that such an approach is not in opposition to a construct-based approach, but rather that it complements such an approach. We need to design test tasks in the light of real-world reading needs and activities, and then consider what abilities their successful completion requires, and thus what constructs they are able to measure.

CHAPTER FIVE

...................................................................................................

# A framework for test design

## Introduction

In the last chapter, I examined at some length the classic approach to test design: the development of our test's construct through the writing of test specifications in terms of a theory of reading, and their realisation through the texts we select, the tasks we require readers to perform, the understandings they exhibit, and the inferences we make from those understandings, typically as reflected in scores.

An alternative approach, and one I propose to explore in this chapter, is to examine what Bachman (1990) calls the target language use situation, and to seek to replicate critical features of this in our assessment procedures.

Recall that the goal of our assessment is typically to know how well a reader reads in the real world. As we have seen, reading in the real world is a complex, varied activity: different readers read all sorts of different texts for all sorts of different purposes with all sorts of different outcomes. In order to be able to relate our measurement or assessment to that real world, we need some sort of framework within which we can compare our test or assessment procedure with the real-world activity and outcome. Once we have such a framework, we can then examine the extent to which our results can generalise beyond the testing situation.

At the same time, however, we should acknowledge that we need to elicit a reading performance in some way if we are to assess a reader's ability or understanding. We thus need a set of test methods (what others might call an elicitation procedure) – we have to get readers to read and to do something with that reading. Whilst such procedures have been traditionally called test methods or techniques – and a great deal of research, as we shall see in Chapter 7, has examined their effect – I propose to describe them in this chapter as 'tasks', following Bachman and Palmer (1996), and for similar reasons.

In fact, approaches which relate pedagogical activities (including assessment) to the real world have quite a long history, reaching an early apotheosis in the work of Munby and his Communicative Needs Processor. Munby's work (1978) was intended to help syllabus de-signers identify those features in real communication settings which need to be taken into account when designing language teaching syllabi. A rather elaborate taxonomy, or better, list of settings, skills, language and so on was developed, as has been briefly described in earlier chapters. In language testing, this approach is best exemplified in the work of Weir, both in his textbooks (Weir, 1990 and 1993), and in the research that led to the development of the Test of English for Educational Purposes (see Alderson *et al.*, 1985, for a review). This approach, and Munby's writings, have been criticised at some length by Mead, Davies and Skehan *inter alia* (see Chapter 1), and there are clear drawbacks to it, as we shall see. It is not a panacea – never-theless, I believe that it offers a useful way of thinking about test design, whatever its theoretical problems. Bachman and Palmer (1996) present a not dissimilar framework, but have developed it further in the context of language testing. Although it has yet to receive thorough empirical investigation and modification, it is likely to be influential for some time to come.

I have so far chosen not to use the framework as an organising principle for the accounts of reading presented in this book for two reasons. The practical reason is that previous research has not been conducted within such a framework, and thus I would have risked falsification of the research, its aims and its outcomes, by presenting it within an alien framework. Secondly, I do not wish to imply, by using such a framework as an organising principle for the whole book, that it is the only, or even the best, approach to understanding reading and its assessment. The fact is that we do not yet know whether it offers any significant empirical advantage over other, more traditional approaches.

## The Bachman and Palmer framework

Bachman and Palmer (1996) set out to describe what they call 'distinguishing characteristics of language use tasks, and to use these characteristics to describe a language use domain' (page 44) – what Bachman earlier called a target language use situation. They claim that most language tests do not seek to generalise to any or all language use domains – that would hardly be possible – but rather test-makers wish to 'make inferences that generalise to those specific domains in which the test-takers are likely to need to use language' (and here the link with Munby's needs analysis procedures seems clearest). They define a target language use domain as 'a set of specific language use tasks that the test taker is likely to encounter outside of the test itself and to which we want our inferences about language ability to generalise' (*loc. cit.*). They distinguish two major domains: real-life and language instruction, and this distinction will be useful for our purposes in thinking about assessing reading. Reading tests are after all used not only to predict real-life reading ability, but are also used for diagnostic and achievement purposes, in which the tester is interested in knowing where a reader's weaknesses lie, for example, in order to devise appropriate remedial instruction, or what stage a reader has reached in their reading development, again for subsequent pedagogical intervention.

Since language tests can be seen, as I have described above, as 'a procedure for eliciting instances of language use from which inferences are made about an individual's language ability' (Bachman and Palmer, 1996:45), then clearly the relationship between language test tasks and tasks in the target language use (TLU) domain is crucial. The Bachman and Palmer framework is intended to enable language testers to describe both language test tasks and TLU tasks.

The framework attempts to provide a description of five aspects of tasks: setting, test rubric, input, expected response and the relationship between input and response. Although it is claimed that this framework is applicable to test tasks and TLU tasks, in practice it is clear that it is intended to aid test development (hence the aspect of test rubric) rather than exhaustively to categorise language use. Indeed, this task characteristic framework is clearly derived from the test method facets of Bachman (1990) but with the aim of generalising beyond tests to TLU domains as described above. A detailed account of the framework is beyond the scope of this chapter, and the interested reader is referred to Bachman and Palmer Chapters 3 (especially pp. 48–57), 6 and 9, as well as the illustrations in Part 3 of that book. Here I concentrate on the main features and their applicability to reading and its assessment.

Figure 5.1 below reproduces Table 3.1 in Bachman and Palmer, which lists what they consider to be relevant task characteristics:

---

**Characteristics of the setting**

Physical characteristics
Participants
Time of task

**Characteristics of the test rubrics**

Instructions
    Language (native, target)
    Channel (aural, visual)
    Specification of procedures and tasks

Structure
    Number of parts/tasks
    Salience of parts/tasks
    Sequence of parts/tasks
    Relative importance of parts/tasks
    Number of tasks/items per part

Time allotment

Scoring method
    Criteria for correctness
    Procedures for scoring the response
    Explicitness of criteria and procedures

**Characteristics of the input**

Format
    Channel (aural, visual)
    Form (language, non-language, both)
    Language (native, target, both)
    Length
    Type (item, prompt)
    Degree of speededness

---

(ctd.)

Vehicle ('live', 'reproduced', both)

Language of input
   Language characteristics
      Organisational characteristics
         Grammar (vocabulary, syntax, phonology, graphology)
         Textual (cohesion, rhetorical/conversational organisation)
      Pragmatic characteristics
         Functional (ideational, manipulative, heuristic,
           imaginative)
         Sociolinguistic (dialect/variety, register, naturalness,
           cultural references and figurative language)
      Topical characteristics

**Characteristics of the expected response**
   Format
      Channel
      Form (language, non-language, both)
      Language (native, target, both)
      Length
      Type (selected, limited production, extended production)
      Degree of speededness

   Language of expected response
      Language characteristics
         Organisational characteristics
            Grammar (vocabulary, syntax, phonology, graphology)
            Textual (cohesion, rhetorical/conversational organisation)
         Pragmatic characteristics
            Functional (ideational, manipulative, heuristic, imaginative)
            Sociolinguistic (dialect/variety, register, naturalness,
              cultural references and figurative language)
         Topical characteristics

**Relationship between input and response**
   Reactivity (reciprocal, non-reciprocal, adaptive)
   Scope of relationship (broad, narrow)
   Directness of relationship (direct, indirect)

Fig. 5.1 Task characteristics (Bachman and Palmer, 1996)

It is hopefully clear from the headings alone that many of these features have already been discussed in previous chapters. The advantage of this particular perspective is that it gives a coherence to the whole which enables one to see relationships between variables and possible interaction effects in a somewhat clearer manner than a mere listing of variables that have been found to be of importance.

I propose to gloss these various features by exemplification with reference to the assessment of reading. Note, though, that the framework was drawn up without reference to a particular 'skill'. Indeed, Bachman and Palmer question the value of a skills-based view of testing, and so we might expect there to be some difficulty in applying some of the above features to the description of reading tasks. Nevertheless, there is value in exploring the extent to which such a general framework can provide useful insights and design principles.

## Characteristics of the setting

*Physical characteristics*

Where somebody is reading can be crucial: in a library; a computer terminal room; on a bus, train or airplane; in a supermarket; in bed or curled up on a sofa. I vividly remember walking past small houses in China in the early 1980s at dusk, and peering through open windows to see children reading textbooks in a crowded living room illuminated only by a 20-watt green coloured electric light bulb, and early in the morning, as I walked to the university to teach, seeing students in the parks reading aloud from English language texts as they walked. Either of these locations is likely to have a considerable (and currently unknown) effect on many aspects of the reading process.

The location is closely linked with lighting conditions, extraneous movement of the text on screen or because of reader or vehicle motion, the noise level of the surroundings and the degree of comfort or discomfort of the environment. Contrast this range of physical conditions with those of the average test setting: usually silent, comfortable temperature and seating, good lighting and so on. Of course, I am not arguing that we should seek to replicate less favourable conditions. We normally attempt to provide favourable physical conditions in order to 'bias for best', and to compensate for the often emotionally charged atmosphere of a testing situation, especially for a high-stakes test. The point is simply that the degree of correspondence between the TLU domain and the test tasks is thereby reduced.

Bachman and Palmer consider that physical characteristics include the degree of familiarity of the materials and test equipment to test-takers or language users: they cite equipment like word processors, audio-visual equipment, or filing systems and computer equipment as examples. I would argue that familiarity is better seen as an interaction of the individual with the physical conditions, but it is nevertheless clearly an important variable. ETS, in their preparations for computer-based TOEFL tests, have undertaken an extensive study of test-takers' familiarity with IT equipment and its relationship with test performance (see Taylor *et al.*, 1998, Kirsch *et al.*, 1998, Eignor *et al.*, 1998). We do not yet know whether IT literacy results in enhanced reading test performance on the computer-based TOEFL. However, one could argue that since IT literacy is likely to enhance reading performance in, say, an office setting, then a more accurate test would deliberately incorporate task characteristics which favoured the IT literate over the IT illiterate!

*Participants*

This includes all those involved in a TLU/test task, their status, relationship to the test-taker and more. In reading tasks, the reader may also have a listener, as in a parent reading a bedtime story to children or a newscaster reading a news bulletin; there will be a hidden participant – the writer – of whom the reader may be well aware, as in the case of reading a letter from a loved one, or a novel or poem by a favourite author. The writer's opinions may be well known to the reader, as in writers of newspaper editorials, or political party manifestos. Or the writer may be anonymous, as in a poison-pen letter, an advertisement or graffiti. The reader's relationship with the writer, and their degree of familiarity with their opinions, past, intentions and so on, is clearly an important part of the reader's background knowledge, which we have seen many times already is demonstrably an important variable in reading.

Interestingly, in testing conditions, texts to be read are often anonymous, with no author attributed, or source from which a writer might be inferred, and the audience for any performance-like reading aloud is somebody who is making a judgement about the performance, rather than paying attention to the message being conveyed. Such conditions might be expected to influence performance and to reduce the correspondence between test task and TLU.

## *Time of task*

This is clearly related to physical conditions: if reading at dusk or later, lighting conditions become crucial. But if reading when drowsy just before going to sleep, a reader might be expected to pay less attention to detail, or to remember what has been read, than when reading when alert. It is hard for testers to control when test-takers might be most alert or least drowsy, but suitable time-tabling is probably more important than task design in taking such variables into account.

## Characteristics of the test rubric

As described, these characteristics seem not to relate to TLU tasks. Bachman and Palmer consider that, whereas in testing instructions are as explicit as possible, in TLU tasks they will often be implicit. They thus think that rubric may be a characteristic where there is relatively little correspondence between language-use tasks and test tasks. However, if re-conceptualised as reading purpose, and associated conditions, the relevance becomes apparent, and I wish to give this characteristic much more importance than is accorded to it in Bachman and Palmer. However, it is clear from previous chapters that relatively little research has to date shown marked effects of varying this characteristic on process or product. This is at least in part due to the fact that many investigations of reading have in fact used tests, and where reading purpose has been manipulated, it has been relatively trivial, and related to reading outcome, rather than to aspects of TLU purposes for reading.

Nevertheless, some test designers have given considerable thought to the relationship between TLU 'instructions', and test task rubrics. In tests like the RSA's CUEFL (reviewed in Alderson *et al.*, 1985), elaborate attempts were made in the test rubrics to simulate situations in which readers had clear purposes for reading. For example, readers might be asked to imagine they were making a visit to a particular town and to read a tourist brochure about that place to glean certain pieces of information, or they might read an extract from a TV schedule in order to see what programmes might be suitable for given purposes or interests.

Such an approach seems very promising indeed, since it enables test developers to think more carefully about reading purposes (and indeed to research the effect of varying purposes or rubrics).

*Instructions*

Readers may have been given explicit instructions for their reading task, as in the case of a school homework assignment or a piece of academic coursework. These may be in the form of a memo from one's boss attached to a draft report, requesting the reader to produce an executive summary of the report, or it may be a request from a spouse to assemble a newly purchased piece of furniture, or from a neighbour to explain a letter received from a solicitor.

In many settings, instructions might be in the reader's second language, or in a language different from the texts to be read, in which case one might expect the reader's understanding of the instructions to influence how well the task is completed, or the nature of the instructions to give extra clues to what the text might contain. In some cases, the instructions might well be to convey in the first language the meaning of a text written in a second or foreign language, as in the case of technical or literary translation, or informal assistance to a second-language speaker wishing to understand public information brochures written in the local language.

The instructions may be conveyed aurally, rather than in writing, as might occur in religious services, for example. The instructions may be self-generated, of course, as in the examples above of reading a TV schedule or tourist brochure, or related directly to text type, as in reading a recipe or instructions for assembling some piece of equipment. If related to text type, such instructions can easily be inferred, or reconstructed by test designers, even if they are implicit (and not necessarily followed) in real life. For example, one often reads recipes, not to cook a meal, but to decide what to cook, whether one has the ingredients, to create a shopping list or to consider the relationship between the dish being described and those who are expected to eat it (as in the case of a dinner party).

In testing, it is usually considered important to ensure that the instructions are as comprehensible as possible, often implying the use of the test-taker's first language. However, in the case of linguistically heterogeneous test populations, as occurs with many proficiency tests (like IELTS or TOEFL), the use of the target language itself is unavoidable at present. Interestingly, however, the advent of computer-based tests opens the possibility of allowing test-takers to select which language they wish test instructions to be presented in, the range of languages simply being limited by practical constraints.

Bachman and Palmer include the degree of specificity of instructions in this task characteristic: their length or brevity, the provision or not of examples, and whether all instructions are presented at once, or are related to particular parts of the test. Common-sense usually suggests that these instructions be entirely explicit, with examples and so on. However, I was very interested, when observing TOEFL test preparation classes in a recent research project (see Alderson and Hamp-Lyons, 1996) to hear the class teacher tell his students that under no circumstances should they waste time reading the instructions to the various sections of the TOEFL test. His rationale was simple: the instructions have not changed in over thirty years, so it would be really bad luck if they were to change on the very day that his students were taking the test! He argued that by ignoring the instructions, students would gain valuable test-taking time. Of course, the implication was that they should be thoroughly familiar with the instructions on how to take the test well in advance of the live experience. This is often one of the main objectives of test preparation classes.

*Structure*

Under this characteristic, Bachman and Palmer include the number of parts or tasks, their salience and sequence, their relative importance and the number of tasks or items per part. They discuss this exclusively with respect to test tasks, but the characteristic can be relevant to, and thus described for, real-life reading also. Indeed, by so doing one might come to see ways in which reading can be integrated into other language use tasks.

For example, one might read a telephone directory's Yellow Pages, under the heading Car Rental, and look for rental agencies that accept a particular credit card. Having found suitable candidates, one might then look for suitably located agencies, and then seek to identify agencies that allow one to drop the car off in a different location. Then one might telephone one or two of these to establish availability and price of cars, fail to find a suitable candidate, and then go back to the Yellow Pages with different criteria in a renewed search. One can imagine devising a test task that followed such a sequence of events, and one might well decide to weight certain of these tasks more than others (for example, identifying a suitably priced car, or an agency that accepted one's credit card) depending upon clearly stated criteria.

Often literacy events – TLU reading tasks – are not undertaken in isolation: a coursework reading assignment leads to note-taking which leads to further reading, to drafting a written paper, re-reading the draft critically, and so on. Reading a company's World Wide Web page might lead to the reader inputting personal data into the computer to request services or goods, and thus to reading further text as the machine interacts with the reader. Reading a letter of complaint from a customer might lead to a discussion about how to respond, before a formal response is drafted.

As we have already discussed, the measurement problem is one of 'muddied measurement', as Weir (1990) calls it: your reading score might be contaminated by your weakness in writing, or your inability to understand the telephone conversation that followed the initial reading. Which is why so many test tasks lack what Bachman and Palmer call authenticity: the link between the TLU task and the test task is weak. Bachman and Palmer imply that a focus on skills rather than tasks leads to such isolation and inauthenticity, and it may be that thinking about TLU task structure – not just test task structure – is one way of rethinking this issue. However, much will depend on the purpose of the reading assessment, as we will discuss in more detail in the next chapter. If the aim is diagnosis of reading skills, or knowledge of a reader's level of understanding of certain sorts of texts, regardless of or separate from their ability to use such understandings, then relative separation of skills is surely called for, however the real-life TLU domain is structured.

An additional problem in testing is achieving reliability, practically. This means that one usually needs more rather than fewer items, or tasks, which often leads to texts being 'milked' for all they can produce in the way of items. For example I well remember an early

RSA CUEFL reading test which presented readers with a Yellow Pages page of car rental agencies, much as described in the above example, but readers were then instructed to answer 12 separate items about the advertisements, which required them to re-read each advertisement, in detail and at length, in a way they never would 'in real life', presumably in an attempt to get a reliable score. The practicality issue is one of efficiency: it is relatively inefficient to require a reader to read a longish text, and then only answer one item or complete one task on it. A test that requires a reader to take five minutes to read a text in order to answer one item is clearly less efficient than one which requires the reader to answer ten items after reading for five minutes. Inevitably, test design is a matter of compromise, where the correspondence between TLU task and test task has to be weighed against measurement and practicality concerns.

## Time allotment

How long a reader might have available for a TLU reading task will be affected by features of the setting and the instructions. The newspaper may have to be read in the time it takes the reader to travel by train to the office in the morning, study or professional reading may have to accommodate a deadline for an associated task like a term paper or a presentation at a meeting. Often, however, in TLU tasks readers are free to decide for themselves how long they will take over reading a novel, a recipe, a magazine or even an academic article. They may choose to read and re-read, or merely to skim-read, depending upon the purpose of reading or other circumstances (familiarity, interest, etc.).

Time allotment is clearly an important variable, but it may be very flexible and hard to determine. In designing tests, we are often obliged to estimate how long it is reasonable to allow or require a person to read a text, with more or less control. (I have already recounted the anecdote of my attempt to control time of exposure to text using an overhead projector; computer-delivered tests allow more precise, although not necessarily more valid, control of time.) We have also seen how Carver believes reading rate to be a crucial and frequently uncontrolled variable in reading assessment.

A distinction is often made between speeded and power tests: in the latter, readers are allowed all the time they need to complete the test, whereas in the former not all test-takers are expected to be able to complete the tasks. Clearly speed of processing and production is an important variable in language ability, although we do not know very much about its effects in relation to the correspondence with TLU tasks. In practice, however, there are very few true power tests: most test designers time their tests to allow roughly 90% of test-takers to complete in time, but do not consider their tests to be speeded. (There is in any case an issue of how best to estimate the reliability of speeded tests, which need not concern us here, but which does worry psychometricians.)

*Scoring method*

All tests require test-takers' responses to be evaluated. This essentially means the prescription, or judgement, of certain understandings or task completions, over other task outcomes. However, in many TLU domains, a reader's understanding may never be known, or not matter, or not be predictable. What might an appropriate understanding be of part of the Bible or the Koran, or of a poem? How many interpretations are legitimate of humorous advertisements or political manifestos? Whose interpretations are to be privileged: the writer's? the reader's? the teacher's? the literary critic's? the subject specialist's? Without wishing to engage in rather sterile post-modernist debate, or to enrage those of my stylistician friends who believe text meaning to be definable, there clearly is an issue here.

There are many TLU reading tasks where we can agree on an appropriate reading – transactional texts or texts used for transactional purposes – or where we can agree on 'literal' meanings whilst disagreeing about inferred interpretations or summaries and appreciations. But there are many others, and not such unusual texts either, where achieving agreement on appropriate interpretations can be very problematic. Test designers often overcome this problem by the use of a particular testing method: the multiple-choice format, where implausible meanings can be constructed in the distractors. Even though one might disagree about other interpretations of the text, one would agree that the given interpretations are incorrect. But then this might introduce a test method facet – the ability to take multiple-choice tests – and a process that one might argue is irrelevant to normal reading, namely having to choose among interpretations that one would not have thought of for oneself during a normal reading process, but which can acquire a degree of plausibility once presented.

One solution to this problem that is sometimes advocated is to consider normal outcomes of relevant, similar TLU tasks, and to allow such outcomes as correct or privileged responses. Thus, in the car rental example, only certain agencies would be selected given certain criteria, in the real world. This may limit the sorts of texts one can use in tests, but it is a useful way of considering how to score responses. Of course, an alternative is to rate responses subjectively, as in the scoring of summaries, for example. Nevertheless, this does not remove the problem, since the making of judgements still implies valuing some responses over others, and it introduces the need to train, or brief, raters, and to establish the extent to which they legitimately agree or disagree with each other (for a discussion of means of establishing rater reliability, see Alderson *et al.*, 1995, Chapters 5 and 6).

An important aspect of this characteristic that Bachman and Palmer mention is the explicitness of criteria and procedures for scoring: the extent to which test-takers are informed about the nature of the scoring criteria. This is usually discussed in relation to writing or speaking tasks, where the importance of such criteria is evident, and where many testers argue that test-takers need to know how they will be judged if they are to perform to the best of their ability. It is less frequently – indeed almost never – discussed with respect to reading test tasks. The test-taker might be told to answer a question 'according to the passage', which implicitly if not directly tells the reader not to use their own background knowledge if it contradicts or supplements information in the passage. Scoring criteria, in other words, are supposedly based on information in the text. In multiple-choice questions, there is always implicitly one correct answer, although the instructions might say something like 'Choose the most appropriate response'. But it is rare for test-takers to be told that their responses will be judged according to the extent to which their interpretation matches that of the test designer, although this is implicit in the notion of a 'correct' response. Good test-takers – those who know how to play the game – know that their task is to do precisely that: to guess or otherwise work out what the expected response is.

A consideration of when in TLU reading tasks the criteria for judgement are made explicit, and when they are left implicit, or do not exist, might help the test designer. In academic settings, either there is conventionally a 'correct' understanding, as when school pupils are expected to read a geography text to learn the facts or a history text to understand the sequences of events or the causes underlying them. In other study settings, readers might explicitly be told that they are expected to provide support from the text for the opinions or judgements they are asked to make about some aspect of the text. Elsewhere, the criteria might be less explicit: the executive summary is expected to cover the main recommendations in the body of the report, but the reader is left to decide how to judge what the main points are and what are subsidiary recommendations. In much reading, however, there are no external criteria for judgement: reading a bedtime story to oneself is different from reading one to one's children. In the latter case, one set of criteria relate to the best way to ensure the child's enjoyment (based often on a knowledge of the child, or past experiences of story reading) or the quickest way to ensure that the child falls asleep. In the former case, the criteria are much more likely to be internal – whether the reader understands to their own satisfaction, or enjoys the reading in whatever way they find enjoyment, and no account need be made to any outside person. Indeed the criteria for success of much personal reading – of fiction, narratives, even study texts – have as much to do with the process as with the product, as we have seen in previous chapters when looking at motivation. Intrinsic motivation and deep reading are regarded as educationally and socially desirable and beneficial aspects of reading, but these are difficult to induce, much less assess externally or to make explicit as criteria by which test performance will be judged.

## Characteristics of the input

Input represents the material which readers and test-takers are expected to process and respond to. Bachman and Palmer discuss input as test items or prompts, but in reading tasks we must consider both the task and the texts to be processed or responded to. We have already seen that the difficulty of test tasks is a function of the interaction between both items and texts. In TLU reading tasks also, it is clear that readers might engage in relatively 'easy' tasks on texts which are 'difficult' if processed differently. Reading a recipe to decide whether to buy certain ingredients is different from reading it to cook a meal, and probably easier. Reading a biology text in order to summarise or remember the main 'facts' is easier than reading the same text in order to identify missing facts or the author's scientific bias. Any consideration of the characteristics of the input must consider text and task separately and in interaction.

Input is considered from the point of view of its format and its language. Format includes channel: aural, visual or both. In TLU reading, texts are visual (or tactile in the case of Braille texts). Test tasks are usually in the same channel, but TLU tasks may be spoken, or simply assumed, as we have seen in the case of instructions (in such cases, the instructions and the task are presumably the same, for example when readers are asked to write a summary or precis of a much longer text).

Its form may be language or non-language or both, and again in reading, often the text is accompanied by pictures, graphs, diagrams or other graphic representations. We have already seen how such combinations in text can lead to processing differences or problems. Children's story books often contain very little language and a great deal of illustration, and children may 'read' the story by reference to the pictures rather than the words. Glossy coffee-table books of travel, art or costumes may be read more for the visual enjoyment than for information conveyed linguistically, although the words may perform an explanatory or supporting function. Multimedia presentations of text on computer screens often combine not only still pictures and drawings but also video clips, sound or animation, and test input which seeks to take full advantage of the opportunities offered by such media is likely to look radically different from simple paper-based input.

Clearly the language of the text and task will be crucial in reading, be it in a TLU task or a test. We have already seen the importance of this characteristic in testing, and have discussed above the possibility of instructions being in a different language from the text. In second-language testing contexts, the relationship between TLU tasks and testing tasks from this perspective may be limited, because of the importance of ensuring that test-takers fully understand the test task. We will come back to this point under the heading of the language of the input.

The length of input is clearly very important in reading. Texts may be a single word, a phrase (as in the case of public warning signs and notices), single sentences (in advertisements) or lists of words or phrases (as in shopping lists or lists of 'jobs to do today'). They may be whole novels, 20-page academic articles, two-page memoranda, two paragraphs on a postcard. Whilst length is related to amount of interpretation needed, this is not necessarily direct: a postcard may be very enigmatic, a novel very explicit. Single sentence advertisements are often ambiguous and humorous, sometimes in ways which require considerable processing time and effort (deliberately, of course, in an attempt to capture and keep the reader's attention).

Test input also varies, although traditionally not as much as TLU input. Until recently it was unusual for reading tests to include public traffic signs, airport direction indicators or other public texts. It is still unlikely that tests will include full novels to be processed during the assessment period, although these are often presented in advance of the assessment, in the form of prescribed reading. In Academic Purpose testing, as in the case of the IELTS or the TEEP for example, it is not unusual for several texts of three or four pages each to have to be read during the test. However, some EAP tests like the TOEFL prefer to use relatively short, single-paragraph texts, in order to be able to sample a larger number of texts on different topics. Clearly there is a trade-off between the amount of time available for testing or assessment, the nature of the processing of texts required by the tasks, and the length and topics of the texts that can be used. Testing, we are again reminded, is inevitably a compromise between the ideal and the practical in our attempt to relate test performance to target language use domains.

Task length will also affect processing difficulty. This is most clearly the case in test tasks, where one wishes to keep the task-processing difficulty and time to a minimum in order to maximise time available for text processing. However, to the extent that TLU tasks are long – although such will usually be implicit rather than explicit – then longer test tasks or items may also be relatively extended, as in the case of the simulation of real reading purposes mentioned above in connection with 'communicative' tests of reading like the CUEFL.

Bachman and Palmer consider the type of input as merely test item or prompt. However, it is clear that text type is an important variable in TLU reading, as we have seen, which we need to include as an important task characteristic. One other place to address text type is under the pragmatic characteristics of the language of input, where Bachman and Palmer include register under sociolinguistic characteristics and ideational and manipulative functions under functional characteristics. Of course, it does not much matter where text type is included as long as it is not forgotten, but the label 'type' under 'form of input' strongly suggests text type ought to come here.

We have examined the effect of text type at some length in Chapters 2 and 3, so little remains to be added here, other than to illustrate for the sake of completeness of the exemplification of the framework. Text types read in TLU domains obviously cover the whole gamut of texts that can be categorised or analysed. These include written hymns and prayers in religious services, obituaries in newspapers, classified advertisements in magazines, notes after telephone conversations, email messages, advertising leaflets, discount coupons, bus direction indicators, train timetables, music festival programmes, price lists, labels on products, directions on medicine, hiking and cycling guides, washing instructions on clothes and much else. The range is only limited by our ability as researchers (especially as ethnographers or anthropologically oriented researchers) to recognise as text those written messages which might often get overlooked if one takes a traditional perspective on reading. When teaching a course on language interpretation, I often get students to complete a diary for 24 hours of everything they have read. The typical list consists of titles of textbooks and academic articles which students have been assigned and occasionally a newspaper or two if they have spent some considerable time reading them. It rarely includes the range of text types listed above, but once students have been made aware that they have indeed processed a far wider range of texts than the ones they have listed, they quickly come to see how pervasive written texts are in our world, they come to realise that their view of 'reading' is limited to study reading, and that the processing of many other text types has to be seen as reading also.

All too many reading tests show a similar bias: the texts they are based on are typically expository texts, although sometimes fictional narrative will also be included, depending upon the test purpose. They will be limited in length, but above all in type. In a sense, they define what their environment considers reading to be, and thus perpetuate a limited genre instead of opening up the assessment of reading to new TLU domains. Again, I hope that using a framework like the Bachman and Palmer framework will facilitate a more open perspective.

In addition, however, it may be that a taxonomy of text types might help test designers to be somewhat more creative in their thinking and their analyses of TLU texts. The following sample taxonomy comes from the DIALANG Project (see Figure 1 in Chapter 4): a

European project which is developing computer-based diagnostic tests of reading, amongst other skills:

### 3.2.2 On the domain of reading

This assessment system focuses on reading comprehension that aims primarily at retrieving *information* from different forms and types of texts.
In the following, the domain of reading is addressed, drawing on a variety of sources.

The figure is based on the one developed originally by Vähäpassi for the IEA International Study of Writing (Gorman *et al.*, 1988), and presents a model that usefully combines aspects of cognitive processing, the purposes of reading, and the content of texts to produce a table whose cells contain various text types/forms. The classification is, of course, not simple and clear cut, i.e. one text may share elements of different forms. Neither is this typology one that necessarily reflects the 'difficulty' of various text types/ forms *per se*, but rather it is an instrument which can be used as an aid for covering adequately the domain of texts. Examples of types of texts classified in some particular cell may be classified in some other cell(s) as well; furthermore, the classification and the examples mentioned are by no means exhaustive (see Fig. 4.1, page 126).

### 3.2.2.1 Text forms

There are different ways of classifying text forms, but one widely used classification is that provided by Werlich (1976, 1988), and this is the main source for the DIALANG approach (see also the specifications for grammar). This classification is based on basic cognitive processes including, for instance, spatial and temporal dimensions. Other, more functionally oriented classifications by Jakobson (1960), Moffet (1968) and Kinneavy (1971) among others, use a very similar range of text forms. The following typology may usefully serve as the basis of text selection (see Fig. 4.2, page 127).

'Type of input' defined as test item or task is more familiar to language testers for, as we have seen, it is commonplace to classify items into types, or test methods. I shall deal with this in more detail in Chapter 7, and so I shall merely mention here that Bachman and Palmer distinguish three major types, under the characteristic of 'expected response'. (However, I would prefer that test methods also be included under 'type of input' as well.) For the record, these are:

- selected response (typically multiple-choice or True–False)
- limited production response (short-answer questions, typically requiring up to a single sentence or utterance)
- extended production response, longer than a single sentence but ranging from two sentences to virtually free written composition.

Finally under Format of Input come the categories of speededness and vehicle. Speededness refers to the rate at which the reader has to process the information in the input, and this obviously overlaps with time allotment, discussed above. Speededness is rarely a crucial criterion in TLU reading, as we have discussed, although clearly one can envisage situations where time is more or less determined. On tests however, and even in classroom assessment procedures, time – speededness – is a practical matter, and as some have argued, also a matter of test construct, i.e. something that should be measured. Some test designers inform test-takers how long they are expected to take in each test section, although rarely item by item or task by task, but an alternative approach is simply to tell test-takers how long they have for the whole test, and to leave them to apportion time to tasks as they think fit. The problem with this latter approach is that some test-takers may misjudge the time they need for certain tasks, and thus underperform on those items/tasks for which they have left insufficient time. One can argue that this introduces the construct-irrelevant variance of ability to judge the time it takes to complete tasks, or even the ability to manage time in general. Others would argue this is indeed relevant to some TLU tasks and thus to the test's construct. Again, reference to relevant TLU tasks might help resolve this dilemma in specific settings.

Vehicle is defined as 'the means by which input is delivered: live, reproduced, or both' (Bachman and Palmer, 1996:53). This characteristic would appear to be more relevant to the testing of listening abilities, but some test developers, notably the Royal Society of Arts in the early days of the CUEFL, argued that facsimiles of 'real texts', like TV schedules, tourist brochures and the like, were more 'valid' than the same texts in revised format, such as different typefaces, different layout, the removal of picture material, page numbers and so on. Many test developers, especially in the British communicative tradition (see also the Oxford Delegacy suite of examinations) have sought to present texts in as 'live' a form as possible, such that their test booklets often look more like the real thing than like a test. It will come as no surprise that the effect of such 'live' presentation on reading test performance is unknown, but in the absence of suitable research, test designers might be best advised to avoid presenting texts as sourceless, inauthentic, de-contextualised, unrecognisable objects, and seek to present them in as 'live' a manner as possible, to maximise the possibility of correspondence between test-task performance and TLU domain.

The second major characteristic of input is its language. We have discussed the language of texts at some length in previous chapters, and so its treatment here will be fairly short. This is not to imply that it is unimportant, as the rest of this book testifies. But it is fairly evident to language testers that the language of the text, and of the items and tasks, is central to test difficulty and thus to the measurement of ability.

Test designers are usually advised to write items in simpler language than the text, as test score users are interested in knowing how well test-takers have processed texts, not items. Rarely is the simplicity of language operationally defined, however, other than by reference, in test specifications or item writer guidelines, to word frequency lists, or to standard pedagogical grammars (which themselves are no guarantee of empirical difficulty).

Bachman and Palmer (1996) categorise the language of input according to the Bachman model of communicative language ability as presented in Bachman (1990). In fact, they claim that the language of input corresponds to the areas of language knowledge and topical knowledge, which they treat under the heading of Characteristics of Individuals. This seems not unreasonable, since what language users need to know and to be able to use is the language of texts. And of course what the test seeks to establish, at least in part, is the match between the individual's language knowledge and the language of the text. And therefore the model needs to accommodate the individual's language knowledge somewhere. However, the individual's language knowledge is generally undetermined – it is often the purpose of the test to determine it. Having the model of communicative language ability in two places – the Characteristics of the Input and the Characteristics of the Individual – introduces a degree of redundancy and unmanageability into the overall framework, on the one hand, and a degree of indeterminacy for the definition of the test construct, on the other hand. Perhaps inevitably, this is compounded by the fact that Bachman and Palmer use the identical categories to classify not only the language of the input but also the language of the expected response and, by inference although not explicitly, the language of the actual response. I shall discuss this further in the next section. Suffice to say at this point that the language characteristics of input (divided into organisational characteristics such as grammar, lexis, graphology, text cohesion, rhetoric so on, as well as pragmatic and sociolinguistic characteristics such as heuristic, imaginative functions, and dialect, naturalness, cultural references) are presented in a fairly non-controversial descriptive framework which does not, however, allow for interaction effects, either within or across the components. This is presumably not the intention, but merely an artefact of the way the model is presented on paper.

The topical characteristics of input (which Bachman and Palmer gloss as personal, cultural, academic or technical information) are not surprisingly nowhere near as well developed as the language of input. Indeed to do so would require not only a theory of knowledge, which presumably implies a theory of all that is in the universe, but also a knowledge of which elements of such a theory are more salient in particular TLU tasks. This may be unfortunate, in that it leaves totally under-specified a crucial aspect of reading in TLU domains or in test tasks, but it is a fact that we simply do not know, and may never know, much about the specific effects of 'topic' in general terms, hence the difficulty of producing a classification scheme. Test developers find no guidance on topic selection in Bachman and Palmer (1996). However, Bachman and Palmer do make the important point that test validity (what they call usefulness) is relative to specific situations, and it is probably only in specific situations, with specified participants in mind, given settings, texts etc., as detailed in this framework, that it makes sense to think of specific topic effects or to investigate them. As already discussed in Chapter 3, when researchers have tried to define topic specificity or generality, they have found it virtually impossible to generalise (see also Douglas, 2000, in a companion volume to this on specific-purpose language testing).

## Characteristics of the expected response

Bachman and Palmer discuss the format of the expected response in a similar way to the way they characterise the format of the input. The channel of the response may be written or spoken, as when a reader reads a text aloud or writes a reply to a letter. The form may be language or non-language or a combination of both. The language may be the reader's first language or the target language, and the length of the response may be single words or extended discourse.

In many TLU tasks, however, the response may be entirely covert, since much reading is silent, private and may give rise to no indication of understanding. What distinguishes test and assessment tasks from such TLU tasks is that the tester seeks to elicit some response even when one would not normally be expected. Thus, reading-test-takers are frequently asked questions about a text where in real life they would not expect to be so asked. This is not infrequently held to be a potential source of invalidity, especially where the tester asks questions that a normal reader would not normally ask themselves. However, to the extent that it is possible to predict the sort of questions that given readers in a given setting might indeed ask themselves, then authenticity might be enhanced.

For example, readers might be asked to read a text about Lancaster University, which describes its location, how easy it is to reach Lancaster by public transport, what accommodation is available for students and what eating and entertainment facilities there might be. One might reasonably expect that somebody reading such a text might be thinking of studying at Lancaster, and that they might wish to know about accommodation and recreation, as well as how to get to the University most conveniently. Questions that assessed whether readers could extract such information might be held to have a degree of authenticity that items aimed at eliciting whether readers had understood the referent of 'its' in line X did not possess. In this example, although readers of such a text might not give any overt response during or after reading, one might expect them to have acquired certain information, or to be able to engage in certain activities with success after understanding the text. Of course, the risk exists of classifying as 'normal' questions items which focus upon information in the text, 'because it is there and therefore readers might be expected to be capable of extracting it'. As ever, it is a matter of judgement, and of degree of plausibility, whether a given set of expected responses are 'natural' or predictable.

Earlier in this chapter, I pointed out that Bachman and Palmer classify type of expected response into three major categories: selected, limited production and extended production. I suggested that this was an appropriate way of thinking about the characteristics of input at least as much as of expected response. Indeed, it seems to me that this is a rather limited view of expected responses, and is specifically designed for the classification of language test tasks. However, if we think about TLU tasks, it is not entirely clear that we can easily identify the type of expected response in such terms, and certainly not independently of rubric.

Clearly, if the instruction in some TLU task requires a reader to write an executive summary after reading a report, this is an extended production, and there might be some value in identifying it as such in Expected Response Characteristics. However, it is entirely predictable from the nature of the instruction, I should have thought, and thus redundant here. In other settings, it might be much more difficult to characterise the type of expected response in terms of, essentially, its length (which is in any case already provided for in the category of length, and so, once again, redundant). The issue is the one addressed in the previous paragraph, namely that many responses to reading are not overt, predictable or can be prescribed, and thus this particular characteristic may not be of much value, even to a test designer, who has already defined the test method under Characteristic of Input (see discussion p. 152ff. above).

As discussed already, Bachman and Palmer characterise the language of the expected response in exactly the same way as the language of the input. In the area of reading, however, the usefulness of this characteristic is less immediately obvious than when a test designer seeks to elicit some language output, as in the testing of writing and speaking. This is partly to do with the lack of predictability of responses, at least in TLU tasks rather than test tasks. It is also because it is not clear that a tester or a participant in a TLU task would judge a reader or the success of reading on the basis of the language used in the response. Obviously the language has to make sense and relate to the meaning of the text, but that seems a relatively trivial point and is in any case not easily covered by the characteristics given. What, for example, does the function of an expected response tell us about a reader's understanding of text?

More relevant is the relationship between the language of the expected response and the language of the input, for example whether the answer to a question can be taken literally from a text, or whether it needs to be paraphrased or summarised in the test-taker's own words. A commonly reported test-taking strategy in a variety of different test methods is for test-takers to scan texts trying to find a match between the language of the item and the language used in the text. To the extent that there is close correspondence, we risk testing test-taking strategies rather than an ability to understand the text (or the question). However, in many TLU reading tasks, readers might be expected to do precisely that. In a history lesson, for example, a pupil might be expected to answer a question about historical facts by citing information in exactly the form in which it is presented in the text, if not in the question. (Note that here we may have stumbled across a characteristic that might be held to obtain between the language of an item and the language of the input text at least as much as between input text and expected response.)

This takes us naturally to the final characteristic that Bachman and Palmer consider, namely the relationship between input and response, as the subject for the next subsection.

### Relationship between input and response

Here Bachman and Palmer seem to mean actual response rather than expected response, since they discuss this characteristic in terms of three aspects: reactivity, scope and directness of relationship.

Reactivity is the extent to which the input or response directly affects subsequent input and responses. Tasks may be reciprocal, where the language user receives feedback on the nature of the response, and the response affects the next input. In most reading tests, such feedback is rarely given, for practical reasons, although the advent of the possibility of immediate feedback from computer-delivered tests makes this an interesting possible future development. However, any feedback is unlikely to result in a change in the next input, except in the case of adaptive tests, which Bachman and Palmer classify as a different type of reactivity.

In TLU reading tasks, however, it is quite conceivable that a participant in the task might give a reader some feedback on the correctness or appropriateness of his interpretation of a text, and then adjust the text being read in the light of that performance or the feedback. The most obvious example is in classroom instruction, where a teacher sees that a child is having difficulty understanding a text, and so asks the child to read the text again more carefully, or gives her a different text to read, and so on. In non-pedagogic settings, an example might be reading a World Wide Web page, which contains a number of 'hotspots'. When readers click on an icon or hot spot, they are presented with another page to read related to that specific hotspot (which of course results in readers essentially reading different texts – a problem for assessment). A low-tech equivalent is the interactive paper-based novel, where readers read part of a story, and then are presented with a choice of different pages to which they can next turn to find a continuation.

The second category of reactivity is 'non-reciprocal', where there is neither feedback nor interaction between language users. Bachman and Palmer consider reading to be an example of non-reciprocal language use 'since the language user's internal and external response to what is read does not change the form of subsequent material in the text' (1996:55). The above examples suggest that this might be an oversimplification, although it is likely that non-reciprocity is the normal case in reading.

The final form of reactivity is adaptivity, where responses do determine subsequent input (easier or more difficult questions, depending upon the correctness of the previous response). Given that there is in principle no reason why readers should not receive feedback on the nature of their response before being presented with a different next input, there seems little reason to consider this a separate case of reactivity from reciprocal language use, except that the reaction comes from a machine, not a language user in the normal sense.

The scope of the relationship between input and response is defined as broad or narrow. A broad scope requires the language user to process a lot of input: the example Bachman and Palmer give is that of a 'main idea' comprehension question that deals with the content of the entire passage, whereas a question that focused on a specific detail or a limited amount of the passage would be narrow in scope. In this case, we could equally well see this as a question of the relationship between text input and task input, as suggested in the previous section.

Finally, we come to the directness of the relationship between expected response (this time) and information in the input or the extent to which the language user must rely on information in the context or in their own knowledge. We have already seen this characteristic addressed in the discussion of literal and inferential questions, or between textually explicit, textually implicit and scriptally implicit questions. As we saw there, the relationship is not always easy to establish, since all language comprehension requires readers to infer, to make assumptions, to use background knowledge.

A direct relationship is one where the response includes primarily information supplied in the input. An indirect task is one where the information is not supplied in the input. Consider, as we did in Chapter 1 the text: *'Sally mopped the floor so the mop was dirty'*, and the task input: *'Was the floor dirty?'* Is the information in the expected response *'Yes'* contained in the input, or in the reader's head?

We also saw that it is extremely difficult to categorise question–text relationships in such a fashion reliably, i.e. with agreement amongst those doing the classification. This task characteristic may be intuitively appealing, but rather difficult to apply in practice. Insofar as language users have to both understand explicitly stated information, and to make inferences and assumptions about information, then this is a relevant, albeit difficult characteristic to identify. It is unclear, however, whether we could say with any confidence that in given TLU settings, readers have to do more of one than the other, which would then allow us to characterise with confidence the relationship between TLU task and test task as more or less authentic because of the prevalence of more direct or more indirect relationships between input and response in one rather than the other. Nevertheless, this provides a useful framework for test developers to consider what a particular task demands of a test-taker.

## Summary

To summarise, I have presented a framework for the analysis of target language use tasks and test tasks, taken from Bachman and Palmer (1996), which represents the most recent thinking in language testing about the relationship between language use and test design. Although I have identified areas of weakness, the advantages of using such a framework greatly outweigh its limitations. Such a framework provides us both with a means of making sense of much of the vast array of research into reading and its assessment, and a starting point for thinking about test design.

In the next chapter, we will look at a few examples where such a framework, supplemented where appropriate, can be used to help develop reading tests for given purposes. Before doing this, however, I need to briefly touch upon another important aspect of the Bachman

(1990) and Bachman and Palmer (1996) models, for the sake of completeness, and in order to provide a further link to the research reported in previous chapters. In particular, in the previous chapter, I illustrated how theories of reading ability are reflected in the constructs that underly test specifications and scales of proficiency. The emphasis, on the other hand, in this chapter has been on tasks and texts rather than ability as such. This should not, however, be taken to imply that 'constructs' are unimportant in the Bachman and Palmer framework, and I have already addressed this issue briefly in my introduction to Chapter 4.

In addition to the framework of task characteristics, Bachman and Palmer (1996) do not forget the individual whose language ability is, after all, being measured. Indeed, in their concept of test usefulness they explicitly focus on the relationship between task characteristics and test-taker characteristics in their notion of 'interactiveness', which they see as an essential element in test validity.

There are many features of individuals which test designers cannot be expected to take into account because they are unpredictable or highly variable (Bachman and Palmer mention mood shifts and fatigue as two such, although one might argue that a test designer could indeed take account of the latter by ensuring that the test is not too long). However, there are many variables to which test designers can in principle pay attention, and Bachman and Palmer consider four main categories of such individual characteristics. These are:

i   Personal characteristics such as age, sex, nationality, resident status, native language, level and type of general education and type and amount of preparation or prior experience with a given test.

ii  Topical knowledge (or knowledge schemata or real-world knowledge, including cultural knowledge). Bachman and Palmer do not discuss this at any length, but we have already seen the importance and complexity of this area in some detail in previous chapters.

iii Affective schemata, which Bachman and Palmer consider as the 'affective or emotional correlates of topical knowledge' (p. 65), and which they consider can either facilitate or limit the responses that test-takers make. They have a much more limited view of affect (referring to 'emotionally charged' or 'controversial topics', for example) than the view of the importance of motivation, anxiety and a host of other affective variables which we have already reviewed in previous chapters.

iv Language ability. This latter is inevitably dealt with at some length, the basic framework for which is taken from Bachman (1990) (and is also encapsulated in the task characteristics above under organisational and pragmatic features of language). For Bachman and Palmer, however, language ability includes not only language knowledge, but also strategic competence: a set of meta-cognitive strategies that manage language use. They see these as essentially three-fold: goal setting, assessment and planning. This aspect of language ability is arguably the least developed in their framework. We shall need to consider it in more depth later, in part because of the importance that research has already attached to metacognition in reading, but also because much of what traditional research into reading processes has investigated would appear to fall into this area.

Bachman and Palmer then suggest that this model of language ability can be cast as a checklist for test design and analysis. In other words, test developers can use such a checklist to help them define and develop their construct, and use it to develop a test design statement, and a test blueprint or a set of specifications (see Alderson *et al.*, 1995, for an account of how such a model can be used in the development of test specifications).

I shall address the process of test development in the next chapter before going on to illustrate the use of the Bachman and Palmer framework in different settings.

..................................................................................................

# CHAPTER SIX

# Tests in the real world:
# test purposes

## Introduction

In Chapter 4 I discussed how constructs of reading have been defined and operationalised. At the end of Chapter 5 I also briefly touched upon aspects other than task characteristics that the development of a test needs to address, namely a definition of what reading ability might be (or language ability applied to written texts, as Bachman and Palmer might prefer). In practice, of course, we have been addressing the issue of the construct of reading throughout this book so far, and we will return to this topic in later chapters, too.

In Chapter 5, I identified a number of task characteristics, initially in target language use domains, using the Bachman and Palmer terminology, and then by extension in test tasks, which need to be taken into account when designing reading tests and assessment procedures.

In this chapter, I present a number of situations in which reading is assessed in relation to uses (i.e. inferences about reading ability, decisions about individuals) that are made based on information from tests or assessment procedures. As already promised in Chapter 1, we shall look at a number of real-world needs for the assessment of reading. First, however, we need briefly to consider the various stages in test development.

## Test development

Bachman and Palmer (1996:87) regard test development as having three main components: design, operationalisation and administration. In design, test developers produce a design statement which covers the purpose of the test, a description of the TLU domain and task types, the characteristics of test-takers, a definition of the test construct, a plan for evaluating test usefulness and an inventory of available resources and a plan for their allocation and management.

At the operationalisation stage, testers select, specify and write: they produce a test blueprint, with details of the test structure (number, salience, sequence and relative importance of parts and number of tasks) and test task specifications (specification of purpose, definition of construct, setting, time allotment, instructions, characteristics of input and expected response and scoring method). Finally the administration phase includes collecting feedback, analysing and archiving the tests and producing test scores.

Although this is a useful characterisation, it involves rather extensive overlap within and across component stages and with the initial description of test task characteristics. An alternative model is taken from Alderson *et al.* (1995) involving the following stages of test construction and evaluation:

- identifying test purpose
- developing test specifications
- guidelines for and training of item/task writers and moderation of their products
- pre-testing, analysis of results and revision of test
- training examiners and administrators
- monitoring examiner reliability
- reporting scores and setting pass marks
- test validation
- post-test reports
- developing and improving tests

In this model, the development of test specifications is seen as central. It is pointed out that specifications exist for a number of different audiences, and these need to be distinguished. Crucially they are written for the guidance of test writers, but they are also needed in somewhat different form by test validators and test users, who include not only teachers and those who will interpret test scores, but also test-takers themselves. Where this model tends to converge with the Bachman and Palmer model is in the aspects of specifications that should be covered. Test specifications, it is suggested, should contain statements covering all or most of the following points:

1 test purpose
2 the learner taking the test (age, sex, level of language proficiency, first language, cultural background, country of origin, educational level and nature of educational reason for taking test, likely personal and professional interests and levels of background knowledge etc.)
3 test level (in terms of test-taker ability)
4 test construct
5 description of suitable language course or textbook
6 number of sections to the test
7 time for each section
8 weighting for each section
9 target language situation(s)
10 text types
11 text length
12 text complexity/difficulty
13 language skills to be tested
14 language elements (structures/lexis/notions/functions)
15 task types
16 number and weight of items
17 test methods
18 rubrics; examples; explicit assessment criteria
19 criteria for scoring
20 description of typical performance at each level
21 description of what candidates at each level can do in the real world                                                                (ctd.)

22 sample papers

23 samples of students' performances on tasks

(Alderson *et al.*, 1995:11–38)

Neither model is perfect, of course, and neither claims comprehensiveness, although the Bachman and Palmer model claims it enables the degree of correspondence to be established between test task and real-life language use. Both, moreover, stress that in particular settings, more or less detail will be needed or will be irrelevant. Both models are also (probably inevitably) a distortion of the actual process of test construction, as each implies linear development, and the treatment of characteristics separately at discrete points in test development. For example, the Alderson *et al.* model might suggest that only when training examiners do we consider scoring methods, but in fact, of course, procedures for scoring, rating scales and mark schemes are drafted at the specification stage, tested during pre-testing and subsequent analysis, and often extensively revised before operational examiner training takes place.

In practice, test development proceeds cyclically: this applies through all stages and for all components of test development, but, as already emphasised, this is especially true for the relationship between test specifications and test tasks. Specifications provide guidance for the drafting of sample tasks, but the difficulties of task development provide feedback to test developers which will usually require modification of test specifications. In one test development project in which I was involved, six different versions of the specifications were developed whilst item writing was going on, as our understanding of the construct developed, and our experience grew with the ability of item writers to interpret and operationalise our specifications. And that was before any test tasks were reviewed by outsiders, or tried out on any test-takers!

Test specifications and tasks will be revised, then, not only in the light of pre-testing, but also in the light of the experience of item writers, test-takers and, crucially, test users. One approach, typical of 1970s needs analyses, is to identify participants in given target language situations and to ask them about the language needs of people in such settings. Thus the informants provide initial input to test specifications. The problem with such approaches is turning the mass of data one collects into usable test specifications. An alternative approach was tried in another test development project, where we

only consulted informants once we had developed our test specifications and sample test tasks, since other research projects had already
investigated language needs in the TLU domain. We asked informants
whether the tasks and specifications we had developed would be
suitable for assessing relevant abilities of participants in given TLU
settings. Comments were then used to help us revise specifications
and tasks before pre-testing (see Clapham and Alderson, 1997, and
Alderson, 1988).

The level of detail contained in test specifications will vary considerably. If the specifications are for the use of one class teacher
devising his own informal reading inventory for his own reading class,
they are likely to be fairly short, with much information implicit in
the setting and not made explicit. In a high-stakes proficiency test,
where a number of item writers will be writing parallel forms of the
test, then much more detail and control over what item writers
produce is necessary.

Much will also depend upon the expertise and experience of item
writers. If they have been trained and have long experience, then it
might be unnecessary to describe exactly how best to write multiple-
choice items, what pitfalls to avoid and so on. However, such expertise cannot always be assumed, even with experienced item writers,
and the development of a detailed item writer's manual (what
Bachman and Palmer call a test blueprint, but with additional detail
about test method effects and best practice in the development of
particular testing techniques) would be very useful.

## Testing situations

I now propose to illustrate the framework expounded in the previous
chapter and the above discussion of test specifications by identifying
TLU and test task characteristics, for a number of assessment settings
and purposes. Chapter 7 presents a complementary discussion of test
methods in more detail.

The first situation illustrates a specific purpose domain, where the
relationship between TLU tasks and test tasks can be fairly easily
established. For further examples of this sort of clear relationship, see
Douglas (2000). The following three situations then present settings
where the relationship between TLU domain and likely test tasks is
not so simple.

## Situation 1

This first situation has a professional setting. The purpose of the test suite is to identify the level of reading ability of employees in the Government Service, specifically the Diplomatic Service. One of the aims of the tests is to encourage diplomats to learn foreign languages, specifically but not only, those spoken in the country where they will be posted. In addition, the tests will be used to identify officers for posting to particular countries, and for assigning them to particular responsibilities or tasks in-country. Candidates will receive a salary supplement, which varies according to the level of ability they have achieved. Tests are devised at five levels of reading ability, from zero to advanced professional.

The test suite is thus for professional purposes, is relatively high stakes, with considerable potential for impact, and is likely to be very formal in administration. Candidates will register for one level at a time, only being eligible to take a higher-level test if they have already passed a lower-level test on a previous occasion. The reading test is also likely to be combined with other measures of language ability, in particular an ability to understand spoken text and to speak in the foreign language. I confine myself here to the written word.

Bachman and Palmer imply that the two lists of TLU and test characteristics should be drawn up separately and then compared point by point for correspondence. In what follows, I juxtapose TLU characteristics with possible test task characteristics for ease of reading.

### Characteristics of the setting

Readers are government officials, usually of a low or medium rank. They are likely to be in their late 20s to mid-40s, but older officials may also be required to take the test as they are considered for promotion or posting. They will be of either sex, with tertiary level education or equivalent professional experience. They will have considerable knowledge of diplomatic procedures and the general demands of their post, but may not have much if any experience of living in the target culture, and their knowledge of the political, commercial, historical or even geographical aspects of the country may be limited, but is considered relevant to an ability to operate effectively at post.

Other participants in the TLU events will be superior officers and peers in other departments at post who need to be briefed as a result of the reading, and occasionally subordinates who need to be given appropriate assignments. Occasionally junior officers and clerks will submit accounts of TLU documents which will need to be checked against the original sources.

Higher-level participants are likely to read paper documents, or on a computer screen, in an office, usually well-lit, comfortable, free from extraneous noise. However, they may also read on public transport, or occasionally in clandestine, uncomfortable settings. They will usually be expected to process documents fairly rapidly, for the main message, or to decide whether they will repay closer scrutiny. Selected documents will have to be read carefully, with less time pressure, but with a much greater need for accuracy in the interpretation of facts and of opinions. Sometimes participants will be required to provide a translation of key parts of documents for superior officers, or to check others' translations.

## Characteristics of the (test) rubrics

Test tasks will need to reflect both major purposes for reading: skim reading, and close and critical reading.

This is likely to be much more important at the upper levels than the lower ones, where reading might be confined to social survival texts, at the level of literal understanding.

Higher-level instructions are usually implicit, the purpose for reading being defined as part of the official's professional duties, but may occasionally be stated explicitly, in the form of a memorandum requesting information or action from a superior, or information in the case of a peer. These requests will be in the participant's own language, and usually, but not always, written.

Officials at the lower levels of achievement will not normally be required to understand target texts in depth for the fulfilment of their official duties, but at higher levels of achievement, they are normally expected to handle a range of texts independently. When such instructions are explicit, their degree of explicitness will vary: sometimes officials will be required to produce a detailed translation by a given deadline, with the main points summarised in an executive summary. More often, they will be expected to check a junior officer's or clerk's translation, to provide a brief summary, and to comment on the relevance of the document to a given policy matter, a proposed plan of action, or for its insight into some historical event. On other occasions, the officials will be reading for background information, to inform themselves about some aspect of the target country, or in order to decide whether to read further. Such purposes will usually be implicit and self-directed.

Test instructions will reflect these two major aspects: implicit and explicit. At the lower levels, test-takers will be required to process relatively straightforward texts and will be tested for their understanding of the main points, factual details and simple inferences. At higher levels, candidates will be expected not merely to understand (progressively more difficult) texts, but also to perform professionally related tasks on them.

For example, at the advanced level the test is structured as follows: there are four major parts, each with a number of tasks. They are equally weighted and clearly distinguished, although two parts are linked by topic and texts.

In Part One, test-takers are required to read several short documents, to identify their main points, and to decide which text is relevant to which department within the diplomatic mission. In Part Two, they are asked to read three somewhat longer texts, each on a different aspect of a related topic, to complete a gapped L1 translation of each, and to answer a number of questions on the particular perspective or bias of each text. In Part Three, they are required by office memo to read a host government statement on immigration policy and to answer a number of questions from a superior officer about the origin, nature and implications of the policy for a number of categories of immigrants. In Part Four, they read a further office memo accompanying a newspaper editorial associated with the official political opposition of the host country, in which they are asked to produce a one-paragraph (maximum 150-word) summary, in L1, of the editorial, together with comments on its relation to the host government's policy outlined in Part Three. Participants are given three hours to complete these four macro tasks, but with no indication of how much time to spend on each part. This time allotment is expected to require test-takers to take strategic decisions about which parts of the texts to concentrate on and whether to read carefully or selectively.

Test-takers are told that they will receive one point each for factually correct or appropriate answers in Parts One, Two and Three, and that their summary and comments in Part Four will be judged according to criteria for accuracy of understanding, and appropriacy of interpretation. They are not told that the summary in Part Four will be read by two trained raters who will be given a mark scheme as well as two five-point scales, one for accuracy, one for appropriacy, containing descriptors for the first, third and fifth point on each scale. Markers are given a detailed mark scheme for Parts One, Two and Three.

## Characteristics of the input

Participants can be expected to read a wide range of texts in the target language. They will be printed or on computer screen, will vary greatly in length, from books to short official announcements, from newspaper editorials to government policy statements, from minutes of official meetings to memoranda of understanding between the two countries, proposals for collaborative projects and the like.

At the lower levels of achievement, the language of these texts will be fairly simple or simplified on occasion, but they will exhibit the main organisational characteristics of the respective genre. However, a relatively restricted set of text types will be tested, with a relatively restricted set of functions: typically ideational, using only the standard variety of the written language. Texts will typically be the sort required for social survival rather than for professional purposes. At higher levels, a wider range of text types will be used, both of a professional as well as an 'everyday' nature, and a wider range of functions, including the manipulative as well as the imaginative, will be included. Whilst most texts, even at the advanced level, will be in the standard written form of the language, some will exhibit the non-standard features typical of genres like popular newspapers or political cartoons, will contain many more cultural references and figurative language, and will be fully authentic in terms of the range and type of language used.

The language of the items/tasks will always be in the candidate's first language; even comprehension questions, as well as simulated tasks, will be in L1, not the target language.

Text topics will relate to the professional interests and responsibilities of test-takers at the more advanced levels, and may require some understanding of the political, commercial, cultural or historical background of the target-language speakers. At the lower levels, however, whilst texts may refer to current affairs or aspects of the target culture, it is not expected that candidates will require specific knowledge in order to be able to understand the texts.

## Characteristics of the expected response

Responses to test tasks at all levels will be in the candidate's first language, as their ability to write in the target language is tested separately. Selected response, limited production and extended production types will all be employed, but in L1; thus some responses will be minimal, as in multiple-choice comprehension questions, others will be longer, up to one sentence in length, and at the higher levels, extended summaries will be required.

The relationship between input and expected response varies. No responses are expected in the target language, but some will be literal translations or close paraphrases in the first language, whereas other responses will constitute major transformations or summaries of the target language into the first language. At the higher levels, candidates will be required to express their own judgements and opinions about target texts in ways which bear little direct relationship to the target texts they are based on.

As the tests are presented in paper and pencil form, there is no reciprocity of relationship between input and expected or actual response. In terms of scope, however, candidates at lower levels will be exposed to input requiring relatively narrow scope – literal comprehension questions, for example – whereas at the upper levels, the scope of the relationship between input and expected response might be extremely broad, as candidates are expected to interpret target texts in light of other texts or their background knowledge. Indeed, at the upper levels, the relationship between input and expected response might be rather indirect precisely because candidates will be expected to use relatively extensive knowledge of the target culture, politics etc. in order to interpret texts.

## Discussion

One of the most important features of this first test situation to note is the fact that the aim of the suite is to identify different levels of readers' ability through different tests. Rather than asking all candidates to take one set of reading texts and tasks, the situation allows test designers to differentiate by task and not just by performance. As we will see in the next testing situation, it is not uncommon to require all candidates to take the same set of tests, and then to discriminate among them according to their performance on the tasks. Lower scores are interpreted to mean lower levels of ability, with some confidence, since all candidates have been exposed to the same tasks. In our first situation, however, test-takers either decide or are required to take a test at a particular level, and either 'pass' or 'fail'.

Whilst it is possible to define levels of performance within each test level (since some who 'pass' the intermediate test will achieve higher or lower scores than others who 'pass'), these differences can be ignored for the sake of deciding a candidate's 'level'. Provided that an established cut-score has been exceeded, all scores are treated as adequate. Although clearly the option exists to treat different 'passing scores' as representing 'better' or 'worse' passes, allowing some candidates to pass with distinction, for example, this possibility is irrelevant to the setting of a pass–fail cut-score.

Similarly, if a cut-score has not been reached, all scores are regarded as inadequate (although it is possible to allow for a borderline review if scores come within a given percentage point of the cut-score).

In such a setting, where different tests are constructed for different levels, it is possible to cover a wide range of text types and tasks across the range of tests in the suite. This is especially useful if, as in our example, we can believe that it is possible to differentiate the sorts of TLU tasks that language users might be expected to perform in the target language use domain, because it means we can have greater confidence that somebody who has progressed through the suite to the higher levels has been fairly thoroughly tested on their reading ability. However, it does imply that we are confident that the different texts and tasks candidates take at the different levels really are different in difficulty from each other. It would be invidious if texts and tasks at level 3, say, proved to be harder than texts and tasks given at a supposedly higher level. Thus test designers need to be especially careful to ensure the increasing difficulty (however measured – see Chapter 3) of the tests. When, as in this first situation, we have a fairly easily described target language use domain, and where we have domains which can be separated, such that we can say with a degree of confidence that higher-level users have to engage with different sorts of texts and different levels of task because of their professional requirements, then we can have reasonable confidence in our differentiation by test task. However, in other settings – see for example the third and fourth situations – our test settings may be so general and our participants so heterogeneous as to make differentiation by potential TLU task very hazardous and speculative. We may then need to appeal to other notions of differentiation (for example, the ALTE framework levels, see Chapter 8).

## Situation 2

Our second situation is in an educational setting. The purpose of the test is to identify those intending postgraduate students who will be at academic risk if studying in the medium of English because of the level of their reading ability in English. The test will be used as only one of several factors in making admissions decisions; others will include the candidate's academic record, academic field already studied, possibly aptitude, ability to pay tuition fees and maintenance costs, and so on. Since the test results will be used by different admissions officers at different academic institutions in a number of English-speaking countries, different cut-scores are required, and the standards are typically determined by each admitting institution, although many expect guidance on what might be an acceptable test performance from the testing agency and the test developers. In addition, since ability to pay tuition and maintenance fees is important, many candidates will be seeking support from governmental agencies or non-governmental organisations (NGOs), such as aid agencies, and many of these agencies will only award scholarships if candidates have a suitable level of English.

The test is thus for educational purposes, and is very high stakes, with considerable potential for impact. It is therefore likely to be very formal in administration. It is also likely to be combined with other measures of academic language ability, in particular an ability to understand and speak the language and to produce adequate academic texts in the foreign language. We again confine ourselves to the written word, and in particular to reading, since many institutions and academic disciplines make different demands on various aspects of language users' communicative competence, and thus wish to differentiate how well a student can read in the language from their ability to understand spoken language, or to write or speak. Different disciplines or institutions will consider reading more or less important than other skills. Hence the justification for a skills-based test.

## Characteristics of the setting

Participants in the TLU domain will be aged anywhere from their mid-20s upwards, with a predominance perhaps of 30- to 40-year-olds. They will be of both sexes, from a whole range of different countries and educational backgrounds (usually not in the medium of English, sometimes at postgraduate level already, although some may only have undergraduate or equivalent qualifications). They will speak a wide variety of first languages, have a wide variety of cultural and social backgrounds, and they will come from, and be intending to study in, a wide variety of academic disciplines. Some will be intending to continue further studies in a subject they have already studied at tertiary level, others will be intending to switch disciplines and to pursue higher studies in a new field (as in former engineering undergraduate students wishing to study management at postgraduate level, for example).

In the target language use setting, their reading will be in libraries, bedrooms, dedicated study rooms or at computer terminals. These will be for the most part, quiet, well lit, with adequate space for taking notes, access to other texts and to some extent to fellow students. Access to academic staff for consultation about their reading will be more restricted, and on the whole language users will be expected to read and study independently. Nevertheless, other participants in the setting will include supervisors or other academics who assign reading tasks and judge outcomes (which include oral presentations of the reading in seminars or tutorials, less formal discussions in seminars, written reviews of literature, critiques of articles or authors, reproduction of learned facts, application of principles or techniques to new settings or to operate equipment).

In addition, reading will occur in a variety of non-academic settings: newspapers on public transport, packaging of goods in supermarkets, announcements for public entertainment; as well as semi-academic settings: instructions, notices, timetables, accommodation guides and the like. In such settings, other participants are those providing the services offered, or those who readers might communicate with after reading.

The time taken to read will vary for the non- or semi-academic tasks: academic reading is typically slow and time-consuming; articles might take three or four hours to read once, and might require re-reading, whole books consderably longer, up to two or three weeks. Laboratory or computer manuals might be consulted briefly but frequently, other academic references like on-line databases might be read occasionally, but for considerable detail.

## Characteristics of the (test) rubrics

As will already be clear from the above, purposes for reading vary considerably in the TLU domain, even if this is narrowly defined as the academic setting. Different academic disciplines will require different sorts of purposes – some are claimed to require very little 'normal' reading at all (as, for example, mathematics or computing) others to need only limited amounts of reading (engineering, chemistry, biology) whereas yet other disciplines (like linguistics, philosophy, literary studies, history) may require critical reading in depth, appreciation of style, textual exegesis and more.

For this reason, it is not uncommon for test developers to distinguish between linguistically demanding, and non-linguistically demanding courses (although the extent to which stereotypes of linguistic demand actually hold true for different disciplines is in need of considerable empirical verification). The different reading purposes of different disciplines can be taken into account if different tests or at least texts are selected for different disciplines (see below); but to the extent that students from different disciplines are expected to take the same test (as in the TOEFL or the latest version of IELTS), then we can expect that either it will be necessary to identify common-core reading purposes, or some students will be advantaged or disadvantaged by the purposes incorporated into the test tasks. In other words, tasks – purposes, rubrics, instructions – will be more or less biased against them.

Given the heterogeneity of the target language user, instructions in both TLU domain and test task will be in the target language. They will normally be in writing in the TLU domain, although assignments may be delivered orally, without visual support, in some lectures.

Reading tasks may be more or less specified, depending upon the reading purpose. If the task is to produce a review of the literature, then the instructions will be fairly general. If the task is to write a critical review of one or two papers, then the instructions are likely to be more explicit. If the task is to write a course paper, in which the focus is on a comparison and contrast of approaches, results or conclusions of a number of articles, or to give one's own opinions or plans in the light of one's reading, then the reading task itself will be more diffuse, more synthetic and less easily related to any specific text or even to particular understandings of individual texts.

Similarly, the structure of the various tasks in the TLU will vary. In the test, it is clear that test developers are limited by the amount of time available. Days or even weeks are unlikely to be available for assessment purposes, especially as many test-takers will be taking the test in their home country before coming to the English-speaking country, and possibly even before having engaged in academic study in English. Thus facile replication of TLU tasks, even if these were homogeneous, is hardly appropriate or even possible.

Decisions about the number, salience, sequence and relative importance of parts/tasks, as well as the number of tasks/items per part, are likely to depend upon practical matters like how much time is available for the test, and much less on what these might look like in the TLU domain. Given that tests of other skills have to be administered as well as the reading test, and that most tests cannot take longer than three hours, for reasons of fatigue in such high-stakes settings, the time available for the reading test is likely to be a major limiting factor and a source of considerable lack of correspondence between TLU tasks and test task – typically, around one hour is the maximum available.

In the TLU tasks, the outcome of reading is assessed in various ways. Readers are expected to become acquainted with the basic facts of their discipline, be they empirical results, statistical procedures or aspects of the history of the discipline. Inaccuracies in understanding or recalling such facts are likely to be penalised. Thus, in test tasks, accuracy of understanding at a literal level is important.

However, at postgraduate level, readers are also expected to be critical in their reading: to detect assumptions, philosophies, theories or prejudices implicit in text, and to relate any account of their readings to their perceptions of such hidden matters. At this level, readers are judged more according to their ability to justify their criticisms than according to the correctness of their interpretation. However, such an ability depends at least partly on readers' understanding of the academic discipline and its history as upon an understanding of language *per se*. If subject matter understanding were legitimately part of the construct to be tested, then this would not matter, but in this test situation, subject matter understanding is measured, admittedly broadly, by other means, and test users expect the language test to test language rather than subject matter knowledge.

In any case, given the heterogeneity of the population, it is impossible to find an academic discipline in which all test-takers could be expected to have roughly equivalent experience or knowledge, or in which it would be legitimate to allow their understanding of the field to interact with their understanding of the language in order to make such relatively high-level judgements. So test developers are obliged to confine the judgements that will be made about readers' understandings to those aspects of interpretation that can be confidently said to be due to language ability, and on which non-specialists, i.e. language testers rather than subject matter specialists, can make adequate judgements of the accuracy of the understanding. This does not confine the tester to assessing literal understanding: identifying main ideas, distinguishing main from subsidiary ideas, detecting bias, authorial opinion, inferring assumptions, and the like will all be important to test, but in contexts where subject matter knowledge is not expected to assist performance.

## Characteristics of the input

In TLU tasks, the texts are written, but may have more or less graphic accompaniment, depending on source and academic discipline. They will vary considerably in length, from short abstracts to book-length texts, and will often be 20 pages in length or more. Readers typically have to read fairly large numbers of such texts for some assignments, and the time spent on such tasks, as already discussed, is necessarily conditioned by the length of the text(s), but is typically perceived as speeded – i.e. under considerable time pressure, working against tight deadlines, rather than leisurely and relaxed.

The tasks which TLU readers are assigned are in the target language, and written responses are also in the target language. Test tasks will also be in the target language rather than the first language, for reasons of practicality as well as TLU faithfulness.

The language of TLU texts is enormously heterogeneous, but rarely simplified (except perhaps in the case of introductory textbooks, which are relatively uncommon at postgraduate level). It is frequently specialised in register, sometimes in genre (technical laboratory reports are not read by all TLU users, for instance); the lexis will be infrequent, the syntax often complex, and the rhetorical features also complex. Standard language rather than non-standard is used and the pragmatic functions are typically ideational and manipulative, either presenting facts or seeking to persuade the reader of a point of view, a philosophy or the correctness of an interpretation.

In the test tasks, it is only possible to simulate such variety if specialist tests can be administered to distinct groups of students, as was attempted in the ELTS test and the early versions of the IELTS test, for example. However, even there, the subject matter groupings were very broad – life and medical sciences, social studies and the like – and were never claimed to be representative of the great variety of registers or at least vocabularies of particular disciplines.

A more practical approach, used by both TOEFL and the current IELTS, is to present a range of texts in various topic areas, either from a range of broadly conceived academic disciplines, as in IELTS, or from a range of non-academic sources such as encyclopaedia entries, books, magazines and newspapers, as in the case of TOEFL. As has been recounted in previous chapters, Clapham's research showed the difficulties attendant upon trying to emulate target language use texts in test input, and the resulting uncontrolled and unpredictable bias in test scores.

## Characteristics of the expected response

In the TLU setting, the expected response will either be invisible (an internal representation of meaning), or it will be in some form of extended written or spoken presentation, in the target language and possibly accompanied by graphic support (OHP slides, graphs, tables). In test tasks, given the need to assess reading separately from writing, expected responses will be much more limited in type, being either selected responses, or short answers – up to a sentence or so – in the target language. More extensive responses, as in the case of a summary, are more likely to form part of a writing test task based upon a related reading input, than to be used to judge the accuracy or reasonableness of a reader's interpretation alone. Nevertheless, it is possible to devise criteria for the assessment of such extended written production which include not only judgements of the accuracy of the language produced, but the accuracy of the interpretation of the input text, independent of the linguistic quality of the written response. In such cases, the criteria for assessment will be explicit, and made available to the candidate as well. However, given the time limit for the reading section of the test battery, the actual summary task will be presented in the writing section, to be based upon one or more texts read (and an understanding of which has already been assessed) in the reading test. The accuracy of the language of the expected response will be largely irrelevant to judgements of understanding.

### Relationship between input and response

In the TLU domain, it is possible for students' understanding – or lack of it – of a text to influence what task or text they will next be assigned. In this sense, the input–response relationship is adaptive. This will not happen in our paper-based test, although if we eventually mount the test on computer, as is happening with the TOEFL at present, then the test can become adaptive and students can be given easier texts or easier tasks if their performance shows them to be finding the test difficult. Currently available reading proficiency tests for this second testing situation are, however, non-reciprocal: all test-takers are expected to read the same texts and to answer the same questions.

The scope of the relationship between input and expected response is both broad and narrow in the TLU and the test tasks: some tasks will focus on detailed understanding of parts of text, others – possibly the majority – will require the language user and test-taker to process large amounts of input. Similarly, the input-expected response relationship will be both direct, in the case of detailed understanding of facts, and indirect, in the case of understanding inferences, assumptions and the like.

### Discussion

An important difference between this testing situation and the previous one has already been alluded to in the previous discussion: here the target population of participants is very heterogeneous, but all test-takers are required to take one test. This means that all test-takers can be measured on a common scale, rank orders can be established and scores can be compared against each other. This is useful for test users, like admissions officers, who are not language experts but who need to know how to interpret test results. As a result, test users generally feel that they 'know' what a TOEFL score of 550 or an IELTS Band of 6.5 'means'. Given the variety of different TLU settings to which participants will be heading, this is an advantage since it means that test users can interpret scores to suit their own institutional requirements, in terms of admissions policies, or in terms of perceived linguistic demands of the academic study in question. Thus, students do not 'pass' or 'fail' these tests, they achieve a score which testifies to their level of proficiency, which is then interpreted in the light of local circumstances, needs and other information about the test-taker before a decision is taken.

A problem is that test users may be more or less competent at interpreting test scores. In my view, it is the responsibility of the test developer to avoid test misuse by offering clear guidelines, based upon appropriate empirical research, which indicates what range of test scores is likely to indicate 'ability to perform adequately in an English-medium setting unhindered by problems of language', or the converse: 'likely to have problems because of language'; and such guidelines should indicate under which circumstances, for which TLU settings or contexts, they obtain, and for which higher or lower scores are likely to be acceptable.

A disadvantage of this testing approach is that test-takers may be more or less disadvantaged by the test content: the correspondence between test tasks and TLU tasks will be much less close for some test-takers than for others. Thus studies of test bias, for or against groups of test-takers, will be an important feature of test monitoring.

A further problem is that different versions of this one test are routinely produced, for security reasons, and it is of crucial importance that test users can have confidence that scores obtained on one test are exactly equivalent to scores obtained on a different version. This may require elaborate test-equating procedures, as well as careful attention to test content. The difficulty here is that test content is relatively less determined than in Situation 1, and therefore the statistical equating procedures become even more important. Discussion of these procedures is beyond the scope of this book, but interested readers can refer to Crocker and Algina (1986) or Holland and Rubin eds. (1982).

# Situation 3

Our third situation is also an educational one: the assessment of reading achievement and progress in classroom settings for both native speakers and second-language users in secondary schools.

The purpose of assessment in this setting is to aid instruction and to identify where readers' strengths and weaknesses might lie. The results of the assessment procedures might be used to adjust teaching, to assign some readers in a class to different tasks from their peers or to place readers into different classes or programmes. This situation is largely low-stakes, and may be able to take advantage of informal rather than formal methods of assessment.

In fact, this 'situation' is far from homogeneous, like the previous situation. However, unlike in Situation 2, we do not need to develop one instrument which will be used in all circumstances. Rather, the assessment procedures developed will need to adapt to aspects of the different settings. The results of the assessment will be used by class-room teachers rather than school authorities or whole school districts, and so informality and practicality are at a premium, and reliability of results is less important.

However, an important aspect of the validity of classroom assess-ment is its relationship to classroom teaching: the content and methods of the teaching, as well as to the atmosphere of the class and the philosophy of the teacher. The relationship with TLU tasks is indirect or non-existent because these are so many and varied that they are indeterminable – after all, reading classes are typically in-tended to prepare learners for life, not for specific TLU tasks. The nature of the classroom teaching is, however, crucial. In what follows, therefore, I concentrate on attempting to characterise a range of different classroom tasks, and only address the nature of assessment directly at the end.

## Characteristics of the setting

Reading takes place in classrooms or at home (or elsewhere), in preparation for classes or as follow-up to classes. In class, reading might be individual or in whole-class settings. In the latter case, individuals might be asked to read sections of text aloud in front of their peers; in the former, individuals might be expected to read silently and to answer teachers' questions as the teacher circulates among class members. Reading might even be in groups, where learners read and discuss their readings with their peers, or complete an assignment based on one or more readings, and the reading itself may have been done in class or elsewhere.

Thus participants may include fellow readers or may only involve the teacher, who may or may not have read the same text. (In the case of extensive reading from a class library, for example, the teachers may be more familiar with some of the books than others, but this familiarity may come from hearing pupils' accounts of their reading, rather than from reading the book themselves.) The teacher may be routinely making judgements about the learners' reading ability, or she may be focusing upon aspects of the reading performance: adequate word recognition, accurate pronunciation of words, intonation indicating an understanding of what is being read aloud, the degree of reader absorption in text which is taken to be an indication of deep reading with intrinsic motivation, and so on.

The time of the task may be short – as in the case of a pupil reading two sentences aloud – or long, where an individual reads a library book over a number of class periods.

## Characteristics of the (test) rubrics

Instructions in such settings will also vary. In many cases, they will be explicit: teachers will assign readers particular tasks, for example to write a brief summary of the library book for the class library diary, or simply to read the next two sentences aloud. The language of such instructions will be in the target language, but may be in the pupils' first language or in their second language if they are non-native speakers of the target language, as often happens in ESL settings, for example. They may be spoken or written; if written, they may be part of a reading programme, such as basal readers in the USA, and thus may be given by the textbook rather than the class teacher herself.

Frequently, classroom activities themselves are test-like – they consist of the teacher asking questions of pupils before they read, whilst they are reading or after their reading. Such questions are likely to influence what pupils pay attention to in their reading, or what they attempt to remember afterwards. In such cases, they will be highly specified.

The activities may, however, be more extensive: they may consist of rather general instructions to design an object based on reading instructions or descriptions, or to conduct a classroom survey based on readings, or to write a project report in which a number of aspects of a geographical region or an historical event are described, and they may even be evaluated by a group of pupils after reading a number of different texts.

Some instructional tasks, then, will have a number of parts, in a specified sequence, whilst others will only require fulfilment of one activity (as in the case of the reading aloud). Pupils may be given one class period or less to complete the task(s), or they may be expected to complete the task out of class, as in homework, for example, and then to bring the result to a subsequent class for discussion or evaluation.

Scoring methods are likely to vary. The criteria for judging successful task completion may be implicit and derivable from the task itself. Reading aloud may conventionally be expected to be judged according to accuracy of word identification, pronunciation and intonation that reflects understanding. But such criteria may not be known by pupils, and indeed the teacher himself may not be fully aware of how he is judging performance, as in the case of intonation.

Assessment criteria may also not relate to understanding but degree of involvement – as in the case of the silent individual reader absorbing himself in a book he is enjoying – or contribution to group-work, as in the case of project work. Such criteria, which may well be made explicit to pupils, may be intended to influence the process of reading and task completion as much as to assess the resulting product (although again we must note the difficulty of inducing the deep reading and intrinsic motivation which is often the goal of individual or extensive reading).

## Characteristics of the input

Texts used in class are, of course, very varied and cover a wide range of text types (as characterised, for example, in Chapter 5) – from simplified basal readers to whole novels, from expository texts in particular subject areas to poems, from newspaper articles to party political manifestoes, religious tracts, advertisements or technical instructions. There has been much discussion, in Britain at least, about language across the curriculum, and the need for teachers of all curricular subjects to see themselves as teachers of language, including reading. And of course it is true that pupils learn to read by reading, and so the texts they cover outside formal language classes are an important influence on their reading ability as well as on their motivation to read. However, describing this set of testing situations, I have in mind the formal language class where reading is explicitly focused on, rather than other curriculum subjects like history, chemistry or social studies.

And it is important to consider to what extent such language or reading classes do indeed cover the whole gamut of possible texts. Considering the range of texts described in Chapter 5, for example, do such classes typically require or encourage pupils to read advertisements, tourist brochures, the covers of CD albums? Is reading seen to include the processing of texts like webpages, electronic databases, science fiction, pornographic stories, cartoons, fanzines, street signs and notices, or even political pamphlets? Might the latter not be seen as the job of the teacher of social studies, rather than the teacher of reading, and some of the others as too trivial or too risky to be read in class? Is critical reading seen as the province of the reading teacher? Or is the reading teacher mainly concerned with teaching literary texts, with acquainting pupils with classic fiction? I suggest that it is likely that reading classes will actually only deal with a subset of the range of possible text types, and this will affect what texts are used as input for reading test/assessment tasks.

Input may well include graphical representations (photos, illustrations, diagrams etc.), but will be in the target language only. If texts vary in length in the teaching, then they should also vary in length for the assessment which, in such informal settings, need not be confined to one class period in any case. However, teachers may also be interested in how quickly pupils can read, and so a degree of speededness may be important in task design. They may, for example, wish to establish and increase pupils' reading (rauding) rates, or to assess their ability to skim or scan-read for gist or specific information.

The language of the input can be expected to exhibit all the normal characteristics of the target language, although texts and tasks may not be highly complex or academic in nature. Some simplification of texts may also occur, for pedagogic reasons, and teachers may well be interested in helping students to understand classic fiction by getting them first to read abridged or simplified versions of otherwise difficult texts. Texts would be expected to cover a range of functions, but perhaps especially the imaginative and manipulative, as well as ideational, and a range of different registers, genres and figurative uses of language would be expected. Topics would be expected to vary, but be within the intellectual capacity of the pupils, their developmental stage and to appeal to or reflect their interests. Texts are likely to be culturally embedded, as part of the aim of many reading classes is to transmit cultural values.

## Characteristics of the expected response

Expected responses will vary, as seen above with instructions. They may be extensive written reports or responses to multiple-choice questions accompanying a basal reader. They will be in the language of the texts, they may be spoken, as in free discussions of a novel, or a reading aloud.

The language of the expected response would not normally be considered to be an important part of the display of understanding or the ability to use textual information for whatever purpose, but it is likely in classroom settings that teachers will encourage pupils to use accurate, appropriate, standard language, and to be imaginative in their responses where appropriate – the ability to use language in such ways might well be included in criteria for evaluating the adequacy of response.

## Relationship between input and response

In many such classroom settings, it is expected that readers are able to understand the language of the texts they read, and they are expected to be able to paraphrase such language, to simplify it, summarise it, express the ideas in alternative ways, and to respond imaginatively and creatively to the language and the topics of the input. Indeed, many classroom tasks focus explicitly on encouraging such creative use of language, and on developing learners' capacity to express and refine their appreciation of the use of language in particular texts, be they advertisements or classic fiction. One of the main aims, indeed, of such classes is often to develop the pupils' metalinguistic abilities: their ability to talk about the language of the texts they read.

The relationship between input and expected response is thus typically often very broad and indirect. Pupils are expected to understand the literal meanings of texts, but required to infer, to go beyond the stated, to assess attitudes, assumptions, prejudices, intentions, as well as to appreciate stylistic devices, humour, irony and the like. Such broad and indirect relationships imply that assessment of the adequacy of response to input will often be a matter of teacher judgement, rather than 'correctness' of interpretation, and teachers may or may not have developed explicit criteria by which they evaluate pupils' responses. Normally, teachers will provide feedback to pupils, thus mediating between reader and text in a reciprocal way, and they may also assign texts to pupils depending upon their perceived progress, thereby making the relationship between input and response an adaptive one.

Often criteria for assessment will remain implicit, to the pupil and to the teacher, and may even be intuitive, rather than definable, and incapable of being captured in a rating scale. This, of course, will present problems in the reliable assessment of interpretations, and will also present pupils with difficulties in understanding exactly what they are expected to do, what an adequate, valued response might be, as well as why such responses are valued or not. It may also present pupils with difficulties in the interpretation of any feedback.

## Assessment characteristics

Essentially so far I have described a range of possible characteristics for classroom instruction in reading at secondary level and have only occasionally touched upon the implications for assessment.

The basic point I wish to make is this: the nature of the assessment of reading in classroom contexts is or should be directly and intimately related to the nature of the instruction. Much instruction is indeed assessment anyway, sometimes quite explicitly so, as when homework assignments are marked and grades are recorded in some form of continuous assessment. Much instruction may be assessment-like, but learners may not be being directly evaluated on their performance, but rather a performance is being elicited in order to help learners understand or improve their understanding of text. Thus, for example, responses to multiple-choice questions on a given text may form the basis of a class discussion of the text, or of the reasonableness or otherwise of the various interpretations contained in the distractors.

In such cases, teachers may be able to accept that various different interpretations are possible, even different answers to multiple-choice questions, provided that the pupils can put forward an adequate justification for their interpretation. What would matter then would be the reasonableness of the interpretation or the adequacy of the justification, rather than the correctness of the response.

When using such tasks for assessment, however, teachers might feel that correctness is more important than during the performance of the task in class. I would suggest that to do so would be to threaten the validity of the assessment, as well as to send the wrong signals to pupils about the difference between learning and assessment. Thus I would expect that a teacher-designed assessment process and associated criteria for evaluation would closely reflect what has been taught and how it has been taught.

Indeed, many informal assessment procedures need not involve separate activities in any case. Rather, they could consist of systematic recording of pupils' responses to class-based tasks. Teachers would sample, randomly or otherwise, pupils' performances, and make a record of how they had performed. Alternatively, teachers might not look to record a 'typical' performance, but rather record when an exceptional performance had occurred, as evidence of progress or of potential.

The difference between assessment and teaching or learning then becomes simply one of systematicity and sampling – teachers explicitly record their impressions of pupils' performance, and they seek to sample it in relevant and fair ways. Thus, for example, it becomes possible to gather a portfolio of pupils' reactions to texts over time, and to use such a portfolio as evidence of progress, effort or interest.

Moreover, in such settings, it becomes feasible to include the learner him- or herself in evaluating their reading. Self-assessments of reading progress are of value in classroom assessment; peer assessments of each other's understandings of texts in, for example, a group task, would be admissible; and a pupil's own comments on their portfolio of readings, interpretations and changes over time would be valued for the insights they could offer into awareness and progress.

The notion of objectivity of interpretation can then be replaced by an explicit encouragement of pupils to allow their own voice to be heard, to be valued and to count towards assessment of achievement.

## Situation 4

In the fourth and final testing situation, I deal with the assessment of reading ability in a foreign language for a national school-leaving examination. This situation relates rather closely to the previous one in that, yet again, it is in an educational context. However, it is a high-stakes situation rather than the low-stakes one just described. In a sense it is the reverse of the previous situation: it represents the assessment of school achievement through public certification, and it concerns school authorities and whole school districts rather than simply individual teachers. Although class teachers are indeed concerned by the results of such assessments and influenced therefore by their importance, the results have social and national significance as well and therefore may be used and misused in a variety of ways for accountability judgements as well as judgements about individuals and for individuals.

However, despite the importance of the assessment context and purpose, it is not necessarily the case that assessment be exclusively by means of formal tests. Indeed, there have been a number of attempts in various settings to combine measures of teacher-based assessment, or continuous assessment, with test-based, externally moderated assessment, in arriving at summative judgements about individuals. In some settings, class-based portfolios and performance assessments are used to make summative judgements.

In what follows, I shall describe an assessment setting, rather than TLU domains. I shall address the 'problem' of final school-leaving examinations and assessments, with particular reference to the assessment of reading in a foreign language. Unlike the previous testing situations, I shall not describe the non-test setting in much detail. Rather I shall take that as given, in that much of what I have described in the third situation might apply to this situation too. What is different is less what happens in class and more who is designing and administering the test or assessment procedures, the importance and impact of those procedures, and the pressures on test developers to 'get it right'. Thus, in this final test situation, I concentrate much more on the tests and their potential impact, and much less on the classroom instructional domain or the TLU domain.

As described in the previous situation, the TLU domains for which final school-leaving examinations are intended, are too varied and unpredictable for them to be of much guidance in test construction.

Secondary school graduates may be entering the world of work, in a wide variety of different settings, or they may plan to continue their studies at tertiary level. They may have no predictable need for the foreign language at all, and even if there is a possible need, it may well be in order to communicate orally rather than to be able to read in the foreign language.

Moreover, whilst test content would hopefully be based on national curricula or syllabuses if these exist, and would be relevant to textbooks used in class and to teaching methods, national curricula and syllabuses are typically very broad and general frameworks, and do not provide very specific guidance to test constructors, and teachers are typically free to use a variety of textbooks and teaching methods. Often, in fact, developers of national school-leaving examinations seek to reflect what they consider to be the best of current practice, and to influence positively what teachers will do in classes. Thus test washback and impact are important considerations in designing tests for this final situation.

Consequently also, test developers are typically conscious of the need to avoid a rigid framework of test content and method over the years. Rather they are encouraged to vary their use of text types, task types and testing methods every year, precisely in order to avoid stereotyping and curricular narrowing. Thus much of what is presented below represents at best one year's examination specifications, and can be expected to vary to some extent year by year.

### Characteristics of the setting

Participants are secondary school pupils in their final year of study, typically aged between 17 and 19, and both sexes are equally represented. Most hope to study at university or college, but the likelihood of this will depend in part on their achieving high scores in this reading test. The test will be taken in familiar surroundings, normally in their own school, probably in a large hall or classroom. Test administrators and invigilators will be school staff, including the pupils' own teachers. They will be seated at individual desks in rows, several feet apart from parallel rows, and collaboration is discouraged.

The reading test will take one hour. The only other (implicit) participant in this setting is the examiner, who will read and judge the pupils' responses. However, the test instructions will assume a number of purposes for reading to motivate test tasks and give an air of authenticity to the reading.

## Characteristics of the (test) rubrics

Test instructions will be written, typically in the target language, in the belief that pupils should be exposed as much as possible to the target language, and that they ought to be able to understand simple test instructions. A countervailing argument is that the instructions should be as simple and understandable as possible and therefore ought to be in the national language. All procedures and tasks are carefully specified, but as simply as possible in order to reduce reading time.

The reading test is divided into six parts, some thematically linked. In Part 1, pupils have to imagine they are visiting England on a school trip, and read a text describing the town they will stay in. Tasks relate to the information in the text and focus on plausible activities the pupils might engage in during their stay. In Part 2, they imagine they are planning a week of entertainment, and read a schedule of entertainments from the local newspaper. Tasks require them to extract information for their plan. In Part 3, they read descriptions of four adolescents living in the target town, and pupils are asked to match lists of interests, occupations, addresses and previous experiences against the descriptions. In Part 4, pupils are required to guess the meaning of underlined nonsense words from the context of a passage, and in Part 5 they are asked to use a facsimile page from an English–English dictionary to identify the meaning of underlined words in another text. In Part 6, pupils are required to respond to conventional comprehension questions about two passages.

The total number of items in the reading test is 40, unevenly distributed across the six sections. Pupils are free to decide how long to spend on each part and item, and are simply told they have one hour to complete this part of the test (there are further sections testing Use of English, Listening, and Writing). At the end of the hour, invigilators remove the test booklets and answer sheets. Pupils are not told how their responses will be scored, simply that they will be awarded one point for each correct answer.

## Characteristics of the input

Some of the written texts are accompanied by illustrations; all are in the target language, as are the tasks/items. Length varies – in Part 1, the text is about 400 words long; in Part 2, two pages, but with only about 150 words; Part 3 is four short paragraph-length descriptions; Part 4 is two long paragraphs; Part 5 is two texts: one a full page of dictionary entries, the second half a page of text; Part 6 contains two two-paragraph texts, one expository and one narrative.

The language of the texts varies, from relatively simple in Parts 1 and 2, to quite complex in Part 6. There are a variety of text types and a number of different topics, although the first three parts are topically linked. Apart from text type, there is little sociolinguistic variation, however, in terms of register or function, and cultural references are confined to the every-day, in the expectation that these will be within the ken if not experience of adolescents.

Most texts look 'authentic' in that their layout and accompanying illustrations are realistic. The test is highly speeded, in the expectation that only the strongest pupils will complete all tasks comfortably in the time available.

## Characteristics of the expected response

Pupils respond in the target language or tick boxes in the multiple-choice sections. They are not expected to answer in more than one sentence, and although the tests are scored by teachers, they are supplied with a list of correct or acceptable answers and are not expected to use any judgement in deciding on the acceptability of responses.

## Relationship between input and response

Limited production responses are expected to be relevant to the topic and task. In normal circumstances (but see the discussion below) responses and input are in a non-reciprocal relationship, however, and the scope of this relationship is fairly narrow and usually direct – pupils are not expected to contribute much background or cultural knowledge, nor to make many judgements about the quality of texts or their relationship to the tasks.

## Discussion

It is important to note the decisions that have to be made in designing this reading test, in the absence of constraints from TLU tasks and in the presence of practical constraints such as time of test, resources available and so on. Texts and tasks chosen represent the test designers' guess that many pupils will either have been on a school trip or will find such a trip a plausible event. The texts themselves will look real and therefore hopefully be motivating and interesting. Reprographic facilities are such that it is possible to reproduce authentic-looking texts.

The first three parts of the test are linked by topic, in the hope of adding a degree of realism and allowing candidates to develop a context within which their understanding of the texts can develop. However, in order not to bias the test as a whole by topic or text type, three further sections use different texts on quite different topics, and focus on skills that appear to teachers and test designers to be useful to FL learners. The need to guess the meaning of words from context is constantly stressed in textbooks used in the school system, and pupils can be expected to have had much practice in this. The use of an English–English dictionary is thought to reflect things pupils will have had to do in class when reading texts. Indeed they may even have been explicitly taught dictionary-use skills, and if not it is expected that the test will have a washback effect in this area. Moreover, the use of an English–English dictionary is deliberately designed to encourage teachers and pupils, when preparing for this test, to use such dictionaries rather than bilingual dictionaries in the belief that the former are more useful to language learners than the latter (please note that I am not advocating this, just stating a design principle).

The school population taking this test is very heterogeneous with respect to language ability. One possible approach to such heterogeneity is to produce three different levels of examination, one called Basic, one Intermediate and the highest level Advanced. However, logistical factors to do with the actual test administration and the difficulties of prior registration might not allow test designers to devise tests at three different levels of difficulty. An alternative approach is that the earlier parts of the test contain easier texts and tasks, which low-level learners ought to be able to complete; the second two parts ought to be completed in the time by intermediate learners; and the last two parts are made deliberately difficult, in the expectation that only advanced learners will complete the tasks successfully.

Note, however, the implications of this second approach: pupils of lower ability will take fewer items/tasks, and therefore not only might this frustrate them and lower their self-esteem, it also means that we can have rather less confidence in the accuracy of the estimation of their ability level than for pupils who have attempted all the items. In a different setting, candidates could be given more time to complete the test, so that it becomes a power test, not a speed test (although this still means that weaker pupils will attempt items intended to be far beyond their ability level); or pupils could take a computer-based adaptive test of reading, which tailors the test to the developing estimation of their ability level. Pupils would then take most items at a level of difficulty close to their ability, and most pupils would respond to roughly the same number of items. In most contexts where school-leaving examinations are administered, this latter scenario is a pipe dream.

A further alternative is that pupils take two reading tests: one more or less as described, and the other in an oral interview. In this latter setting, they are given texts to read during the test rather than before it, but as their responses to questions reveal their ability, the examiner adjusts the difficulty of texts and questions to suit. This is in Bachman and Palmer's terms either a reciprocal or an adaptive test. Of course, it would take more testing time, and require trained administrators and questions at known levels of difficulty. It would rely on examiners reporting results accurately, and an ability within the system to combine and report both sorts of reading scores.

Yet another alternative is to combine an externally devised and administered test with internal assessments of reading ability, much as described in the third situation. This allows a rich and ongoing picture of ability to complement the external measurement. Indeed, in the UK, internal assessment of this nature, with a degree of external moderation of standards of assessing, was the norm for examinations of English ability for a number of years, until the then Conservative government decreed that school-based coursework could only constitute a maximum of 25% of marks allotted to pupils in school-leaving examinations. Such decisions were taken less on evidence of lack of validity and reliability than on grounds of prejudice and expedience.

Test methods vary deliberately in this fourth situation, both in order to avoid biasing test results in favour of pupils who might be better at, or more familiar with, one method than others, and in order to maximise positive washback. It is believed that concentrating on one method, say multiple-choice, will encourage teachers and pupils to ignore other exercise/test types and to learn techniques for taking multiple-choice tests.

Because of the inclusion of constructed response items, there is some opportunity for pupils to respond in their own words. Markers are not allowed to mark the responses of their own pupils. They are instructed not to penalise responses which show an understanding of the text and task, but are expressed in 'incorrect' language. They are also supplied with a mark scheme/key which they are expected to follow rather than using their professional judgement as English teachers, in the interests of reliability. If markers encounter any responses which are not on the list of acceptable or unacceptable responses, they are required to refer these to the examination authorities for a decision, and mark schemes are amended accordingly.

Some teachers might find this offensive, and accuse the authorities of not respecting their judgements and devaluing the professionalism of teachers. However, one of the reasons why central examinations are needed is precisely because experience shows that teachers' judgements can be biased and unreliable and unacceptably variable for high-stakes decisions. Universities and employers complain that the results from school-based examinations are unbelievable, and many universities develop their own entrance examinations in response. Thus it is important to ensure reliability of marking across the nation if results are to be believed.

Ideally, marking would be done centrally, with considerable control over standards, but this could involve teachers travelling long distances, at great expense. One alternative is for teams of markers to be recruited regionally and trained in advance of the test session. Mark schemes would be trialled exhaustively during pre-testing. Marking would take place in regional centres (not in each school), and Regional Chief Examiners would be appointed to monitor the marking in their local centre. When unexpected responses are encountered, these would be communicated by telephone immediately to each centre, and a proportion of papers already marked would be scrutinised in case such unexpected responses had been marked inappropriately before notification.

Another alternative might be to engage in double marking, where the first marking is done locally, and the second round is central. In some settings, a few days after the test has been administered, the teachers' association publishes a marking key produced on the basis of scoring a few hundred actual responses from the test administration. This key is sent to schools to guide teachers in their local marking, and is also used as the central markers' guideline. Additions to the key are announced and discussed in an examiners' meeting before the centralised markers start work.

Whatever system is adopted, reliable marking involves a degree of expense, time and people, and it is important that the need for these, and the consequences of unreliable marking, be made clear.

## Summary

In this chapter, I have presented a brief overview of the test development process, before concentrating on illustrating how the relationship between target language use and test tasks can be established by use of a framework of task characteristics.

I have explored a number of different real-world purposes for the assessment of reading, and discussed the implications for the design of tests or other assessment procedures. I have also emphasised the central importance of establishing test specifications as a framework for test development.

However, I do not wish the reader to finish this chapter with the impression that all a test designer has to do is to consider TLU domains and seek to mirror them in test specifications. Firstly, as some of the testing situations described have hopefully shown, this will be difficult if not impossible in some settings. Secondly, it may be the case that the TLU domain is indeterminate, and recourse must be had to the domain of classroom instruction, or to the relationship with a given syllabus, or to a given theory of reading ability or what skills underly it, rather than to TLU domains. Thirdly, and importantly, the writing of test specifications, even when acknowledged to be cyclical or iterative, is only one part of test design. Once the specifications are ready and test tasks have been developed, they will need to be edited, revised, trialled, analysed, revised, retrialled and possibly reanalysed, before they can be put into operation. Obviously this is an extensive process, which will apply to high-stakes settings rather than to low-stakes ones. Nevertheless, the principle applies to all tests and assessment procedures: you never produce a good test without revisions, trialling and critical inspection on the basis of empirical results. And fourthly, a very important consideration, and part of this revision process, is the potential and frequent discrepancy between expected responses and actual responses. Test designers have expectations that may not be borne out in practice. Test-takers may misinterpret instructions or tasks, may provide alternative inter-pretations of texts, and may respond in unexpected but acceptable ways to tasks. Test developers have to be open to such unexpected events. In particular, they must investigate the response validity of their procedures. They must give their test tasks to respondents, and explore to what extent the responses reveal processes and outcomes which are what was intended, and to what extent they reveal different processes and different outcomes.

We have already seen the importance of this when investigating whether test items do or do not measure particular skills, and we have concluded that responding to test tasks is itself a highly complex process which may vary from reader to reader, test-taker to test-taker. What matters in assessment is how we interpret how test-takers have responded, not whether the expected response has been given or not. An approach to task design that concentrates on task characteristics at the expense of response processes and their interpretation risks overlooking important aspects of test validity. In the next chapter we begin the process of looking at responses by discussing testing tech-niques in action, and what it is that they might prove to be capable of measuring, in both the process and product of reading.

CHAPTER SEVEN

......................................................................................................

# Techniques for testing reading

## Introduction

In this chapter I shall use the terms 'test method', 'test technique' and 'test format' more or less synonymously, as the testing literature in general is unclear as to any possible difference between them. Moreover, it is increasingly commonplace (for example in test specifications and handbooks) to refer to 'tasks' and 'task types', and to avoid the use of the word 'technique' altogether. I feel, however, that there is value in conceiving of tasks differently from techniques: Chapters 5 and 6 have illustrated at length what is meant by 'task'. A task can take a number of different formats, or utilise a number of different techniques. These are the subject of the current chapter.

Many textbooks on language testing (see, for example, Heaton, 1988; Hughes, 1989; Oller, 1979; Weir, 1990 and 1993) give examples of testing techniques that might be used to assess language. Fewer discuss the relationship between the technique chosen and the construct being tested. Fewer still discuss in any depth the issue of test method effect, and the fact that different testing techniques or formats may themselves test non-linguistic cognitive abilities or give rise to affective responses, both of which are usually thought to be extraneous to the testing of language abilities. Moreover, it is conceivable that different testing techniques permit the measurement of different aspects of the construct being assessed. Therefore, it is important to consider what techniques are capable of assessing, as well as what they might typically assess.

It is also usual in testing textbooks to make a distinction between the method and the texts used to create tests. However, this distinction is not always helpful, since there may be a relationship between the text type and the sort of technique that can be used. For instance, it is difficult to see the value in using cloze techniques or summary tasks based on texts like road signs. In this chapter, therefore, I shall illustrate the use of particular techniques with different texts, and I shall briefly discuss the relationship between text type and test task.

Many books on language teaching assert that there is a significant difference between teaching techniques and testing techniques. However, I believe that this distinction is overstated, and that the design of a teaching exercise is in principle similar to the design of a test item. There are differences (for a discussion of these, see Alderson in Nuttall, 1996) but in general these mean that the design of test items is more *difficult* than the design of exercises, but not in principle any different. The point of making this statement is to encourage readers to see *all* exercises as potential test items also. Excellent sources for ideas on test items for reading are books on the teaching of reading and the design of classroom activities – see in particular Grellet (1981) and Nuttall (1982 and 1996). The difference is not so much the materials themselves as the way they are used and the purpose for which they are used. The primary purpose of a teaching/learning task is to promote learning, while the primary purpose of an assessment task is to collect relevant information for purposes of making inferences or decisions about individuals – which is not to say that assessment tasks have no potential for promoting learning, but simply that this is not their primary purpose.

## No 'best method'

It is important to understand that there is no one 'best method' for testing reading. No single test method can fulfil all the varied purposes for which we might test. However, claims are often made for certain techniques – for example, the cloze procedure – which might give the impression that testers have discovered a panacea. Moreover, the ubiquity of certain methods – in particular the multiple-choice technique – might suggest that some methods are particularly suitable for the testing of reading. However, certain methods are commonplace merely for reasons of convenience and efficiency, often at the expense of validity, and it would be naive to assume that because a method is widely used it is therefore 'valid'. Where a method is widely advocated and indeed researched, it is wise to examine all the research and not just that which shows the benefits of a given method. It is also sensible to ask whether the very advocacy of the method is not leading advocates to overlook important drawbacks, for rhetorical effect. It is certainly sensible to assume that no method can possibly fulfil all testing purposes.

Multiple-choice (four-option) questions used to be by far the commonest way of assessing reading. Jack Upshur is believed to have said of the multiple-choice technique: 'Is there any other way of asking a question?' The technique even dominated textbooks for teaching reading and, in fact, some interesting exercises were developed with this technique. For example, Munby's ESL reading textbook *Read and think* (Munby, 1968) uses multiple-choice exclusively, but the author has carefully designed each distractor in each question to represent a plausible misinterpretation of some part of the text. The hope was that if a learner responded with an incorrect choice, the nature of his misunderstanding would be immediately obvious, and could then be 'treated' accordingly.

> Multiple-choice questioning can be used effectively to train a person's ability to think . . . It is possible to set the distractors so close that the pupil has to examine each alternative very carefully indeed before he can decide on the best answer . . . When a person answers a comprehension question incorrectly, the reason for his error may be intellectual or linguistic or a mixture of the two. Such errors can be analysed and then classified so that questioning can take account of these areas of difficulty. Here is an attempt at classifying the main areas of comprehension error:
>
> 1 Misunderstanding the plain sense
>
> 2 Wrong inference
>
> 3 Reading more into the text than is actually there, stated or implied
>
> 4 Assumption, usually based on personal opinion
>
> 5 Misplaced aesthetic response (i.e. falling for a 'flashy' phrase)
>
> 6 Misinterpreting the tone (or emotional level) of the text
>
> 7 Failing to understand figurative usage
>
> 8 Failing to follow relationships of thought

9 Failing to distinguish between the general idea (or main point) and supporting detail

10 Failing to see the force of modifying words

11 Failing to see the grammatical relationship between words or groups of words

12 Failing to take in the grammatical meaning of words.

(Munby, 1968:xii–xiii)

The 1970s saw the advent, in ESL, of the advocacy of the use of the cloze procedure to produce cloze tests which were claimed to be not only tests of general language proficiency, but also of reading. In fact, the procedure was first used with native speakers of English in order to assess text readability, but it was soon used to test such subjects' abilities to understand texts as well, and was only later used to assess 'general language proficiency', especially of a second or foreign language. Cloze tests are, of course, very useful in many situations because they are so easy to prepare and score. Their validity as tests of reading is, however, somewhat controversial, as I discuss below.

Recent years have seen an increase in the number of different techniques used for testing reading. Where multiple-choice prevailed, we now see a range of different 'objective' techniques, and also an increase in 'non-objective' methods, like short-answer questions, or even the use of summaries which have to be subjectively evaluated. Test constructors often have to use objective techniques for practical reasons, but there is a tendency for multiple-choice to be avoided if at all possible (although the use of computer-based testing has resulted in a, hopefully only temporary, resurgence of multiple-choice techniques – see Alderson, 1986, and Alderson and Windeatt, 1991, for comments on this).

The description of the IELTS Test of Academic Reading illustrates the range of techniques that are now being employed in the testing of reading:

A variety of questions are used, chosen from the following types:
multiple-choice;
short-answer questions;
sentence completion;
notes/summary/diagram/flow chart/table completion;
choosing from a 'heading bank' for identified paragraphs/sections
of the text; (ctd.)

identification of writer's view/attitudes/claims: yes/no/not given;
classification;
matching lists;
matching phrases.

(International English Language Testing System
Handbook, 1999, and Specimen Materials, 1997)

What is also interesting about IELTS is that multiple methods are
employed on any one passage, unlike many tests of reading where the
understanding of one passage is assessed by only one testing technique. The Specimen Materials give the following examples:

**Passage 1**: Multiple-matching, single word or short-phrase responses; completion of gapped summary with up to three words
per gap; information transfer; four-option multiple-choice.

**Passage 2**: multiple-matching; yes/no/not given; short-answer
responses.

**Passsage 3**: yes/no/not given; information transfer: a) diagram
completion with short phrase; b) table completion with short
phrases.

It is now generally accepted that it is inadequate to measure the
understanding of text by only one method, and that objective
methods can usefully be supplemented by more subjectively evaluated techniques. Good reading tests are likely to employ a number of
different techniques, possibly even on the same text, but certainly
across the range of texts tested. This makes good sense, since in real-
life reading, readers typically respond to texts in a variety of different
ways. Research into and experience with the use of different techniques will certainly increase in the future, and it is hoped that our
understanding of the potential of different techniques for measuring
different aspects of reading will improve. The following sections deal
with what is currently known about some of the more commonly
used techniques for testing reading.

## Discrete-point versus integrative techniques

Testers may know exactly what they want to test, and wish to test this
specifically and separately. In other situations they may simply want
to test 'whether students have understood the text satisfactorily'. On
the one hand, they may wish to isolate one aspect of reading ability,

or one aspect of language, whereas on the other, they want a global overview of a reader's ability to handle text.

The difference between these two approaches can be likened to the contrast between discrete-point or analytic approaches, and integrative or integrated approaches. In discrete-point approaches, the intention is to test one 'thing' at a time, in integrative approaches, test designers aim to gain a much more general idea of how well students read. In the latter case, this may be because we recognise that 'the whole is more than the sum of the parts'. It may also be simply because there is not the time to test one thing at a time, or the test's purpose may not require a detailed assessment of a student's understanding or skills.

Some argue that a discrete approach to testing reading is flawed, and that it is more appropriate not to attempt to analyse reading into component parts, which will perhaps inevitably distort the nature of reading. They believe that a more global, unitary, approach is more valid.

Some claim that the cloze test is ideal for this because it is often difficult to say what the cloze technique tests. Others are more sceptical and say that it is precisely because we do not know what 'the cloze test as a whole' tests that we cannot claim that it is testing a unitary skill (see Alderson, 1983; Bachman, 1985; Oller, 1973; and Jonz, 1991, for differing positions in this debate).

## The cloze test and gap-filling tests

Cloze tests are typically constructed by deleting from selected texts every n-th word (n usually being a number somewhere between 5 and 12) and simply requiring the test-taker to restore the word that has been deleted. In some scoring procedures, credit may also be given for providing a word that makes sense in the gap, even if it is not the word which was originally deleted. One or two sentences are usually left intact at the beginning and end of the text to provide some degree of contextual support.

Gap-filling tests are somewhat different (see below) in that the test constructor does not use a pseudo-random procedure to identify words for deletion: she decides, on some rational basis, which words to delete, but tries not to leave fewer than five or six words between gaps (since such a lack of text can make gaps unduly difficult to

restore). Unfortunately, although these two types of test are potentially very different from each other, they are frequently confused by
both being called 'cloze tests', or the gap-filling procedure is known
as the 'rational' cloze technique. I strongly recommend that the term
'cloze test' be confined to those tests that are produced by the application of the pseudo-random deletion procedure described above. All
other gap-filling tests should not be called 'cloze tests' since they
measure different things.

Here is an example of a cloze test constructed by deleting every
sixth word beginning with the first word of the second sentence (note
that research shows that reliable results will only be achieved if a
minimum of 50 deletions are created):

> The fact is that one cloze test can be very different from another
> cloze test based on the same text. 1) .......... pseudo-random con-
> struction procedure guarantees that 2) .......... test-writer does not
> really know 3) .......... is being tested: she simply 4) .......... that if
> enough gaps are 5) .........., a variety of different skills 6) ..........
> aspects of language use will 7) .......... involved, but inevitably this
> is 8) .......... Despite the claims of some 9) .........., many cloze items
> are not 10) .......... to the constraints of discourse 11) .......... much
> as to the syntactic 12) .......... of the immediately preceding
> context. 13) .......... depends upon which words are 14) .........., and
> since the cloze test 15) .......... has no control over the 16) .......... of
> words, she has minimal 17) .......... over what is tested.

Quite different cloze tests can be produced on the same text by beginning the pseudo-random deletion procedure at a different starting
point. Research has shown that the five different versions of a cloze
test produced by deleting every fifth word, starting at the first word,
then the second word and so on, lead to significantly different test
results. Test this for yourself by beginning the every-sixth-word deletion pattern on the above example with the word 'pseudo-random',
'construction', 'procedure', 'guarantees' or 'that'.

What an individual cloze test measures will depend on which individual words are deleted. Since the test constructor has no control
over this once the starting point has been chosen, it is not possible to
predict with confidence what such a test will measure: the hope is
that, by deleting enough words, the text will be sampled adequately.
However, since the technique is word-based, many reading skills may
not be assessed by such deletions. Many cloze items, for example, are
not constrained by long-range discourse, but by the immediately

adjacent sentence constituents or even the preceding two or three words. Such items will not measure sensitivity to discourse beyond the sentence or even the phrase. Since the test constructor has no control over which words are deleted, she has minimal control over what is tested. In the example above, items 1, 2 and 3 appear to be constrained syntactically, whereas items 4 and 5 might be measuring sensitivity to semantics as well as syntax. None of these, however, can be said to be constrained by larger units of discourse than the sentence, whereas arguably items 8 and 14 may measure sensitivity to the topic of the text, but not necessarily to the meaning of the whole passage. Item 9 is fairly open-ended and some responses (for example 'researchers' rather than 'people') might show a greater sensitivity to the text as a whole. Item 17 on the other hand, whilst requiring an item from the open class of nouns, is constrained by the need for coherence with the preceding clause.

An alternative technique for those who wish to know what they are testing is the gap-filling procedure, which is almost as simple as the cloze procedure, but much more under the control of the tester.

In the examples below, two versions have been produced from the same passage: Example 1 deletes selected content words with the intention of testing an understanding of the overall meaning of the text, Example 2 deletes function words with the intention of testing mainly grammatical sensitivity.

**Example 1**

Typically, when trying to test overall understanding of the text, a tester will delete those words which seem to carry the 1) .......... ideas, or the cohesive devices that make 2) .......... across texts, including anaphoric references, connectors, and so on. However, the 3) .......... then needs to check, having deleted 4) .......... words, that they are indeed restorable from the remaining 5) .......... . It is all too easy for those who know which words have been 6) .......... to believe that they are restorable: it is very hard to put oneself into the shoes of somebody who does not 7) .......... which word was deleted. It therefore makes sense, when 8) .......... such tests, to give the test to a few colleagues or students, to see whether they can indeed 9) .......... the missing words. The hope is that in order to restore such words, students 10) .......... to have understood the main idea, to have made connections across the text, and so on. As a result, testers have a better idea of what they are trying to test, and what students need to do in order to complete the task successfully.

**Example 2**

Typically, when trying to test overall understanding 1) .......... the text, a tester will delete those words 2) .......... seem to carry the main ideas, or 3) .......... cohesive devices that make connections 3) .......... texts, including anaphoric references, connectors, and so 4) .......... However, the tester then needs 5) .......... check, having deleted key words, that they 6) .......... indeed restorable from the remaining context. It 7) .......... all too easy for those who know 8) .......... words have been deleted to believe 9) .......... they are restorable: it is very hard to put oneself 10) .......... the shoes of somebody who does not know which word 11) .......... deleted. It therefore makes sense, when constructing 12) .......... tests, to give the test to a few colleagues or students, 13) .......... see whether they can indeed restore the missing words. The hope 14) .......... that in order to restore such words, students need to have understood the main idea, to have made connections across the text, 15) .......... so on. As a result, testers have a better idea of what they are trying to test, and what students need to do in order to complete the task successfully.

Thus, an overall understanding of the text may be tested by removing those words which are essential to the main ideas, or those words which carry the text's coherence. The problem with constructing gap-filling tests like this is that the test constructor knows which words have been deleted and so may tend to assume that those words are essential to meaning. Pre-testing of these tests is necessary, with a careful analysis of responses for their plausibility, in order to explore what they reveal about respondents' understanding.

A variant on both cloze and gap-filling procedures is to supply multiple choices for the students to select from. Two versions are common: one is where the options (three or four) for each blank are inserted in the gap, and students simply choose among them. The other is for the choices to be placed after the text, again in one of two ways: either all together in one bank, usually in alphabetic order, or separately grouped into fours, and identified against each numbered blank by means of the same number. The 'banked cloze' procedure (sometimes called a 'matching cloze' procedure) is actually quite difficult to construct since one has to ensure that a word which is intended as a distractor for one gap is not, in fact, possible in another blank. Possibly for this reason, many test designers prefer the variant where each set of three or four options is separately numbered to match the numbered blanks..

The disadvantages of all variants where candidates do not supply a missing word are similar to those of multiple-choice techniques.

## Multiple-choice techniques

Multiple-choice questions are a common device for testing students' text comprehension. They allow testers to control the range of possible answers to comprehension questions, and to some extent to control the students' thought processes when responding. Pages xiv to xxii of Munby's (1968) textbook give an extensive illustration and discussion of this. In addition, of course, multiple-choice questions can be marked by machine.

However, the value of multiple-choice questions has been questioned. By virtue of the distractors, they may present students with possibilities they may not otherwise have thought of. This amounts to a deliberate tricking of students and may be thought to result in a false measure of their understanding. Some researchers argue that the ability to answer multiple-choice questions is a separate ability, different from the reading ability. Students can learn how to answer multiple-choice questions, by eliminating improbable distractors, or by various forms of logical analysis of the structure of the question. For example, Alderson *et al.* (1995) cite the following item:

> (After a text on memory)
> *Memorising is easier when the material to be learned is*
> *a) in a foreign language*
> *b) already partly known*
> *c) unfamiliar but easy*
> *d) of no special interest*
>
> Common sense and experience tell us that a) is not true, that d) is very unlikely and that b) is probably the correct answer. The only alternative which appears to depend on the text for interpretation is c) since 'unfamiliar' and 'easy' are both ambiguous.
> (Alderson *et al.*, 1995: 50)

Test-coaching schools are said to teach students specifically how to become test-wise and how to answer multiple-choice questions. Some cultures do not use multiple-choice questions at all, and those students who are unfamiliar with such a testing method may fare unusually badly on multiple-choice tests.

The construction of multiple-choice questions is a very skilled and time-consuming business. To write plausible but incorrect options that will attract the weaker reader but not the better reader is far from easy. Even experienced test constructors have to pre-test their questions, analyse the items for difficulty and discrimination, and either reject or modify those items that have not performed well. Many testing textbooks give advice on the construction of such questions – see, for example, Alderson *et al.* (1995:45–51).

A further serious difficulty with multiple-choice questions – possibly even with the Munby-style questions referred to earlier – is that the tester does not know why the candidate responded the way she did. She may have simply guessed at her choice, or she may have a totally different reason in mind from that which the test constructor intended when writing the item – including the distractors. She may even simply have employed test-taking strategies to eliminate implausible choices, and been left with only one choice. Of course, researchers can explore the processes test-takers engage in when validating their tests, but there is no guarantee that any given test-taker will in fact use processes that were shown to be commonly used.

Thus it is possible to get an item correct for the 'wrong' reason – i.e. without displaying the ability being tested – or to get the item wrong (choosing a distractor) for the 'right' reason – i.e. despite having the ability being tested (for a discussion of this see Alderson, 1990c). This may be true for other test techniques also, but the problem is compounded in multiple-choice items as test-takers are only required to tick the correct answer. If candidates were required to give their reasons for making their choice as well, the problem might be mitigated, but then the practical advantage of multiple-choice questions in terms of marking would be vitiated.

An interesting variant on multiple-choice is the example reprinted on the following pages. In this example, note that the test-taker has the same set of options to choose from (1–10) for each item. Moreover, since the response that is required is *not* a short-answer question, the reader has to read and understand the relevant paragraphs and cannot get the item correct from background knowledge alone. In addition, the questions that are asked are of the sort that a reader reading a text like this might plausibly ask himself about such a text, thereby enhancing at least the face validity of the test (see the discussion below about texts and tasks).

QUESTION 1

You are thinking of studying at Lancaster University. . Before you make a decision you will wish to find out certain information about the University. Below are ten questions about the University. Read the questions and then read the information about Lancaster University on the next page.

Write the letter of the paragraph where you find the answer to the question on the answer sheet.

Note:  Some paragraphs contain the answer to more than one question.

1.  In which part of Britain is Lancaster University?

2.  What about transport to the University?

3.  Does a place on the course include a place to live?

4.  Can I cook my own food in college?

5.  Why does the University want students from other countries?

6.  What kind of courses can I study at the University?

7.  What is the cost of living like?

8.  Can I live outside the University?

9.  Is the University near the sea?

10.  Can I cash a cheque in the University?

(ctd.)

LANCASTER UNIVERSITY - A FLOURISHING COMMUNITY

Since being granted its Royal
Charter on 14 September, 1964, The
University of Lancaster has grown
into a flourishing academic community attracting students from many
overseas countries.' The University
now offers a wide range of first
degree, higher degree and diploma
A courses in the humanities, management and organisational sciences,
sciences and social sciences. Extensive research activities carried
out by 470 academic staff have contributed considerably to the University's international reputation in
these areas.

The University is situated on an
attractive 250-acre parkland site in
a beautiful part of North-West
England. As one of Britain's modern
universities Lancaster offers its
4,600 full-time students specially
B designed teaching, research and
computer facilities, up-to-date
laboratories and a well stocked
library. In addition eight colleges
based on the campus offer students
2,500 residential places as well as
social amenities. There is also a
large sports complex with a heated
indoor swimming pool, as well as a
theatre, concert hall and art
gallery.

INTERNATIONAL COMMUNITY
Lancaster holds an established place
in the international academic comm-
C unity. Departments have developed
links with their counterparts in
overseas universities, and many
academic staff have taught and
studied in different parts of the
world.

From the beginning the University
has placed great value on having
students from overseas countries
studying and living on the campus.
D They bring considerable cultural and
social enrichment to the life of the
University. During the academic
year 1981/82 460 overseas undergraduates and postgraduates from 70
countries were studying at
Lancaster.

ACCOMMODATION AND COST OF LIVING
Overseas single students who are
offered a place at Lancaster and
accept by 15 September will be able
to obtain a study bedroom in college
E on campus during the first year of
their course. For students accepting places after that date every
effort will be made to find a room
in college for those who want one.

Each group of rooms has a well
equipped kitchen for those not
F wishing to take all meals in
University dining rooms. Rooms are
heated and nearly all have wash
basins.

Living at Lancaster can be significantly cheaper than at universities
in larger cities in the United Kingdom. Students do less travelling
since teaching, sports, cultural and
G social facilities as well as shops,
banks and a variety of eating
facilities are situated on the
campus. The University is a lively
centre for music and theatre
performed at a professional and
amateur level. The University's
Accommodation Officer helps students
preferring to live off campus find
suitable accommodation, which is
available at reasonable cost within
a 10-kilometre radius of the campus.

THE SURROUNDING AREA
The University campus lies within
the boundary of the city of Lancaster
with its famous castle overlooking
the River Lune, its fifteenth century
H Priory Church, fine historic buildings,
shops, cinemas and theatres. The near-
by seaside resort of Morecambe also
offers a range of shops and entertainment.

From the University the beautiful
tourist areas of the Lake District
with its mountains, lakes and
valleys, and the Yorkshire Dales are
I easily reached. The M6 motorway
links the city to the major national
road network. Fast electric trains
from London (Euston) take approx-
imately three hours to reach Lancaster.
Manchester, an hour away by car, is
the nearest international airport.

Fig. 7.1 A variation on the multiple-choice technique

# Alternative objective techniques

Recent language tests have experimented with a number of objectively, indeed machine-markable techniques for the testing of reading (for a discussion of some of these techniques in the context of computer-based testing, see Alderson and Windeatt, 1991).

## Matching techniques

One objective technique is multiple matching. Here two sets of stimuli have to be matched against each other as, for example, matching headings for paragraphs to their corresponding paragraph, titles of books against extracts from each book, and so on. Fig. 7.2, reproduced on the next two pages, is an example of multiple matching from the Certificate in Advanced English.

4

SECOND TEXT/QUESTIONS 18-23

For questions **18-23**, you must choose which of the paragraphs **A - G** on page **5** fit into the numbered gaps in the following magazine article. There is one extra paragraph which does not fit in any of the gaps. Indicate your answers **on the separate answer sheet.**

# DOLPHIN RESCUE

*Free time isn't in the vocabulary of British Divers' Marine Life Rescue teams; one fairly normal weekend recently spilled over into three weeks, as a seal move turned into a major dolphin rescue.*

To find a beached and stranded dolphin is a rarity; to nurse one back from the brink of death, and reintroduce it into the wild, is almost unheard of. Only two cases have occurred in Britain, the most recent of which involved a rescue team from British Divers' Marine Life Rescue. They started the weekend trying to relocate a 9ft bull seal and finished it fighting to save a dolphin's life after the Sea Life Centre on the south coast had informed them that a dolphin was beached at Mudeford (pronounced Muddyford) near Bournemouth.

The dolphin was found by a lady, who must have heard the message telling anyone who found it what to do. The animal was kept wet and its blowhole clean. Mark Stevens of the rescue team says: "The dolphin would have certainly been in a worse condition, if not dead, if that lady hadn't known what to do."

"I can't thank those people enough. The woman even gave us her lemonade so we could have a much-needed drink." The Sea Life Centre had hastily moved several large tope and the odd stingray from their quarantine tank, and the dolphin was duly installed.

By 1 a.m. the team were running out of energy and needed more help. But where do you find volunteers at that time of night? Mark knew of only one place and called his friends at the local dive centre.

The team allowed the photographers in for a few minutes at a time, not wanting to stress the creature too much. They had to walk a fine line between highlighting the animal's ordeal and being detrimental to its health.

How a striped dolphin got stranded in Mudeford isn't clear because they are primarily an ocean-going, rather than an inshore, species. Theories suggest that he was chucked out of his pod (group of dolphins) for some reason and, maybe chasing fish or attracted by the sounds coming from the Mudeford water festival, wandered into the bay by accident.

It took several days before the dolphin was comfortable enough to feed itself – in the meantime it had to be tube-fed. Fish was mashed up and forced down a tube inserted into the dolphin's stomach. It's not a nice procedure, but without it the dolphin would have died. Eventually he started to feed and respond to treatment.

His health improved so much that it was decided to release him, and on Tuesday, 24th August, the boat *Deeply Dippy* carried the dolphin out past the headland near the Sea Life Centre. The release, thankfully, went without a hitch; the dolphin hung around the area for a while before heading out to sea. And that was the end of another successful operation.

0150/1 W96

(ctd.)

**5**

**A**  He actually started toying with the team and trying to gain attention. He would increase his heart rate and show distress so a team member had to quickly suit up to check him over. But as the person entered the pool, his heart rate returned to normal.

**B**  It is large but has only a small opening so, once in, getting out isn't easy. The boats at the event would have panicked the creature and it ended up beached, battered and drained of energy.

**C**  The story actually appeared in several national newspapers as well as the local press. Publicity is very important for charities like the Marine Life Rescue, providing precious exposure which pleases the sponsor companies and highlights the team's work.

**D**  Luck then seemed to be on the team's side when a double-glazing van-driver stopped to investigate. The driver offered his services to transport the dolphin back to the Sea Life Centre and a lady spectator gave the team a brand new cooler box to store valuable water to keep the dolphin moist.

**E**  However, by the time they arrived, the dolphin had started to swim unsupported. The press picked up on the story and descended on the Sea Life Centre wanting stories, pictures and any information they could get hold of. And they wanted a name. Mark and the other team members had a hasty think and came up with 'Muddy' – after all, it was found at Mudeford.

**F**  Now the battle to save its life could begin, but a transportation problem arose. How do you get a grown dolphin back to the Sea Life Centre without a vehicle big enough?

**G**  The creature was so weakened by the ordeal that it could not even keep itself afloat and had to be walked in the tank to stop it from just sinking to the bottom and drowning. Most people can only walk a dolphin for around 20 minutes to half an hour. Holding a 150 kg animal away from your body and walking through water at sea temperature saps your strength.

**Remember to put your answers on the separate answer sheet.**

**[Turn over**

Fig. 7.2  Multiple matching (Certificate in Advanced English)

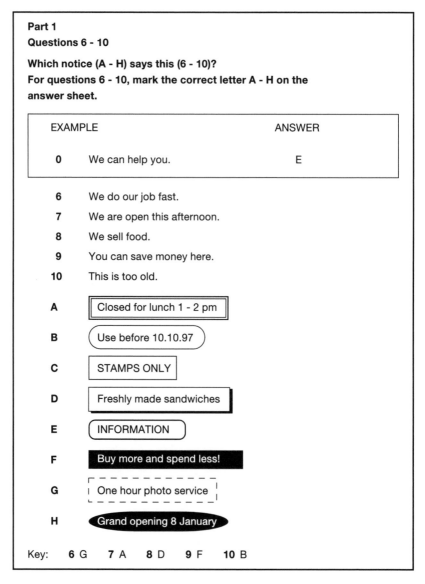

Part 1
Questions 6 - 10

Which notice (A - H) says this (6 - 10)?
For questions 6 - 10, mark the correct letter A - H on the answer sheet.

| EXAMPLE | | ANSWER |
|---|---|---|
| 0 | We can help you. | E |

6    We do our job fast.
7    We are open this afternoon.
8    We sell food.
9    You can save money here.
10   This is too old.

A    Closed for lunch 1 - 2 pm

B    Use before 10.10.97

C    STAMPS ONLY

D    Freshly made sandwiches

E    INFORMATION

F    Buy more and spend less!

G    One hour photo service

H    Grand opening 8 January

Key:    6 G    7 A    8 D    9 F    10 B

Fig. 7.3 Multiple matching (Key English Test)

In effect, these are multiple-choice test items, but with a common set of eight choices, all but one of which act as distractors for each 'item'. They are as difficult to construct as banked cloze, since it is important to ensure that no choice is possible unintentionally. It is also important to ensure that more alternatives are given than the matching task requires (i.e. than the number of items) to avoid the danger that once all but one choice has been made, there is only one possible final choice. It is also arguable that matching is subject to the same criticism as multiple-choice, in that candidates may be distracted by choices they would not otherwise have considered.

## Ordering tasks

In an ordering task, candidates are given a scrambled set of words, sentences, paragraphs or texts as in Fig. 7.4 overleaf, and have to put them into their correct order.

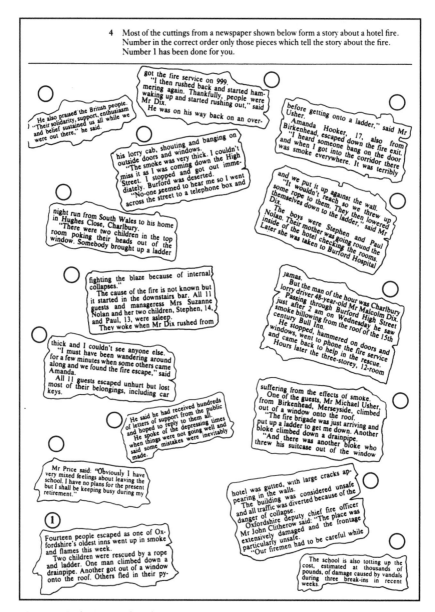

4  Most of the cuttings from a newspaper shown below form a story about a hotel fire.
Number in the correct order only those pieces which tell the story about the fire.
Number 1 has been done for you.

got the fire service on 999.
"I then rushed back and started ham-
mering again. Thankfully, people were
waking up and started rushing out," said
Mr Dix.
He was on his way back on an over-

He also praised the British people.
"Their solidarity, support, enthusiasm
and belief sustained us all while we
were out there," he said.

before getting onto a ladder," said Mr
Usher.
Amanda Hooker, 17, also from
Birkenhead, escaped down the fire exit.
"I heard someone bang on the door
and when I got into the corridor there
was smoke everywhere. It was terribly

his lorry cab, shouting and banging on
outside doors and windows.
"The smoke was very thick. I couldn't
miss it as I was coming down the High
Street. I stopped and got out immediately. Burford was deserted.
"No-one seemed to hear me so I went
across the street to a telephone box and

and we put it up against the wall.
"It wouldn't reach so we threw up
some rope to them. They then lowered
themselves down to the ladder," said Mr
Dix.
The boys were Stephen and Paul
Nolan. Their mother was going round the
inside of the hotel checking the rooms.
Later she was taken to Burford Hospital

night run from South Wales to his home
in Hughes Close, Charlbury.
"There were two children in the top
room poking their heads out of the
window. Somebody brought up a ladder

fighting the blaze because of internal
collapses."
The cause of the fire is not known but
it started in the downstairs bar. All 11
guests and manageress Mrs Suzanne
Nolan and her two children, Stephen, 14,
and Paul, 13, were asleep.
They woke when Mr Dix rushed from

james.
But the man of the hour was Charlbury
lorry driver 48-year-old Mr Malcolm Dix.
Passing through Burford High Street
just after 2 am on Wednesday he saw
smoke billowing from the roof of the 15th
century Bull Inn.
He stopped, hammered on doors and
windows, went to phone the fire service
and came back to help in the rescue.
Hours later the three-storey, 12-room

thick and I couldn't see anyone else.
"I must have been wandering around
for a few minutes when some others came
along and we found the fire escape," said
Amanda.
All 11 guests escaped unhurt but lost
most of their belongings, including car
keys.

He said he had received hundreds
of letters of support from the public
and hoped to reply to them all.
He spoke of the depressing times
when things were not going well and
said some mistakes were inevitably
made.

suffering from the effects of smoke.
One of the guests, Mr Michael Usher,
from Birkenhead, Merseyside, climbed
out of a window onto the roof.
"The fire brigade was just arriving and
put up a ladder to get me down. Another
bloke climbed down a drainpipe.
"And there was another bloke who
threw his suitcase out of the window

Mr Price said: "Obviously I have
very mixed feelings about leaving the
school. I have no plans for the present
but I shall be keeping busy during my
retirement."

①
Fourteen people escaped as one of Oxfordshire's oldest inns went up in smoke
and flames this week.
Two children were rescued by a rope
and ladder. One man climbed down a
drainpipe. Another got out of a window
onto the roof. Others fled in their py-

hotel was gutted, with large cracks appearing in the walls.
The building was considered unsafe
and all traffic was diverted because of the
danger of collapse.
Oxfordshire deputy chief fire officer
Mr John Clitherow said: "The place was
extensively damaged and the frontage
particularly unsafe.
"Our firemen had to be careful while

The school is also totting up the
cost, estimated at thousands of
pounds, of damage caused by vandals
during three break-ins in recent
weeks.

Fig. 7.4 Ordering task: The Oxford Delegacy Examinations in English as a
Foreign Language

Although superficially attractive since they seem to offer the possibility of testing the ability to detect cohesion, overall text organisation or complex grammar, such tasks are remarkably difficult to construct satisfactorily. Alderson *et al.* (1995:53) illustrate the problems involved where unanticipated orders prove to be possible.

> The following sentences and phrases come from a paragraph in an adventure story. Put them in the correct order. Write the letter of each in the space on the right.
>
> Sentence D comes first in the correct order, so D has been written beside the number 1.
>
> A  it was called 'The Last Waltz'          1..D....
> B  the street was in total darkness          2.......
> C  because it was one he and Richard had learnt at school  3.......
> D  Peter looked outside                     4.......
> E  he recognised the tune                    5.......
> F  and it seemed deserted                    6.......
> G  he thought he heard someone whistling     7.......
>
> (Alderson *et al.*, 1995:53)

Although an original text obviously only has one order, alternative orderings frequently prove to be acceptable – even if they were not the author's original ordering – simply because the author has not contemplated other orders and has not structured the syntax of the text to make only one order possible (through the use of discourse markers, anaphoric reference and the like). Thus test constructors may be obliged either to accept unexpected orderings, or to rewrite the text in order to make only one order possible. In the above example, as Alderson *et al.* point out, there are at least two ways of ordering the paragraph. The answer key gives 1:D, 2:G, 3:E, 4:C, 5:A, 6:B, 7:F, but 1:D, 2:B, 3:F, 4:G, 5:E, 6:C, 7:A is also acceptable.

Problems are also presented by partially correct answers: if a student gets four elements out of eight in correct sequence, how is such a response to be weighted? And how is it to be weighted if he gets three out of eight in the correct order? Once partial credit is allowed, marking becomes unrealistically complex and error-prone. Such items are, therefore, frequently marked either wholly right or wholly wrong, but, as Alderson *et al.* (1995:53) say: 'the amount of effort involved in both constructing and in answering the item may not be considered to be worth it, especially if only one mark is given for the correct version'.

## Dichotomous items

One popular technique, because of its apparent ease of construction, are items with only two choices. Students are presented with a statement which is related to a target text and have to indicate whether this is True or False, or whether the text agrees or disagrees with the statement. The problem is, of course, that students have a 50% chance of getting the answer right by guessing alone. To counteract this, it is necessary to have a large number of such items. Some tests reduce the possibility of guessing by including a third category such as 'not given', or 'the text does not say', but especially with items intending to test the ability to infer meaning, this can lead to considerable confusion.

**Part 4**
**Questions 26 - 32**

Read the article about a young actor.
Are sentences 26 - 32 'Right' (A) or 'Wrong' (B)?
If there is not enough information to answer 'Right' or
'Wrong', choose 'Doesn't say' (C).
For questions 26 - 32, mark A, B, or C on the answer sheet.

### SEPTEMBER IN PARIS

This week our interviewer talked to the star of the film
'September in Paris', Brendan Barrick.

*You are only 11 years old. Do you get frightened when there are lots of
photographers around you?*

No, because that always happens. At award shows and things like
that, they crowd around me. Sometimes I can't even move.

*How did you become such a famous actor?*

I started in plays when I was six and then people wanted me for
their films. I just kept getting films, advertisements, TV films and
things like that.

*Is there a history of acting in your family?*

Yes, well my aunt's been in films and my dad was an actor.

*You're making another film now – is that right?*

Yes! I'm going to start filming it this December. I'm not sure if
they've finished writing it yet.

*What would you like to do for the rest of your life?*

Just be an actor! It's a great life.

| EXAMPLE | ANSWER |
|---|---|
| 0   Brendan is six years old now.<br>A   Right      B   Wrong      C   Doesn't say | **B** |

26   A lot of people want to photograph Brendan.
     A   Right      B   Wrong      C   Doesn't say

27   Brendan's first acting job was in a film.
     A   Right      B   Wrong      C   Doesn't say

28   Brendan has done a lot of acting.
     A   Right      B   Wrong      C   Doesn't say

29   Brendan wanted to be an actor when he was four years old.
     A   Right      B   Wrong      C   Doesn't say

30   Some of Brendan's family are actors.
     A   Right      B   Wrong      C   Doesn't say

31   Brendan's father is happy that Brendan is a famous actor.
     A   Right      B   Wrong      C   Doesn't say

32   Brendan would like to be a film writer.
     A   Right      B   Wrong      C   Doesn't say

Key:   **26** A   **27** B   **28** A   **29** C   **30** A   **31** C   **32** B

Fig. 7.5  Right/Wrong/Doesn't say items (Key English Test)

## Editing tests

Editing tests consist of passages in which errors have been introduced, which the candidate has to identify. These errors can be in multiple-choice format, or can be more open, for example by asking candidates to identify one error per line of text and to write the correction opposite the line. The nature of the error will determine to a large extent whether the item is testing the ability to read, or a more restricted linguistic ability. For example:

| | |
|---|---|
| Editing tests consist of passages in which error have been | 1)....... |
| introduce, which the candidate has to identify. These errors | 2)....... |
| can been in multiple-choice format, or can be more open, for | 3)....... |
| example by asking candidates to identifying one error per line | 4)....... |
| of text and to write the correction opposite to the line. The | 5)....... |
| nature of the error will determine to a larger extent whether | 6)....... |
| the item is testing the ability to read, or the more restricted | 7)....... |
| linguistic ability. | |

The UK Northern Examinations Authority employs a variant of such a technique, which resembles a gap-filling or cloze-elide task (see below). Words are deleted from text, but are not replaced by a gap. Candidates have to find where the missing word is (a maximum of one per line, but some lines are intact), and then write in the missing word. For example:

| | |
|---|---|
| Editing tests consist of passages which errors have been | 1)....... |
| introduced, which the candidate has identify. These errors | 2)....... |
| can be in multiple-choice format, or can be more open, | |
| by asking candidates to identify one error per line text and | 3)....... |
| to write the correction opposite the line. The nature of the | |
| error will determine to large extent whether the item is | 4)....... |
| testing the ability to read, or a more restricted linguistic | |
| ability. | |

Such a task could be said to be similar to a proof-reading task, which is often the 'real-life' justification for editing tasks more generally. It is likely that the technique enables the assessment of only a restricted range of abilities involved in 'real' reading, but much more research is needed into such techniques before anything conclusive can be said about their value.

## Alternative integrated approaches

### The C-test

The C-test is based upon the same theory of closure or reduced redundancy as the cloze test. In C-tests, the second half of every second word is deleted and has to be restored by the reader. For example:

> It i.... claimed th.... this tech.......... is ..... more reli.... and compre....... measure o....... understanding th....... cloze te...... It h..... been sugg...... that t..... technique i..... less sub..... to varia....... in star....... point f....... deletion a....... is mo...... sensitive t...... text diffi.......

It is claimed that this technique is a more reliable and comprehensive measure of understanding than cloze tests. It has been suggested that the technique is less subject to variations in starting point for deletion and is more sensitive to text difficulty. Many readers, however, find C-tests even more irritating to complete than cloze tests, and it is hard to convince people that this method actually measures understanding, rather than knowing how to take a C-test. For instance, in the above example, test-takers need to know that there are either exactly the same number of letters to be restored in a word as are left intact (*i....* = *is; th.....* = *that*); or one more letter is required (*tech.....* = *technique)*. Yet occasionally other longer or shorter completions might be acceptable (*varia.....* = *variation* or *variations*). Deciding whether to delete a single letter (*'a'* above) or not introduces an element of judgement into the test construction procedure which might be said to violate the 'objective' deletion procedure. For further details of this procedure, see the classic articles by Klein-Braley and Raatz (1984), Klein-Braley (1985), and a more recent paper by Dörnyei and Katona (1992).

### The cloze elide test

A further alternative to the cloze technique was invented by Davies in the 1960s and was known as the 'Intrusive Word Technique' (Davies, 1975, 1989). It was later rediscovered in the 1980s and labelled the 'cloze-elide' technique, although it has also variously been labelled 'text retrieval', 'text interruption', 'doctored text', 'mutilated text' and 'negative cloze' (Davies, personal communication, 1997). In this procedure the test writer *inserts* words into text, instead of deleting them. The task of the reader is to delete each word 'that does not belong'. The test-taker is awarded a point for every word correctly deleted, and points are deducted for words wrongly deleted (that were indeed in the original text).

> Tests are actually a very difficult to construct in this way. One has to be sure over that the inserted words do not belong with: that it is not possible to interpret great the text (albeit in some of different way) with the added words. If so, candidates will not be therefore able to identify the insertions.

Tests are actually very difficult to construct in this way. One has to be sure that the inserted words do not belong: that it is not possible to interpret the text (albeit in some different way) with the added words. If so, candidates will not be able to identify the insertions. Davies attempted to address this problem by using Welsh words inserted into English texts in the first part of his Intrusive Word test. This then presents the problem that it is possible to identify the insertion on the basis of its morphology or 'lack of Englishness' without necessarily understanding the text.

Another issue is where exactly is one to insert the words? Using pseudo-random insertion procedures, certainly when target language words are being inserted, often results in plausible texts, and in any case, risks the danger that candidates might identify the insertion principle and simply count words! A rational insertion procedure is virtually inevitable, but the test constructor still has to intuit what sort of comprehension is required in order to identify the insertion, and since he knows which word was inserted it is often impossible to put oneself in the shoes of the candidate (as discussed above, gap-filling tests suffer from the same problem). See also Manning (1987) and Porter (1988).

The best use of this technique may be as Davies originally intended: not as a measure of comprehension, but as a measure of the speed with which readers can process text. He assumed that some degree of text understanding, however vaguely defined that might be, would be necessary in order to identify the insertions, and so the candidates were simply required to identify as many insertions as possible in a limited period of time. The number of correctly identified insertions, minus the number of incorrectly identified items, was taken as a measure of reading speed.

## Short-answer tests

A semi-objective alternative to multiple-choice is the short-answer question (which Bachman and Palmer, 1996, classify as a 'limited production response type'). Test-takers are simply asked a question which requires a brief response, in a few words, as in the example below (not just Yes/No or True/False). The justification for this technique is that it is possible to interpret students' responses to see if they have really understood, whereas on multiple-choice items students give no justification for the answer they have selected and may have chosen one by eliminating others.

> There was a time when Marketa disliked her mother-in-law. That was when she and Karel were living with her in-laws (her father-in-law was still alive) and Marketa was exposed daily to the woman's resentment and touchiness. They couldn't bear it for long and moved out. Their motto at the time was 'as far from Mama as possible'. They had gone to live in a town at the other end of the country and thus could see Karel's parents only once a year.                    (Text from Kundera, 1996:37)
>
> Question: What is the relationship between Marketa and Karel?
> Expected answer: husband and wife

The objectivity of scoring depends upon the completeness of the answer key and the possibility of students responding with answers or wordings which were not anticipated (for example, 'lovers' in the above question). Short-answer questions are not easy to construct. The question must be worded in such a way that all possible answers are foreseeable. Otherwise the marker will be presented with a wide range of responses which she will have to judge as to whether they demonstrate understanding or not.

In practice, the only way to ensure that the test constructor has removed ambiguities in the question, and written a question which requires certain answers and not others, is to try it out on colleagues or students similar to those who will be taking the test. It is very difficult to predict all responses to and interpretations of short-answer questions, and therefore some form of pre-testing of the questions is essential wherever possible.

One way of developing short-answer questions with some texts is to ask oneself what questions a reader might ask, or what information the reader might require, from a particular text. For example:

## OTHER SAVERS FROM OXFORD

|  | SAVER RETURN | | WITH RAILCARD | |
|---|---|---|---|---|
|  | OFF-PEAK DAYS | PEAK DAYS | OFF-PEAK DAYS | PEAK DAYS |
| Bournemouth | £12.00 | £15.00 | £7.92 | £9.90 |
| Bristol T.M. | £9.70 | £12.00 | £6.41 | £7.92 |
| Exeter | £17.00 | £21.00 | £11.22 | £13.86 |
| Glasgow | £33.00 | £40.00 | £21.78 | £26.40 |
| Leeds | £20.00 | £25.00 | £13.20 | £16.50 |
| Liverpool | £16.00 | £21.00 | £10.56 | £13.86 |
| Manchester | £16.00 | £22.00 | £10.56 | £14.52 |
| Newcastle | £30.00 | £38.00 | £19.80 | £25.08 |
| Nottingham | £13.50 | £16.50 | £8.91 | £10.89 |
| Preston | £19.00 | £24.00 | £12.54 | £15.84 |
| Sheffield | £16.00 | £19.50 | £10.56 | £12.87 |
| Shrewsbury | £12.00 | £15.00 | £7.92 | £9.90 |
| Swansea | £18.00 | £23.00 | £11.88 | £15.18 |
| Torquay | £22.00 | £26.00 | £14.52 | £17.16 |
| Worcester* | £6.80 | £8.40 | £4.49 | £5.55 |

*Cheaper fares for a day out – ask for details.

| PEAK DAYS | OFF-PEAK DAYS |
|---|---|
| FRIDAYS | MONDAYS TO THURSDAYS (except 23 May and 22 August) |
| SATURDAYS 25 May, 29 June to 24 August inclusive | SATURDAYS Until 18 May, 1 to 22 June and from 31 August |
| SUNDAYS 30 June to 25 August | SUNDAYS Until 23 June and from 1 September |
| THURSDAYS 23 May and 22 August | |

## SAVERS

   Savers from Oxford really are fantastic value as you will see from our prices below.
   Savers are the cheapest way to travel by train over longer distances. And they are valid for return the same day or any time up to a month.
   There are a few restrictions on the use of Savers on busy peak trains to the west of England or via London. If you avoid the peak times you're virtually free to travel whenever you like – wherever you like.
   Oxford Travel Centre will have full details to help you plan your journey with a Saver. Do check your travel arrangements in advance as by adjusting your times and dates of travel it's possible to obtain maximum benefit from the range of Saver fares.

## INFORMATION

### TELEPHONE ENQUIRIES

For information on train services, fares and other facilities please telephone:
Oxford 722333
Daily                    08.00 to 20.00
Please wait for a reply as enquiries are answered in strict rotation on an automatic call queuing system.
You can hear a recorded summary of main trains and fares to London by dialling the appropriate number.
Oxford 249055
Information is constantly updated about any significant alterations to timetabled services. For a summary of the national situation on main InterCity routes dial Traveline on 01-246 8030.

### RADIO AND TV

For local rail travel news, particularly at times of disruption, tune into:
Radio Oxford                    202MW
                               1485KHz
                               95.2MHz
Alternatively Ceefax (BBC1) provides teletext rail travel news on index pages 164, 165 and 166.
Or see Oracle (ITV) on index page 186.
See index page 125 for BR Money-saving offers.
If you use Prestel, you will find information on page 221.

### TRAVEL CENTRE

We've staff waiting to help you plan your journey at your local British Rail Travel Centre:
Oxford Travel Centre, Forecourt, Oxford Station.
Open Mon-Fri        08.00 to 19.45
        Sat         08.00 to 18.45
        Sun         09.00 to 19.00

### RAILCARDS

Railcards can get you discount travel on many journeys. Valid for 12 months from date of purchase, a Railcard may be used as often as you like. Young Person, Senior Citizen, Family and Disabled Persons Railcards each cost £12. There's also a £7 card for Senior Citizens, giving discounts on Cheap Day Returns only.

### CHILDREN

Children under 16 travel at half price. Children under 5 travel free.
And remember, that up to 4 children can travel for just £1 each with an adult holding a Family, Senior Citizen or Annual Season Ticket Railcard.

### DISABLED

Some stations have ramped access and specially adapted waiting rooms and toilets. Most InterCity coaches have wide doors with hand rails; some have removable seats. For assistance with your travel arrangements ring: Oxford 722333.

### KIDS OUT – QUIDS IN

This summer treat the children to an enjoyable day out with our special offer in to London. One passenger pays the 2nd class cheap day return fare and up to 4 others (one must be a child) travel for £1 each.
Ask for a leaflet containing full details.

## VALIDITY OF SAVERS

Savers featured in this folder are valid for travel by any train except:
To West of England
Mondays to Thursdays – InterCity trains timed to depart Reading before 10.00 hrs; and on the 17.09 service from Reading.
Fridays – InterCity trains timed to depart Reading before 10.00 hrs, and between 16.25 and 18.25 from Reading; also only valid to stations in Cornwall on the 19.21 train from Reading.
Sleepers – Savers not valid on the 00.36 train from Reading Saturday mornings in July and August.
Return by any train
South coast
Mondays to Fridays on trains timed to depart Reading before 09.00 hrs.
Return by any train except on the 17.46 train from Didcot.
Savers are not valid on the following services:
Special Excursion trains
Motorail Services
Railair Coach Links
Golden Rail Holidays
These Saver tickets are not valid for travel via LONDON.
Valid for 2nd class travel only. In the event of use for 1st class travel, the Board reserve the right to require payment in full of the appropriate 1st class fare.
You may not break your journey.
Overnight journeys started on a permitted day may continue into the following day.
InterCity Saver tickets used for one direction only travel carry no refund entitlement.
Savers are subject to the British Railways Board's Conditions of Carriage except where specifically excluded.

(ctd.)

**Remember that you may use your English-English dictionary**

(*You are advised to spend about 25 minutes on this question*)

2. Use the information printed opposite (an extract from a British Rail leaflet about Saver fares from Oxford) to answer the following questions.

(a) You want a Saver Return to Sheffield on a Sunday in July. What's the fare?

.........................................................................................................................

(b) You want to travel to Worcester as cheaply as possible just for a day. Does the leaflet tell you how much it will cost?

.........................................................................................................................

(c) At what rate does one unaccompanied child of 8 have to pay to travel by train?

.........................................................................................................................

(d) You want information about times of trains to Birmingham. Which of the two Oxford numbers given should you dial?

.........................................................................................................................

(e) If you dial Oxford 249055, you will be given information about trains to which city?

.........................................................................................................................

(f) How much does a Disabled Person's Railcard cost? ..........................................................

(g) You bought a Railcard on 1st January, 1985. Can you use it tomorrow?

.........................................................................................................................

(h) Oracle is a teletext information service. What information is given on index page 186?

.........................................................................................................................

(i) Can you use a Saver ticket if you want to go away and return in three weeks' time?

.........................................................................................................................

(j) Can you use Saver tickets on every train? ..........................................................................

(k) If you don't use the return half of your Inter-City Saver ticket, can you get your money back?

.........................................................................................................................

(l) Is a Saver ticket valid for 1st class travel? .......................................................................

(m) Can you use a Saver ticket if you travel from Oxford to York through London?

.........................................................................................................................

(n) It's 7.30 p.m. on a Sunday evening. Can you get information at the Oxford Travel Centre?

.........................................................................................................................

(o) If you use a Saver ticket, can you break your journey and continue it the next day?

.........................................................................................................................

Fig. 7.6 Short-answer questions that readers might ask themselves of this text (The Oxford Delegacy, Examinations in English as a Foreign Language)

## The free-recall test

In free-recall tests (sometimes called immediate-recall tests), students are asked to read a text, to put it to one side, and then to write down everything they can remember from the text. The free-recall test is an example of what Bachman and Palmer (1996) call an extended production response type.

This technique is often held to provide a purer measure of comprehension, since test questions do not intervene between the reader and the text. It is also claimed to provide a picture of learner processes: Bernhardt (1983) says that recalls reveal information about how information is stored and organised, about retrieval strategies and about how readers reconstruct the text. Clearly, the recall needs to be in the first language, otherwise it becomes a test of writing as well as reading – Lee (1986) found a different pattern of recall depending on whether the recall is in the first language or the target language. Yet many studies of EFL readers have had readers recall in the target language.

How are recalls scored? One system sometimes used is Meyer's (1975) recall scoring protocol, based on case grammar. Texts are divided into idea units, and relationships beween idea units are also coded – e.g. comparison–contrast – at various levels of text hierarchy. Bernhardt (1991:201–208) gives a detailed example. Unfortunately, although such scoring templates, where text structure is fully recorded, are reasonably comprehensive, it reportedly takes between 25 and 50 hours to develop one template for a 250-word text, and then each student recall protocol can take between half an hour to an hour to score! This is simply not practical for most assessment purposes, however useful it might be for reading research.

An alternative is simply to count idea units and ignore structural or meaning relationships. The comprehension score is then the number of 'idea units' from the original text that are reproduced in the free recall. An idea unit is somewhat difficult to define ('complete thought' is not much more helpful than 'idea unit'), and this is rarely adequately addressed in the literature.

To illustrate how idea units might be identified, the first paragraph of this section might be said to contain the following idea units:

1  Free-recall tests are sometimes called immediate-recall tests.

2  In free-recall tests, students read a text.

3  Students put the text to one side.

3  Students write down all they can remember.

4  Bachman and Palmer (1966) call this test an extended production response type test.

However, it must be acknowledged that an alternative is to treat every content word or phrase as potentially containing a separate idea. The first paragraph would thus have at least 15 idea units:

1  free recall

2  immediate recall

3  tests

4  students

5  read

6  one

7  text

8  put aside

9  write

10  all

11  remember

12  Bachman

13  Palmer

14  1996

15  extended production response

An alternative is to analyse the propositions in the text based on pausal units, or breath groups (a pausal unit has a pause at the beginning and end during normal oral reading). The propositions in these units are listed, and then student recall protocols are checked for presence or absence of such units. Oral reading by expert readers can be used for the initial division into pausal units. Scoring reportedly takes 10 minutes per protocol. In addition, each unit can be ranked according to the judged importance of the pausal unit to the text (on a scale of four). Bernhardt (1991:208–217) gives a full example of such a 'weighted propositional analysis'. Correlations between the Meyer system and the simple system were .96 for one text, but only .54 for a second text. Using the weighted system increased the latter correlation to a respectable .85. Bernhardt points out that such scoring can take place using a computer spreadsheet, which then enables the user to sort information, providing answers to somewhat more qualitative questions like: 'What types of information are the best readers gathering? Are certain readers reading more from one type of proposition than from another?' and so on. Whatever mark scheme is used, it is important to establish the reliability of the judgement of numbers of idea units, by some form of inter-rater correlation.

It might be objected that this is more a test of memory than of understanding, but if the task follows immediately on the reading, this need not be the case. Some research has shown, however, that instructions to test-takers need to be quite explicit about how they will be evaluated. Riley and Lee (1996) showed that if readers were asked to write a summary of a passage rather than simply to recall the passage, significantly more main ideas were produced than in simple recall protocols. The recall protocols contained a higher percentage of details than main ideas. Thus simply counting idea units which had been accurately recalled risks giving a distorted picture of understanding. Research has yet to show that the weighted scoring scheme gives a better picture of the quality of understanding.

### The summary test

A more familiar variant of the free-recall test is the summary. Students read a text and then are required to summarise the main ideas, either of the whole text or of a part, or those ideas in the text that deal with a given topic. It is believed that students need to understand the main ideas of the text, to separate relevant from irrelevant ideas, to organise their thoughts about the text and so on, in order to be able to do the task satisfactorily.

Scoring the summaries may, however, present problems: does the rater, as in free recall, count the main ideas in the summary, or does she rate the quality of the summary on some scale? If the latter, the obvious problem that needs to be addressed is that of subjectivity of marking. This is particularly acute with judgements about summaries, since agreeing on the main points in a text may prove well nigh impossible, even for 'expert' readers. The problem is, of course, intensified if the marking includes a scheme whereby main ideas get two points, and subsidiary ideas one point. One way of reaching agreement on an adequate summary of a text is to get the test constructors and summary markers to write their own summaries of the text, and then only to accept as 'main ideas' those that are included by an agreed proportion of respondents (say 100%, or 75%). Experience suggests, however, that this often results in a lowest common denominator summary which may be perceived by some to be less than adequate.

However, this problem may disappear if readers are given a task/reading purpose, for which some textual information is demonstrably more important and relevant than other information. In addition, if the summary can relate to a real-world task, the adequacy of the response will be easier to establish.

You are writing a brief account of the eruption of Mount St Helens for an encyclopaedia. Summarise in less than 100 words the events leading up to the actual eruption on May 18.

**READING PASSAGE 1**

The Spectacular Eruption of Mount St. Helens

**A** The eruption in May 1980 of Mount St. Helens, Washington State, astounded the world with its violence. A gigantic explosion tore much of the volcano's summit to fragments; the energy released was equal to that of 500 of the nuclear bombs that destroyed Hiroshima in 1945.

**B** The event occurred along the boundary of two of the moving plates that make up the Earth's crust. They meet at the junction of the North American continent and the Pacific Ocean. One edge of the continental North American plate over-rides the oceanic Juan de Fuca micro-plate, producing the volcanic Cascade range that includes Mounts Baker, Rainier and Hood, and Lassen Peak as well as Mount St. Helens.

**C** Until Mount St. Helens began to stir, only Mount Baker and Lassen Peak had shown signs of life during the 20th century.

According to geological evidence found by the United States Geological Survey, there had been two major eruptions of Mount St. Helens in the recent (geologically speaking) past: around 1900B.C., and about A.D.1500. Since the arrival of Europeans in the region, it had experienced a single period of spasmodic activity, between 1831 and 1857. Then, for more than a century, Mount St. Helens lay dormant.

**D** By 1979, the Geological Survey, alerted by signs of renewed activity, had been monitoring the volcano for 18 months. It warned the local population against being deceived by the mountain's outward calm, and forecast that an eruption would take place before the end of the century. The inhabitants of the area did not have to wait that long. On March 27, 1980, a few clouds of smoke formed above the summit, and slight tremors were felt. On the 28th, larger and darker clouds, consisting of gas and ashes, emerged and climbed as high as 20,000 feet. In April a slight lull ensued, but the volcanologists remained pessimistic. Then, in early May, the northern flank of the mountain bulged, and the summit rose by 500 feet.

**E** Steps were taken to evacuate the population. Most - campers, hikers, timber-cutters - left the slopes of the mountain. Eighty-four-year-old Harry Truman, a holiday lodge owner who had lived there for more than 50 years, refused to be evacuated, in spite of official and private urging. Many members of the public, including an entire class of school children, wrote to him, begging him to leave. He never did.

(ctd.)

F    On May 18, at 8.32 in the morning, Mount St. Helens blew its top, literally. Suddenly, it was 1300 feet shorter than it had been before its growth had begun. Over half a cubic mile of rock had disintegrated. At the same moment, an earthquake with an intensity of 5 on the Richter scale was recorded. It triggered an avalanche of snow and ice, mixed with hot rock - the entire north face of the mountain had fallen away. A wave of scorching volcanic gas and rock fragments shot horizontally from the volcano's riven flank, at an inescapable 200 miles per hour. As the sliding ice and snow melted, it touched off devastating torrents of mud and debris, which destroyed all life in their path. Pulverised rock climbed as a dust cloud into the atmosphere. Finally, viscous lava, accompanied by burning clouds of ash and gas, welled out of the volcano's new crater, and from lesser vents and cracks in its flanks.

G    Afterwards, scientists were able to analyse the sequence of events. First, magma - molten rock - at temperatures above 2000°F. had surged into the volcano from the Earth's mantle. The build-up was accompanied by an accumulation of gas, which increased as the mass of magma grew. It was the pressure inside the mountain that made it swell. Next, the rise in gas pressure caused a violent decompression, which ejected the shattered summit like a cork from a shaken soda bottle. With the summit gone, the molten rock within was released in a jet of gas and fragmented magma, and lava welled from the crater.

H    The effects of the Mount St. Helens eruption were catastrophic. Almost all the trees of the surrounding forest, mainly Douglas firs, were flattened, and their branches and bark ripped off by the shock wave of the explosion. Ash and mud spread over nearly 200 square miles of country. All the towns and settlements in the area were smothered in an even coating of ash. Volcanic ash silted up the Columbia River 35 miles away, reducing the depth of its navigable channel from 40 feet to 14 feet, and trapping sea-going ships. The debris that accumulated at the foot of the volcano reached a depth, in places, of 200 feet.

I    The eruption of Mount St. Helens was one of the most closely observed and analysed in history. Because geologists had been expecting the event, they were able to amass vast amounts of technical data when it happened. Study of atmospheric particles formed as a result of the explosion showed that droplets of sulphuric acid, acting as a screen between the Sun and the Earth's surface, caused a distinct drop in temperature. There is no doubt that the activity of Mount St. Helens and other volcanoes since 1980 has influenced our climate. Even so, it has been calculated that the quantity of dust ejected by Mount St. Helens - a quarter of a cubic mile - was negligible in comparison with that thrown out by earlier eruptions, such as that of Mount Katmai in Alaska in 1912 (three cubic miles). The volcano is still active. Lava domes have formed inside the new crater, and have periodically burst. The threat of Mount St. Helens lives on.

Fig. 7.7 A 'real-world' summary task. Text from International English Language Testing System Specimen Materials, task written by author

An obvious problem is that students may understand the text, but be unable to express their ideas in writing adequately, especially within the time available for the task. Summary writing risks testing writing skills as well as reading skills. One solution might be to allow candidates to write the summary in their first language rather than the target language. The problem remains, however, if the technique is being used to test first-language reading, or if markers cannot understand the test-takers' first language. One solution to this problem of the contamination of reading with writing is to present multiple-choice summaries, where the reader's task is to select the best summary out of the answers on offer.

For
Examiner's
Use

**TASK 2**

You are interested in helping students to improve their writing skills.

You have found the following extract from a teacher's resource book and you would like to summarize it for your colleagues.

**Read the extract and then complete the tasks that follow in Section A and Section B.**

### WRITERS AND WRITING

1 Successful writing depends on more than the ability to produce clear and correct sentences. I am interested in tasks which help students to write whole pieces of communication, to link and develop information, ideas, or arguments for a particular reader or group of readers. Writing tasks which have whole texts as their outcome relate appropriately to the ultimate goal of those learners who need to write English in their social, educational, or professional lives. Some of our students already know what they need to be able to write in English, others may be uncertain about the nature of their future needs. Our role as teachers is to build up their communicative potential and we can do this by encouraging the production of whole texts in the classroom.

2 Perhaps the most important insight that recent research into writing has given us is that good writers appear to go through certain processes which lead to successful pieces of written work. They start off with an overall plan in their heads. They then think about what they want to say and who they are writing for. They then draft out sections of the writing and as they work on them they are constantly reviewing, revising, and editing their work. In other words, we can characterize good writers as people who have a sense of purpose, a sense of audience, and a sense of direction in their writing. Unskilled writers tend to be much more haphazard and much less confident in their approach.

3 The process of writing also involves communicating. Most of the writing that we do in real life is written with a reader in mind - a friend, a relative, a colleague, an institution, or a particular teacher. Knowing who the reader is provides the writer with a context without which it is difficult to know exactly what or how to write. In other words, the selection of appropriate content and style depends on a sense of audience. One of the teacher's tasks is to create contexts and provide audiences for writing. Sometimes it is possible to write for real audiences, for example, a letter requesting information from an organization. Sometimes the teacher can create audiences by setting up 'roles' in the classroom for tasks in which students write to each other.

4 But helping our students with planning and drafting is only half of the teacher's task. The other half concerns our response to writing. Writing requires a lot of conscious effort from students, so they understandably expect feedback and can be discouraged if it is not forthcoming or appears to be entirely critical. Learners monitor their writing to a much greater extent than their speech because writing is a more conscious process. It is probably true, then, that writing is a truer indication of how a student is progressing in the language. Responding positively to the strengths in a student's writing is important in building up confidence in the writing process. Ideally, when marking any piece of work, ticks in the margin and commendations in the comments should provide a counterbalance to the correction of 'errors' in the script.

0770/2 S97

(ctd.)

**5** There is a widely held belief that in order to be a good writer a student needs to read a lot. This makes sense. It benefits students to be exposed to models of different text types so that they can develop awareness of what constitutes good writing. I would agree that although reading is necessary and valuable it is not, on its own, sufficient. My own experience tells me that in order to become a good writer a student needs to write a lot. This is especially true of poor writers who tend to get trapped in a downward spiral of failure; they feel that they are poor writers, so they are not motivated to write and, because they seldom practise, they remain poor writers.

**6** This situation is made worse in many classrooms where writing is mainly relegated to a homework activity. It is perhaps not surprising that writing often tends to be an out-of-class activity. Many teachers feel that class time, often scarce, is best devoted to aural/oral work and homework to writing, which can then be done at the students' own pace. However, students need more classroom practice in writing for which the teacher has prepared tasks with carefully worked out stages of planning, drafting, and revision. If poorer writers feel some measure of success in the supportive learning environment of the classroom, they will begin to develop the confidence they need to write more at home and so start the upward spiral of motivation and improvement.

**7** Another reason for spending classroom time on writing is that it allows students to work together on writing in different ways. Group composition is a good example of an activity in which the classroom becomes a writing workshop, as students are asked to work together in small groups on a writing task. At each stage of the activity the group interaction contributes in useful ways to the writing process, for example:

(a) brainstorming a topic produces lots of ideas from which students have to select the most effective and appropriate;

(b) skills of organization and logical sequencing come into play as students decide on the overall structure of the piece of writing.

**8** Getting students to work together has the added advantage of enabling them to learn from each others' strengths. Although the teacher's ultimate aim is to develop the writing skills of each student individually, individual students have a good deal to gain from collaborative writing. It is an activity where stronger students can help the weaker ones in the group. It also enables the teacher to move around, monitoring the work and helping with the process of composition.

(Adapted from *Writing* by Tricia Hedge,
Resource Books for Teachers, OUP)

**[Turn over**

(ctd.)

For Examiner's Use

**Section B**

Choose the summary [(a), (b), or (c)] which best represents the writer's ideas.

Tick (✔) one box only.

(a) Writing tasks which help students to write complete texts are important since they develop communicative abilities. In order to succeed in their writing, students need to have an overall plan, in note form, and to have thought about who they are writing for. It is important that they read more because it develops their awareness of what constitutes good writing, and it also improves their own ability to write. Teachers can help in the writing process by getting students to work in groups and by monitoring and providing support. Group composition is a classroom activity which will help to improve students' confidence. ☐

(b) More classroom time should be spent on writing complete texts. It is only with practice that students will improve their writing and it is possible for them to work together in class, helping one another. Successful writers tend to follow a particular process of planning, drafting and revision. The teacher can mirror this in the classroom with group composition. The teacher should also provide students with a context for their writing and it is important that feedback both encourages and increases confidence. ☐

(c) Students can improve their writing ability and increase their confidence by participating in collaborative writing sessions in the classroom. It is possible for students to help one another during these sessions as they discuss their ideas about the correct way of phrasing individual sentences. The teacher's role during the actual writing is to monitor and provide support. An essential aspect of developing students' writing skills is the response of the teacher; it is important that traditional error correction should be balanced with encouragement. ☐

0770/2 S97
[Turn over

Fig. 7.8 A multiple summaries task, using the multiple-choice technique (Cambridge Examination in English for Language Teachers)

## The gapped summary

One way of overcoming both these objections to summary writing is the gapped summary. Students read a text, and then read a summary of the same text, from which key words have been removed. Their task is to restore the missing words, which can only be restored if students have both read and understood the main ideas of the original text. It should, of course, not be possible to complete the gaps without having read the actual text. An example of a gapped summary test on the Mount St Helens text in Fig. 7.7 is given below.

---

*Questions 5 - 8*

*Complete the summary of events below leading up to the eruption of Mount St. Helens. Choose NO MORE THAN THREE WORDS from the passage for each answer.*

*Write your answers in boxes 5-8 on your answer sheet.*

In 1979 the Geological Survey warned ...(5)... to expect a violent eruption before the end of the century. The forecast was soon proved accurate. At the end of March there were tremors and clouds formed above the mountain. This was followed by a lull, but in early May the top of the mountain rose by ...(6)... . People were ...(7)... from around the mountain. Finally, on May 18th at ...(8)..., Mount St. Helens exploded.

---

Fig. 7.9 Gapped summary (International English Language Testing System)

Scoring students' responses is relatively straightforward (as with gap-filling tests) and the risk of testing students' writing abilities is no more of a problem than it is with short-answer questions. In tests of second- or foreign-language reading, furthermore, the summary and required responses can even be in the test-takers' first language.

A further modification is to provide a bank of possible words and phrases to complete the gapped summary (along the lines of the banked gap-filling or cloze tests mentioned earlier) or to constrain responses to one or two words taken from the passage. See Fig. 7.10, on pages 241/42.

# Reading passage

*Job satisfaction and personnel mobility*

*Europe, and indeed all the major industrialized nations, is currently going through a recession. This obviously has serious implications for companies and personnel who find themselves victims of the downturn. As Britain apparently eases out of recession, there are also potentially equally serious implications for the companies who survive, associated with the employment and recruitment market in general.*

*During a recession, voluntary staff turnover is bound to fall sharply. Staff who have been with a company for some years will clearly not want to risk losing their accumulated redundancy rights. Furthermore, they will be unwilling to go to a new organization where they may well be joining on a 'last in, first out' basis. Consequently, even if there is little or no job satisfaction in their current post, they are most likely to remain where they are, quietly sitting it out and waiting for things to improve. In Britain, this situation has been aggravated by the length and nature of the recession – as may also prove to be the case in the rest of Europe and beyond.*

*In the past, companies used to take on staff at the lower levels and reward loyal employees with internal promotions. This opportunity for a lifetime career with one company is no longer available, owing to 'downsizing' of companies, structural reorganizations and redundancy programmes, all of which have affected middle management as much as the lower levels. This reduction in the layers of management has led to flatter hierarchies, which, in turn, has reduced promotion prospects within most companies. Whereas ambitious personnel had become used to regular promotion, they now find their progress is blocked.*

*This situation is compounded by yet another factor. When staff at any level are taken on, it is usually from outside and promotion is increasingly through career moves between companies. Recession has created a new breed of bright young graduates, much more self-interested and cynical than in the past. They tend to be more wary, sceptical of what is on offer and consequently much tougher negotiators. Those who joined companies directly from education feel the effects most strongly and now feel uncertain and insecure in mid-life.*

*In many cases, this has resulted in staff dissatisfaction. Moreover, management itself has contributed to this general ill-feeling and frustration. The caring image of the recent past has gone and the fear of redundancy is often used as the prime motivator.*

*As a result of all these factors, when the recession eases and people find more confidence, there will be an explosion of employees seeking new opportunities to escape their current jobs. This will be led by younger, less-experienced employees and the hard-headed young graduates. 'Headhunters' confirm that older staff are still cautious, having seen so many good companies 'go to the wall', and are reluctant to jeopardize their redundancy entitlements. Past experience, however, suggests that, once triggered, the expansion in recruitment will be very rapid.*

*The problem which faces many organizations is one of strategic planning; of not knowing who will leave and who will stay. Often it is the best personnel who move on whilst the worst cling to the little security they have. This is clearly a problem for companies, who need a stable core on which to build strategies for future growth.*

(ctd.)

> *Whilst this expansion in the recruitment market is likely to happen soon in Britain, most employers are simply not prepared. With the loss of middle management, in a static marketplace, personnel management and recruitment are often conducted by junior personnel. They have only known recession and lack the experience to plan ahead and to implement strategies for growth. This is true of many other functions, leaving companies without the skills, ability or vision to structure themselves for long-term growth. Without this ability to recruit competitively for strategic planning, and given the speed at which these changes are likely to occur, a real crisis seems imminent.*

**Questions 9–13**

The paragraph below is a summary of the last section of the reading passage. Complete the summary by choosing *no more than two words* from the reading passage to fill each space. Write your answers in boxes 9–13 on your answer sheet.

*Example*                                         *Answer*

Taking all of these various ...                   factors

into consideration

when the economy picks up and people ... **9** ..., there will be a very rapid expansion in recruitment. Younger employees and graduates will lead the search for new jobs, older staff being more ... **10** ... Not knowing who will leave creates a problem for companies; they need a ... **11** ... of personnel to plan and build future strategies. This is a serious matter, as ... **12** ... is often conducted by inexperienced staff, owing to the loss of many middle management positions. This inability to recruit strategically will leave many companies without the skills and vision to plan ahead and ... **13** ... to achieve long term growth.

Fig. 7.10 Banked choice, gapped summary task (International English Language Testing system)

Alderson *et al.* (1995:61) conclude that such tests 'are difficult to write, and need much pretesting, but can eventually work well and are easier to mark'.

## Information-transfer techniques

Information-transfer techniques are a fairly common testing (and teaching) technique, often associated with graphic texts, such as diagrams, charts and tables. The student's task is to identify in the target text the required information and then to transfer it, often in some transposed form, on to a table, map or whatever. Sometimes the answers consist of names and numbers and can be marked objectively; other times they require phrases or short sentences and need to be marked subjectively.

**PEOPLE AND ORGANISATIONS: THE SELECTION ISSUE**

**A**   In 1991, according to the Department of Trade and Industry, a record 48,000 British companies went out of business. When businesses fail, the post-mortem analysis is traditionally undertaken by accountants and market strategists. Unarguably organisations do fail because of undercapitalisation, poor financial management, adverse market conditions etc. Yet, conversely, organisations with sound financial backing, good product ideas and market acumen often underperform and fail to meet shareholders' expectations.   The complexity, degree and sustainment of organisational performance requires an explanation which goes beyond the balance sheet and the "paper conversion" of financial inputs into profit making outputs. A more complete explanation of "what went wrong" necessarily must consider the essence of what an organisation actually is and that one of the financial inputs, the most important and often the most expensive, is *people.*
**B**   An organisation is only as good as the people it employs. Selecting the right person for the job involves more than identifying the essential or desirable range of skills, educational and professional qualifications necessary to perform the job and then recruiting the candidate who is most likely to possess these skills or at least is perceived to have the ability and predisposition to acquire them. This is a purely person/skills match approach to selection.
**C**   Work invariably takes place in the presence and/or under the direction of others, in a particular organisational setting. The individual has to "fit" in with the work environment, with other employees, with the organisational climate, style of work, organisation and culture of the organisation. Different organisations have different cultures (Cartwright & Cooper, 1991;1992). Working as an engineer at British Aerospace will not necessarily be a similar experience to working in the same capacity at GEC or Plessey.
**D**   Poor selection decisions are expensive. For example, the costs of training a policeman are about £20,000 (approx. US$30,000). The costs of employing an unsuitable technician on an oil rig or in a nuclear plant could, in an emergency, result in millions of pounds of damage or loss of life. The disharmony of a poor person-environment fit (PE-fit) is likely to result in low job satisfaction, lack of organisational commitment and employee stress, which affect organisational outcomes  i.e. productivity, high labour turnover and absenteeism, and individual outcomes i.e. physical, psychological and mental well-being.
**E**   However, despite the importance of the recruitment decision and the range of sophisticated and more objective selection techniques available, including the use of psychometric tests, assessment centres etc., many organisations are still prepared to make this decision on the basis of a single 30 to 45 minute unstructured interview. Indeed, research has demonstrated that a selection decision is often made within the first four minutes of the interview. In the remaining time, the interviewer then attends exclusively to information that reinforces the initial "accept" or "reject" decision. Research into the validity of selection methods has consistently demonstrated that the unstructured interview, where the interviewer asks any questions he or she likes, is a poor predictor of future job performance and fares little better than more controversial methods like graphology and astrology. In times of high unemployment, recruitment becomes a "buyer's market" and this was the case in Britain during the 1980s.
**F**   The future, we are told, is likely to be different. Detailed surveys of social and economic trends in the European Community show that Europe's population is falling and getting older. The birth rate in the Community is now only three-quarters of the level needed to ensure replacement of the existing population. By the year 2020, it is predicted that more than one in four Europeans will be aged 60 or more and barely one in five will be under 20. In a five-year period between 1983 and 1988 the Community's female workforce grew by almost six million. As a result, 51% of all women aged 14 to 64 are now economically active in the labour market compared with 78% of men.
**G**   The changing demographics will not only affect selection ratios. They will also make it increasingly important for organisations wishing to maintain their competitive edge to be more responsive and accommodating to the changing needs of their workforce if they are to retain and develop their human resources. More flexible working hours, the opportunity to work from home or job share, the provision of childcare facilities etc., will play a major role in attracting and retaining staff in the future.

(ctd.)

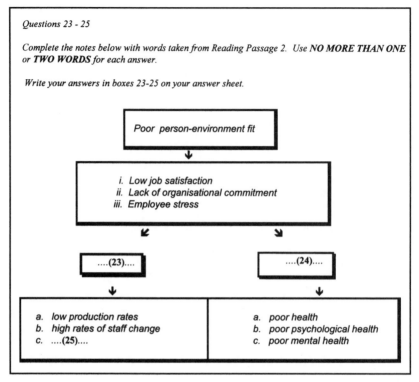

Fig. 7.11 Information transfer: text diagram/notes (International English Language Testing System)

READING PASSAGE 3

You should spend about 20 minutes on **Questions 30–38** *(p. 247) which are based on the following Reading Passage 3.*

# "The Rollfilm Revolution"

The introduction of the dry plate process brought with it many advantages. Not only was it much more convenient, so that the photographer no longer needed to prepare his material in advance, but its much greater sensitivity made possible a new generation of cameras. Instantaneous exposures had been possible before, but only with some difficulty and with special equipment and conditions. Now, exposures short enough to permit the camera to be held in the hand were easily achieved. As well as fitting shutters and viewfinders to their conventional stand cameras, manufacturers began to construct smaller cameras intended specifically for hand use.

One of the first designs to be published was Thomas Bolas's 'Detective' camera of 1881. Externally a plain box, quite unlike the folding bellows camera typical of the period, it could be used unobtrusively. The name caught on, and for the next decade or so almost all hand cameras were called 'Detectives'. Many of the new designs in the 1880s were for magazine cameras, in which a number of dry plates could be pre-loaded and changed one after another following exposure. Although much more convenient than stand cameras, still used by most serious workers, magazine plate cameras were heavy, and required access to a darkroom for loading and processing the plates. This was all changed by a young American bank clerk turned photographic manufacturer, George Eastman, from Rochester, New York.

Eastman had begun to manufacture gelatine dry plates in 1880, being one of the first to do so in America. He soon looked for ways of simplifying photography, believing that many people were put off by the complication and messiness. His first step was to develop, with the camera manufacturer William H. Walker, a holder for a long roll of paper negative 'film'. This could be fitted to a standard plate camera and up to forty-eight exposures made before reloading. The combined weight of the paper roll and the holder was far less than the same number of glass plates in their light-tight wooden holders. Although roll-holders had been made as early as the 1850s, none had been very successful because of the limitations of photographic materials then available. Eastman's rollable paper film was sensitive and gave negatives of good quality; the Eastman-Walker roll-holder was a great success.

The next step was to combine the roll-holder with a small hand camera; Eastman's first design was patented with an employee, F. M. Cossitt, in 1886. It was not a success. Only fifty Eastman detective cameras were made, and they were sold as a lot to a dealer in 1887; the cost was too high and the design too complicated. Eastman set about developing a new model, which was launched in June 1888. It was a small box, containing a roll of paper-based stripping film sufficient for 100 circular exposures 6 cm in diameter. Its operation was simple: set the shutter by pulling a wire string; aim the camera using the V line impression in the camera top; press the release button to activate the exposure; and turn a special key to wind on the film. A hundred exposures had to

(ctd.)

be made, so it was important to record each picture in the memorandum book provided, since there was no exposure counter. Eastman gave his camera the invented name 'Kodak' - which was easily pronounceable in most languages, and had two Ks which Eastman felt was a firm, uncompromising kind of letter.

The importance of Eastman's new roll-film camera was not that it was the first. There had been several earlier cameras, notably the Stirn 'America', first demonstrated in the spring of 1887 and on sale from early 1888. This also used a roll of negative paper, and had such refinements as a reflecting viewfinder and an ingenious exposure marker. The real significance of the first Kodak camera was that it was backed up by a developing and printing service. Hitherto, virtually all photographers developed and printed their own pictures. This required the facilities of a darkroom and the time and inclination to handle the necessary chemicals, make the prints and so on. Eastman recognized that not everyone had the resources or the desire to do this. When a customer had made a hundred exposures in the Kodak camera, he sent it to Eastman's factory in Rochester (or later in Harrow in England) where the film was unloaded, processed and printed, the camera reloaded and returned to the owner. "You Press the Button, We Do the Rest" ran Eastman's classic marketing slogan; photography had been brought to everyone. Everyone, that is, who could afford $25 or five guineas for the camera and $10 or two guineas for the developing and printing. A guinea ($5) was a week's wages for many at the time, so this simple camera cost the equivalent of hundreds of dollars today.

In 1889 an improved model with a new shutter design was introduced, and it was called the No. 2 Kodak camera. The paper-based stripping film was complicated to manipulate, since the processed negative image had to be stripped from the paper base for printing. At the end of 1889 Eastman launched a new roll film on a celluloid base. Clear, tough, transparent and flexible, the new film not only made the roll-film camera fully practical, but provided the raw material for the introduction of cinematography a few years later. Other, larger models were introduced, including several folding versions, one of which took pictures 21.6 cm x 16.5 cm in size. Other manufacturers in America and Europe introduced cameras to take the Kodak roll-films, and other firms began to offer developing and printing services for the benefit of the new breed of photographers.

By September 1889, over 5,000 Kodak cameras had been sold in the USA, and the company was daily printing 6-7,000 negatives. Holidays and special events created enormous surges in demand for processing: 900 Kodak users returned their cameras for processing and reloading in the week after the New York centennial celebration.

(ctd.)

*Questions 30 - 34*

*Complete the diagram below. Choose **NO MORE THAN THREE WORDS** from the passage for each answer.*

*Write your answers in boxes 30-34 on your answer sheet.*

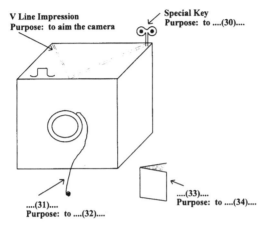

**V Line Impression**
**Purpose: to aim the camera**

**Special Key**
**Purpose: to ....(30)....**

....**(31)**....
**Purpose: to ....(32)....**

....**(33)**....
**Purpose: to ....(34)....**

*Questions 35 - 38*

*Complete the table below. Choose **NO MORE THAN THREE WORDS** from the passage for each answer.*

*Write your answers in boxes 35-38 on your answer sheet.*

| Year | Developments | Name of person/people |
|------|--------------|----------------------|
| 1880 | Manufacture of gelatine dry plates | .....(35)..... |
| 1881 | Release of 'Detective' camera | Thomas Bolas |
| .....(36)..... | The roll-holder combined with .....(37)..... | Eastman and F.M.Cossitt |
| 1889 | Introduction of model with .....(38)..... | Eastman |

Fig. 7.12 Information transfer: labelling diagram and table completions (International English Language Testing System)

One of the problems with these tasks is that they may be cognitively or culturally biased. For example, a candidate might be asked to read a factual text and then to identify in the text relevant statistics missing from a table and to add them to that table. Students unfamiliar with tabular presentation of statistical data often report finding such tasks difficult to do – this may be more an affective response than a reflection of the 'true' cognitive difficulty of the task, but whatever the cause, such bias would appear to be undesirable. One could, however, argue that since people have to carry out such tasks in real life, the bias is justified and is, indeed, an indication of validity, since such candidates would be disadvantaged by similar tasks in the real world.

A possibly related problem is that such tasks can be very complicated. Sometimes the candidates spend so much time understanding what is required and what should go where in the table that performance may be poor on what is linguistically a straightforward task – the understanding of the text itself. In other words, the information-transfer technique adds an element of difficulty that is not in the text.

One further warning is in order: test constructors sometimes take graphic texts already associated with a text, for example a table of data, a chart or an illustration, and then delete information from that graphic text. The students' task is to restore the deleted information. The problem is that in the original text verbal and graphic texts were complementary: the one helps the other. A reader's understanding of the verbal text is assisted by reference to the (intact) graphic text. Once that relationship has been disrupted by the deletion of information, then the verbal text becomes harder – if not impossible – to understand. The test constructor may need to add information to the verbal text to ensure that students reading it can indeed get the information they need to complete the graphic text.

## 'Real-life' methods: the relationship between text types and test tasks

The disadvantage of all the methods discussed so far is that they bear little or no relation to the text whose comprehension is being tested nor to the ways in which people read texts in normal life. Indeed, the purpose for which a student is reading the test text is simply to respond to the test question. Since most of these test methods are unusual in 'real-life reading', the purpose for which readers on tests are reading, and possibly the manner in which they are reading, may not correspond to the way they normally read such texts. The danger is that the test may not reflect how students would understand the texts in the real world.

We have seen how important reading purpose is in determining the outcome of reading (Chapter 2). Yet in testing reading, the only purpose we typically give students for their reading is to answer our questions, to demonstrate their understanding or lack of it. The challenge for the person constructing reading tests is how to vary the reader's purpose by creating test methods that might be more realistic than cloze tests and multiple-choice techniques. Admittedly, short-answer questions come closer to the real world, in that one can imagine a discussion between readers that might use such questions, and one can even imagine readers asking themselves the sorts of questions found in short-answer tests. The problem is, of course, that readers do not usually answer somebody else's questions: they generate and answer their own.

An increasingly common resolution of the problem of what method to use that might reflect how readers read in the real world is to ask oneself precisely that question: what might a normal reader do with a text like this? What sort of self-generated questions might the reader try to answer? For example, if the student is given a copy of a television guide and asked to answer the following questions:

---

a) You are watching sport on Monday afternoon at around 2 p.m. Which sport?

b) You are a student of maths. At what times could you see mathematics programmes especially designed for university students?

c) You like folk songs. Which programme will you probably watch?

d) Give the names of three programmes which are not being shown for the first time on this Monday.

e) Give the name of one programme which will be televised as it happens and not recorded beforehand.

f) Which programme has one other part to follow?

g) Give the names and times of two programmes which contain regional news.

h) You are watching television on Monday morning with a child under 5. Which channel are you probably watching?

i) Why might a deaf person watch the news on BBC 2 at 7.20? What other news programme might he watch?

j) You have watched 22 episodes of a serial. What will you probably watch on Monday evening?

k) Which three programmes would you yourself choose to watch to give you a better idea of the British way of life? Why?

---

Fig. 7.13 'Real-life' short-answer questions (The Oxford Delegacy Examinations in English as a Foreign Language)

What distinguishes this sort of test technique from the test methods discussed already is that the test writer has asked herself: what task would a reader of a text like this normally have? What question would such a reader normally ask herself? In short, there is an attempt to match *test task* to *text type* in an attempt to measure 'normal' comprehension. More reading testers are now attempting to devise tasks which more closely mirror 'real-life' uses of texts.

The CCSE (Certificates in Communicative Skills in English, UCLES 1999 – see also Chapter 8) include a Certificate in Reading. This test aims to use communicative testing techniques:

> Wherever possible the questions involve using the text for a purpose for which it might actually be used in the 'real world'. In other words, the starting point for the examiners setting the tests is not just to find questions which can be set on a given text, but to consider what a 'real' user of the language would want to know about the text and then to ask questions which involve the candidates in the same *operations*. (Teachers' Guide, 1990:9)

I have considered the relationship between tasks and texts at some length in Chapters 5 and 6. One sort of realistic test technique that might be considered is the information-transfer type of test.

*Directions:* Read the labels in figure 3.4 quickly to determine which have food additives.

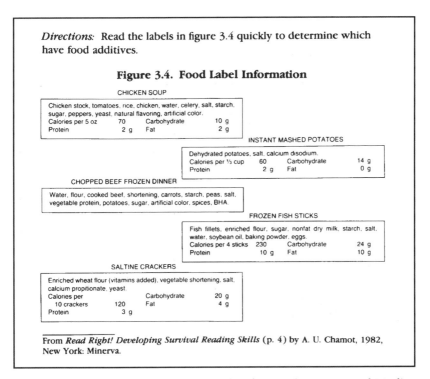

**Figure 3.4. Food Label Information**

From *Read Right! Developing Survival Reading Skills* (p. 4) by A. U. Chamot, 1982, New York: Minerva.

Fig. 7.14 Realistic tasks on real texts (Read Right! Developing Survival Reading Skills)

3.  **(b)**  On the map below, various places are marked by a series of letters. For example, the place numbered 5 in the leaflet is marked E on the map. Using information given in the leaflet write, against each **number** printed under the map, the corresponding **letter** given on the map.

(ctd.)

### 1

#### ROYAL NAVAL AIR STATION, YEOVILTON

Just off the A303 near Ilchester, Somerset
The largest collection of historic military aircraft under one roof in Europe. Numerous ship and aircraft models, photographs, paintings, etc., plus displays, including the Falklands War. Also Concorde 002, with displays and test aircraft showing the development of supersonic passenger flight.
Flying can be viewed from the large free car park and picnic area. Children's play area, restaurant, gift shop. Facilities provided for the disabled.

Open daily from 10a.m. until 5.30p.m. or dusk when earlier. Telephone: Ilchester (0935) 840565

### 2

#### Coldharbour Mill, Uffculme

An 18th century mill set in Devon's unspoilt Culm valley where visitors can watch knitting wool spun and cloth woven by traditional methods. These high quality products can be purchased in the mill shop. Other attractions include the original steam engine and water wheel, restaurant, and attractive water-side gardens.
Open 11a.m.-5p.m. Easter-end of September; daily. October to Easter. Times subject to change—for details please phone Craddock (0884) 40960. Situated at Uffculme midway between Taunton and Exeter, 2 miles from M5 Junction 27. Nearest town, Cullompton.

### 3

THE WEST COUNTRY GARDEN — OPEN TO THE WORLD
★ 50 acres of Stately Gardens
★ James Countryside Museum
★ Exhibition on life of Sir Walter Ralegh
★ Children's Adventure Playground & teenage assault course
★ Temperate and Tropical Houses
★ Meet the Bicton Bunny
★ Bicton Woodland Railway
★ NEW -- Bicton Exhibition Hall
★ Special events throughout the Summer.
Facilities for the disabled; self service restaurant, Buffet and Bar. Open 1st April to 30th September 10a.m.-6p.m. Winter 11a.m.-4p.m. (Gardens only). Situated on A376 Newton Poppleford-Budleigh Salterton Road. Tel: Colaton Raleigh (0395) 68465.

### 4

Off the A376 near Budleigh Salterton
Tel: Colaton Raleigh 68521, 68031 (Craftsmen).

**Otterton Mill** brings stimulus and tranquility in an enchanting corner of Devon. The mill, with its partly wooden machinery, some of it 200 years old, is turned by the power of the River Otter. Explanations and slides show you how it works. We sell our flour, bread and cakes and you can sample them in the Duckery licensed restaurant.
★ Changing exhibitions 8 months of the year.
★ Craftsmen's workshops in the attractive mill courtyard.
★ A well-stocked shop with British crafts, many made at the mill.

Open Good Friday-end of Oct.     10.30a.m.-5.30p.m.
Rest of the year                2.00p.m.-5.00p.m.

(ctd.)

⑤ E

## AND PLEASURE GARDEN

**A welcome** awaits you high on the hillside. Enjoy the flower garden with delightful views, play Putting and Croquet, ride on the Live Steam Miniature Railway through the exciting tunnel. Lots of fun in the Children's Corner. Enjoy the Exhibition of Model Railways and garden layout. Take refreshments at the Station Buffet and in the "Orion" Pullman Car. Model and Souvenir Shops, car parking, toilets. Modest entrance charges. Exhibition & Garden open all year Mon-Fri. 10a.m.-5.30p.m. Sats. 10a.m.-1p.m. Full outdoor amenities from 26 May-Oct: inc. Spring & Summer Bank Hols. Sundays, 27 May then from 22 July-2 Sept. inclusive. **BEER, Nr. SEATON, DEVON.**　　　**Tel: Seaton 21542**

⑥

Seaton to Colyton, via Colyford
**Visiting Devon?** Then why not come to Seaton where the unique narrow gauge Electric Tramway offers open-top double deck cars. Situated in the Axe Valley the Tramway is an ideal place to see and photograph the wild bird life, for which the river is famous.
**Colyton:** is the inland terminus 3 miles from Seaton. An old town with many interesting features.
**Party Booking:** Apply to Seaton Tramway Co., Harbour Road, Seaton, Devon.
**Tramway Services:** Seaton Terminus, Harbour Road, Car Park:—Tramway operates daily from Easter to end of October, with a limited Winter service. Ring 0297 21702 or write for information.

⑦

A collection of rare breeds and present day British Farm Animals are displayed in a beautiful farm setting with magnificent views over the Coly Valley. Roam free over 189 acres of natural countryside and walk to prehistoric mounds.
Attractions
- Licensed Cafe
- Pony Trekking
- Donkey and Pony Rides
- Devonshire Cream Teas
- Covered Farm Barn
  for rainy days
- Picnic anywhere
- Nature Trails
- Pet's Enclosure
- Gifts/Craft Shop
- 18-hole Putting Green
- 'Tarzan's Leap'

Open Good Friday until 30th September
10.00a.m.-6.00p.m. daily (except Saturdays).
**Farway Countryside Park, Nr. Colyton, Devon**
**Tel: Farway 224/367**
DOGS MUST BE KEPT ON LEADS

⑧

Chard, Somerset Tel: Chard 3317

**This old corn mill** with its working water wheel and pleasant situation by the River Isle houses a unique collection of bygones well worth seeing.

The licensed restaurant offers coffee, lunches and excellent cream teas. Good quality craft shop. Free admission to restaurant, craft shop, car park and toilets. Coaches by arrangement only.

Open all year except for Christmas period.
Monday-Saturday 10.30-6.00;
Sundays 2.00-7.00 (6.00 in winter).
1 mile from Chard on A358 to Taunton.

Fig. 7.15 Information transfer: Realistic use of maps and brochure texts (The Oxford Delegacy Examinations in English as a Foreign Language)

We have seen in Chapter 2 how important the choice of text is to an understanding of the nature of reading, how text type and topic can have considerable influence on reading outcomes as well as process, and how the influence of other variables, most notably the reader's motivation and background knowledge, is mediated by the text being read. Similarly in the assessment of reading, the text on which the assessment is based has a potentially major impact on the estimate of a reader's performance and ability. This is so for three main reasons: the first is the one alluded to above, namely the way in which text mediates the impact of other variables on test performance. The second lies in the notion that the task a reader is asked to perform can be seen as that reader's purpose in reading. Thus, since we know that purpose greatly affects performance (see Chapter 2), devising appropriate tasks is a way of developing appropriate and varied purposes for reading. And since purpose and task both relate to the choice of text, a consideration of text type and topic is crucial to content validity. The third reason also relates to the way in which the tasks that readers are required to perform relate to the text chosen. I have already suggested that some techniques are unlikely to be suitable for use with certain text types. The implication is that there is a possibility of invalid use of task, depending upon the text chosen.

There is, however, a positive angle to this issue also: thinking about the relationship between texts and potential tasks is a useful discipline for test constructors and presents possibilities for innovation in test design, as well as for the improved measurement of reading. I suggest that giving thought to the relationship between text and task is one way of arriving at a decison as to whether a reader has read adequately or not.

Earlier approaches to the assessment of reading appear not to have paid much attention to the relationship between text and test question. Most test developers probably examined a text for the 'ideas' it contained (doubtless within certain parameters such as linguistic complexity, general acceptability and relevance of topic and so on) and then used text content as the focus for test questions. Texts would be used if they yielded sufficient 'things' to be tested: enough factual information, main ideas, inferrable meanings and so on.

A more recent alternative aproach is to decide what skills one wishes to test, select a relevant text, and then intuit which bits of the text require use of the target skills to be read. (The problem of knowing what skills are indeed required in order to understand all or part of any text was discussed in Chapter 2 of this book.) Still, however, the relationship between text and test question is relatively tenuous: the text is a vehicle for the application of the skill, or the 'extraction of ideas'.

I suggest that a 'communicative' alternative is, first, to select texts that target readers would plausibly read, and then to consider such texts and ask oneself: what would a normal reader of a text like this do with it? Why would they be reading it, in what circumstances might they be reading the text, how would they approach such a text, and what might they be expected to get out of the text, or to be able to do after having read it? The answers to these questions may give test constructors ideas for the type of technique that it might be appropriate to use, and to the way in which the task might be phrased, and outcomes defined.

Such an approach has become increasingly common as testers have broadened their view of the sorts of texts they might legitimately include in their instruments. Earlier tests of reading typically included passages from the classics of literature in the language being tested, or from respectable modern fiction, typically narrative or descriptive in nature, or occasionally from scientific or pseudo-scientific expository texts. Texts chosen were usually between 150 and 350 words in length, were clearly labelled as extracts from larger pieces, and were usually almost entirely verbal, without illustrations or any other type of graphic text.

More recent tests frequently include graphic texts – tables, graphs, photographs, drawings – alongside the text, which may or may not be appropriate for use in information-transfer techniques. Most notably, however, texts are increasingly taken from authentic, non-literary sources, are presented in their original typography or format, or in facsimiles thereof, and in their original length. They often include texts of a social survival nature: newspapers, advertisements, shopping lists, timetables, public notices, legal texts, letters and so on. Such texts clearly lend themselves to more 'authentic' assessment tasks and thus, some argue, to potentially enhanced validity and generalisability to non-test settings.

Even tests that include traditional techniques endeavour to achieve greater authenticity in the relation between text and task, for example, by putting the questions before the text in order to encourage candidates to read them first and then scan the text to find each answer (thereby giving the reader some sort of reading purpose).

## Informal methods of assessment

So far, we have discussed techniques that can be used in the formal, often pencil-and-paper-based, assessment of reading. However, a range of other techniques exists that are frequently used in the more informal assessment of readers. These are of particular relevance to instruction-based ongoing assessment of readers, especially those learning to read, those with particular reading disabilities, and learners in adult literacy programmes. In the latter environment in particular, there is often a strong resistance to formal testing or assessment procedures, since the learners may associate tests with previous failure, since it may be difficult to measure progress by formal means, since the teachers or development workers themselves often view tests with suspicion (not always rationally) and since often, as Rogers says, 'training for literacy is not just a matter of developing skills. It is more a question of developing the right attitudes, especially building up learners' confidence' (Rogers, 1995, in the Foreword to Fordham *et al.*, 1995:vi).

Indeed, as Barton (1994a) points out, in adult literacy schemes in Britain there was until recently a conscious attempt to avoid external evaluation and assessment. He advises parents and educators to be wary of standardised tests, especially those which 'isolate literacy from any context or simulate a context' (p. 211), and to rely more on teachers' assessments and children's own self-assessments. And Ivanic and Hamilton (1989) believe that adults' assessments of their own literacy are defined by their current needs and aspirations in varying roles and contexts, not by independent measures and objective tests.

Assessment techniques in common use include getting readers to read aloud and making impressionistic judgements of their ability or using checklists against which to compare their performance; doing formal or informal miscue analyses of reading-aloud behaviour; interviewing readers about their reading habits, problems and performance, either on the basis of a specific reading performance or with the aid of diaries; the use of self-report techniques, including think-alouds, diaries and reader reports, to assess levels of reading achievement and proficiency.

In the second-language reading context, Nuttall (1996) does not recommend regular formal testing of extensive reading. Not only will different readers be reading different books at any one time, but also, she believes, testing extensive reading can be damaging if it makes students read less freely and widely, and with less pleasure. Instead, she suggests, records of which students have read which books can provide sufficient evidence for progress in extensive reading, especially if the books in a class library are organized according to difficulty levels. Thus students' developing reading abilities are shown by their moving up from one level to the next. She gives the following example of a useful assessment of level of reading ability, for extensive reading:

> Homer reads mainly at level 4 but has enjoyed a few titles from level 5. Keen on war stories and travel books.
>
> (Nuttall, 1996:143)

To gather such information, either teachers could make detailed observations of students' reading and their responses, or they might supplement records of which books had been read by information on reading habits – e.g. from personal reading diaries or Reading Diets (see below), from responses to questionnaires (possibly given at the end of each library book) or to informal interview questions about enjoyment. Similarly, if it was not thought to be too demotivating, the cloze technique could be used on sample passages selected from library books, to assess whether readers had understood texts at the given level.

Fordham *et al.* (1995) present a range of possible approaches and methods for assessment within the context of adult literacy programmes for development. Group reviews/meetings are suggested as being 'one of the simplest amd most effective ways of obtaining a wealth of information', and especially to 'depersonalise' individual difficulties. Example questions given tend to focus on an evaluation of the programme rather than individual progress or achievement (e.g. 'Are you enjoying the programme? Have you found it too slow? too fast? Are you benefiting as you expected to?' and so on (Fordham *et al.*, 1995:108).

However, no doubt such questions could reveal individual difficulties as well as concerns, which could be taken up in individual interviews, the second general approach the authors suggest. Here it is noted that different cultures may object to individual interviews or interviewers, and that it is essential that individuals feel comfortable being interviewed (either by the teacher or development worker, or by their peers). Open-ended, *wh*-questions are recommended as more useful than closed questions, and interviewers are advised to have available a record of the individual's work (see below) for reference.

Two other approaches useful in this sort of assessment are observation of classes as well as casual conversations and observations. The former should be undertaken on the understanding that its purpose is support, not judgement, since teachers are often uncomfortable with being observed by outsiders. Casual conversations – in tea-breaks, before or after class and in chance encounters – as well as observation of non-verbal behaviour like gestures and facial expressions, whilst not classed as 'methods', are held to provide very useful information which can be followed up later, presumably by means of the other approaches mentioned.

In assessing reading (only one of the 'literacy skills' mentioned), Fordham *et al.* suggest a number of ways of 'checking on reading' – presumably 'checking' is less formal and threatening than 'assessing' or 'testing'. These include:

- talking with learners about progress;
- reading aloud (but with a caution that this is different from reading silently, and some readers may be very shy about performing in public);
- miscue analysis: 'this is one way to assess fluency and to discover what strategies a reader is using for tackling a new word or deriving meaning from a text. But it is not a test of any other form of reading skill' (p. 111);
- checking how far a reader gets in a passage during silent reading (whilst reading for understanding);
- answering questions on a passage (possibly in pairs, orally);
- cloze procedure or gap-filling exercises, whose main value the authors see as providing an opportunity to talk with readers about why they responded as they did, thus possibly giving insights into how they approach the reading task;
- paired reading;
- 'real-life situations', rather than 'tests' (where learners are encouraged to report on how they have understood words in new contexts outside the class);
- Reading Diets – notes or other records (by the learner or the teacher) of all the learner's reading activities during a particular period, leading to comparisons over time;

• asking questions like 'have they been able to read something which they could not have coped with previously? What have they read? Do they dare to try reading something now that they would have avoided before?'

Critical of standardised tests for viewing literacy as skills-based, and thereby supposedly divorcing literacy from the contexts in which it is used, Lytle *et al.* (1989) describe what they call a 'participatory approach' to literacy assessment in which learners are centrally involved. This participatory assessment involves various aspects – the description of practices, the assessment of strategies, the inclusion of perceptions and the discussion of goals. Thus, learners are encouraged to describe the various settings in which they engage in literacy activities, partly in order to explore the social networks in which literacy is used. Learners' strategies for dealing with a variety of literacy texts and tasks are documented in a portfolio of literacy activities. Learners' own views of their literacy learning and history, and what literacy means for them, are explored in interviews and learners are encouraged to identify and prioritise their own goals and purposes for literacy learning.

The methods used for such assessment are described in Lytle *et al.*, as are the problems that arose in their implementation. Involving learners actively in their own assessment created new roles and power relationships among and between students and staff, which many found uncomfortable. Some of the methods used – e.g. portfolio creation – were much more time-consuming than traditional tests, and were therefore resisted by some. And because the procedures were fairly complex, staff needed more training in their use. Thus, the difficulties involved in the introduction and use of less familiar, more informal and possibly more complex procedures should not be overlooked when their use is advocated instead of more traditional testing and assessment procedures.

A very important and frequently advocated method is the systematic keeping of records of activities and progress, sometimes in Progress Profiles like those used by the ALBSU (Adult Literacy Basic Skills Unit) in the UK (Holland, 1990); see opposite.

| Aims | Elements | | |
|---|---|---|---|
| To read Samuel's letters | To practise reading his writing | To practise reading other letters and notes | To learn to spell his name and address so that I can write back |
| Look at the Elements and shade in the amount you have achieved ▶ | | | |
| To write a note for my mother that she can read | To spell my mother's name and address | To practise my writing so that it will look neat | To find my spelling mistakes for myself |
| Look at the Elements and shade in the amount you have achieved ▶ | | | |
| I want to add up what I must pay at the shop | To add up the different things I want to buy | To check if I have enough money to pay for them | To check if the shop gives me the right money back (change) |
| Look at the Elements and shade in the amount you have achieved ▶ | | | |

How have you used what you have learned?

I can read my son's letters on my own.
I wrote a note to my mother.
I checked my money at the shop — I was right.

PROGRESS

Fig. 7.16 A progress profile (Adult Literacy Basic Skills Unit)

Teachers frequently keep records of their learners' performance, based on observation and description of classroom behaviours. If entries are made in some formal document or in some systematic fashion over a substantial period of time – say, a school year or more – then a fairly comprehensive profile can be built up and serve as a record of monitored progress. One such system is the Literacy Profile Scales, developed initially in Victoria, Australia, and since used in a number of English-speaking contexts for recording the reading development of first-language readers (Griffin *et al.*, 1995); see opposite.

## Reading Profile Class Record

Class ............................ School ....................................................................

Teacher ....................................................................................................

**Band**

| | |
|---|---|
| **I** | Is skillful in analyzing and interpreting own response to reading. Can respond to a wide range of text styles. |
| **H** | Is clear about own purpose for reading. Reads beyond literal text and seeks deeper meaning. Can relate social implications to text. |
| **G** | Reads for learning as well as pleasure. Reads widely and draws ideas and issues together. Is developing a critical approach to analysis of ideas and writing. |
| **F** | Is familiar with a range of genres. Can interpret, analyze and explain responses to text passages. |
| **E** | Will tackle difficult texts. Writing and general knowledge reflect reading. Literary response reflects confidence in settings and characters. |
| **D** | Expects and anticipates sense and meaning in text. Discussion reflects grasp of whole meanings. Now absorbs ideas and language. |
| **C** | Looks for meaning in text. Reading and discussion of text shows enjoyment of reading. Shares experience with others. |
| **B** | Recognizes many familiar words. Attempts new words. Will retell story from a book. Is starting to become an active reader. Interested in own writing. |
| **A** | Knows how a book works. Likes to look at books and listen to stories. Likes to talk about stories. |

Fig. 7.17 Literacy Profile Scales: record keeping (The Reading Profile Class Record, Australian Curriculum Studies Association, Inc.)

## Reading Profile Rocket

Class ........................................... School ...........................................

Teacher ........................................ Student .........................................

Is clear about own purpose for reading. Reads beyond literal text and seeks deeper meaning. Can relate social implications to text.

Is familiar with a range of genres. Can interpret, analyze and explain responses to text passages.

Expects and anticipates sense and meaning in text. Discussion reflects grasp of whole meanings. Now absorbs ideas and language.

Recognizes many familiar words. Attempts new words. Will retell story from a book. Is starting to become an active reader. Interested in own writing.

**I** · · · · · · Is skillful in analyzing and interpreting own response to reading. Can respond to a wide range of text styles.

**H** · · · · · ·

**G** · · · · · · Reads for learning as well as pleasure. Reads widely and draws ideas and issues together. Is developing a critical approach to analysis of ideas and writing.

**F** · · · · · ·

**E** · · · · · · Will tackle difficult texts. Writing and general knowledge reflect reading. Literary response reflects confidence in settings and characters.

**D** · · · · · ·

**C** · · · · · · Looks for meaning in text. Reading and discussion of text shows enjoyment of reading. Shares experience with others.

**B** · · · · · ·

**A** · · · · · · Knows how a book works. Likes to look at books and listen to stories. Likes to talk about stories.

50% of the Grade ☐ students can be located within this range. Norms for all grades can be identified by locating the 'box' from the box and whisker plot in Chapter 13 for the relevant skill.

■ The student is estimated to be at about this location on the profile. See the worked example for writing shown on pages 106–8.

Fig. 7.18 Literacy Profile Scales: reporting results (The Reading Profile Rocket, Australian Curriculum Studies Association, Inc.)

Such records are compiled from a number of 'contexts for observation', which include reading conferences (where the teacher may discuss part of a book with a reader, listen to the student reading aloud, or encourage self assessment), reading logs (a student- or teacher-maintained list of books the student has read), retelling of what has been read (where the teacher makes judgements about what or how much the student has understood), cloze activities and notes from classroom observation, together with information gleaned from project work and portfolios. Teachers are also encouraged to discuss the student's reading with parents, for further insights. The use of such a rich variety of sources enables teachers to develop considerable insight into the progress students are making.

The profiles themselves are essentially scales of development (in this case, not only in Reading but also in Writing, Spoken Language, Listening and Viewing). The scales are divided into nine bands – A (lowest) to I (highest) – containing detailed descriptions and a 'nutshell' (summary) statement. The profiles are intended to be descriptive of what students can do, rather than prescriptive of what should happen, or of standards that must be reached. Teachers are encouraged initially to use the nutshell statements, in a holistic way, and then to use the detailed bands as indicative of a cluster of behaviours that they judge to be present or not, based on their observations and records of individual children; see overleaf.

| Reading band **B** | Recognizes many familiar words. Attempts new words. Will retell story from a book. Is starting to become an active reader. Interested in own writing. |
|---|---|
| Reading profile record | School .................................... Class ...... <br> Name ........................................ Term ...... |

## Reading band A                    COMMENT

**Concepts about print**
Holds book the right way up. Turns pages from front to back. On request, indicates the beginnings and ends of sentences. Distinguishes between upper- and lower-case letters. Indicates the start and end of a book.

**Reading strategies**
Locates words, lines, spaces, letters. Refers to letters by name. Locates own name and other familiar words in a short text. Identifies known, familiar words in other contexts.

**Responses**
Responds to literature (smiles, claps, listens intently). Joins in familiar stories.

**Interests and attitudes**
Shows preference for particular books. Chooses books as a free-time activity.

## Reading band B                    COMMENT

**Reading strategies**
Takes risks when reading. 'Reads' books with simple, repetitive language patterns. 'Reads', understands and explains own 'writing'. Is aware that print tells a story. Uses pictures for clues to meaning of text. Asks others for help with meaning and pronunciation of words. Consistently reads familiar words and interprets symbols within a text. Predicts words. Matches known clusters of letters to clusters in unknown words. Locates own name and other familiar words in a short text. Uses knowledge of words in the environment when 'reading' and 'writing'. Uses various strategies to follow a line of print. Copies classroom print, labels, signs, etc.

**Responses**
Selects own books to 'read'. Describes connections among events in tests. Writes, role-plays and/or draws in response to a story or other form of writing (e.g. poem, message). Creates ending when text is left unfinished. Recounts parts of text in writing, drama or artwork. Retells, using language expressions from reading sources. Retells with approximate sequence.

**Interests and attitudes**
Explores a variety of books. Begins to show an interest in specific type of literature. Plays at reading books. Talks about favorite books.

## Reading band C                    COMMENT

**Reading strategies**
Rereads a paragraph or sentence to establish meaning. Uses context as a basis for predicting meaning of unfamiliar words. Reads aloud, showing understanding of purpose of punctuation marks. Uses picture cues to make appropriate responses for unknown words. Uses pictures to help read a text. Finds where another reader is up to in a reading passage.

**Responses**
Writing and artwork reflect understanding of text. Retells, discusses and expresses opinions on literature, and reads further. Recalls events and characters spontaneously from text.

**Interests and attitudes**
Seeks recommendations for books to read. Chooses more than one type of book. Chooses to read when given free choice. Concentrates on reading for lengthy periods.

## Suggested new indicators

*VIEWING   LISTENING   SPOKEN LANGUAGE   WRITING   READING   I H G F E D C B A*

Fig. 7.19 Reporting literacy: overall ('nutshell') statements (Australian Curriculum Studies Association, Inc.)

For a more detailed discussion of scales of reading development, see the next chapter.

An important point frequently stressed by Griffin *et al.* (1995) is the formative value of the variety of assessment procedures and the literacy profiles they present. Since they claim that building a literacy profile 'is an articulation of what teachers see and do in ordinary, everyday classrooms', then not only should recording information become a routine part of a teacher's work, but also the information gathered can be used to inform and guide subsequent teaching and learning activities: 'The process of compiling profile data can be of formative use in that it may help the teaching and learning process' (*ibid.*, p. 7). They also claim that moderation of teacher judgements, where teachers compare the evidence they have gathered and the justifications they give for their judgements, can also be valuable for both formal and informal teacher development. And importantly, they emphasise that profiles can be motivating for students, since the emphasis is on positive achievements, students are given responsibility for compiling aspects of the profile, and teachers find them motivating in identifying positive aspects of student learning. They give a number of illustrative, practical class-based examples of how profiles can be used to answer key questions like 'What can the students do? What rate of progress are they making? and How do they compare with their peers and with established standards?' (*ibid.*, pp. 105–113, and 121–128). The point they emphasise is the way in which the information gathered (which they exemplify) can feed directly into teaching, and be based directly on the student's work.

For further examples of the use of profiles and portfolios in the assessment of reading in a foreign language, see the Language Portfolios for students of language NVQ (National Vocational Qualification) units (McKeon and Thorogood, 1998), or the examples of different methods of alternative assessment given in the TESOL Journal, Autumn 1995 (for example, Huerta-Macías, 1995; Gottlieb, 1995; or McNamara and Deane, 1995).

Informal methods of assessing reading are frequently claimed to be more sensitive to classroom reading instruction, and thus more accurate in diagnosing student readers' strengths and weaknesses. One such set of methods is known, especially in the United States, as Informal Reading Inventories, or IRIs. They are frequently advocated by textbook writers and teacher trainers:

Reading authorities agree that the informal reading inventory represents one of the most powerful instruments readily available
to the classroom teacher for assessing a pupil's instructional
reading level.        (Kelly, 1970:112, cited in Fuchs *et al.*, 1982)

However, despite the advocacy, the evidence for validity and reliability is fairly slim. Correlations between IRIs and student reading
levels, and standardised reading tests and similar placements vary:
most often in favour of the standardised tests.

IRIs are typically based on selections from graded readers. Readers
are asked to read aloud the selected passage, and teachers estimate
the word accuracy and comprehension of the reading. Surprisingly,
whilst traditional criteria for evaluating word accuracy and comprehension are 95% and 77% respectively, not only has little research
justified these cut-offs, some authors recommend quite different standards: Smith (1959) uses 80% and 70%; Cooper (1952) suggests 95%
and 60% in the primary grades and 98% and 70% for the intermediate
grades; Spache uses 60% and 75% as his lower limits! (All cited in
Fuchs *et al.*, 1982.)

Fuchs *et al.* (1982) review the topic and report their own study into
IRIs. The traditional 95% accuracy criterion performed as well as a
number of other cut-off criteria. High correlations were found
between these different criteria and teacher placements, suggesting
no advantage for one criterion over another. However, a cross-classifi-
cation analysis showed large numbers of students to be misclassified
by IRIs in comparison with both standard achievement tests and
teacher placements, by a number of different cut-offs.

On average, ten passages had to be selected from a basal reading
book before two passages consistent with the mean for the whole
book could be identified. Intratext variation is to be expected and so
the authors are critical of the lack of guidance to teachers on how to
select passages for the IRI.

IRIs are attractive because of their apparent simplicity and
practicality, but their lack of validity is worrisome. Fuchs *et al.*
advocate the development of parallel IRIs, and the aggregation of
results after multiple administrations over a number of days, thereby
sampling a number of passages from readers and allowing a range of
performances.

Perhaps inevitably in contexts where such informal, teacher- or
classroom-based techniques are used or advocated, little reference is
made to their validity, accuracy or reliability, and much more is made

of their 'usefulness' and 'completeness', and the need to actively involve the learners, especially if they are adults, in assessing their own reading. For example, Fordham *et al.* (1995) claim that 'adults learn best when they actively participate in the learning process and similarly the best way to assess their progress is to involve them in the process' (p. 106). They also encourage teachers to assess using the same sorts of activities used in teaching, and to use wherever possible 'real activities' for assessment: 'for example, the way in which learners actually keep accounts; or how frequently and for what purposes they use the post office' (p. 106). (As we have seen, this is much more difficult for reading than for other literacy 'skills'.) Nevertheless, much of what they advocate reflects principles and procedures advocated throughout this book and is not fundamentally different from good practice in testing generally, always provided that minimum standards of reliability and validity are assured.

> Asessing literacy is a process of identifying, recognising and describing progress and change. If we are concerned only with measuring progress, we tend to look only for evidence that can be quantified, such as statistics, grades and percentages. If, however, we ask learners to describe their own progress, we get qualitative responses, such as 'I can now read the signs in the clinic' or 'I read the lesson in church on Easter Sunday'. If learning is assessed in both qualitative and quantitative ways the information produced is more complete and more useful.
> (Fordham *et al.*, 1995:106–107)

I hope that the reader will see that I do not share this characterisation of measurement as mere statistics or the other straw men that it is often claimed to be. I see assessment as a process of describing. Judgement comes later, when we are trying to interpret what it is we have described or observed or elicited. Nevertheless, the perspective brought to assessment by those in adult literacy, portfolio assessment and profiles and records of achievement is a potentially useful widening of our horizons. Sadly, in writings like Fordham *et al.*, no evidence is presented to show that the approaches, methods or techniques being advocated do actually mean something, do actually result in more complete descriptions, can actually be repeated, or used, or even interpreted.

An extensive discussion of such alternative methods of assessment is beyond the scope of this volume, but is well documented elsewhere (see, for example, Anthony *et al.*, 1991; García and Pearson, 1991;

Goodman, 1991; Holt, 1994; Newman and Smolen, 1993; Patton, 1987; and Valencia, 1990). Despite the current fashion for portfolio assessment and the impression created by enthusiasts like Huerta-Macías (1995) that alternative assessment is new, it has in fact a surprisingly long history: Broadfoot (1986) provides an excellent overview and review of profiles and records of achievement going back to the 1970s in Scotland, and I refer the reader to Broadfoot for a full account of a theoretical rationale and many examples of schemes in operation.

## Summary

In this chapter, I have presented and discussed a number of different techniques for the assessment of reading. I have emphasised the danger of test method effects, and thus the risk of biasing our assessment of reading if we only use one or a limited number of techniques. Different techniques almost certainly measure different aspects of the reading process or product and any one technique will be limited in what it allows us to measure – or observe and describe. Given the difficulty, of which we are repeatedly aware in this book, of the private and silent nature of reading, the individual nature of the reading process, and the often idiosyncratic yet legitimate nature of the products of comprehension, any single technique for assessment will necessarily be limited in the picture it can provide of that private activity. Any one technique will also, and perhaps necessarily, distort the reading process itself. Thus any insight into reading ability or achievement is bound to be constrained by the techniques used for elicitation of behaviour and comprehension. Whilst we should seek to relate our instruments and procedures as closely as possible to real-world reading, as outlined in Chapters 5 and 6, we should always be aware that the techniques we use will be imperfect, and therefore we should always seek to use multiple methods and techniques, and we should be modest in the claims we make for the insight we gain into reading ability and its development, be that through formal assessment procedures or more informal ones.

In the next chapter, I shall discuss the notion of reading development in more detail: what changes as readers become better readers, and how this can be described or operationalised.

...........................................................................................

# CHAPTER EIGHT

# The development of reading ability

## Introduction

As we have seen in earlier chapters, researchers into, and testers of, reading, have long been concerned to identify differences between good and poor readers, the successful and the unsuccessful. Much research into reading has investigated reading development: what changes as readers become more proficient, as reading ability develops with age and experience. Theories of reading are frequently based upon such research, although they may not be couched in terms of reading development. Constructs of reading ability can also be expressed in terms of development: what changes in underlying ability as readers become more proficient. In earlier chapters, I have been concerned to explore the constructs of reading that underly test specifications and frameworks for development. In this chapter, I will explore the longitudinal aspect of the construct of reading, by looking at views of how reading ability develops over time.

Testers need to describe to users what those who score highly on a reading test can do that those who score low cannot, to aid score interpretation. In addition, since different reading tests are frequently developed for readers at different stages of development, there is a need for detailed specifications of tests at different levels, to differentiate developing readers. Thus designers of reading tests and assessment procedures have had to operationalise what they mean by reading development. Considering such assessment frameworks, scales of reading performance and tests of reading can therefore provide useful insights into test construction as well as a different perspective on reading and the constructs of reading.

In this chapter I shall look at ways in which test developers and others have defined the nature of, and stages in, reading development. I shall examine a number of widely used frameworks, scales and tests for reporting reading development and achievement, and consider the theoretical and practical bases for and implications of these levels.

First I shall examine two examples of reading within the UK national framework of attainment, one for reading English as a first language (in its 1989 and 1994 versions) and one for reading modern foreign languages, in order to contrast how reading is thought to develop in a first language and in a foreign language. I shall then describe various reading scales, in particular the ACTFL Proficiency Guidelines, and associated empirical research; the Framework of ALTE (Association of Language Testers in Europe); and draft band descriptors for reading performance on the IELTS test. Finally I shall describe two suites of foreign-language reading tests: the Cambridge main suite of examinations in English as a Foreign Language; and the Certificates of Communicative Skills in English.

This chapter does not attempt to be exhaustive in its coverage or even representative of the many different frameworks, scales and tests that exist internationally. It does, however, seek to be illustrative of different approaches to characterising reading development.

## National frameworks of attainment

Many national frameworks of attainment in reading exist, but I shall illustrate using an example from the UK. Such frameworks are used to track achievement, as well as to grade schools, and are often controversial (see Brindley, 1998). However, I am less concerned with the controversy here, and more concerned to describe how such frameworks conceptualise reading development in a first language, as well as in a foreign language.

### (i) Reading English as a first language

The National Curriculum for England and Wales includes attainment targets for English, which includes Reading. Official documents present descriptions of the types and range of performance which pupils working at a particular level should characteristically demonstrate.

There are ten levels of performance, and four Key Stages when formal tests and assessment procedures have to be administered to pupils. Key Stage 1 is taken at age 7, Key Stage 2 at age 11, Key Stage 3 at age 14 and Key Stage 4 is equivalent to the General Certificate of Secondary Education (GCSE) which is the first official school-leaving examination, at age 16. It is claimed that 'the great majority of pupils should be working at Levels 1 to 3 by the end of Key Stage 1, Levels 2 to 5 by the end of Key Stage 2 and Levels 3 to 7 by the end of Key Stage 3. Levels 8 to 10 are available for the most able pupils at Key Stage 3.'

The 1989 version of the Attainment Targets contained considerable detail in its descriptions of levels, but as a result of teacher protest, Sir Ron Dearing revised and simplified these in the 1994 version. To show the difference between the two versions, consider the descriptions of Level 1 below:

**1989: Level 1**

Pupils should be able to:

i   Recognise that print is used to carry meaning, in books and in other forms in the everyday world.

ii  Begin to recognise individual words or letters in familiar contexts.

iii Show signs of a developing interest in reading.

iv  Talk in simple terms about the content of stories, or information in non-fiction books.

**1994: Level 1**

In reading aloud simple texts pupils recognise familiar words accurately and easily. They use their knowledge of the alphabet and of sound–symbol relationships in order to read words and establish meaning. In these activities they sometimes require support. They express their response to poems and stories by identifying aspects they like.

The 1994 version is arguably much easier to demonstrate, and for teachers to test or assess, since the 1989 version gives little indication of how, for example, a pupil can be considered to have recognised that print is used to carry meaning.

To see how reading is thought to develop by Level 5, consider the following two versions:

**1989: Level 5**

i   Read a range of fiction and poetry, explaining their preferences in talk and writing.

ii  Demonstrate, in talking about fiction and poetry, that they are developing their own views and can support them by reference to some details in the text, *e.g. when talking about characters and actions in fiction.*

iii Recognise, in discussion, whether subject matter in non-literary and media texts is presented as fact or as opinion.

iv  Select reference books and other information materials, *e.g. in classroom collections or the school library or held on a computer,* and use organisational devices, *e.g. chapter titles, subheadings, typeface, symbol keys,* to find answers to their own questions.

v   Recognise and talk about the use of word play, *e.g. puns, unconventional spellings etc.,* and some of the effects of the writer's choice of words in imaginative uses of English.

**1994: Level 5**

Pupils show understanding of a range of texts, selecting essential points and using inference and deduction where appropriate. In their responses, they identify key features and select sentences, phrases and relevant information to support their views. They retrieve and collate information from a range of sources.

It is interesting to see that whereas for Level 1, the descriptions are different, rather than simplified, for Level 5, considerable simplification has occurred in the 1994 version, with a considerable loss of detail. This is unfortunate because the more detailed targets may provide more guidance to test writers and teachers conducting assessments, although of course such detail risks being not only prescriptive but also simply inaccurate in its assumption of a hierarchy of development.

In addition, what pupils read, and how their reading is to be encouraged, is also defined at the various Key Stages. The 1994 version distinguishes between texts by length, simplicity (undefined), type (literary, non-fiction) and response – from recognition to understanding major events and main points, to location and retrieval of information, to inferencing and deducing, to giving personal responses and to summarising and justifying, leading to critical response to literature, analysis of argument and recognition of inconsistency.

There is an emphasis on the importance of the development of reading habits, leading to independence in reading and to pupils' selecting texts for their own purposes, be they informative or entertaining. The importance of motivation, of pupils being encouraged to read texts they will relate to, that will encourage learning to read as well as reading to learn, is clearly paramount, especially in the early stages.

Later, pupils are to be exposed to progressively more challenging texts, and it is interesting to note that challenge is defined in terms of subject matter (which 'extends thinking'), narrative structure, and figurative language. This is quite unlike the progression we will see in foreign-language reading, where the emphasis is on more complex language – syntax and organisation – and less familiar vocabulary. For first-language readers there is also an emphasis on 'well-written text' – although this is not defined – and 'the literary heritage'. The wide variety of texts to which pupils should be exposed and through exposure to which reading is assumed to develop, is evident, especially by Key Stages 3 and 4, where emphasis is placed on literary texts, with much less definition of the sorts of non-fiction, expository and informative text that pupils should be encouraged and able to read.

This suggests that native English readers are more likely to have their reading development assessed, at least in the English section of the curriculum, through fictional and literary texts, than through other text types. Whilst it is clearly the case that expository texts will have to be read in other subject areas, it appears less likely that pupils will be assessed in those subject areas on their ability to process the information at varying levels of delicacy or inference, rather than on their knowledge of facts and their ability to manipulate information using subject matter knowledge.

To summarise the view of first-language reading development presented by this Framework, in early stages of reading, children learn sound–symbol correspondences, develop a knowledge of the alphabet and of the conventions of print, and their word recognition ability increases in terms of number of words recognised, and speed and accuracy of recognition. This aspect of development is assumed to be largely complete by Key Stage 2 (age 11), although mention is still made of pupils' ability to use their knowledge of their language in order to 'make sense of print'. Pupils should also develop an understanding of what print is and what purposes it can serve, and their confidence in choosing texts to read and to read new unfamiliar material is growing.

By Key Stage 2 not only is confidence growing, but so is sensitivity, awareness and enthusiasm: sensitivity both to implied meanings (reading between the lines) and to language use; awareness of text structure (which seems rather similar to sensitivity to language use) and of thematic and image development; and enthusiasm for reading in general. Readers are becoming more interactive with text ('asking and answering questions'), are able to distinguish more and less important parts of text and develop an ability to justify their own interpretation.

Key Stages 3/4 expect further development of all these areas – ability to pay attention to detail and overall meaning, increasing insight, distinguishing fact and opinion, and so on. A new element – the ability to follow the thread of an argument and identify both implications and inconsistencies – comes partly out of the earlier 'ability to summarise' and 'sensitivity to meanings beyond the literal', but also suggests increasing cognitive, rather than purely 'reading' or 'linguistic', development (much as the earlier ability to justify one's own interpretations seems to require an increase in logical thinking and expression).

The overall picture is then of an increasingly sensitive and aware response to increasingly subtle textual meanings, and an increasingly sophisticated ability to support one's developing interpretations, some of which is linked to an increased awareness of the use of language to achieve desired effects.

The relevance of this to a developing ability to read in a foreign language remains a moot point, if foreign-language readers have already developed such sensitivities in their first language (as we have discussed at some length in earlier chapters). Certainly, however, the development of tests of such sensitivity would greatly facilitate an investigation of the relevance and role of such awarenesses and abilities in foreign-language reading.

## (ii) Modern foreign languages

The Attainment Targets for Modern Foreign Languages in the National Curriculum for England and Wales provide a framework for the assessment of modern foreign language proficiency which is interesting for its contrast with the view of reading development in a first language.

The Targets are relevant only to Key Stages 3 and 4, since the learning of the first foreign language usually begins at age 11. Pupils are said to progress from understanding single words at Level 1, to short phrases (Level 2), to short texts (Level 3), to a range of written material (Levels 5 to 8) which includes authentic materials from Level 5, unfamiliar contexts (Level 6), and some complex sentences (Level 7). Interestingly, Level 8 seems little different from earlier Levels in this regard.

In terms of understanding, pupils develop from matching sound to print (Level 2) to identifying main points (Level 3) and some details (Level 4). Whilst they are said to understand 'likes, dislikes and feelings' at Level 2, Level 5 claims they now understand 'opinions' and at Level 6 pupils can now understand 'points of view'. By Level 8 they can 'recognise attitudes and emotions'.

The scanning of written material (for interest) is first mentioned at Level 5, but already at Level 3 they are said to 'select' texts.

Independence appears to begin at Level 3 (although 'independence of what' is unclear, since pupils still use dictionaries and glossaries at Level 3, and even at Level 4 dictionaries are used alongside the guessing of the meaning of unknown words). Level 6 mentions their competence to read independently, and Level 8 mentions their reading for personal interest. Confidence is also shown in reading aloud by Level 5, and in deducing the meaning of unfamiliar language by Level 6.

It is hard to see how any reader could be better than the 'exceptional performance' described in these Attainment Targets for foreign-language reading, and I wonder how this differs from what good readers would do in their first language:

> Pupils show understanding of a wide range of factual and imaginative texts, some of which express different points of view, issues and concerns, and which include official and formal material. They summarise in detail, report, and explain extracts, orally and in writing. They develop their independent reading by selecting and responding to stories, articles, books and plays, according to their interests.

In this section, we have examined frameworks for the measurement of developing reading ability, in a first as well as in a foreign language.

We have seen that the main difference between the two appears to be in the emphasis in the latter on the increased complexity of language that can be handled, as well as on an increasing range of texts. Development in cognitive complexity, however, is more characteristic of first-language reading development. However, it is important to emphasise that at present these frameworks represent a theoretical or curricular approach, rather than an empirically grounded statement of development.

## Reading scales

There have been many attempts to define levels of language proficiency by developing scales, with detailed descriptions of each point, level or band, on the scale. Some of these, such as the American Council for the Teaching of Foreign Languages (ACTFL), the closely related Australian Second Language Proficiency Ratings (ASLPR) or The Council of Europe Common European Framework are well known, others are less well known.

### (i) The ACTFL proficiency guidelines

The ACTFL proficiency guidelines provide detailed descriptions of what learners at given levels can do with the language: these are labelled as Novice, Intermediate, Advanced and Superior, with gradations like Low, Mid or High, giving nine different levels in all, for all four skills. The definitions of reading proficiency are said to be in terms of text type, reading skill and task-based performance, which are supposedly 'cross-sectioned to define developmental levels'. As Lee and Musumeci put it:

> A specific developmental level is associated with a particular text type and particular reading skills. By the definition of hierarchy, high level skills and text types subsume low ones so that readers demonstrating high levels of reading proficiency should be able to interact with texts and be able to demonstrate the reading skills characteristic of low levels of proficiency. Conversely, readers at low levels of the proficiency scale should neither be able to demonstrate high level skills nor interact with high level texts.
>
> (Lee and Musumeci, 1988:173)

| Level | Text type | Sample texts | Reading skill |
|-------|-----------|--------------|---------------|
| 0/0+ | Enumerative | Numbers, names, street signs, money denomination, office/shop designations, addresses | Recognize memorized elements |
| 1 | Orientated | Travel and registration forms, plane and train schedules, TV/radio program guides, menus, memos, newspaper headlines, tables of contents, messages | Skim, scan |
| 2 | Instructive | Ads and labels, newspaper accounts, instructions and directions, factual reports, formulaic requests on forms, invitations, introductory and concluding paragraphs | Decode, classify |
| 3 | Evaluative | Editorials, analyses, apologia, certain literary texts, biography with critical interpretation | Infer, guess, hypothesize, interpret |
| 4 | Projective | Critiques of art or theater performances, literary texts, philosophical discourse, technical papers, argumentation | Analyse, verify, extend, hypothesize |

(Lee and Musumeci, 1988:174)

These guidelines are widespread and influential, at least in the USA. However, some controversy surrounds them, since they are based on *a priori* definitions of levels, with no empirical basis to validate the *a priori* assumptions.

Allen *et al.* (1988) point out that the ACTFL Proficiency Guidelines are based on the premise that reading proficiency increases according to particular grammatical features and function/type of text. The ACTFL text typologies allegedly range from simple to complex (Child, 1987). A simple text might be a friendly letter or a popular magazine article, and more difficult texts might be formal business letters or serious newspaper articles. Allen *et al.* argue that this perspective is limited because it does not take the reader and his/her knowledge into account, and therefore cannot give an adequate view of comprehension or, they argue, reading development.

They claim that much discussion of second-language reading focuses upon text, not behaviour. Reading materials are typically 'graded' – in other words are ordered in terms of difficulty, estimates of which are either arrived at intuitively or by devices such as readability formulae, measures of lexical density ('the more frequent the word, the easier'). The assumption is that second-language reading development is a matter of moving from easier to more difficult texts.

Allen *et al.*'s research, investigating reading of French, Spanish and German in ninth to twelfth grade secondary school students in the USA, selected authentic texts appropriate for the various grade levels according to the ACTFL Guidelines. Their results showed that regardless of proficiency and grade level, students were able to capture some meaning from all of the texts, despite their teachers' expectations. Their results did not show a sequence of difficulty or a text hierarchy as implied by the ACTFL Guidelines. They suggest that the interaction between reader and text is much more complex than the Guidelines suggest: 'text-based factors such as "type of text" do little to explain the reading abilities of second language learners' (Allen *et al.*, 1988:170). However, they also conclude that whilst even low-level learners were able to extract some information from authentic texts, 'as learning time increases, so does the ability to gather ever increasing amounts (of propositions, i.e. information) from text' (*ibid.*, p. 170). But even low-level learners were able to cope with long texts (250–300 words) – shorter does not necessarily mean easier (since longer texts may be more cohesive and more interesting). They conclude that making inferences about developing ability on the basis of supposedly increasing difficulty of text is invalid, especially if this hierarchy of supposed difficulty relates to text type.

Lee and Musumeci (1988) confirmed these findings, failing to discover any significant difference between texts across different levels of learners of Italian. Although text types were significantly different, the order of difficulty did not follow the ACTFL Guidelines' predictions: a level 1 text was as difficult as a level 3 and a level 5 text! Similarly, the predicted level of skill difficulty was not achieved: skill two was more difficult than skills one, three or four! No evidence was found for the hierarchy of text type, the hierarchy of skill, nor for the belief that performance on higher level tasks subsumes lower ones.

Lee and Musumeci suggest that levels of skill based on increasing cognitive difficulty (which the ACTFL skills seem to be) might not account for levels of reading proficiency when readers are at roughly the same cognitive level, whereas linguistically based reading skills might differentiate such readers.

Furthermore, levels of second- and foreign-language reading proficiency for literate, academically successful adults might be different
from levels for learners who are *not* yet literate in their first language,
or who are not academically successful, and different again from the
developmental levels of first-language reading of cognitively imma-
ture children.

## (ii) The ALTE framework for language tests

ALTE (The Association of Language Testers in Europe) has developed
a framework of levels for the comparison of language tests, particularly for those produced by ALTE members. A useful Handbook
(ALTE, 1998) describes the various examinations of ALTE members,
not only in terms of these levels, but also skill by skill. Interested
readers should consult the Handbook for details of examinations in
Catalan, Danish, Dutch, English, Finnish, French, German, Greek,
Irish Gaelic, Italian, Letzeburgish, Norwegian, Portuguese, Spanish
and Swedish.

It is useful to briefly consider the generic descriptions of ALTE
levels for Reading at this point, not only because of their relationship
to the Council of Europe levels (Levels 1, 2 and 3 relate to Waystage,
Threshold and Vantage respectively) but also because they represent
a potentially influential view of developing reading proficiency. In
what follows, all references are to the 1998 Handbook.

ALTE presents a general description of what a learner can do at a
particular level, before describing this in detail for each skill, which
occasionally helps to clarify the detail of the skill, in terms of purposes
and contexts for language use (e.g. Level 1: language for survival,
everyday life, familiar situations; compared with Level 4: access to the
press and other media, and to areas of culture), hence details of this
general description are given in the ALTE document for each level
before the detailed descriptions of Reading.

For each level, ALTE distinguishes three main areas of use: social
and travel contexts, the workplace, and studying, and although the
level descriptions are broadly comparable for each context, the implication is that a model of developing reading ability needs to distinguish between such contexts, or to specify reading ability in each one
separately. This distinction reflects the fact that ALTE members
produce tests relevant in some way to these different contexts, or

which are targeted at these contexts, and for which therefore they feel the need to provide information which can be interpreted by users in such contexts. Thus there is little advantage in telling a business employer that a candidate for a job has sufficient German to read cash machine notices, when what the employer needs to know is whether they can deal with standard letters (Level 1).

What is unclear from the documentation, however, is whether ALTE considers that stepped profiles of reading ability are possible. Thus for instance, could a candidate be at Reading Level 3 for social and travel contexts, but only Level 1 for studying? The differentiation of the three major **contexts** suggests that this may be an important dimension to consider when thinking about or trying to measure reading ability.

A second dimension of developing reading ability is **the texts** that can be handled at a given level. Thus at Level 1, candidates can:

> ... read such things as road signs, store guides and simple written directions, price labels, names on product labels, common names of food on a standard sort of menu, bills, hotel signs, basic information from adverts for accommodation, signs in banks and post offices and on cash machines and notices related to use of the emergency services.          (ALTE, 1998)

By Level 4, candidates can 'understand magazine and newspaper articles' and 'in the workplace, they can understand instructions, articles and reports' and 'if studying, reading related to the user's own subject area presents problems only when abstract or metaphorical language and cultural allusions are frequent'.

This description makes clear that a differentiation between levels is not simply a matter of **text type** (which might appear to be the case from the Level 1 description) but also of **language** (concrete versus abstract), **cultural familiarity** or unfamiliarity and **subject matter/ area** (within or outside the reader's knowledge).

The **nature of the information** that can be understood varies, from 'basic information from factual texts' (Level 1) to 'a better understanding' and 'most language ... most labels' and 'understanding ... goes beyond merely being able to pick out facts and may involve opinions, attitudes, moods and wishes' (Level 2), to 'the general meaning' and 'their understanding of ... written texts should go beyond being able to pick out items of factual information, and they should be able to distinguish between main and subsidiary points and between the general topic of a text and specific detail' (Level 3), to (NOT) 'humour or complex plots' (Level 4), to (NOT) 'culturally remote references' (Level 5).

This mention of what readers can and cannot do introduces another dimension of the description of development: the **positive** and the **negative**. The ALTE descriptions include both statements about what readers **can do** at a level and what they **cannot do**, although this does not vary systematically.

This lack of systematicity in use of the dimensions that occur presents problems for a *post hoc* construction of a theory of reading development, which is what we could be said to be attempting here. This is not to say, however, that it does not provide useful guidance both to test developers and to those who wish to know what a given test and a given score or grade tells about a particular candidate's reading ability.

Other dimensions along which the ALTE Framework classifies reading development include **predictability of use** ('standard letters, routine correspondence, subject matter predictable, predictable topics, respond appropriately to unforeseen as well as predictable situations') – a dimension which appears to relate also to familiarity and subject knowledge. **Speed** is occasionally mentioned, although never defined ('If given enough time' – Level 2, but is often expressed **negatively**: 'reading speed for longer texts is likely to be slow' – Level 2, or 'reading speed is still slow for a postgraduate level of study' – Level 5).

**Length of text** is another dimension, such that more advanced readers are said to be able to handle longer texts than lower-level readers: 'users at this level can read texts which are longer than the very brief signs, notices, etc, which are characteristic of what can be handled at the two lower levels'. (Level 3). Again, however, this dimension is neither defined for any level, nor is it mentioned systematically through the levels. **Amount of reading** that can be handled is also an issue, even for more advanced readers: 'The user still has difficulty getting through the amount of reading required on an academic course' (Level 4).

Awareness of **register**, politeness and formality appears to develop (Level 3), and the ability to 'handle the main **structures** with some **confidence**' (Level 3) or 'with **ease and fluency**' (Level 4) is a dimension mentioned in the more advanced stages in particular. Mention is made of **simplicity** and **complexity** of text (simplicity not being defined), and of the need for simplified texts (Level 2), but these are not systematically contrasted with **authentic** texts, since even at Level 1, readers are said to be able to handle 'real' texts. The need for support in text processing is also a feature of lower-level readers, who are said to rely more on dictionaries.

Thus, in summary, we see that the development of reading, according to ALTE, needs to be seen in terms of context, text, (possibly) text type, language, familiarity of subject matter (and reader knowledge of subject matter), and can be expressed negatively in terms of what readers cannot yet do, or positively, in terms of what they can now or already do. Development appears to involve an increase in confidence, speed, awareness, length and amount of text, as well as the simplicity and predictability of texts and the nature of the information (basic, general, specific, opinion, humour) that can be understood in text.

The ALTE Framework represents an interesting set of hypotheses about reading development, based upon the test development experience of ALTE members, which could provide a very fruitful basis for further research into empirical dimensions of foreign-language reading development.

### (iii) Band descriptors of foreign-language academic reading performance

Urquhart (1992) surveys many attempts to devise scales of reading, as part of his attempt to devise a scale for The International English Language Testing System (IELTS) on which readers might be placed. However, the attempt is fraught with difficulties.

Firstly, as Alderson (1991) points out, scales of reading ability or performance that are user-oriented, i.e. that are intended to help people understand test scores, must relate to test content. It is unacceptable to claim, as ACTFL and ASLPR do, that a high-level reader can read newspaper editorials, if they have not been tested on such abilities or texts. Without evidence that they have been so tested, the descriptor associated with any given level is open to challenge and at best represents an indirect inference from behaviours of 'typical' readers at that level.

Thus, secondly, descriptors of performance at given levels must derive both from test specifications – the blueprint for the test – and from an inspection of actual test content. The latter, however, is only

a sample of the former, and thus test-based descriptions of performance will lack generalisabilty, however 'accurate' they might be in
terms of test performance.

In fact, the literature attempting to develop scales of reading
performance is remarkably non-empirical and speculative. Urquhart's
own attempt to identify relevant dimensions on which readers might
be differentiated is speculative, based upon his knowledge of reading
theory and reading research, and remains unvalidated, albeit
interesting.

The components of the draft band scales he proposes include text,
task and reader factors, as follows:

- Text factors:
  text type: expository, argumentative etc.
  discourse: comparison/contrast; cause/effect etc.
  text: accessibility – signalling, transparent vs. opaque
  length
- Task factors:
  complexity: narrow/wide; shallow/deep
  paraphrasing: simple matching/paraphrasing
- Reader factors:
  flexibility: matching performance to task
  independence: choosing dominant or submissive role; holist or
    serialist

The draft bands Urquhart illustrates contain detailed descriptions of
the different variables in each factor, for each of eight different levels.
However, an inspection of the descriptors reveals the familiar problems in many such scales of lack of specificity. Quantifiers and
comparative adjectives have no absolute value, and even relative
values are difficult to determine. What is 'reasonably'? 'some'? 'considerable'? Or even: 'shorter'? 'more demanding'? Clearly such terms
need definition, anchoring or at least exemplifying if the bands are to
be meaningful or useful, much less valid.

Interestingly, however, Urquhart also draws a picture of a competent and a marginal reader, as seen by a test user, in this case a
postgraduate tutor, who might need to make a decision about the
adequacy of a reading score. This tutor might judge adequacy of a
reader in the following way, which Urquhart suggests we try to build
into our band scales:

## Two portraits (postgraduate student readers)

### The good reader

This student gives every sign of having covered all the required reading, with no complaints and no evidence of being stretched. In seminars and tutorials specifically devoted to a particular article, she shows evidence of having extracted both gist and details. She is able to express what the tutor considers to be reasonable opinions about the article. These opinions may be in line with, or opposed to, those of the original author. More generally, she is able to cite articles appropriate to a particular discussion and use them to further her own argument.

In independent research, she is able to select articles relevant to her purposes. In her writing, she can incorporate quotations from the article appropriately; she can also paraphrase the information in the article. She shows that she is aware of the case being put forward by the writer, and of the evidence the writer uses to support this case. She can extrapolate what the writer says to a different context, of more particular relevance to herself. When necessary, she can cite flaws in the writer's argument, or produce evidence to support her own position.

### The marginal reader

This student may complain that the reading assigned on the course is too much, that it takes too long to get through. He is reluctant to talk in seminars devoted to an article, and may admit to 'not having understood all of it', or may state that it was very difficult. He is often unable to identify the point of view seemingly expressed in the article, though he may be able to mention factual points, i.e. what the author says about X,Y,Z.

In dissertation work, the choice of articles read does not seem entirely appropriate. The student may well cite long passages from articles, without integrating these into his own work to any marked degree. There is little comment on the passages quoted; they are generally introduced by 'X says. . .'. There is little, or no attempt to paraphrase text. Occasionally he quotes in support of an argument a text which, while being on the appropriate topic, does not support his own argument, and at worst may be in direct opposition.

(Urquhart, 1992:34–35)

To my knowledge no other attempt to describe reading performance has taken the perspective of the test user, and this fledgling attempt by Urquhart is worthy of replication in other contexts and further experimentation.

In this section, we have examined a number of scales of reading ability, which are interestingly suggestive of how reading might develop in a first as well as in a second language, but we have also seen that empirical evidence for the increasing difficulty of tasks and texts, and associated development of reading ability, is hard to come by. This implies that much more empirical investigation is needed before we can be confident that the scales do indeed reflect reading development.

## Suites of tests of reading

Another way of looking at how reading proficiency is thought to develop is to examine a set of language tests, to see what changes as the test levels advance. Perhaps the best known such set of language examinations are the Cambridge Examinations in English as a Foreign Language. UCLES produce proficiency tests in EFL at five different levels in what they call their 'main suite':

- Key English Test (KET)
- Preliminary English Test (PET)
- First Certificate in English (FCE)
- Certificate in Advanced English (CAE)
- Certificate of Proficiency in English (CPE).

In addition, UCLES also produce The Cambridge Certificates in Communicative Skills in English (CCSE), at four levels.

I shall describe how each of these suites operationalises a view of reading development, in turn.

### (i) The UCLES main suite

In what follows I describe the details for each test and discuss the implications for a view of reading development.

## 1. Key English Test (KET)

KET is based on the Council of Europe Waystage specification (Council of Europe, 1990), i.e. what may be achieved after 180–200 hours of study. Language users at this level are said to be able to read simple texts of the kind needed for survival in day-to-day life or while travelling in a foreign country.

The 1998 Handbook lists the language functions tested ('language purposes'): transactions such as ordering food and drink, making purchases; obtaining factual information; and establishing social and professional contacts. Topics candidates will be expected to deal with (personal and concrete) are also listed (e.g. house, home and environment; daily life, work and study, weather, places, services and so on).

Texts used in KET include signs, notices or other very short texts 'of the type usually found on roads, in railway stations, airports, shops, restaurants, offices, schools etc.; forms; newspaper and magazine articles; notes and short letters (of the sort that candidates may be expected to write)'.

Even though this is the lowest test in the UCLES suite, the Key English Test uses authentic texts, but adapts these to suit the level of the student. Reading is tested alongside Writing in a paper that takes 70 minutes and involves 56 questions. The reading test is divided into five parts.

Part 1 tests the ability to understand the main message of signs, notices or other very short texts found in public places. Questions might ask where one might see such signs, who the notices are intended for, or they might require a paraphrase of their general meaning.

Part 2 tests candidates on their knowledge of vocabulary, for example they may have to match definitions to words.

Part 3 tests 'the ability to understand the language of the routine transactions of daily life': in effect, pseudo-conversations.

Part 4 tests the ability to understand the main ideas and some details of longer texts (about 180 words), again from sources like newspapers and magazines, but adapted. Examples in the handbook include a weather forecast and an interview with an actor.

Part 5 tests knowledge of grammatical structure and usage in the context of similar texts to those in Part 4.

Two of the three remaining parts, focusing on writing, require candidates to complete gapped texts (e.g. notes or letters), and to transfer information from one text to another e.g. a text about a person and a visa application form for that same person. Both these parts clearly involve the ability to read as well, even if the focus is on correct written production.

No further information is given on text processing operations, skills or levels of understanding. Clearly this reading test focuses on simple short texts, on gathering essential information, but also on the understanding of language: vocabulary and grammar being explicitly tested. The sources for/difficulty of these language elements are not specified, other than to say that focus is on 'structural elements such as verb forms, determiners, pronouns, prepositions and conjunctions. Understanding of structural relationships at the phrase, clause sentence or paragraph level may be required' (*ibid.* 1998:12). The rationale for their selection is unstated, for example whether it relates to research into the linguistic components of reading development or to second-language acquisition research.

## 2. Preliminary English Test (PET)

PET is based on the Threshold Level of the Council of Europe (Council of Europe, 1990), and it is thought to require 375 hours of study to attain this level. PET is defined in terms of what a Threshold User can deal with: for reading, the text types which can be 'handled include: street signs and public notices, product packaging, forms, posters, brochures, city guides and instructions on how to do things as well as informal letters and newspaper and magazine texts such as articles, features and weather forecasts' (Handbook, 1997:6). It is claimed that PET reflects the use of language in real life.

For Reading, the Handbook sets out PET's aims as follows:

> Using the structures and topics listed in this Handbook, candidates should be able to understand public notices and signs; to read short texts of a factual nature and show understanding of the content; to demonstrate understanding of the structure of the language as it is used to express notions of relative time, space, possession, etc.; to scan factual material for information in order to perform relevant tasks, disregarding redundant or irrelevant

material; to read texts of an imaginative or emotional character and to appreciate the central sense of the text, the attitude of the writer to the material and the effect it is intended to have on the reader.

(Handbook, 1997:9)

It is interesting to note the inclusion of the ability to process syntax and semantic notions in this description of reading ability. This may in part be due to the test's close relationship with the Council of Europe's Threshold Level. Indeed, several pages of the Handbook are taken up listing an inventory of functions, notions and communicative tasks covered by the test as a whole, and an inventory of grammatical areas that may be tested, of topics and of lexis.

Topics, not surprisingly, relate to the Council of Europe topics: personal identification, environment, free time, travel, health and body care, shopping, services, language, house and home, daily life, entertainment, relations with other people, education, food and drink, places and weather.

Reading is tested alongside Writing in Paper 1, which takes 90 minutes in total. The reading section is divided into five parts, as follows:

Part 1: texts are signs, labels or public notices. Candidates are advised to consider the situation in which the text would appear and to guess its purpose. They do not need to understand every word (five multiple-choice questions).

Part 2: a number of short factual texts, against which other short texts have to be matched (normally eight texts, with five shorter texts against which to do the matching).

Part 3: a series of texts or one text, containing practical information. 'The type of task with which people are confronted in real life' (*ibid.*:13): 'the task is made more authentic by putting the questions before the text in order to encourage candidates to read them first and then scan the text to find each answer'.

Part 4: a text going beyond factual information, with multiple-choice questions aiming at general comprehension (gist), writer's purpose, reader's purpose, attitude or opinion, and detailed and global meaning. 'Candidates will need to read the text very carefully indeed' (*ibid.*:13).

Part 5: a short text, an extract from a newspaper article or a letter or story, containing numbered blanks to be completed from multiple-choice options. This part is designed to 'test vocabulary and grammatical points such as connectives and prepositions'.

It is claimed that students' understanding of notices depends on language not cultural knowledge, and that the whole reading component 'places emphasis on skimming and scanning skills'.

## 3. The First Certificate in English (FCE)

The FCE examination has been described in Chapter 4, and the reader is referred to that chapter for details of the test.

## 4. The Certificate in Advanced English (CAE)

CAE's test of Reading in Paper 1 tests 'a variety of reading skills including skimming, scanning, deduction of meaning from context and selection of relevant information to complete the given task' (Handbook, 1998:7). The level of the test is within Level 4 of the ALTE Framework:

> Learners at this level can develop their own interests in reading both factual and fictional texts . . . Examinations at Level Four may be used as proof of the level of language necessary to work at a managerial or professional level or follow a course of academic study at university level.           (Handbook, 1998:6)

However, the test appears not to have been designed with professional or study TLU domains specifically in mind. Four texts are selected, from a range of text types including 'informational, descriptive, narrative, persuasive, opinion/comment, advice/instructional, imaginative/journalistic and sources include newspapers, magazines, journals, non-literary books, leaflets, brochures, etc'. In addition, leaflets, guides and advertisements may be included, and plans, diagrams and other visual stimuli are used 'where appropriate' to illustrate.

With respect to the language of the texts it is said that, for Part 2 of the Reading Paper, 'practice is needed in a wide range of linguistic devices which mark the logical and cohesive development of a text, e.g., words and phrases indicating time, cause and effect, contrasting arguments; pronouns, repetition; use of verb tenses' (*ibid.* 1998:11).

The test focuses on:

- the ability to locate particular information, including opinion or attitude, by skimming and scanning a text (Part One);

- understanding how texts are structured and the ability to predict text development (Part Two);
- detailed understanding of the text, including opinions and attitudes, distinguishing between apparently similar viewpoints, outcomes, reasons (Part Three);
- the ability to locate specific information in a text (Part Four).

(1998:11–12)

One of the difficulties there is in understanding how one test in the suite differs from another – that is, what view of reading development is reflected in the tests – is that different words are used to describe texts, processes, skills and operations across the suite. It thus becomes somewhat difficult to see what changes as one progresses up through the suite.

An inspection of sample papers for FCE and CAE suggests that the language of the texts becomes more difficult, with increasingly arcane vocabulary, the syntax and organisation is unsimplified, and the language of the questions/tasks is less controlled. The CAE tasks are not radically different from FCE, and are not more obviously related to 'the real world', as the Specifications claim. Readers at the CAE level may read harder texts and read faster, but only a detailed content analysis, coupled with empirical data on item performance, would throw light on how successful CAE readers have developed beyond their FCE stage of proficiency.

### 5. The Certificate of Proficiency in English (CPE)

CPE is described in the 1998 Handbook as indicating a level of competence which 'may be seen as proof that the learner is able to cope with high level academic work', and CPE is recognised as fulfilling English language entrance requirements by the majority of British universities. 'It is also widely recognised throughout the world by universities, institutes of higher education, professional bodies and in commerce and industry as an indication of a very high level of competence in English' (CPE Handbook, 1998:6).

However, the test does not appear to be based upon an analysis of TLU domains as discussed in Chapters 5 and 6. Paper 1 (Reading Comprehension) is very traditional. It contains two sections: Section A, with 25 multiple-choice (four-option) questions 'designed to assess the candidate's knowledge of vocabulary and grammatical control' based on discrete sentences, and Section B, with 15 multiple-choice (four-option) questions, based on three or more texts. Only Section B can be considered to reflect the construct of reading as it is developed and discussed in this book. Since FCE originally also had this format, but then was recently changed, as noted in Chapter 4, we can expect CPE to change, too, in the future, to a more up-to-date view of what reading is.

Sources for texts in Section B include 'literary fiction and non-fiction, newspapers, magazines, journals, etc.' Usually one text is literary and the other two non-literary. The non-literary texts 'are more expository or discursive and taken from non-fiction texts aimed at the educated general reader. Subjects recently have included the media, the philosophy of science, archaeology, education and the development of musical taste, for example' (CPE Handbook, 1998:11).

Section A is described as testing the following areas of linguistic competence: 'semantic sets and collocations, use of grammar rules and constraints, semantic precision, adverbial phrases and connectors, and phrasal verbs' (*ibid*. 1998:11).

Section B tests 'various aspects of the texts, e.g. the main point(s) of the text, the theme or gist of part of the text, the writer's opinion or attitude, developments in the narrative, the overall purpose of the text, etc.' (*ibid*. 1998:11).

Clearly the CPE view of reading development is closely related to the development of grammatical and semantic sensitivity, as much as to the ability to process more complex and literary texts.

An overview of the main suite as provided in Figure 8.1 below operationalises the tests' view of reading development.

| | **Expected hours instruction required** |
|---|---|
| KET | 180–200 |
| PET | 375 |
| FCA | Not stated |
| CAE | Not stated |
| CPE | Not stated |
| | **Time** |
| KET | 70 mins (inc Writing) |
| PET | 90 mins (inc Writing) |
| FCE | 75 mins (Reading only) |
| CAE | 75 mins |
| CPE | 60 mins |

(ctd.)

**Number of items**
KET    40
PET    35
FCE    35
CAE    40/50
CPE    40 (25 of which are Structure)

**Number of texts**
KET    Not stated: 13 short, 2 longer, 10 conversations, 5 words
PET    13 short, 3 longer
FCE    4/5
CAE    4
CPE    3

**Average text length**
KET    Not stated ('longer' text said to be 180 words)
PET    Not stated
FCE    350–700 words
CAE    450–1200 words
CPE    450–600 words

**Total text length**
KET    Not stated
PET    Not stated
FCE    1900–2300 words
CAE    3000 words
CPE    1500–1800 words

**Topics**
KET    House, home and environment; daily life, work and study, weather, places, services
PET    Personal identification, environment, free time, travel, health and body care, shopping, services, language, house and home, daily life, entertainment, relations with other people, education, food and drink, places and weather. (Long citation from Council of Europe lists)
FCE    Not stated
CAE    Not stated; 'it is free from bias, and has an international flavour'
CPE    Not stated: claims topics 'will not advantage or disadvantage certain groups and will not offend according to religion, politics or sex'

**Authenticity**
KET    Authentic, adapted to candidate level
PET    Authentic, adapted to level
FCE    Semi-authentic
CAE    Authentic in form
CPE    Not stated

(ctd.)

| | |
|---|---|
| | **Texts** |
| KET | Signs, notices or other very short texts 'of the type usually found on roads, in railway stations, airports, shops, restaurants, offices, schools etc'; forms; newspaper and magazine articles; notes and short letters |
| PET | Street signs and public notices, product packaging, forms, posters, brochures, city guides and instructions on how to do things, informal letters, newspaper and magazine texts such as articles, features and weather forecasts, texts of an imaginative or emotional character, a short text, an extract from a newspaper article or a letter or story |
| FCE | Informative and general interest, advertisements, correspondence, fiction, informational material (e.g. brochures, guides, manuals, etc), messages, newspaper and magazine articles, reports |
| CAE | Informational, descriptive, narrative, persuasive, opinion/comment, advice/instructional, imaginative/journalistic. Sources include newspapers, magazines, journals, non-literary books, leaflets, brochures, leaflets, guides, and advertisements, plans, diagrams and other visual stimuli |
| CPE | Narrative, descriptive, expository, discursive, informative, etc. Sources include literary fiction and non-fiction, newspapers and magazines. |
| | **Skills/ability focus** |
| KET | The ability to understand the main message, knowledge of vocabulary, the ability to understand the language of the routine transactions of daily life, the ability to understand the main ideas and some details of longer texts, knowledge of grammatical structure and usage |
| PET | Using the structures and topics listed, able to understand public notices and signs; to show understanding of the content of short texts of a factual nature; to demonstrate understanding of the structure of the language as it is used to express notions of relative time, space, possession, etc; to scan factual material for information in order to perform relevant tasks, disregarding redundant or irrelevant material; to read texts of an imaginative or emotional character and to appreciate the central sense of the text, the attitude of the writer to the material and the effect it is intended to have on the reader. Ability to go beyond factual information, general comprehension (gist), writer's purpose, reader's purpose, attitude or opinion, and detailed and global meaning. Candidates will need to read the text very carefully indeed |
| FCE | Candidates' understanding of written texts should go beyond being able to pick out items of factual information, and they should be able to distinguish between main and subsidiary points and between the gist of a text and specific detail, to show understanding of gist, detail and text structure and to deduce meaning and lexical reference, ability to locate information in sections of text |
| CAE | A wide range of reading skills and strategies:<br>Forming an overall impression by skimming the text |

(ctd.)

Retrieving specific information by scanning the text
Interpreting the text for inference, attitude and style
Demonstrating understanding of the text as a whole
Selecting relevant information required to perform a task
Demonstrating understanding of how text structure operates
Deducing meaning from context

CPE  The candidate's knowledge of vocabulary and grammatical control
Understanding structural and lexical appropriacy
Understanding the gist of a written text and its overall function and message
Following the significant points, even though a few words may be unknown
Selecting specific information from a written text
Recognising opinion and attitude when clearly expressed
Inferring opinion, attitude and underlying meaning
Showing detailed comprehension of a text
Recognising intention and register

Fig. 8.1 Foreign language reading development, as revealed by UCLES' main suite exams (University of Cambridge Local Examinations Syndicate)

## (ii) Certificates of Communicative Skills in English (CCSE)

The fact that different interpretations or operationalisations are possible of the construct of reading development is illustrated particularly well by the other suite of tests that UCLES produces: the Certificates in Communicative Skills in English (CCSE). Unlike the main suite, which has in a sense grown organically and is still unifying rather disparate views of language ability within its hierarchy, the CCSE is based upon a unified view of the development of language proficiency, from a communicative perspective, and thus presents a potentially very interesting and different view of reading development.

The CCSE is offered at four levels, which are said to correspond to the main suite examinations roughly as follows:

• Level 1: Preliminary English Test (PET)
• Level 2: Grade C/D in the First Certificate in English (FCE)
• Level 3: Certificate in Advanced English (CAE)
• Level 4: Grade B/C in Cambridge Proficiency in English (CPE)

There are tests in the four macro-skills of Reading, Writing, Speaking and Listening, at each level. Unlike the main-suite examinations, however, students can take the CCSE in as many skills as they wish and they can enter for different skills at different levels. Thus it is possible for a candidate only to take a Reading test at Level 1, or to take a Reading test at Level 3 and a Writing test at Level 2, and so on. Candidates are simply awarded a Pass or Fail at each level, and the detailed specifications of the tests indicate what it means to 'pass' at each level.

A very interesting feature of the tests is that the same collection of authentic material (genuine samples reproduced in facsimile from the original publication) is used at all four levels, although not all texts in the booklet are used at all levels. But there are occasions when the same text may be used at different levels, using different tasks, requiring a different reading skill. In other words, reading development is seen not as a progression from inauthentic to authentic texts, or even from text to text, rather it is recognised that readers at all levels will need to read authentic texts. What will differ is what they are expected to be able to do with those texts. Interestingly it is said that complete overlap between text and task across two levels (in other words, the repeat of text and task at adjacent levels) is also included to monitor the 'reliability and validity' of the test.

> Tasks may involve candidates in working with the following text types:
>
> At all levels:
> leaflet; advertisement; letter; postcard; form; set of instructions; diary entry; timetable; map; plan; newspaper/magazine article.
>
> At levels 3/4 only:
> newspaper feature; newspaper editorial; novel (extract); poem.                                    (CCSE Handbook, 1999)

Tasks involve using the text for a purpose for which it might be used in the real world, wherever possible, at all levels. 'In other words, the starting point for the examiners setting the tests is not just to find questions which can be set on a given text, but to consider what a 'real' user of the language would want to know about the text and then to ask questions which involve the candidates in the same *text processing operations*' (*ibid.* 1999:10).

At all levels, formats may be closed (multiple-choice or True/False) or open (single word, phrase, notes or short reports). At lower levels, however, candidates will have to write only single words or phrases, at higher levels connected writing may be required. Thus, although it is claimed that during marking focus is always on the receptive skill, one aspect of reading development appears to be the ability to do more with the text in terms of production.

'Text processing operations' (not, note, 'skills') are partially differentiated by level and partly common across levels. At Levels 3/4 only, tasks may involve:

- Deciding whether a text is based on e.g. fact, opinion or hearsay.

- Tracing (and recording) the development of an argument.

- Recognising the attitudes and emotions of writers as revealed implicitly by the text.

- Extracting the relevant points to summarise the whole text, a specific idea or the underlying idea.

- Appreciating the use made of e.g. typography, layout, images in the communication of a message.                      (*ibid.* 1999:11)

Thus only relatively advanced readers are expected to be able to distinguish fact from opinion, follow an argument, summarise or appreciate non-verbal devices. At all levels, however, readers are expected to be able to engage in the following text-processing operations. In other words, readers are not thought to develop according to their ability to:

- Locate and understand specific information in a text.

- Understand the overall message (gist) of a text.

- Decide whether a particular text is relevant (in whole or in part) to their needs in completing the task.

- Decide whether the information given in a text corresponds to information given earlier.

- Recognise the attitudes and emotions of the writer when these are expressd overtly.

- Identify what type of text is involved (e.g. advertisement, news report, etc.).

- Decide on an appropriate course of action on the basis of the information in a text.                      (*ibid.* 1999:11)

It is certainly interesting to note the lack of a claim that readers' skills develop in the use of such operations. One is left wondering, however, given the overlap across texts, the commonality among many text processing operations and the lack of any distinctions made between Levels 1 and 2 or between Levels 3 and 4, exactly what model of reader development does in fact underly this set of examinations.

# Degree of Skill: Certificate in Reading

In order to achieve a pass at a given level, candidates must demonstrate the ability to complete the tasks set. Tasks will be based on the degree of skill in language use specified by these criteria.

| Degree of Skill | Level 1 | Level 2 | Level 3 | Level 4 |
|---|---|---|---|---|
| COMPLEXITY | Does not need to follow the details of the structure of the text. | The structure of a simple text will generally be perceived but tasks should depend only on explicit markers. | The structure of a simple text will generally be perceived and tasks may require understanding of this. | The structure of the text followed even when it is not signalled explicitly. |
| RANGE | Needs to handle only the main points. A limited amount of significant detail may be understood. | Can follow most of the significant points of a text including some detail. | Can follow most of the significant points of a text including most detail. | Can follow all the points in a text including detail. |
| SPEED | Likely to be very limited in speed. Reading may be laborious. | Does not need to pore over every word of the text for adequate comprehension. | Can read with considerable facility. Adequate comprehension is hardly affected by reading speed. | Can read with great facility. Adequate comprehension is not affected by reading speed. |
| FLEXIBILITY | Only a limited ability to match reading style to task is required at this level. | Sequences of different text types, topics or styles may cause initial confusion. Some ability to adapt reading style to task can be expected. | Sequences of different text types, topics cause few problems. Good ability to match reading style to task. | Sequences of different text types, topics and styles cause no problems. Excellent ability to match reading style to task. |
| INDEPENDENCE | A great deal of support needs to be offered through the framing of the tasks, the rubrics and the context that are established. May need frequent reference to dictionary for word meanings. | Some support needs to be offered through the framing of the tasks, the rubrics and the contexts that are established. The dictionary may still be needed quite often. | Minimal support needs to be offered through the framing of the tasks, the rubrics and the contexts that are established. Reference to dictionary will only rarely be necessary. | No allowances need to be made in framing tasks, rubrics and establishing contexts. Reference to dictionary will be required only exceptionally. |

Fig 8.2  Degree of skill in reading (Certificate in Communicative Skills in English)

The Handbook attempts to answer this question by distinguishing the four levels according to the degree of skill in language use required by the reading tasks (see Fig. 8.2 on the previous page). The degree of skill is classified according to complexity, range, speed, flexibility and independence, as follows.

Thus, tasks are said to require progressively more of candidates in terms of 'the complexity of information to be extracted from a text, the range of points to be handled from a text, the speed at which texts can be processed, the flexibility in matching reading style to task, and the degree of independence of the reader from support in terms of signposting and rubrics in the design of the task, and from the use of dictionaries for word meanings' (*ibid.* 1999:11).

Of these, complexity, range and independence seem to relate to linguistic features of the text, to the information conveyed by the language, and to the reader's growing linguistic ability. The only aspect which does not relate so directly to linguistic proficiency might be flexibility. Although reading style is not defined, it could be argued that part of reading development is seen as increased ability to deploy reading styles appropriately.

This need not amount to a claim that readers develop new styles as they progress, but simply that they are increasingly able to use them, possibly as a result of increasing language proficiency and thus independence from the language of the text. This seems a not unreasonable position and accords fully with the research we have discussed in earlier chapters as to the transfer of reading ability from first language to second language. In such a view, reading development in a foreign language is closely linked to the development of language proficiency, which would certainly justify to some extent what I have called the traditional view of reading reflected in the current CPE and the older version of FCE, namely that syntactic and lexical/semantic competence is an essential part of reading ability. CCSE takes a different view (or possibly, since this is not stated, is unconcerned to measure linguistic competence separately, since this will be engaged and thus measured, through direct measures of reading ability). This existence of two different views presents a wonderful opportunity to investigate the empirical implications of either approach.

In summary, CCSE is an interesting attempt to define what is meant by foreign-language reading development. The specifications in the Handbook show deliberate and considerable overlap across levels.

Unlike other systems, CCSE recognises that many text types will be accessed by readers at any level and therefore development is not characterised in terms of text that can be processed: what will differ is what readers can do with the text. However, CCSE also recognises that even 'low-level' readers will have to do things in the real world with text, and therefore it makes little attempt to order these by difficulty or in developmental terms.

CCSE seems to believe that differentiation will occur amongst developing readers in the degree to which they are able to deploy skills. These are couched less as cognitive skills and are more related to the linguistic information which is being processed and the speed with which it is processed. This definition of the construct seems intuitively to make sense for foreign-language readers, even if it is not explicitly tied into a theory of reading development. The sample tests themselves illustrate how the construct is operationalised, in a very user-friendly way.

As we have seen with the ACTFL Guidelines, however, research is needed to see whether the beliefs of test developers with respect to reading development are empirically justified. Given the overlap across levels in CCSE, the suite offers an exciting opportunity to put such beliefs to the test.

## Summary

It is possible to continue this presentation and analysis of reading tests, scales of reading performance and frameworks for the assessment of reading, at some length. Certainly there are many such tests and scales which I could have presented and which sometimes illustrate novel features. But this chapter must stop somewhere!

In this chapter, I have attempted to illustrate and discuss a range of issues that arise when examining operationalisations of the reading construct, and I hope that the chapter has provided sufficient exemplification to allow readers to consider either adopting one of these approaches, or developing a similar framework to suit their own purposes.

In addition, what this chapter illustrates, I believe, is the importance of being as specific as possible in one's claims of what does develop as readers progress, the necessity of avoiding vague terminology or overlapping levels, and the importance of the provision of sample tests or at least sample items that show how the concepts contained in the scales, the framework descriptions and the test specifications are actually operationalised.

Furthermore, I have emphasised the importance of empirical verification of one's view of progression. The research that has been conducted on the ACTFL Guidelines is to be commended for addressing this issue head-on. Of course, it raises very difficult matters, some of which are probably unresolvable because much of the difficulty of test items stems from the interaction of items with individual readers. However, this is not sufficient reason for not researching the claims that underly the tests, scales and frameworks we have looked at. It is my fervent hope that this chapter might stimulate test developers into investigating empirically their claims of development and progression, and reading researchers into using tests, scales and frameworks that already exist as a basis for further research into reading development.

CHAPTER NINE

......................................................................................................

# The way forward

## Assessing the interaction between reader and text: processes and strategies

This chapter will be more speculative in nature, and will explore how aspects of the reading process that have been recently considered to be important can be assessed. Language testing has traditionally been much more concerned with establishing the products of comprehension than with examining the processes. Even those approaches that have attempted to measure reading skills have in effect inferred a 'skill' from the relationship between a question or a task, and the text. Thus the 'skill' of understanding the main idea of a passage is inferred from a correct answer to a question which requires test-takers to identify the main idea of that passage. There is little experience, especially in large-scale testing, of assessing aspects of processes and strategies during those processes. I shall therefore have recourse to non-testing sources for ideas on how process might be assessed. In particular, I will look at how reading strategies have been taught or learned, how researchers have identified aspects of process through qualitative research techniques, and how scholars have explored the use of metalinguistic and metacognitive abilities and strategies.

In suggesting that we should look further afield than traditional testing and assessment practices in order to develop ways of assessing processes and strategies, this chapter inevitably leads into a discussion of directions in which assessment might develop in future, including the use of information technology.

## Process

In Chapters 1, 2 and 4 we have examined the nature of the reading process at some length and drawn conclusions relevant to an articulation of a construct of reading that incorporates a view of reading as a process. I have illustrated how test specifications, scales of reading ability and actual test items exemplify reading constructs, including skills and the reader's interaction with text. We have also seen the difficulty of separating considerations of readers and their ability from the nature of the text and the task associated with any reading activity or reading assessment. Inevitably, much of what has been illustrated reflects a view of the process as well as of the outcomes of that process.

This final chapter, however, builds upon earlier accounts of the reading process by looking particularly at what have been termed 'strategies' for reading, and speculates on future directions in reading assessment. But first a reminder of the problems of assessing 'process'.

We saw in Chapter 2 the difficulties associated with trying to isolate individual reading skills and the likelihood that these skills interact massively in any 'reading' or response to a question or task. Indeed, this is one of the reasons why the research into skills is so inconclusive. The test constructors have not established that their test questions do indeed tap the processes they are claimed to. We have already seen that some research shows that judges find it difficult to agree on what skills are being tested by reading items (Alderson, 1990b). Whilst there is other research (Bachman *et al.*, 1996) which shows that judges can be trained to identify item content using a suitably constructed rating instrument, it still does not follow that the processes the test-taker engages in reflect those that the reader–judge thinks will be engaged, or that s/he engages in as an expert reader.

Several studies have replicated the Alderson (1990b) study that showed the difficulty of testing individual skills in isolation. Allan (1992) conducted a series of studies aimed at investigating ways in which reading tests might be validated by gathering information on the reading process. One study asked judges to decide what a test item was measuring. His judges did not agree on the level of skill (higher or lower order), and only in 50% of the cases did they agree on the precise skill being tested. He concludes that using panels of judges is unlikely to produce reliable results and suggests that 'judges who are asked to comment upon what is likely to be measured by particular items shoud be supplied with think-aloud protocols from pilot trials of test prototypes'.

Li (1992) used introspective data to show, firstly, that subjects seldom reported using one skill alone in answering test questions, secondly that when the skills used corresponded to the test constructor's intentions, the students did not necessarily get the answer correct and, thirdly, that students answered correctly whilst using skills that the test constructor had not identified. He grouped his results into two types: predicted and unpredicted.

What he called 'predicted results' were (i) the expected skill (with or without other skills) leading to a correct answer; (ii) unexpected skills leading to a wrong answer. What he called 'unpredicted results' were (i) the expected skill (with or without other skills) leading to a wrong answer; and (ii) unexpected skills leading to a correct answer. He found as many predicted results as unpredicted.

Li concluded that the use of the assigned skill does not necessarily lead to success, and that several different skills, singly or in combination, may lead to successful completion of an item. Thus, items do not necessarily test what the constructor claims, individuals can show comprehension in a variety of (unpredicted) ways, and the use of the skill supposedly being tested may lead to the wrong answer. Yet again, this emphasises the difficulty of reliably tapping the reading process, at least as defined by the use of particular skills, through reading comprehension questions.

It may still be possible that reading items can be carefully designed to measure one or more claimed skill – for some readers. The problem occurs if some readers do not call upon that supposedly measured skill when responding. When analysing test or research results, the 'valid' or intended responses to items are added to the invalid or unintended responses. It is then not surprising if the analysis of such aggregation fails to show clearly that a skill is being tested separately. In other words, such items might be measuring the skill for some readers, but not for others and so would inevitably not load on a separate factor. Perhaps we need to rethink the way we design our data collection and aggregation procedures, in order to group responses together in ways that reflect how students have actually processed the items. Mislevy and Verhelst (1990) and Buck *et al.* (1996) have developed different methodologies for exploring this area, which would repay careful analysis (see Chapter 3).

However, this is only a problem for tests of reading if such tests are based on a multi-divisible view of reading, which they need not be. Indeed, most second-language reading tests do not depend upon multi-divisibility – whilst test developers may very well try to write items that aim to test some skills more than others or to get at different levels of understanding of text, it may not much matter whether they succeed if scores are not reported by subskill.

Usually reading test scores are reported globally, with no claim to being able to identify weaknesses or strengths in particular skills. It is only when we claim to have developed diagnostic tests that this dilemma becomes problematic. All that reading test developers need do is to state that every attempt has been made to include items that cover a range of skills and levels of understanding, in order to be as comprehensive in their coverage of the construct as possible. Given that much research shows that expert judges find it hard to agree on what skills are being tested by individual items, it would be hard to contradict or even to verify such claims anyway.

However, if we are interested in assessing the process of reading, and we have a multi-divisible view of that process, then we do appear to be faced with problems, if we want to be able to say that x reader shows an ability to process text appropriately, or has demonstrated y skills during the assessment process.

## Strategies

Recent approaches to the teaching of reading have emphasised the importance of students acquiring strategies for coping with texts. ESL reading research has long been interested in reader strategies: what they are, how they contribute to better reading, how they can be incorporated into instruction. These have been labelled and classified in various ways. Yet as Grabe (2000) shows clearly, the term is very ill-defined. He asks (*ibid.* 10–11) very pertinent questions: what exactly is the difference between a skill and a strategy? between a level of processing and a level of meaning? How are 'inferencing skills' different from 'strategies' like 'recognising mis-comprehension' or 'ability to extract and use information, to synthesize information, to infer information'? Is 'the ability to extract and use information' the same strategy (skill?) as 'the ability to synthesize information'? Grabe correctly identifies the need for terminological clarification and recategorisation.

Nevertheless, however confused the field, claims to teach strategies, skills, abilities remain pervasive and persuasive, and challenge those who would wish to test what is taught. Can tests measure strategies for reading?

This is a very difficult and interesting area. Interesting, because if we could identify strategies we might be able to develop good diagnostic tests, as well as conduct interesting research. Difficult, firstly, because, as pointed out above, we lack adequate definitions of strategies. Difficult, secondly, because the test-taking process may inhibit rather than encourage the use of some of the strategies identified: would all learners be willing to venture predictions of text content, for example? Difficult, thirdly, because testing is prescriptive: responses are typically judged correct or incorrect, or are rated on some scale. But it is very far from clear that one can be prescriptive about strategy use. Good readers are said to be flexible users of strategies. Is it reasonable to force readers into only using certain strategies on certain questions? Is it possible to ensure that only certain strategies have been used? We find ourselves back with the skills dilemma.

Buck (1991) attempted to measure prediction and comprehension monitoring in listening, and found that he was obliged to accept virtually any answer students gave that bore any relationship with the text (and some that did not). Items that can allow any reasonable response are typically very difficult to mark.

As I have said, the interest in strategies stems in part from an interest in characterising the process of reading rather than the product of reading. In part, however, it also stems from the literature on learning strategies more generally. I shall digress somewhat to deal with this latter area first, before looking at how reading strategies have been identified and 'taught'.

## Learner strategies

The 1970s and 1980s saw considerable interest in learner strategies in language learning: for a useful overview as well as a report of research studies, see Wenden and Rubin (1987).

Stern defines strategies as 'the conscious efforts learners make' and as 'purposeful activities' (in Wenden and Rubin, 1987:xi). However, Wenden points out that in the literature, 'strategies have been referred to as "techniques, tactics, potentially conscious plans, consciously employed operations, learning skills, basic skills, functional skills, cognitive abilities, language processing strategies, problem-solving procedures". These multiple designations point to the elusive nature of the term' (Wenden, 1987:7).

She distinguishes three different questions that strategy research has addressed: 'What do L2 learners do to learn a second language? How do they manage or self-direct these efforts? What do they know about which aspects of the L2 learning process?', and she thus classifies strategies as:

1 referring to language learning behaviours

2 referring to what learners know about the strategies they use

3 referring to what learners know about aspects of L2 learning other than the strategies they use.

Wenden lists six characteristics of the language-learning behaviours that she calls strategies:

1 Strategies refer to specific actions and techniques: i.e. are not characteristics of a general approach (e.g. 'risk-taker').

2 Some strategies will be observable, others will not ('making a mental comparison').

3 Strategies are problem-oriented.

4 Strategies contribute directly and indirectly to language learning.

5 Sometimes strategies may be consciously deployed, or they can become automatised and remain below the level of consciousness.

6 Strategies are behaviours that are amenable to change: i.e. unfamiliar ones can be learned.                    (Wenden, 1987:7–8)

In the same volume, Rubin classifies as strategies 'any set of operations, steps, plans, routines used by the learner to facilitate the obtaining, storage, retrieval and use of information' (1987:19). She distinguishes among:

- **cognitive learning strategies** (clarification/verification; guessing/inductive inferencing; deductive reasoning; practice; memorisation; and monitoring);

- **metacognitive learning strategies** (choosing, prioritisation, planning, advance preparation, selective attention and more);

- **communication strategies** (including circumlocution/paraphrase, formulae use, avoidance strategies and clarification strategies)
- **social strategies**                    (Rubin, 1987:20 passim)

These distinctions reflect a distinction frequently made between cognitive and metacognitive strategies (Brown and Palinscar, 1982). The latter involve thinking about the process, planning and monitoring of the process and self-evaluation after the activity (see below).

## Reading strategies

It will be clear that much of what are called language use or learning strategies are not directly relevant to the study of reading. Indeed, much of the strategy literature concentrates on oral interaction, listening and writing, and has much less insight to offer in the area of reading comprehension. Nevertheless, there are ways in which the categories of language-learning or language-use strategies developed in other areas might be relevant to an understanding of reading, whether or not they have been explicitly researched in the context of reading. For example, monitoring one's developing understanding of text, preparing in advance how to read and selectively attending to text are clearly relevant to reading. Paraphrasing what one has understood in order to see whether it fits into the meaning of the text, or deductively analysing the structure of a paragraph or article in order to clarify the author's intention might prove to be effective metacognitive strategies in order to overcome comprehension difficulties.

Much of the research into, and teaching of, reading strategies remains fairly crude, however, and frequently fails to distinguish between strategies as defined more generally in the strategy literature, and 'skills' as often used in the reading literature. One of the few examples in Wenden and Rubin (1987) of strategy research in reading is the work of Hosenfeld, who identifies contextual guessing as distinguishing successful from unsuccessful second-language readers. She also identifies a metacognitive strategy where readers evaluate the appropriateness of the logic of their guess. Rubin cites the following strategies identified in Hosenfeld's study of Cindy: How to be a Successful Contextual Guesser.

1 Keep the meaning of a passage in mind while reading and use it to predict meaning.

2 Skip unfamiliar words and guess their meaning from remaining words in a sentence or later sentences.

3 Circle back in the text to bring to mind previous context to decode an unfamiliar word.

4 Identify the grammatical function of an unfamiliar word before guessing its meaning.

6 Examine the illustration and use information contained in it in decoding.

7 Read the title and draw inferences from it.

8 Refer to the side gloss.

12 Recognize cognates.

13 Use knowledge of the world to decode an unfamiliar word.

14 Skip words that may add relatively little to total meaning.

(Hosenfeld, 1987:24)

The ability to infer the meaning of unknown words from text has long been recognised as an important skill in the reading literature. What Hosenfeld (1977, 1979, 1984) offers is a data-based gloss on components of this process as reported by young readers during think-alouds. It is unclear, however, why such a skill is now classified as a 'strategy'.

An example of this tendency to reclassify as strategies variables that have long been known to be important in reading is Thompson (1987). He examines briefly the role of memory in reading, and emphasises the important effects of background knowledge and the rhetorical structure of the text on processing. He reports (page 52) several studies of first-language readers, including Meyer et al. (1980) who describe good ninth-graders using the same overall structure of the text as the author in organising their recall whilst poor readers did not; Whaley (1981), who shows how good readers activate a schema before reading a story whilst poor readers did not; and Eamon (1978/9), who reports good readers recalling more topical information by evaluating it with respect to its relevance to the overall structure of the passage (see also Chapters 1 and 2). It should be noted, however, that this research was not couched in terms of reading strategies, but simply sought to characterise the differences between good and weaker readers in L1.

Claiming that no research has been done on L2 reading strategies,

Thompson nevertheless lists reading strategies, which he says can be taught in order to improve comprehension in L1, and which he implies can lead to efficient L2 reading. These are:

i    identifying text structure, via a flow-chart or a hierarchical summary;

ii   providing titles to texts before reading;

iii  using embedded headings as advanced organisers;

iv  pre-reading questions;

v    generation of story-specific schema from general problem-solving schema for short stories (questions readers ask themselves);

vi  use of visual imagery;

vii reading a story from the perspective of different people or participants.

Many of these activities we have seen in earlier chapters. Now they appear to be being presented as reading strategies. This underlines the need for greater clarity in deciding what are strategies and what are skills, abilities or other constructs. The language-learning literature cited above suggests that a distinguishing feature of strategies might be the degree of consciousness with which they are deployed.

## Characterisation of strategies in textbooks and by teachers

In my attempt to identify which aspects of which skills, processes or strategies might be measurable, or at least assessable, I now examine how various textbooks operationalise such constructs and turn them into exercises. Earlier approaches (Grellet, 1981; Nuttall, 1982) emphasised reading skills, which I have discussed at some length in earlier chapters. Here I mention them in order to show their similarity with more recent approaches. Grellet is not a handbook on reading, but a typology of exercises for the teaching of reading. Nevertheless, the book has been influential, and it is interesting to look at her use of the term 'strategy' and 'skill':

> We apply different reading strategies when looking at a notice board to see if there is an advertisement for a particular type of flat and when carefully reading an article of special interest in a scientific journal. Yet locating the relevant advertisement on the board and understanding the new information contained in the

article demonstrates that the reading purpose in each case has been successfully fulfilled. In the first case, a competent reader will quickly reject the irrelevant information and find what he is looking for. In the second case, it is not enough to understand the gist of the text; more detailed comprehension is necessary.

(Grellet, 1981:3)

Here Grellet seems to relate strategy to purpose for reading (although these are not identical) and locating information occurs as a result of a number of different processes, depending on the purpose. How strategies relate to rejecting irrelevant information, understanding gist and detailed information is not clear. Nor is the extent to which strategies are conscious or un/subconscious.

She distinguishes four 'ways' of reading: skimming, scanning, extensive and intensive reading, although she points out that these are not mutually exclusive. She makes frequent reference to Munby in her classification and labelling of reading skills (pp. 4–5). Her approach to reading as a process is clearly influenced by the work of Goodman and Smith, and she sees reading as a constant process of guessing: hypothesising, skimming, confirming guesses, further prediction and so on. She classifies the reading comprehension exercises she presents in Figure 9.1, overleaf. This division is reflected in the organisation of the book into four parts: techniques (which Grellet calls 'reading skills and strategies'), how the aim is conveyed, understanding meaning, and assessing the text.

Strategies, then, appear under 'skills' or 'techniques', although as Grellet points out, there is a certain amount of overlapping between these four parts. In short, we never really get a clear idea of what 'strategies' might be and how they might be different from what has traditionally been considered to be parts of reading ability.

What is valuable about Grellet, however, is the wealth of illustration of these techniques, skills or strategies. In practice, most of the illustrations could function not only as exercises, but as test items or assessment procedures, emphasising the point already made several times in this book that it is often difficult to make a clear distinction between a test item and an exercise. Thus for a source of ideas on what tests of particular skills or strategies might look like, Grellet is as useful a reference as many testing manuals.

To give three examples, deducing the meaning of unfamiliar lexical items (referred to above as both a skill and a strategy), scanning and predicting. Lexical inferencing is taught in Exercise 5 (Fig. 9.2):

| Reading techniques | How the aim is conveyed | Understanding meaning | Assessing the text |
| --- | --- | --- | --- |
| 1 SENSITIZING | 1 AIM AND FUNCTION OF THE TEXT | 1 NON-LINGUISTIC RESPONSE TO THE TEXT | 1 FACT VERSUS OPINION |
| 1 Inference: through the context / Inference: through word-formation | 1 Function of the text | 1 Ordering a sequence of pictures | 2 WRITER'S INTENTION |
| 2 Understanding relations within the sentence | 2 Functions within the text | 2 Comparing texts and pictures | |
| 3 Linking sentences and ideas: reference / Linking sentences and ideas: link-words | 2 ORGANIZATION OF THE TEXT: DIFFERENT THEMATIC PATTERNS | 3 Matching | |
| 2 IMPROVING READING SPEED | 1 Main idea and supporting details | 4 Using illustrations | |
| 3 FROM SKIMMING TO SCANNING | 2 Chronological sequence | 5 Completing a document | |
| 1 Predicting | 3 Descriptions | 6 Mapping it out | |
| 2 Previewing | 4 Analogy and contrast | 7 Using the information in the text | |
| 3 Anticipation | 5 Classification | 8 Jigsaw reading | |
| 4 Skimming | 6 Argumentative and logical organization | 2 LINGUISTIC RESPONSE TO THE TEXT | |
| 5 Scanning | 3 THEMATIZATION | 1 Reorganizing the information: reordering events / Reorganizing the information: using grids | |
| | | 2 Comparing several texts | |
| | | 3 Completing a document | |
| | | 4 Question-types | |
| | | 5 Study skills: summarizing / Study skills: note-taking | |

Fig. 9.1 Reading comprehension exercise-types (Grellet, 1981:12–13)

Exercise 5

*Specific aim:* To train the students to infer the meaning of unfamiliar words.

*Skills involved:* Deducing the meaning of unfamiliar lexical items through contextual clues.

*Why?* This kind of exercise (cloze exercise) will make the students realize how much the context can help them to find out the meaning of difficult or unfamiliar words.

Read the following paragraph and try to guess the meaning of the word '*zip*'.

*Zip* was stopped during the war and only after the war did it become popular. What a difference it has made to our lives. It keeps people at home much more. It has made the remote parts of the world more real to us. Photographs show a country, but only *zip* makes us feel that a foreign country is real. Also we can see scenes in the street, big occasions are *zipped*, such as the Coronation in 1953 and the Opening of Parliament. Perhaps the sufferers from *zip* are the notable people, who, as they step out of an aeroplane, have to face the battery of *zip* cameras and know that every movement, every gesture will be seen by millions of people. Politicians not only have to speak well, they now have to have what is called a '*zip* personality'. Perhaps we can sympathize when Members of Parliament say that they do not want debates to be *zipped*. (From *Britain in the Modern World* by E. N. Nash and A. M. Newth)

*zip* means ☐ cinema
☐ photography
☐ television
☐ telephone

Fig. 9.2 Exercise in lexical inferencing – deducing the meaning of unfamiliar words (Grellet, 1981:32)

Note that Exercise 7, has the same aim of teaching the ability to deduce the meaning of unknown words from context and is simply an every-eighth-word cloze test!

Exercise 7

*Specific aim:* ⎫ Same as for exercise 5 but this time about one word out of
*Skills involved:* ⎬ eight has been taken out of the text and must be deduced
*Why?* ⎭ by the students.

Read the following text and complete the blanks with the words which seem most appropriate to you.

## What is apartheid?

It is the policy of ........................ Africans inferior, and separate from Europeans. ........................ are to be kept separate by not being ........................ to live as citizens with rights in ........................ towns. They may go to European towns to ........................ , but they may not have their families ........................ ; they must live in 'Bantustans', the ........................ areas. They are not to ........................ with Europeans by ........................ in the same cafés, waiting-rooms, ........................ of trains, seats in parks. They are not to ........................ from the same beaches, go to the ........................ cinemas, play on the same game- ........................ or in the same teams.

Twelve per cent of the ........................ is left for the Africans to live and ........................ on, and this is mostly dry, ........................ , mountainous land. ........................ the Africans are three-quarters of the people. They are ........................ to go and work for the Europeans, not ........................ because their lands do not ........................ enough food to keep them, but also ........................ they must ........................ money to pay their taxes. Each adult ........................ man has

to pay £1 a year poll tax, and ten shillings a year ........................ for his hut. When they ........................ into Europeans areas to work ........................ are not allowed to do ........................ work; they are hewers of wood and drawers of water, and their ........................ is about one-seventh of what a European ........................ earn for the same ........................ of work.

If a European ........................ an African to do skilled work of the kind ........................ for Europeans, ........................ as carpentry, both the European and his ........................ employee may be fined £100. Any African who takes part in a strike may be ........................ £500, and/or sent to ........................ for three years.

(From *Britain in the Modern World*, by E. N. Nash and A. M. Newth)

Here are the answers as an indication:
keeping – they – allowed – European – work – there – native – mix – sitting – compartments – bathe – same – fields – land – farm – poor – yet – forced – only – grow – because – earn – African – tax – go – they – skilled – wage – would – kind – employs – reserved – such – African – fined – prison

Fig. 9.3 Exercise in lexical inferencing through a cloze task (Grellet, 1981:34)

Secondly, look at the following Exercise 3 as an example of an exercise teaching students reference skills – scanning.

Exercise 3

*Specific aim:*    To train students to use the text on the back cover of a book, the preface and the table of contents to get an idea of what the book is about.

*Skills involved:*  Reference skill.

| | |
|---|---|
| *Why?* | It is often important to be able to get a quick idea of what a book is about (e.g. when buying a book or choosing one in the library). Besides, glancing through the book, the text on the back cover, in the preface and in the table of contents gives the best idea of what is to be found in it. |

You have a few minutes to skim through a book called *The Rise of The Novel* by Ian Watt and you first read the few lines written on the back cover of the book, the table of contents and the beginning of the preface. What can you tell about the book after reading them? Can you answer the questions that follow?

1  For what kind of public was the book written?
2  The book is about

☐ reading                    ☐ eighteenth century
☐ novelists          in the  ☐ Middle Ages
☐ literature in general      ☐ nineteenth century

3  What major writers are considered in this book?
4  The main theory of the author is that the form of the first English novels resulted from:
   ☐ the position of women in society
   ☐ the social changes at that time
   ☐ the middle class

Fig. 9.4 Exercise in scanning (Grellet, 1981:60)

Finally, consider the anticipation Exercise 2 – a True–False test:

Exercise 2

*Specific aim:*  ⎫
*Skills involved:* ⎬ Same as for exercise 1 but a quiz is used instead of
*Why?*  ⎭ questions.

Decide whether the following statements are true or false.

a)  The first automatons date back to 1500.
b)  The French philosopher Descartes invented an automaton.
c)  The first speaking automatons were made around 1890.
d)  In the film *Star Wars* the most important characters are two robots.
e)  One miniature robot built in the United States can imitate most of the movements of an astronaut in a space capsule and is only twelve inches tall.
f)  Some schools have been using robot teachers for the past few years.
g)  One hospital uses a robot instead of a surgeon for minor operations.
h)  Some domestic robots for the home only cost £600.

i) A robot is used in Ireland to detect and disarm bombs.
j) Some soldiers-robots have already been used for war.

What is your score?

Fig. 9.5 Exercise in prediction (Grellet, 1981:62)

Of course the extent to which these exercises can be used as test items depends on the extent to which we can be prescriptive about correct or best answers, a point I have already made several times.

Silberstein (1994) is aimed at practising and student teachers of English as a Second Language, written by somebody who has considerable experience of writing textbooks for teaching second-language reading, and training reading teachers. The book has nothing to say about assessment, but many of the classroom techniques she proposes and illustrates could be adapted to assessment contexts. Those I shall discuss here, however, are techniques for teaching strategies where one might consider that no one correct answer exists, and therefore they present problems for assessment, as discussed above.

Prediction strategies are frequently held to be important for readers to learn, both to engage their background knowledge and to encourage learners to monitor their expectations as the text unfolds. Such strategies were particularly popular following the work of Smith and Goodman and the notion of reading as a psycholinguistic guessing game (see Chapter 1). One example Silberstein gives is as follows:

**The Changing Family**

Below is part of an article about the family [*LSA* 10(3)(Spring 1987)]. Read the article, stopping to respond to the questions that appear at several points throughout. Remember, you cannot always predict precisely what an author will do, but you can use knowledge of the text and your general knowledge to make good guesses. Work with your classmates on these items, defending your predictions with parts of the text. Do not worry about unfamiliar vocabulary.

# The Changing Family by Maris Vinovskis

1. Based on the title, what aspect of the family do you think this article will be about? List several possibilities.

Now read the opening paragraph to see what the focus of the article will be.

There is widespread fear among policymakers and the public today that the family is falling apart. Much of that worry stems from a basic misunderstanding of the nature of the family in the past and lack of appreciation for its strength in response to broad social and economic changes. The general view of the family is that it has been a stable and relatively unchanging institution through history and is only now undergoing changes; in fact, change has always been characteristic of it.

**The Family and Household in the Past**

2. This article seems to be about the changing nature of the family throughout history. Is this what you expected?

3. The introduction is not very specific, so you can only guess what changing aspects of the family will be mentioned in the next section. Using information from the introduction and your general knowledge, check (✓) those topics from the list below that you think will be mentioned:

_____ a. family size　　　　　　　　_____ f. the family throughout the world
_____ b. relations within the family　 _____ g. the economic role of the family
_____ c. the definition of a family　　_____ h. sex differences in family roles
_____ d. the role of family in society　_____ i. the role of children
_____ e. different family customs　　 _____ j. sexual relations

Now read the next section, noting which of your predictions is confirmed.

In the last twenty years, historians have been re-examining the nature of the family and have concluded that we must revise our notions of the family as an institution, as well as our assumptions about how children were perceived and treated in past centuries. A survey of diverse studies of the family in the West, particularly in seventeenth-, eighteenth-, and nineteenth-century England and America shows something of the changing role of the family in society and the evolution of our ideas of parenting and child development. (Although many definitions of *family* are available, in this article I will use it to refer to kin living under one roof.)

4. Which aspects of the family listed above were mentioned in this section?

_____

_____

5. Which other ones do you predict will be mentioned further on in the article?

_____

6. What aspects of the text and your general knowledge help you to create this prediction?

_____

_____

(ctd.)

7. Below is the topic sentence of the next paragraph. What kind of supporting data do you expect to find in the rest of the paragraph? How do you think the paragraph will continue?

_____

_____

_____

    Although we have tended to believe that in the past children grew up in "extended households" including grandparents, parents, and children, recent historical research has cast considerable doubt on the idea that as countries became increasingly urban and industrial, the Western family evolved from extended to nuclear (i.e., parents and children only).

The rest of the paragraph is reprinted below. Read on to see if your expectations are confirmed.

    Historians have found evidence that households in pre-industrial Western Europe were already nuclear and could not have been greatly transformed by economic changes. Rather than finding definite declines in household size, we find surprisingly small variations, which turn out to be a result of the presence or absence of servants, boarders, and lodgers, rather than relatives. In revising our nostalgic picture of children growing up in large families, Peter Laslett, one of the foremost analysts of the pre-industrial family, contends that most households in the past were actually quite small (mean household size was about 4.75). Of course, patterns may have varied somewhat from one area to another, but it seems unlikely that in the past few centuries many families in England or America had grandparents living with them.

8. Were your predictions confirmed?

9. Look again at the list of topics you saw in Question 3. Now *skim* the rest of the article; check (✓) the topics that the author actually discusses.

| | | | |
|---|---|---|---|
| ____ a. family size | | ____ f. the family throughout the world | |
| ____ b. relations within the family | | ____ g. the economic role of the family | |
| ____ c. the definition of a family | | ____ h. sex differences in family roles | |
| ____ d. the role of family in society | | ____ i. the role of children | |
| ____ e. different family customs | | ____ j. sexual relations | |

Activity from *Reader's Choice* (2nd ed., pp. 236–238) by E. M. Baudoin, E. S. Bober, M. A. Clarke, B. K. Dobson, and S. Silberstein, 1988, Ann Arbor, Mich.: University of Michigan Press. Reading passage from "The Changing Family" by Maris Vinovskis, 1987, *LSA*, 10 (3), Ann Arbor: The University of Michigan.

Fig. 9.6 Teaching prediction strategies (Baudoin *et al.*, 1988)

Note that whilst accurate predictions can be made only with hindsight, other predictions are reasonable in the light of the text up to the point where the prediction is made, and therefore it is virtually impossible to be prescriptive about correct answers. However, the teacher can encourage students to justify their predictions and should be able to make judgements, possibly on a pre-prepared scale, about the reasonableness of the prediction. The teacher can also rate students on the quality of their justifications. Thus the quality of prediction strategies can arguably be assessed, if not tested.

Critical reading is said to involve a number of strategies, which students might use to recognise the limitations on objectivity in writing. Thus, identifying the function of a piece of writing, recognising authors' presuppositions and assumptions, distinguishing fact from opinion, recognising an intended audience and point of view and evaluating a point of view are all important to critical reading, but often difficult to test objectively. Certainly, as we have seen in Munby's *Read and think* (see Chapter 7), there are ways in which multiple-choice options can be devised to trap students who make illegitimate inferences or evaluations, but often there is no one correct interpretation, especially in the case of elaborative inferences rather than bridging inferences. In such circumstances, teachers can again make judgements on the reasonableness of readers' opinions and interpretations and the way in which they argue for or against a point of view. One example of such an exercise is the following:

---

**Advertisement for Smokers' Rights**

## Smoking in Public: Live and Let Live

Ours is a big world, complex and full of many diverse people. People with many varying points of view are constantly running up against others who have differing opinions. Those of us who smoke are just one group of many. Recently, the activism of non-smokers has reminded us of the need to be considerate of others when we smoke in public.

But, please! Enough is enough! We would like to remind non-smokers that courtesy is a two-way street. If you politely request that someone not smoke you are more likely to receive a cooperative response than if you scowl fiercely and hurl insults. If you speak directly to someone, you are more likely to get what you want than if you complain to the management.

Many of us have been smoking for so long that we sometimes forget that others are not used to the aroma of burning tobacco. We're human, and like everyone else we occasionally offend unknowingly. But most of us are open to friendly suggestions and comments, and quite willing to modify our behavior to accommodate others.

Smokers are people, too. We laugh and cry. We have hopes, dreams, aspirations. We have children, and mothers, and pets. We eat our hamburgers with everything on them and salute the flag at Fourth of July picnics. We hope you'll remember that the next time a smoker lights up in public.

Just a friendly reminder from your local Smokers Rights Association.

From: *Reader's Choice* (2nd ed., p. 82) by E. M. Baudoin, E. S. Bober, M. A. Clarke, B. K. Dobson, and S. Silberstein, 1988, Ann Arbor, Mich.: University of Michigan Press.

---

(ctd.)

*Directions:* Below you will find portions of the editorial, followed by a list of statements. Put a check (√) next to each of the statements that reflects the underlying beliefs or point of view of the original text.

1. Ours is a big world, complex and full of many diverse people. People with many varying points of view are constantly running up against others who have differing opinions. Those of us who smoke are just one group of many.

_____ a. Smokers are simply another minority in the U.S., such as Greek Americans.
_____ b. Smoking can be thought of as a point of view rather than as a behavior.
_____ c. People should like smokers.
_____ d. Smokers are people, too.

2. We would like to remind nonsmokers that courtesy is a two-way street. If you politely request that someone not smoke, you are more likely to receive a cooperative response than if you scowl fiercely and hurl insults. If you speak directly to someone, you are more likely to get what you want than if you complain to the management.

_____ a. Nonsmokers have not been polite to smokers.
_____ b. Nonsmokers should not complain to the management.
_____ c. Smokers have been uncooperative.
_____ d. If nonsmokers were not so impolite, smokers would be more cooperative.

3. Smokers are people, too. We laugh and cry. We have hopes, dreams, aspirations. We have children, and mothers, and pets.... We hope you'll remember that the next time a smoker lights up in public.

_____ a. Smokers are not always treated like people.
_____ b. Nonsmokers should be nicer to smokers because they have mothers.
_____ c. We should remember smokers' mothers when they light up in public.
_____ d. Having a pet makes you a nice person.

**Evaluating a Point of View**
1. *Directions:* Check (√) all of the following that are assumptions of this passage.

_____ Secondary smoking (being near people who smoke) can kill you.
_____ A major reason smokers are uncooperative is that nonsmokers are not polite.
_____ Smokers are people, too.

2. Now look at the statements listed under Item 1 above. This time, check all those with which you agree.

**Class Discussion**
1. Do you agree with the presuppositions and point of view of this editorial?
2. Is this the same opinion you had before you read the text?
3. What do you think made the passage persuasive?
4. Unpersuasive?

Fig. 9.7 An exercise in critical reading (Baudoin *et al.*, 1988)

Note that some of the options do not have correct answers but are designed for debate. That does not mean, however, that teachers or students could not assess opinions for their reasonableness in relation to the text.

For a final example of how textbooks describe and exemplify the skills and strategies they are attempting to teach, let us look at some examples taken from a textbook aiming to teach Advanced Reading (Tomlinson and Ellis, 1988). Task 2 page 2 is intended to help readers identify the author's position and is, in effect, a multiple-choice test:

---

**Task 2**

> **This activity is designed to help you identify the general position which the writer takes up in the passage.**

Use the quotations below, taken from the passage, to decide which of the following best describes the position that the writer takes up on male/female language differences.

The writer's position is

☐ a  that research into male/female language differences supports our preconceptions about the differences
☐ b  that there are no real male/female language differences
☐ c  that male/female language differences are far greater than we might expect
☐ d  that the most important male/female language differences relate to the question of social control

1  'Because we think that language also *should* be divided into masculine and feminine we have become very skilled at ignoring anything that will not fit our preconceptions.'

2  'Of the many investigators who set out to find the stereotyped sex differences in language, few have had any positive results.'

3  'Research into sex differences and language may not be telling us much about language, but it is telling us a great deal about gender, and the way human beings strive to meet the expectations of the stereotype.'

4  'Although as a general rule many of the believed sex differences in language have not been found ... there is one area where this is an exception. It is the area of language and power.'

---

Fig. 9.8 Exercise in identifying author's position – multiple choice (Tomlinson and Ellis, 1988)

It is intended to be used as a preparation for reading the text. In a test, either the four quotations from the text or the text itself could be used.

Task 1 (Extensive reading) on the same text is often seen on tests of reading: matching headings to sections of text – this is claimed to teach (test) the strategy of identifying textual organisation:

---

**Extensive reading**

**Task 1**

> **The purpose of this activity is to encourage you to look at how the writer has organized the passage into sections.**

The passage can be divided into three main sections, each dealing with a separate issue. These issues are:

1 Myths about sex differences in language
2 Sex differences in language and power
3 Sex differences in language and learning

Skim through the passage and write down the line numbers where each section begins and ends.

---

(ctd.)

To do this activity you don't need to read every sentence in the passage. Before you start, discuss with your teacher what is the most effective way of reading to complete the task.

# Don't talk, listen!

'In mixed-sex classrooms, it is often extremely difficult for females to talk, and even more difficult for teachers to provide them with the opportunity'. Dale Spender looks at some myths about language and sex differences.

Ours is a society that tries to keep the world sharply divided into masculine and feminine, not because that is the way the world is, but because that is the way we believe it *should* be. It takes unwavering belief and considerable effort to keep this division. It also leads us to make some fairly foolish judgments, particularly about language.

Because we think that language also *should* be divided into masculine and feminine we have become very skilled at ignoring anything that will not fit our preconceptions. We would rather change what we hear than change our ideas about the gender division of the world. We will call assertive girls unfeminine, and supportive boys effeminate, and try to change them while still retaining our stereotypes of masculine and feminine talk.

This is why some research on sex differences and language has been so interesting. It is an illustration of how wrong we can be. Of the many investigators who set out to find the stereotyped sex differences in language, few have had any positive results. It seems that our images of serious taciturn male speakers and gossipy garrulous female speakers are just that: images.

Many myths associated with masculine and feminine talk have had to be discarded as more research has been undertaken. If females do use more trivial words than males, stop talking in mid-sentence, or talk about the same things over and over again, they do not do it when investigators are around.

None of these characteristics of female speech have been found. And even when sex differences have been found, the question arises as to whether the difference is in the eye—or ear—of the beholder, rather than in the language.

Pitch provides one example. We believe that males were meant to talk in low pitched voices and females in high pitched voices. We also believe that low pitch is more desirable. Well, it has been found that males tend to have lower pitched voices than females. But it has also been found that this difference cannot be explained by anatomy.

If males do not speak in high pitched voices, it is not usually because they are unable to do so. The reason is more likely to be that there are penalties. Males with high pitched voices are often the object of ridicule. But pitch is not an absolute, for what is considered the *right* pitch for males varies from country to country.

Some people have suggested that gender differentiation in America is more extreme than in Britain. This perhaps helps to explain why American males have deeper voices. (Although no study has been done, I would suspect that the voices of Australian males are even lower.) This makes it difficult to classify pitch as a sex difference.

It is also becoming increasingly difficult to classify low pitch as more desirable. It is less than 20 years since the *BBC Handbook* declared that females should not read the news, because their voices were unsuitable for serious topics.

(ctd.)

Presumably women's voices have been lowered in that 20 years, or high pitch is not as bad as it used to be.

Research into sex differences and language may not be telling us much about language, but it is telling us a great deal about gender, and the way human beings strive to meet the expectations of the stereotype. Although as a general rule many of the believed sex differences in language have not been found (and some of the differences which have been found by gender-blind investigators cannot be believed) there is one area where this is an exception. It is the area of language and power.

When it comes to power, some very interesting sex differences have been found. Although we may have been able to predict some of them, there are others which completely contradict our beliefs about masculine and feminine talk.

The first one, which was to be expected, is that females are more polite. Most people who are without power and find themselves in a vulnerable position are more polite. The shop assistant is more polite than the customer; the student is more polite than the teacher; the female is more polite than the male. But this has little to do with their sex, and a great deal to do with their position in society.

Females are required to be polite, and this puts the onus on them to accommodate male talk. This is where some of the research on sex differences in language has been surprising. Contrary to our beliefs, it has been found repeatedly that males talk more.

When it comes to husbands and wives, males not only use longer sentences, they use more of them. Phylis Chesler has also found that it is difficult for women to talk when men are present—particularly if the men are their husbands.

Although we might all be familiar with the sight of a group of women sitting silently listening to a male speaker, we have rarely encountered a group of men sitting quietly listening to a female speaker. Even a study of television panel programmes has revealed the way that males talk, and females accommodate male talk; men are the talkers, women the polite, supportive and encouraging listeners.

If females want to talk, they must talk to each other, for they have little opportunity to talk in the presence of men. Even when they do talk, they are likely to be interrupted. Studies by Don Zimmerman and Candace West have found that 98 per cent of interruptions in mixed sex talk were performed by males. The politeness of females ensures not only that they do not interrupt, but that they do not protest when males interrupt them.

The greater amount of man-talk and the greater frequency of interruptions is probably something that few of us are conscious of: we believe so strongly in the stereotype which insists that it is the other way around. However, it is not difficult to check this. It can be an interesting classroom exercise.

It was an exercise I set myself at a recent conference of teachers in London. From the beginning the men talked more because although there were eight official male speakers, there were no female ones. This was seen as a problem, so the organizing committee decided to exercise positive discrimination in favour of female speakers from the floor.

At the first session—with positive discrimination—there were 14 male speakers and nine female: at the second session there were 10 male speakers and four female. There was almost twice as much man talk as woman talk. However, what was interesting was the impression people were left with about talk. The stereotypes were still holding firm. Of the 30 people consulted after the sessions, 27 were of the opinion that there had been more female than male speakers.

(ctd.)

This helps to explain some of the contradictions behind sex differences in language. On the one hand we believe that females talk too much; on the other hand we have ample evidence that they do not talk as much as males. But the contradiction only remains when we use the same standard for both sexes; it disappears when we introduce a double standard, with one rule for females and another for males.

A talkative female is one who talks about as often as a man. When females are seen to talk about half as much as males they are judged to be dominating the talk. This is what happened at the conference. Although females were less than half of the speakers, most people thought they had dominated the talk.

This double standard was not confined to the general session; it was also present in the workshop on sexism and education. At the first workshop session there were 32 females and five males. When the tape was played afterwards, it was surprising to find that of the 58 minutes of talk 32 were taken up by males.

It was surprising because no one realized, myself included, just how much the males were talking. Most people were aware that the males had talked disproportionately but no one had even guessed at the extent. We all, male and female alike, use the double standard. Males have to talk almost all the time before they are seen to be dominating the talk.

There are numerous examples of the ways in which males can assume the right to talk in mixed-sex groups. Not only can they use their power to ensure that they talk more, but that they choose the topic. The polite female is always at a disadvantage.

It is not polite to be the centre of conversation and to talk a lot—if one is female. It is not polite to interrupt—if one is female. It is not polite to talk about things which interest you—if one is

female. It *is* polite to accommodate, to listen, to be supportive and encouraging to male speakers—if one is female.

So females are kept in their place. They enjoy less rights to talk. Because they have less power and because politeness is part of the repertoire of successful feminine behaviour, it is not even necessary to force females to be quiet. The penalties are so great if they break the rule, they will obligingly monitor themselves.

In the past few years, a lot of attention has been paid to the role of language and learning, but the assumption has been that the sexes have enjoyed equal rights to talk. Yet it is quite obvious that females do not have equal access to talk outside the classroom, so it would be surprising if this was reversed in the school.

However, if talking for learning is as important as Douglas Barnes maintains it is, then any teacher in a mixed-sex class who upholds the social rules for talk could well be practising educational discrimination. Such teachers would be allowing boys to engage in talk more frequently than girls.

In looking at talk, it becomes clear that there are differences in girls' single-sex and mixed-sex schools. In single-sex schools (providing, of course, that the teacher is female), females are not obliged to defer to male authority, to support male topics, to agree to interruptions, or to practise silence; or to make the tea while the males make the public speeches.

'Free speech' is available to females in a way which is not available in mixed-sex schools. This could be the explanation for the frequently claimed superior achievement of females in single-sex schools; free to use their language to learn, they learn more.

In mixed-sex classrooms it is often extremely difficult for females to talk, and even more difficult for teachers to provide them with the opportunity. This is not because teachers are supremely

(ctd.)

sexist beings, but because they are governed by the same social rules as everyone else.

It is appropriate for normal boys to demand more of the teachers' time, and they cannot always modify this situation. Male students in the classroom conform to expectations when they are boisterous, noisy and even disruptive; female students conform when they are quiet and docile; teachers conform when they see such behaviour as gender appropriate.

When questioned, some teachers have stated, in fairly hostile terms, that the girls in their classrooms talk all the time—to each other! This of course is a logical outcome under the present rules for talk: females do not get the same opportunity to talk when males are around. If females want to talk, they experience difficulties if they try to talk with males.

In visiting classrooms, I have often observed the teacher engaged in a class discussion with the boys, while the girls chat unobtrusively to one another. I have seen girls ignored for the whole lesson, while the teacher copes with the demands of the boys. I have heard boys praised for volunteering their answers, while girls have been rebuked for calling out.

Angela Parker has found that not only do males talk more in class, but that both sexes believe that 'intellectual argumentation' in the classroom is a masculine activity. If girls believe that it is unfeminine for them to speak up in class, they will probably take silence in preference to a loss of femininity—particularly during adolescence.

I asked a group of girls at an Inner London secondary school whether they thought it was unfeminine to speak up in class. They all agreed. The girls thought it natural that male students should ask questions, make protests, challenge the teacher and demand explanations. Females on the other hand should 'just get on with it'— even when they, too, thought the work was silly, or plain boring.

Although it is unlikely that teachers deliberately practise discrimination against their students on the grounds of sex, by enforcing the social rules for talk they are unwittingly penalizing females. But this situation is not inevitable. There is no physical reason, no sex difference, which is responsible for the relative silence of females. As John Stuart Mill stated, this asymmetry depends upon females willingly conceding the rights to males.

Perhaps teachers can help females to be a little less willing to be silent in mixed-sex classrooms. Perhaps they can help females to enjoy the same rights to talk as males. But we would have to change our stereotypes.

## Task 2

> The aim of this activity is to help you identify the theme and purpose of the passage.

Answer these questions in groups. Make sure that you are able to justify your answers.

1   Which of the following would make the best title for the passage?

☐   a   How men discriminate against women in talk
☐   b   Changing our stereotypes of males and females
☐   c   Recent research into sex differences in language
☐   d   Sex inequalities in classroom talk

Fig. 9.9 Exercise in identifying textual organization (Tomlinson and Ellis, 1988)

The Teacher's Guide advises teachers to 'discuss the kinds of strategies needed to skim effectively: for an example, reading the first and last lines of each paragraph to identify the topics dealt with' (page 117). Other 'strategies' are not given.

This and the first example raise the crucial question: to what extent does either example teach the strategy in question? Firstly, of course, readers can get the answer correct for the wrong reason. Secondly, however, in Figure 9.9 readers may *not* use the strategy exemplified in the Teacher's Guide and yet be perfectly capable of getting the correct answer. How has the exercise/item taught or tested a strategy?

One interesting feature of the book is that for each exercise an indication is given of what is being taught/learned/practised, as follows:

1 In this activity you will practise scanning the information in the text in order to find specific information. (p. 44)

2 The purpose of this activity is to encourage you to look at how the passage has been organized into sections. (p. 45)

3 The aim of this activity is to help you to consider who the intended audience of the passage is. (p. 45)

4 In this activity you will consider the attitude which the writer takes to the content of the article. (p. 51)

5 In this activity you will consider your own response to both the content of the text and also the way that it is written. (p. 52)

6 This activity is designed to help you explore the characters in the extract and the techniques of characterization used by the author. (p. 56)

and so on. In so far as these rubrics are intended to help students reflect on what they are learning and to be conscious of how they are doing what they are expected to do, this could be argued to be metacognitive in nature, by raising awareness of what the cognitive processes in reading are. However, the exercises are essentially intended to draw attention to features of the text or the intended outcomes and do not explicitly offer advice on the process of getting to those outcomes.

Nevertheless, it is interesting to examine how they achieve what they claim to achieve: the item types used would not look out of place in a test of reading. For the scanning activity (Activity 1 above), readers are asked to read quickly through the text and put a tick against each sentence that is true according to the text.

For Activity 2, students are asked to write the numbers of the lines where each section of the text starts and ends, readers having been told that there are three main sections and having been given the topic of each section.

Activity 3 is a multiple-choice item:

> Who do you think this passage was written for?
> a the educated general reader
> b trained scientists
> c trained linguists
> d students studying linguistics

Students are asked to make a list of clues used to arrive at the answer.

Somewhat less test-like, although still usable in an assessment procedure where justifications would be sought, is the following exercise for Activity 4:

> What is the writer's attitude to the parrot experiment in the passage? Describe his attitude by ringing the appropriate number on each of the scales below.
>
> The writer's attitude to the parrot experiment can be described as:

| | | | | | | |
|---|---|---|---|---|---|---|
| sceptical | 1 | 2 | 3 | 4 | 5 | convinced |
| dismissive | 1 | 2 | 3 | 4 | 5 | supportive |
| bored | 1 | 2 | 3 | 4 | 5 | interested |
| frivolous | 1 | 2 | 3 | 4 | 5 | serious |
| biased | 1 | 2 | 3 | 4 | 5 | objective |
| critical | 1 | 2 | 3 | 4 | 5 | uncritical |

Even Activity 5, requiring personal response, could be evaluated for greater or lesser acceptability, although, of course, the student's ability to write, to justify responses and interpretations and so on, is also being assessed by items like this: *'Why is it important to demonstrate that the parrot is capable of "segmentation" (Paragraph 5)? Do you think that the parrot experiment has demonstrated that Alex is capable of segmentation?'*

Finally, Activity 6 includes the following two tasks. The Teacher's Guide gives detailed answers to each of these tasks, suggesting that even such apparently open-ended items can be assessed fairly objectively.

> 1 Use the list of adjectives below to describe the characters in the following table:

| Bigwig | Hazel | Fiver | Chief Rabbit |
|--------|-------|-------|--------------|
| ........ | ........ | ........ | ........ |
| ........ | ........ | ........ | ........ |
| ........ | ........ | ........ | ........ |
| neurotic | trusting | dutiful | confident |
| superior | forgetful | sensible | clairvoyant |

2  Find evidence from the passage to support each of the following statements.

   a  Fiver is not respected much by the other rabbits

   b  Hazel is respected by the other rabbits

   c  The Chief Rabbit is getting out of touch with the affairs of the warren

   d  The Chief Rabbit doesn't like being disturbed

   e  Bigwig is a little frightened of the Chief Rabbit

   f  Hazel has complete confidence in his brother

The authors emphasise that there may be more than one plausible answer to many tasks, but nevertheless provide answers to the tasks in the back of the book, for the teacher's benefit. They frequently stress that other answers may be acceptable as well, but this nevertheless implies that criteria for judging acceptability exist, and that the teacher, or peer students, are capable of making such judgements. Thus, once again, whilst some of the techniques used may not lend themselves to objective marking, it is assumed that acceptability of responses can be judged and therefore such exercises could indeed be used in test and assessment procedures, provided an acceptable degree of agreement can be reached amongst markers. How practical it would be to use such exercises as assessment procedures is a separate issue.

As we have discussed in Chapter 7, a major limitation on what can be tested or assessed is the method used for the assessment. If objectively scorable methods must be used, then greater ingenuity needs to be employed to devise non-trivial questions that assess such abilities as Activities 5 and 6 above. However, if resources allow non-objective scoring to be used, then the possibilities for assessing skills such as those listed above increase. Tomlinson and Ellis and the authors cited in Silberstein have managed to devise tasks as exercises which I claim can equally well be used as test items, provided that reliability and validity can be demonstrated. Of course, the need to ensure that unexpected answers are judged consistently remains, but this is true of any open-ended item and does not of itself invalidate the use of such techniques in assessment.

## Strategies during test-taking

Testers have recently attempted to investigate what strategies might be being used by students when answering traditional test items. Allan (1992) used introspections gathered in a language laboratory to investigate strategies used to answer multiple-choice questions on a TOEFL reading test and concluded that students did indeed tend to use predicted strategies on multiple-choice items, but not on free-response items (whether or not they got the item correct). Thus multiple-choice questions (mcq) might be thought to be more appropriate if specific strategies are to be tested. However, mcq items engaged strategies which focused more on the stem and alternatives, whereas free-response strategies centred more on the test passage and the students' knowledge of the topic. In addition, mcq items engaged test-wiseness strategies.

Allan concluded from the introspections that certain categories of questions engage a narrow range of strategies: a) identifying the main idea and b) identifying a supporting idea. On the other hand, 'two different categories of question engage a wider range of reading strategies: a) ability to draw an inference and b) ability to use supporting information presented in different parts of the passage'. He states: 'test designers cannot make a strong case that a) their questions are likely to engage predicted strategies in readers or that b) using the predicted strategies will normally lead to the correct answer'.

A further study by Allan examined the strategies reported by students taking a gap-filling test, and discovered that it was common for answers to be supplied with reference only to the immediate context. Allan (1992) claimed that the gap-filling format 'appears to shift the students' focus from reading and understanding the main ideas of the text to puzzle-solving tactics which might help to fill in the blanks'.

Storey (1994, 1997) confirmed the finding that even in 'discourse cloze' (a gap-filling test where elements carrying discourse meaning rather than phrase- or clause-bound meaning are deleted), test-takers tended to confine themselves to sentence-level information in order to fill blanks and did not tend to go beyond the sentence, despite the test constructor's intention. Indeed, Storey argues that the use of introspective procedures is essential to test validation, since 'it can reveal aspects of test items which other techniques cannot, provide guidelines for the improvement of items and throw light on the construct validity of the test by examining the processes underlying test-taking behaviour' (Storey, 1994:2).

Although language-testing researchers are increasingly using qualitative research methods to gain insights into the processes that test-takers engage in when responding to test items, this is not the same as trying to model processes of reading in the design of assessment procedures, which I shall attempt to address in the next section.

## Insights into process: methods for eliciting or assessing?

All too many assessment procedures are affected by the use of test methods suitable for high-stakes, large-volume, summative assessment – the ubiquitous use of the multiple-choice test, for example. Yet such methods may be entirely inappropriate for the diagnosis of reading strengths and difficulties and for gaining insights into the reading process, although we have already seen a possible exception in the work of Munby in *Read and think* (above and Chapter 7).

I have discussed how exercises intended to teach reading strategies might offer insights into how strategies might be assessed. I shall now turn to other sources for ideas on what methods might be used to gain insights into readers' processes and to facilitate their assessment. In particular, qualitative research methods and other methods used by reading researchers might offer promise for novel insights.

As we shall see, such procedures cannot be used in large-scale testing, or in any setting where the test results are high stakes, since it is relatively easy to cheat. However, if the purpose of the testing or assessment is to gain insight into readers' processes, or to diagnose problems that readers might be having in their reading, then such procedures appear to hold promise. Indeed, diagnostic testing in general would benefit greatly from considering the sorts of research procedures used by reading researchers in experimental settings.

Furthermore, the availability of cheap microprocessing power makes the use of computers even more attractive as a means of keeping track of a reader's process, as we shall see in the penultimate section of this chapter.

## Introspection

Introspective techniques have been increasingly used in reading research, both in the first language and in second- and foreign-language reading, as a means of gaining insight into the reading process.
We have also seen in the previous section how introspections can be very useful for giving insights into strategy use in answering traditional test items, and thus may be potentially useful for the validation of tests of processes and strategies. Might such techniques also lend themselves to use for assessment purposes?

Cohen, in Wenden and Rubin (1987), describes how learners' reports of their insights about the strategies they use can be gathered. He points out that the data is necessarily limited to those strategies of which learners can become consciously aware. He distinguishes self-report ('What I generally do') from self-observation ('What I am doing right now or what I have just done') from self-revelation (think-aloud, stream-of-consciousness data, unedited, unanalysed). In a more recent overview article, Cohen (1996) suggests ways in which verbal reports can be fine-tuned to provide more insightful and valid data. Issues addressed include the immediacy of the verbal reporting, the respondent's role in interpreting the data, prompting for specifics in verbal report, guidance in verbal reporting and the reactive effects of verbal reporting.

Data can be collected in class or elsewhere, in a language laboratory, for example, as Allan (1992) did. Readers may introspect alone, in a group or in an interview setting, and the degree of recency of the event being introspected upon to the process of introspection is obviously an important variable.

Introspection can take place orally or in writing, and can be open-ended or in response to a checklist (see below for a discussion of the value of such closed items). And the degree of external intervention will vary from none, as in learner diaries, to minimal as in the case of an interviewer prompting 'What are you thinking?' in periods of silence during a think-aloud session, to high, as in the case of introspective or self-report questionnaires, for example.

The amount of training required is an issue, and most research shows that short training sessions are essential for the elicitation of useful data. Cavalcanti (1983), for example, found that if left alone to introspect, informants would read aloud chunks of text and then retrospect, and she had to train them to think aloud when they noticed that a pause in their reporting had occurred.

The need for such training suggests that not all informants can introspect usefully, which makes this perhaps a limited technique for use in assessment procedures where comparisons of individuals or groups are required outcomes. In diagnostic testing, however, such outcomes may not be needed.

Allan (1992, 1995) discovered that many students were not highly verbal and found it difficult to report their thought processes. To overcome this, he attempted to use a checklist of predicted skills or strategies, but found that a) the categories were unclear to students, and b) that using the checklist risked skewing responses to those the checklist writer had thought of. He attempted a replication of Nevo's (1989) use of a checklist of strategies, but with an interesting variation. He developed two checklists, one with 15 strategies and a category 'Other' for any strategy not contained on the list. The second checklist deleted the strategy which had been most frequently reported on the first checklist, thus leaving 14 strategies and the 'Other' category. If the checklist was valid, he argued, the most frequently reported strategy in Checklist 1 ought to appear frequently under 'Other' in checklist 2. It did not! He thus questions the validity of checklists. Although he feels that checklists may be useful, he advocates careful construction and piloting.

One interesting way of getting information from students on their reading process is reported by Gibson. He asked his Japanese students, reading English as a Foreign Language, to complete a cloze test in a language laboratory. 'On hearing a bleep through their headphones (the bleeps were more or less at random as I had no way to predict the speed with which informants would work through the passage) they had to circle J or E on their paper to indicate whether they were thinking in Japanese or English at that moment. Some circled E quite consistently, but it later became clear that they had not been distinguishing between sounding out the English text in their heads and actually thinking about the cloze deletions. About 40% of the total choices of J or E were left unmade, which doesn't inspire much confidence in informants' ability to judge which language they're working in at any given time' (personal communication).

Although such methods were not used to assess a reader's process, it is not inconceivable that they could be. For example, they might be used to elicit specific information about the process by being linked, for example, to a tracking of eye movements, so that a think-aloud might be prompted when a particular part of the text had been reached.

A less hi-tec version of such a technique is reported by Cavalcanti (1983) where readers were asked to report what they were thinking when they saw a particular symbol in the text. Such techniques would allow detailed exploration of processing problems associated with particular features of text and the strategies that readers use to overcome such problems.

## Interviews and talk-back

Harri-Augstein and Thomas (1984) report on the use of a 'reading recorder', flowcharts and talk-back sessions, in order to gain insight into how students are reading text. They describe the Reading Recorder, which is a piece of equipment which keeps track of where in a text a reader actually is at any point in time. The record of this reading – the reading record – can then be laid over the text and related to a flow diagram of the structure of the text, so that places where readers slowed down, back-tracked, skipped and so on can be related to the information in and organisation of the text they were reading. Finally, readers are interviewed about their reading record, to explore their own accounts of their reasons for their progression through the text. This stimulated recall often results in useful information about what the reader was thinking at various points in time. What they call 'the conversational paradigm' is aimed at

> . . . enabling readers to arrive at personal descriptions of their reading process, so that they can reflect upon and develop their competence. Such descriptions include:
>
> 1 Comments on how learners map meaning onto the words on a page;
> 2 Terms expressing personally relevant criteria for assessing comprehension;
> 3 Personally acceptable explanations of how learners invent, review and change meaning until a satisfactory outcome is achieved. (Harri-Augstein and Thomas, 1984:253)

The description of the process takes place at various levels of text – word, sentence, paragraph, chapter. The reading records show essentially how time was spent, revealing changes in pace, hesitations, skipping, backtracking, searching and note-making. A number of basic patterns are shown (smooth read, item read, search read, think session and check read) which combine to produce reading strategies of greater or lesser effectiveness. When mapped onto an analysis of the text, then questions can be answered, or at least explored, like:

- What was in the first 50 lines that made the reader pause after reading them?
- Why were lines 60–67 so difficult to read?
- Why did the reader go back to line 70 after line 120?
- Why was it so easy then to read from line 120 to the end?

Conversational investigations may show that the first 50 lines contained an introduction, the next 20 explained the author's intentions in detail, referring to previous research, and so on. It is also possible to relate reading strategies captured in this way to reading outcomes, and to show how on given texts or text types certain strategies may lead, for individual readers, to certain sorts of outcome. As learners explore their process of reading by relating their behaviour to the text and reconstruct the original reading experience, 'an evaluative assessment leads to a review of the reader/learner's purpose, strategy and outcome' (*ibid.*:265).

Latterly, more sophisticated equipment, computer-controlled, linked to eye-movement photography, has enabled the capture of much fine-grained detail of behaviour, which can be combined with records of latencies and analyses of text to provide useful diagnostic information on readers' processes (see below on computer-based testing and assessment).

### Classroom conversations

We have already seen in Chapter 7 the use of reading conferences as informal assessment procedures. The simple conversation between an assessor – usually the teacher – and a reader, or readers in a group, can be used in class, but not in large-scale testing situations. In such conversations, readers can be asked about what texts they have read, how they liked them, what the main ideas of the texts were, what difficulties they have experienced, and what they have found relatively unproblematic, how long it has taken them to read, why they have chosen the texts they have, whether they would read them again, and so on. Obviously the questions would have to be selected and worded according to the aim of the assessment. Some might be geared to gaining a sense of how much reading learners did, or what sort of reading they most enjoyed or found most difficult, challenging and so on. Questions might remain at a fairly general level if what was being attempted was more of a survey of reading habits, or they might be more detailed and focused on particular texts or part of texts, if information was needed on whether readers had understood particular sections or had used particular strategies to overcome difficulties.

The wording of the questions would need to be checked for comprehensibility and for their ability to elicit the information required, but the advantage of this sort of conversation about reading is that it allows the investigator or assessor to experience when the informant has not understood the question, or misunderstood it, and to reformulate or devise some other way of eliciting the same information.

How can such conversations be used to assess or to gain insight into processes and strategies? One way, as has already been hinted at, is to accompany the conversation with some record of the reading being discussed: a video- or audio-tape, a reading record or even a text with reader notes in the margin (Schmidt and Vann, 1992). Then recall of processes and strategies could be stimulated on the basis of the record. Where readers show evidence of experiencing difficulty or misunderstanding, for example, they can be asked:

- What was the nature of the difficulty?
- Why did you not understand?
- What *did* you understand?
- Did you notice that you had not understood or had misunderstood?
- How did you notice this?
- What did you do (could you have done) about this misunderstanding?

In the process of such exploratory, relatively open-ended conversations, it is entirely plausible that unexpected responses and insights will emerge, which is much less likely with more structured and closed techniques.

Garner *et al.* (1983) discuss a 'tutor' method for externalising the mental processes of test-takers. They ask readers to assume teaching roles, i.e. to tutor younger readers, and assume that the tutor will have to externalise the process of answering questions to help the younger reader. (Their aim was to study externalised processes, not teaching outcomes.)

Both weak and successful 6th grade readers were selected to tutor 4th grade readers. The focus was on the tutors helping the younger readers to answer comprehension questions on a text whose topic was expected to be unfamiliar to either. Good and poor comprehenders were distinguished by the number of look-backs they encouraged their tutees to engage in. Good comprehenders were also better at differentiating their tutees' use of text to answer text-based questions from questions that were reader-based – i.e. required the reader to answer from his or her own experience or knowledge. Similarly, good comprehenders encouraged more sampling of text than simply re-reading it from start to finish. Good comprehenders demonstrated awareness of why, when and where look-backs should be used. Poor comprehenders did not. Good comprehenders demonstrated a sophis-ticated look-back strategy. This tutor method would appear to hold considerable promise for insights into strategy use and metacognition.

## Immediate-recall protocols

Also in Chapter 7, we saw the use of free recall, or immediate recall, as a method of assessing understanding, and I reported Bernhardt's belief that such protocols can be used for insight into reading processes. Basing her analysis on a model – not dissimilar to the framework presented in this book – of text and reader (what she calls 'knowledge') factors, Bernhardt (1991:120ff) identifies three text-based factors and three knowledge-based factors that influence the reading process. These are: word recognition, phonemic/graphemic decoding and syn-tactic feature recognition, for the former, and intratextual perception, metacognition and prior knowledge, for the latter. She collected data on students' understanding of texts in German and Spanish by getting them to recall the texts immediately after reading, and she then ana-lysed the protocols to show these factors at work (*ibid.* 123–168).

A lack of prior knowledge about standard formats for business letters is shown to lead to misinterpretations about who is writing to whom. Parenthetical comments in the protocols show readers using metacognition to struggle to make sense of the text. Once they start an interpretation, however, they tend to adhere to that interpretation and ignore important textual features.

Problems with syntax impede comprehension, and attempts to parse sentences in order to fit ongoing interpretations lead to meanings rather remote from the author's original meaning. Even minor syntactic errors (misinterpreting singular nouns as plurals, for example) lead to misinterpretations. Ambiguous vocabulary often affected readers' comprehension, but even phonemic and graphemic features, like the similarity between 'gesprochen' and 'versprochen', 'sterben' and 'streben', led to unmonitored misinterpretations. The lack of prior knowledge was found to be a problem, but interestingly the existence of relevant prior knowledge also led to misinterpretations, as readers let their prior perceptions influence their interpretation, despite relevant textual features.

Bernhardt is, however, at pains to point out that no single factor in the model can accurately account for the reader's overall comprehension. Rather, comprehension is characterised by a complex set of interacting processes as the reader tries to make sense of the text. 'Although certain elements in the reading process seem to interact more vigorously at certain times than others, all of them contribute to the reader's evolving perception of texts' (Bernhardt, 1991:162).

In addition to showing how an analysis of immediate-recall protocols can yield useful insights into how readers are interpreting and misinterpreting texts, Bernhardt argues that the information so yielded can be used for instructional purposes as well: in other words, analysis of immediate-recall protocols can serve diagnostic and formative assessment ends. Bernhardt suggests that teachers can use student-generated data – through the recall protocol – for later lessons that can address cultural, conceptual and grammatical features that seem to have interfered with understanding. She proposes that a practical way of doing this is for one student to be asked to read his/her recall and then other students could participate in the analysis and discussion. Berkemeyer (1989) also illustrates the diagnostic use of such protocols.

The rather obvious limitation from the point of view of much large-scale or even classroom assessment is that such techniques are time-consuming to apply. A similar criticism applies to a method that used to be popular, but is now less so: miscue analysis.

## Miscue analysis

Miscues are experienced when, in reading aloud, the observed response is different from the expected response, that is the actual word or words on the page (Wallace, 1992). Researchers in the 1970s made frequent use of so-called miscue analysis, elicited through reading-aloud tasks, in order both to study the reading process and to assess young first-language readers. Some researchers have also applied this technique to second-language readers (see Rigg, 1977).

Goodman advocates the analysis of miscues, including omissions, as windows on the reading process, as a tool in analysing and diagnosing how readers make sense of what they struggle to read (see Goodman, 1969; Goodman and Burke, 1972; Goodman, 1973).

Miscues include omissions of words from text. Goodman and Gollasch (1980) present an account of the reasons why readers omit words from text during their readings-aloud. They argue that omissions are integral to the reader's quest for meaning, and when meaning is disrupted, omissions are as likely to result from loss of comprehension as to create it. Non-deliberate omissions may show the reader's strengths in constructing meaning from text. Some are transformations of text, revealing linguistic proficiency, others show a recognition of redundancy, since their omission has little impact on meaning, whereas others occur at points where the information presented in the word omitted is unexpected and unpredictable. Some may arise from dialect or first-language differences from the language of the text, and others may be seen as part of a strategy of avoiding the risk of being wrong.

One of the obvious problems with miscue analysis is that the recording and analysis of the miscues, involving detailed comparison of observed responses with expected responses, is time-consuming. Typically, articles reporting miscue analyses deal with only one or two subjects and present results in considerable detail. Such analyses are unlikely to be practical for classroom assessment purposes, although Davies claims that miscue analysis is widely used in first- and second-language reading classes, and she presents examples of how the miscues might be recorded and analysed (Davies, 1995:13–20).

In addition, the analysis is necessarily subjective. Although detailed manuals were published to guide and train teachers in miscue analysis (see, for example, Goodman and Burke, 1972), ultimately the reasons adduced by the analyst/teacher for the miscues are speculative and often uninformative. Miscues are analysed for their graphemic, phonemic, morphological, syntactic and semantic similarity with expected responses, but why such responses were produced is a matter of inference or guesswork. Readers may indeed have mistaken one word for another, perhaps because they were anticipating one interpretation when the text took an unexpected turn. However, such wrong predictions are a normal part of reading and do not reveal much about an individual's strategies without further information or conversation.

Because miscues focus on word-level information, much information relevant to an understanding of reading remains unexplored, such as text organisation, the developing inferences that readers are making, the monitoring and evaluating that they are making of their reading and so on. In fact, miscue analysis seems limited to early readers in its usefulness and is less useful for enabling a full characterisation and diagnosis of the reading process. And of course the whole procedure is based upon oral reading, where readers may not be reading for comprehension but performance. Silent reading is likely to result in quite different processes.

## Self-assessment

Self-assessment is increasingly seen as a useful source of information on learner abilities and processes. Metastudies of self-assessment in a foreign-language context (Ross, 1998) show correlations of the order of .7 and more between a self-assessment of foreign-language ability and a test of that ability. We have already seen the use of self-assessment in Can-Do statements to get learners' views of their abilities in reading. For example, the DIALANG project referred to in Chapter 4 uses self-assessment tools for placement and comparison purposes.

The same DIALANG self-assessment tools also contain statements which could be argued to be attempting to gather information about learners' reading strategies. Thus

> Level A1  I can understand very short, simple texts, putting to-
> gether familar names, words and basic phrases, by, for
> example, re-reading parts of the text.
> Level B1  I can identify the main conclusions in clearly written ar-
> gumentative texts.

and:

> Level B1  I can recognise the general line of argument in a text but not necessarily in detail.
>
> Level B2  I can read many kinds of texts quite easily, reading different types of text at different speeds and in different ways according to my purpose in reading and the type of text.
>
> Level C1  I can understand in detail a wide range of long, complex texts of different types provided I can re-read difficult sections.

One can envisage self-assessment statements being written, based on a taxonomy of reading strategies, which could offer considerable potential for research into the relationship between self-assessed abilities and measured ability. These would be useful even if it proved impossible to devise tests of strategies, since self-assessed strategy use could be related to specific test performance, especially if the self-assessment addressed not only traits (i.e. statements about general states of affairs or abilities), but also states (i.e. the process which the informant had just undergone when taking a test of reading). Such self-assessments might be very useful tools for the validation of reading tests by allowing us to explore the relationship between what items are intended to test, and the processes which candidates reported they had undergone. (They would, of course, ideally be accompanied and triangulated by other sources of data on process, especially introspective data.) Indeed, Purpura (1997) and Alderson and Banerjee (1999) have devised self-assessment inventories of language learning and language use strategies, including measures of reading, for use in examining the relationship between test-taker characteristics and test-taker performance.

## Miscellaneous methods used by researchers

Chang (1983) divides methods used to study reading into two: simultaneous and successive. Simultaneous methods examine the process of encoding; successive methods look at memory effects and the coded representation. He further distinguishes between obtrusive methods, which might be held to distort what they measure, and unobtrusive measures, whose results might be more difficult to interpret. He presents a useful table (Fig. 9.10 below) of different methods in this two-way categorization (e.g. probe reaction times; shadowing over headphones whilst reading; eye–voice span; recall, recognition, question answering; electromyography; eye movements; reading time and so on.

| | Disruption to Reading | | | |
|---|---|---|---|---|
| Time of Measurement | Obtrusive | | Unobtrusive | |
| | Technique | Issue | Technique | Issue |
| simultaneous | probe RT (Britton et al., 1978) | cognitive capacity | electromyography (Hardyck & Petronovich, 1970) | subvocalization |
| | shadowing (Kleiman, 1975) | phonological code | ERPs (Kutas & Hillyard, 1980) | context |
| | eye-voice span (Levin & Kaplan, 1970) | syntactic structure | eye movements (Rayner, 1975) | perceptual span |
| | search (Krueger, 1970) | familiarity of letter springs | reading time (Aaronson & Scarborough, 1976) | instructions |
| successive | recall (Thorndyke, 1977) | story structure | transfer (Rothkopf & Coatney, 1974) | text difficulty |
| | RSVP (Forster, 1970) | underlying clausal structure | | |
| | recognition (Sachs, 1974) | exact wording vs. meaning | | |
| | question answering (Rothkopf, 1966) | adjunct questions | | |

Fig. 9.10 Methods used to study reading (Chang, 1983:218)

## Encoding time

We have seen (Chapter 2) that some models of reading assume that the allocation of attention to elementary processes such as encoding is at the expense of more global processes involved in comprehension. Thus if slow encoding is indicative of greater attentional demand, slow encoding could be an indirect cause of lower comprehension. Martinez and Johnson (1982) investigate the use of encoding time as an indicator of part of the process of reading. They report that above-average adult first-language readers perform better than average readers on a task involving encoding sets of unrelated letters to which they were exposed for brief durations. They thus suggest that encoding time is a good predictor of reading proficiency. They further suggest the use of encoding time as a possible diagnostic tool.

## Word-identification processes

Researchers have distinguished two word-identification processes in reading: the phonological and the orthographic (see Chapter 2). Skill at identifying words is aided by information from comprehension during reading and from the printed visual symbols. The latter involves phonological as well as orthographic information. Phonological processes require awareness of phoneme–grapheme correspondences and the word's phonological structure. But orthographic processes apppear to be more word-specific. Orthographic knowledge involves memory for specific visual/spelling patterns (and is sometimes refered to as lexical knowledge).

Barker *et al.* (1992) investigate the role of orthographic processing skills on five different reading tasks. The purpose of the study was to explore the independence of orthographic identification skills over other skills in several different reading tasks. Their measures are fairly unusual and different from common testing procedures. Skills were measured as follows:

a **Phonological processing skill**

i phonological choice: children view two non-word letter strings and decide which one is pronounced like a real word (e.g. 'saip' vs. 'saif'). Pairs are presented on screen, and latencies and accuracy measures are gathered for 25 pairs (the correlation between latency and number of errors was .20).

ii phoneme deletion task: the experimenter pronounces a word and asks the child what word remains after one phoneme is deleted. E.g. 'trick', and the child is asked to delete 'r' (to produce 'tick'). Two sets of 10 words are administered, where one set requires deletion from a blend, and the other ten deletion of the final phoneme. The score is the total of correct answers divided by 20.

**b  Orthographic processing skill**

i orthographic choice: the child is required to pick the correct spelling from two choices that sound alike (e.g. 'bote' and 'boat'). This is designed to measure knowledge of conventional spelling patterns. 25 pairs of a real word and a nonsense alternative are given. The data are the median reaction times for correct responses and the number of response errors.

ii homophone choice task: the child is first read a sentence such as 'what can you do with a needle and thread?', then is shown two real homophones on screen (e.g. 'so' and 'sew'). The child chooses the word that represents the answer to the question. Median reaction times are calculated for correct responses and number of errors.

Although such measures are used with beginning first-language readers, they may suggest ways in which we could assess second-language readers' skills. If research establishes their usefulness, I can see considerable diagnostic potential, for example, possibly in conjunction with similar measures in the first language.

Yamashita (1992) reports on the use of word-recognition measures for Japanese learners of English. She developed an interesting battery of computer-based tests to examine Japanese learners' of English word-recognition skills: recognition of real words, of pseudo-English words, of non-words, of numbers, as well as measures of the identification of the meaning of individual words, and the understanding of simple sentences. She concluded that foreign-language skills that do not require the manipulation of meaning do not relate to foreign-language reading comprehension. Interestingly, word-recognition efficiency did not relate to foreign-language reading ability, nor to reading speed. This suggest that word-recognition efficiency and the ability to guess the meaning of unknown words from context might be quite unrelated skills.

## Word-guessing processes

Sometimes the ability to guess the meaning of unknown words from context is considered a skill, at other times it is called a strategy. Nevertheless, however we choose to classify lexical abilities and guessing, they are clearly an important component of the reading process, and so looking at how they have been operationalised or measured by researchers should provide insights into possible assessment procedures.

Alderson and Alvarez (1977) report the use of a series of exercises intended to develop context-using skills. Traditional exercises include getting learners to pay attention to morphology and syntax in order to guess word class or function. Alderson and Alvarez construct contexts based upon semantic relations between words and encourage learners to guess the 'meaning' of nonsense words using such semantic information:

### hyponymy
'Michael gave me a beautiful bunch of flowers: roses, dahlias, marguerites, chrysanthemums, *nogs* and orchids.'

'Even in the poorest parts of the country, people usually have a table, some chairs, a *roup* and a bed.'

'Over the last 20 years, our family has owned a great variety of *wurgs*: poodles, dachshunds, dalmatians, Yorkshire terriers and even St Bernards.'

### opposites – incompatability
'If I don't buy a blue car, then I might buy a *fobble* one.'

### gradable antonymy
'These reactions proceed from the group as a whole, and can assume a great variety of forms, from putting to death, corporal punishment, expulsion from the tribe to the expression of ridicule and the *nurdling of cordwangles*.'

### complementarity
'Well, if it isn't a *mungle* horse, it must be female.'

### synonymy and textual cohesion
'If you asked an average lawyer to explain our courts, the *nerk* would probably begin like this: our *frugs* have three different functions. One *blurk* is to determine the facts of a particular case. The second function is to decide which laws apply to the facts of that particular *durgle*.'

Such exercises could be used as assessment procedures, to see whether students are able to detect and use semantic relations in order to guess meaning from context.

Carnine *et al.* (1984) investigate the extent to which different sorts of contextual information aid getting the meaning of unknown words from context, with 4th, 5th and 6th grade first-language readers. Explicitness of clue and learner age were the variables investigated: explicitness varying from synonyms to contrasts (by antonym plus 'not') to inference relationships; and the closeness or distance of the clue from the unknown word.

Determining the meaning of unfamiliar words is easier when they are presented in context (same words in isolation versus in passages); deriving meaning from context is easier when the contextual information is closer to the unknown word; and when it is in synonym form than when in inference form; and older students respond correctly more often, whether the words are in isolation or in context.

### Metacognition

We have seen in Chapter 2 the importance of metacognition in the reading process and have discussed the research of Block (1992), amongst others. With first-language readers, evidence suggests that comprehension monitoring operates rather automatically and is not readily observable until some failure to comprehend occurs. Older and more proficient readers have more control over this monitoring process than younger and less proficient readers; good readers are more aware of how they control their reading and are more able to verbalise this awareness (Forrest-Pressley and Waller, 1984). They also appear more sensitive to inconsistencies in text, although even good readers do not always notice or report all inconsistencies, perhaps because they are intent on making text coherent. Good readers tend to use meaning-based cues to evaluate whether they have understood what they read whereas poor readers tend to use or over-rely on word-level cues, and to focus on intrasentential rather than intersentential consistency. Useful research and possibly assessment methods could involve building inconsistencies into text and investigating whether and how readers notice these.

Block (1992) compared proficient native and ESL readers with less proficient native and ESL readers in a US college. She collected verbal protocols and inspected how they dealt with a referent problem and a vocabulary problem. As reported in Chapter 2, she concludes that less proficient readers often did not even recognise that a problem existed, and they usually lacked the resources to attempt to solve the problem. They were frequently defeated by word problems and tended to emphasise them, whereas more proficient readers appeared not to worry so much if they did not understand a word. One strategy of proficient readers was to decide which problems they could ignore and which they had to solve.

Research has revealed the relationship between metacognition and reading performance. Poor readers do not possess knowledge of strategies and are often not aware of how or when to apply the knowledge they do have. They often cannot infer meaning from surface-level information, have poorly developed knowledge about how the reading system works and find it difficult to evaluate text for clarity, consistency and compatibility. Instead, they often believe that the purpose of reading is errorless word pronunciation and that good reading includes verbatim recall.

Duffy *et al.* (1987) show how low-group 3rd grade first-language readers can be made aware of the mental processing involved in using reading skills as strategies (metacognitive awareness) and how such students then become more aware of lesson content and of the need to be strategic when reading. They also scored better on traditional (standardised), nontraditional and maintenance measures of reading achievement.

Their measures were interesting, as follows, and remind us of the simple classroom conversations advocated above:

**Measures of student awareness**

i Lesson interviews to determine awareness of lesson content: what teachers taught (declarative knowledge); when to use it (situational knowledge); how to use it (procedural knowledge). Five students were interviewed after each lesson, with three levels of questions:

1 What can you remember of the lesson?

2 What were you learning in the lesson I just saw? When would you use what the teacher was teaching you? How do you do what you were taught to do?

3 Repetition of (2) with examples from the lesson.

Raters rated the answers from the transcripts, on a scale of 0–4.

ii Concept interviews. Three students were randomly selected from each class and were interviewed at the end of the school-year. Four questions were asked:

1 What do good readers do?

2 What is the first thing you do when you are given a story to read?

3 What do you do when you come to a word that you do not know?

4 What do you do when you come upon a sentence or story you do not understand?

Ten rating categories were developed and scores assigned on a 7-point rating scale for each category. Two raters marked the transcripts of the interviews.

**Reading Characteristic**
Involves intentionality
Involves effort
Is systematic
Is self-directed
Involves problem-solving
Uses skills & rules to get meaning
Is enjoyable
Is a meaning-getting activity
Involves conscious processing
Involves selection of strategies

Fig. 9.11 Scales for rating student awareness (Duffy *et al.*, 1987)

## Measures of achievement

Finally, in this miscellany of interesting methods used by researchers, I want to draw attention to the non-traditional measures of student achievement used by Duffy *et al.* in the study cited above. Their achievement measures were interesting, because they might be said to throw light on process or components of process as well as on 'achievement'.

### 1 Supplemental Achievement Measure (SAM)

Part I: use of skill in isolated situations
For example: Read the sentence. Decide what the base word is for the italicized word. 'Jan and Sandy were *planning* a special trip to the sea this summer.' Now choose the base word for the italicized word. Put an X before the correct answer:

☐ plane
☐ planned
☐ plan

Part II: rationale for choice
For example:
I am going to read a question and four possible answers. Choose the best answer. Put an X before the best answer.

You just chose a base word. How did you decide which base word was the right one for the italicized word in the sentence?

☐ I looked for the word that looked most like the word in the sentence
☐ I just knew what the base word was
☐ I took off the ending and that helped me find the base word that would make sense
☐ I thought about the sea and that was a clue that helped me choose the base word.

It is claimed that Part II measures students' awareness of their reasoning as they did the task (although no details are given of how the responses were scored).

### 2 Graded Oral Reading Paragraph Test (GORP)
This 'non-traditional' test is claimed to measure whether students, when confronted with a blockage while comprehending connected text, reported using a process of strategic mental reasoning to restore the meaning.

> Two target words are embedded in a 3rd grade passage: 'grub' – expected to be unknown – and 'uncovered'. The first is tested in advance of the passage, by asking students to pronounce the word and use it in a sentence. The student is then given the passage, asked to read it aloud and told to remember what was read. Students' self-corrections were noted and then, after the reading, self-reports were elicited about the self-corrections. Students were then asked a) the meaning of 'grub' and how this meaning was determined, b) how they would figure out the meaning of 'uncovered'. The verbal reports both for self-corrections and for the embedded words were rated for whether they focused on word recognition or meaning, and whether they reflected strategic mental processing.

Clearly such intensive methods would be difficult to implement for assessment, unless very specific diagnostic information was required – transcribing and rating protocols is very time-consuming. Nevertheless, one can imagine adaptations of such measures, perhaps as part of the focus of a simple read-aloud task for which the text has particular words or structures embedded in it which are predicted to cause certain sorts of processing problems. Raters would then score for success on encoding those words.

## Computer-based testing and assessment

Inevitably in a final chapter looking at the way forward as well as synthesising recent approaches, it is necessary to consider the role of information technology in the assessment of reading. I have several times commented on the role of the computer in assessing reading, and in this penultimate section I need to explore this some more.

There are many opportunities for exploitation of the computer environment which do not easily exist with paper-and-pencil tests. The possibility of recording response latencies and time on text or task opens up a whole new world of exploration of rates of reading, of word recognition, and so on which are not available, or only very crudely, in the case of paper-based tests. The computer's ability to capture every detail of a learner's progress through a test – which items were consulted first, which were answered first, in what sequence, with what result, which help and clue facilities were used, with what effect and so on (see Alderson and Windeatt, 1991, for a discussion of many of these) – the possibilities are almost endless and the limitation is more likely to be on our ability to analyse and interpret the data than on our ability to capture data.

However, as Chapelle points out in a discussion of the validity of using computers to assist in the assessment of strategies in second-language acquisition research, it is important to establish that the variables measured by the computer are indeed related to the use of the hypothesised strategies: 'The investigation of strategy issues relies on the validity of the measurement used to assess strategies' (Chapelle, 1996:57). For example, in Jamieson and Chapelle (1987), response latency was taken to be an index of planning and advanced preparation in a study of the relationship between advanced preparation and cognitive style, but little independent evidence was gathered that delays in response time did in fact measure planning rather than lack of interest or wandering attention. Chapelle advocates the use of learner self-reports, expert judgements, correlations with other valid measures, behavioural observation and like measures to legitimise, or validate, the inferences made from computer-captured data.

It may be that the development of diagnostic tests of skills could be facilitated by being delivered by computer. Tests can be designed to present clues and hints to test-takers as part of the test-taking procedure. Use of these can be monitored in order not only to understand the test-taking process, but also to examine the response validity of the answers. Information would then be used only from those items where the student had indeed engaged in the intended process. Conceivably, unintended processing of items, if it could be detected, could be used diagnostically too.

Computer-based tests of reading allow the possibility of developing measures of rate and speed, which may prove very useful, especially in the light of recent research into the importance of automaticity.

An issue occasionally discussed in the literature (see Bernhardt, 2000, for example) is whether readers of different language backgrounds should be assessed differently, as well as having different expectations of development associated with their test performance. Given the differential linguistic distances between, say English and Spanish on the one hand, and Arabic and Chinese on the other hand, it is not surprising that some research shows students with Spanish as their first language to be better readers in English than those whose first language is Arabic or Chinese.

An interesting possibility for computer-based testing is that it might be feasible to allow learners from one language background to take a different test of second-language reading from those of another language background, by simple menu selection on entry to the test – the restriction is our ability to identify significant differences and to write items to test for these. Theory is not so well advanced yet, but this may be a case where the development of computer-based reading tests and the examination of differential item functioning might contribute to the development of theory.

In addition, the future availability of tests on the Internet will make available a range of media and information sources that can be integrated into the test, thereby allowing the testing of information accessing and processing skills, as well as opening up tests to a variety of different input 'texts'.

Computer-based adaptive tests (tests whose items adjust in difficulty to ongoing test performance) offer opportunities not only for more efficient testing of reading, but also for presenting tests that are tailored to readers' ability levels, and that do not frustrate test-takers by presenting them with items that are too difficult or too easy. It is also possible to conceive of learner-adaptive tests: where the candidate decides whether to take an easier or a more difficult next item based on their estimate of their own performance to date (or indeed based upon the immediate feedback that such an adaptive computer test can provide).

However, there are also limitations. The most obvious problem for computer-based tests of reading is that the amount of text that can be displayed on screen is limited, and the video monitor is much less flexible in terms of allowing readers to go back and forth through text than the printed page. In addition, screen reading is more tiring, slower, influenced by a number of variables that do not affect normal print (colour combinations, for example, or the need for more white space between words, the need for larger font size and so on: see Chapters 2 and 3). All these variables might be thought to affect the extent to which we are safe to generalise from computer-based reading to print literacy elsewhere.

As pointed out in Chapter 2, it is true that much reading does take place on screen – the increased use of the word-processor, the use of email, access to the World-Wide Web, computer-based instruction and even computer-based testing are all real and increasingly important elements of literacy, at least in much of the Western world. And it is probably true that future generations will be much more comfortable reading from screen than current generations, who are still adapting to the new media. It is certainly the case that many of my colleagues prefer to print out their emails and read them from paper, to reading long messages on screen. Even though I regularly use word-processors I also print out my drafts and edit them by hand on paper before transferring my amendments back into electronic form.

It is precisely such descriptions of how people use literacy – in this case in interaction with computers – that we need in order to be able to discuss sensibly the validity of computer-based tests of reading. That, then, is clearly one area where an analysis of target language use domains (as discussed in Chapter 5), possibly using the ethnographic research techniques that many literacy researchers use – see, for example, Barton and Hamilton (1998) – could be very helpful.

A further worry in computer-based testing is the effect of test method: all too many computer-based tests use the multiple-choice technique, rather than other, more innovative, interesting or simply exploratory test methods. However, the DIALANG project referred to above and in Chapter 4 is seeking to implement many of the ideas in Alderson (1990) and Alderson and Windeatt (1991), and attempting to reduce the constraints of computer-based scoring, whilst maximising the opportunities provided by computer-based, and especially Internet-delivered, tests. Alderson (1996) discusses the advantages that might be gained by using computer corpora in conjunction with computer-based tests, and suggests ways in which such corpora could be used at all stages of test design and construction, as well as for scoring.

Despite the possible limitations, the advantage of delivering tests by computer is the ease with which data can be collected, analysed and related to test performance. This may well enable us to gain greater insights into what is involved in taking tests of reading, and in its turn this might lead to improvements in test design and the development of other assessment procedures.

## Summary

In this chapter, I have been much more tentative and speculative than in earlier chapters. This is perhaps inevitable when dealing with the way forward. It is, after all, difficult to predict developments in a field as complex and as widely researched and assessed as reading. It is also, however, as I have pointed out, because of the nature of the subject. Not only are reading processes mysterious and imperfectly understood; even the terms 'skill', 'strategy' and 'ability' are not well defined in the field, are often used interchangeably and one person's usage contradicts another's. I have no wish to add confusion to this area, and so I have chosen not to present my own definition – which would doubtless itself be inadequate. I have instead used terms interchangeably, or used the terms that the authors I have cited use themselves. Above all, however, I have exemplified and illustrated what I consider to be relevant 'things' when considering process.

We have seen that the testing and assessment field is no less confused than other areas of reading research and instruction. Indeed, it has largely avoided assessing process, in order to concentrate on product, with the possible exception of 'skills'. And we have ample evidence for the unsatisfactory nature of our attempts to operationally define these.

Where we might find more useful insights into the assessment of strategies has been in the area of informal assessment, rather than formal tests, and I remind the reader that the discussion of informal techniques in Chapter 7 is as relevant to this issue as is the discussion in this chapter. However, as I pointed out in Chapter 7, much more research is needed into what Bachman and Palmer (1996) call the usefulness – the validity, reliability, practicality, impact – of these less formal techniques before we can assess their value in comparison with more 'traditional techniques'. Advocacy is one thing; evidence is another. In the area of informal techniques, qualitative methods, teacher- or learner-centred procedures, it is essential that much more research be conducted, both so that we can understand better what additional insights they can provide into reading processes over and above what traditional approaches can provide, and also so that we can consider to what extent we can improve those traditional techniques using insights gained from the alternative procedures.

One way in which this can happen has already been stressed throughout this book: the use of qualitative methods, like think-alouds, immediate recall, interviews, self-assessment and the like, with test-takers, *about* their test performance, in order to begin to get a better understanding of why test-takers responded the way they did, how they understood both the tasks and the texts, and how they feel that their performance does or does not reflect their understanding of that text/those texts, and their literacy in other areas also.

I have suggested that in order to gain insights into methods, techniques or procedures for assessing process, we should look closely (and critically) at which teaching/learning exercises are advocated and developed in textbooks and teacher manuals. A better understanding of how such exercises actually work in class and what they are capable of eliciting will help not only assessment but also instruction.

I have also suggested that we consider the research techniques used by reading researchers, not only for the insight they give into how aspects of process are operationalised, but also for ideas for assessment procedures. In this book, I have constantly emphasised that how researchers operationalise their constructs crucially determines the results they will gather and thus the conclusions they can draw and the theories they develop. If their operationalisation of aspects of process seem inadequate, or trivial, then any resulting theory or model will be equally inadequate. And I have also stressed that the methods we use for assessing and testing reading, including the processes and strategies, can throw light on what the reading process is. It is therefore incumbent on testers in the broadest sense to experiment with novel and alternative procedures and to research their effects, their results and their usefulness, in order to contribute to a greater understanding of the nature of reading.

I have thus emphasised the need to explore new methods and technologies, especially both the IT-based and the ethnographic, conversational and qualitative. However, it is important always to bear in mind the need for validity, reliability and fitness for purpose. The fascination with the novel does not absolve us from the need to validate and to justify our methods, our results and our interpretation of the results, and to consider the washback, consequences and generalisability of our assessments.

## Conclusion

In this book, I have attempted to show how research into reading can help us define our constructs for assessment and what remains to be known. I have shown how assessment can provide insights into constructs and how much more needs to be done. I have attempted to be fairly comprehensive in my overview of research and development in both areas, and widely illustrative of techniques and approaches. Inevitably, however, especially in a field as vast as reading, I have been selective, sometimes consciously, sometimes unconsciously, through ignorance. Particularly in this final chapter I have felt the need to read more, to identify the latest insights from research or assessment, to explore innovative suggestions and assertions. However, as with every chapter in this book, I have had to call a halt somewhere: there will always be some avenue unexplored, some research neglected, some proposals ignored. I hope that readers will forgive omissions and be stimulated to contribute themselves through research or assessment to a greater understanding of how we might best, most fairly and appropriately, and most representatively, assess how well our clients, students, test-takers – those we serve and hope to assist – read, understand, interpret and use written text.

I have offered no panaceas, no best method, not even a set of practical guidelines for item writing or text selection. I believe that this would be useful, but in given contexts, rather than in generalised form. I also believe it would involve much more illustration and exemplification than I have space for in this volume. What I have done, I hope, is offered a way of approaching test design through the application of the most recent theories and research in test design generally, shown how it might be applied to the assessment of reading, shown its limitations in some contexts, but offered other ways of thinking about how traditional testing approaches might be complemented and validated. I hope to have thrown light on what is a complex process, offered ways of looking at techniques for assessment and for viewing reading development. Above all, I hope the reader has gained a sense of what is possible, not just what appears to be impossible, and that you will feel encouraged to explore further and to research and document your explorations, in the expectation that only by so doing can we inform and improve our practices in the testing and assessment of reading.

# Bibliography

Abdullah, K. B. (1994). *The critical reading and thinking abilities of Malay secondary school pupils in Singapore.* Unpublished PhD thesis, University of London.

Adams, M. J. (1991). *Beginning to read: thinking and learning about print.* Cambridge, MA: The MIT Press.

Alderson, J. C. (1978). *A study of the cloze procedure with native and non-native speakers of English.* Unpublished PhD thesis, University of Edinburgh.

Alderson, J. C. (1979). The cloze procedure as a measure of proficiency in English as a foreign language. *TESOL Quarterly* 13, 219–227.

Alderson, J. C. (1981). Report of the discussion on communicative language testing. In J. C. Alderson and A. Hughes (eds.), *Issues in Language Testing.* vol. 111. London: The British Council.

Alderson, J. C. (1984). Reading in a foreign language: a reading problem or a language problem? In J. C. Alderson and A. H. Urquhart (eds.), *Reading in a Foreign Language.* London: Longman.

Alderson, J. C. (1986). Computers in language testing. In G. N. Leech and C. N. Candlin (eds.), *Computers in English language education and research.* London: Longman.

Alderson, J. C. (1988). New procedures for validating proficiency test of ESP? Theory and practice. *Language Testing* 5 (2), 220–232.

Alderson, J. C. (1990a). *Innovation in language testing: can the microcomputer help?* (Language Testing Update Special Report No 1). Lancaster: University of Lancaster.

Alderson, J. C. (1990b). Testing reading comprehension skills (Part One). *Reading in a Foreign Language* 6 (2), 425–438.

Alderson, J. C. (1990c). Testing reading comprehension skills (Part Two). *Reading in a Foreign Language* 7 (1), 465–503.

Alderson, J. C. (1991). Bands and scores. In J. C. Alderson and B. North (eds.), *Language testing in the 1990s: the communicative legacy.* London: Macmillan/Modern English Publications.

Alderson, J. C. (1993). The relationship between grammar and reading in an English for academic purposes test battery. In D. Douglas and C. Chappelle (eds.), *A new decade of language testing research: selected papers from the 1990 Language Testing Research Colloquium.* Alexandria, VA: TESOL.

Alderson, J. C. (1996). Do corpora have a role in language assessment? In J. Thomas and M. Short (eds.), *Using corpora for language research.* Harlow: Longman.

Alderson, J. C., and Alvarez, G. (1977). The development of strategies for the assignment of semantic information to unknown lexemes in text. *MEXTESOL.*

Alderson, J. C., and Banerjee, J. (1999). Impact and washback research in language testing. In C. Elder *et al.* (eds.), *Festschrift for Alan Davies.* Melbourne: University of Melbourne Press.

Alderson, J. C., Clapham, C., and Steel, D. (1997). Metalinguistic knowledge, language aptitude and language proficiency. *Language Teaching Research* 1 (2), 93–121.

Alderson, J. C., Clapham, C., and Wall, D. (1995). *Language test construction and evaluation.* Cambridge: Cambridge University Press.

Alderson, J. C., and Hamp-Lyons, L. (1996). TOEFL preparation courses: a study of washback. *Language Testing* 13 (3), 280–297.

Alderson, J. C., Krahnke, K., and Stansfield, C. (eds.). (1985). *Reviews of English language proficiency tests.* Washington, DC: TESOL Publications.

Alderson, J. C., and Lukmani, Y. (1989). Cognition and reading: cognitive levels as embodied in test questions. *Reading in a Foreign Language* 5 (2), 253–270.

Alderson, J. C., and Urquhart, A. H. (1985). The effect of students' academic discipline on their performance on ESP reading tests. *Language Testing* 2 (2), 192–204.

Alderson, J. C., and Windeatt, S. (1991). Computers and innovation in language testing. In J. C. Alderson and B. North (eds.), *Language testing in the 1990s: the communicative legacy.* London: Macmillan/Modern English Publications.

Allan, A. I. C. G. (1992). *EFL reading comprehension test validation: investigating aspects of process approaches.* Unpublished PhD thesis, Lancaster University.

Allan, A. I. C. G. (1995). Begging the questionnaire: instrument effect on readers' responses to a self-report checklist. *Language Testing* 12 (2), 133–156.

Allen, E. D., Bernhardt, E. B., Berry, M. T., and Demel, M. (1988). Comprehension and text genre: an analysis of secondary school foreign language readers. *Modern Language Journal* 72 (163–172).

ALTE (1998). *ALTE handbook of European examinations and examination systems*. Cambridge: UCLES.

Anderson, N., Bachman, L., Perkins, K., and Cohen, A. (1991). An exploratory study into the construct validity of a reading comprehension test: triangulation of data sources. *Language Testing* 8 (1), 41–66.

Anthony, R., Johnson, T., Mickelson, N., and Preece, A. (1991). *Evaluating literacy: a perspective for change*. Portsmouth, NH: Heinemann.

Ausubel, D. P. (1963). *The psychology of meaningful verbal learning*. New York: Green and Stratton.

Bachman, L. F. (1985). Performance on the cloze test with fixed-ratio and rational deletions. *TESOL Quarterly* 19 (3), 535–556.

Bachman, L. F. (1990). *Fundamental considerations in language testing*. Oxford: Oxford University Press.

Bachman, L. F., Davidson, F., Lynch, B., and Ryan, K. (1989). *Content analysis and statistical modeling of EFL Proficiency Tests*. Paper presented at the The 11th Annual Language Testing Research Colloquium, San Antonio, Texas.

Bachman, L. F., Davidson, F., and Milanovic, M. (1996). The use of test method characteristics in the content analysis and design of EFL proficiency tests. *Language Testing* 13 (2), 125–150.

Bachman, L. F., and Palmer, A. S. (1996). *Language testing in practice*. Oxford: Oxford University Press.

Balota, D. A., d'Arcais, G. B. F., and Rayner, K. (eds.). (1990). *Comprehension processes in reading*. Hillsdale, NJ: Lawrence Erlbaum Associates.

Barker, T. A., Torgesen, J. K., and Wagner, R. K. (1992). The role of orthographic processing skills on five different reading tasks. *Reading Research Quarterly* 27 (4), 335–345.

Bartlett, F. C. (1932). *Remembering*. Cambridge: Cambridge University Press.

Barton, D. (1994a). *Literacy: an introduction to the ecology of written language*. Oxford: Basil Blackwell.

Barton, D. (ed.). (1994b). *Sustaining local literacies*. Clevedon: Multilingual Matters.

Barton, D., and Hamilton, M. (1998). *Local literacies: reading and writing in one community*. London: Routledge.

Baudoin, E. M., Bober, E. S., Clarke, M. A., Dobson, B. K., and Silberstein, S. (1988). *Reader's Choice*. (Second ed.) Ann Arbor, MI: University of Michigan Press.

Beck, L. L., McKeown, M. G., Sinatra, G. M., and Loxterman, J. A. (1991). Revising social studies text from a text-processing perspective: evidence of improved comprehensibility. *Reading Research Quarterly* 26 (3), 251–276.

Benesch, S. (1993). Critical thinking: a learning process for democracy. *TESOL Quarterly* 27 (3).

Bensoussan, M., Sim, D., and Weiss, R. (1984). The effect of dictionary usage on EFL test performance compared with student and teacher attitudes and expectations. *Reading in a Foreign Language* 2 (2), 262–276.

Berkemeyer, V. B. (1989). Qualitative analysis of immediate recall protocol data: some classroom implications. *Die Unterrichtspraxis*, vol. 22, pp. 131–137.

Berman, I. (1991). *Can we test L2 reading comprehension without testing reasoning?* Paper presented at the The Thirteenth Annual Language Testing Research Colloquium, ETS, Princeton, New Jersey.

Berman, R. A. (1984). Syntactic components of the foreign language reading process. In J. C. Alderson and A. H. Urquhart (eds.), *Reading in a Foreign Language*. London: Longman.

Bernhardt, E. B. (1983). Three approaches to reading comprehension in intermediate German. *Modern Language Journal* 67, 111–115.

Bernhardt, E. B. (1991). A psycholinguistic perspective on second language literacy. In J. H. Hulstijn and J. F. Matter (eds.), *Reading in two languages* vol. 7, pp. 31–44. Amsterdam: Free University Press.

Bernhardt, E. B. (2000). If reading is reader-based, can there be a computer-adaptive test of reading? In M. Chalhoub-Deville (ed.), *Issues in computer-adaptive tests of reading*. Cambridge: Cambridge University Press.

Bernhardt, E. B., and Kamil, M. L. (1995). Interpreting relationships between L1 and L2 reading: consolidating the linguistic threshold and the linguistic interdependence hypotheses. *Applied Linguistics* 16 (1), 15–34.

Block, E. L. (1992). See how they read: comprehension monitoring of L1 and L2 readers. *TESOL Quarterly* 26 (2), 319–343.

Bloom, B. S., Engelhart, M. D., Furst, E. J., Hill, W. H., and Kratwohl, D. R. (eds.) (1956). *Taxonomy of educational objectives: cognitive domain*. New York: David McKay. (See also Bloom, B. S. *et al.* (eds.), Taxonomy of educational objectives. *Handbook I: Cognitive Domain*. London: Longman, 1974.)

Bormuth, J. R. (1968). Cloze test readability: criterion reference scores. *Journal of Educational Measurement* 5, 189–196.

Bossers, B. (1992). *Reading in two languages*. Unpublished PhD thesis, Amsterdam: Vrije Universiteit.

Bransford, J. D., Stein, B. S., and Shelton, T. (1984). Learning from the perspective of the comprehender. In J. C. Alderson and A. H. Urquhart (eds.), *Reading in a Foreign Language*. London: Longman.

Brindley, G. (1998). Outcomes-based assessment and reporting in language learning programmes: a review of the issues. *Language Testing*, vol. 15, 1, 45–85.

Broadfoot, P. (ed.). (1986). *Profiles and records of achievement.* London: Holt, Rinehart and Winston.

Brown, A., and Palinscar, A. (1982). Inducing strategic learning from texts by means of informed self-control training. *Topics in Learning and Learning Disabilities* 2 (Special issue on metacognition and learning disabilities), 1–17.

Brown, J. D. (1984). A norm-referenced engineering reading test. In A. K. Pugh and J. M. Ulijn (eds.), *Reading for professional purposes.* London: Heinemann Educational Books.

Brumfit, C. J. (ed.). (1993). *Assessing literature.* London: Macmillan/Modern English Publications.

Buck, G. (1991). The testing of listening comprehension: an introspective study. *Language Testing* 8 (1), 67–91.

Buck, G., Tatsuoka, K., and Kostin, I. (1996). *The subskills of reading: rule-space analysis of a multiple-choice test of second-language reading comprehension.* Paper presented at the Language Testing Research Colloquium, Tampere, Finland.

Bügel, K., and Buunk, B. P. (1996). Sex differences in foreign language text comprehension: the role of interests and prior knowledge. *The Modern Language Journal* 80 (i), 15–31.

Canale, M., and Swain, M. (1980). Theoretical bases of communicative approaches to second language teaching and testing. *Applied Linguistics*, vol. 1, 1, 1–47.

Carnine, D., Kameenui, E. J., and Coyle, G. (1984). Utilization of contextual information in determining the meaning of unfamiliar words. *Reading Research Quarterly* XIX (2), 188–204.

Carr, T. H., and Levy, B. A. (eds.). (1990). *Reading and its development: component skills approaches.* San Diego: Academic Press.

Carrell, P. L. (1981). *Culture-specific schemata in L2 comprehension.* Paper presented at the Ninth Illinois TESOL/BE Annual Convention: The First Midwest TESOL Conference, Illinois.

Carrell, P. L. (1983a). Some issues in studying the role of schemata, or background knowledge, in second language comprehension. *Reading in a Foreign Language* 1 (2), 81–92.

Carrell, P. L. (1983b). Three components of background knowledge in reading comprehension. *Language Learning* 33 (2), 183–203.

Carrell, P. L. (1987). Readability in ESL. *Reading in a Foreign Language* 4 (1), 21–40.

Carrell, P. L. (1991). Second-language reading: Reading ability or language proficiency? *Applied Linguistics* 12, 159–179.

Carrell, P. L., Devine, J., and Eskey, D. (eds.). (1988). *Interactive approaches to second-language reading.* Cambridge: Cambridge University Press.

Carroll, J. B. (1969). From comprehension to inference. In M. P. Douglas (ed.),

*Thirty-Third Yearbook, Claremont Reading Conference*. Claremont, CA: Claremont Graduate School.

Carroll, J. B. (1971). *Defining language comprehension: some speculations* (Research Memorandum). Princeton, NJ: ETS.

Carroll, J. B. (1993). *Human cognitive abilities*. Cambridge: Cambridge University Press.

Carroll, J. B., Davies, P., and Richman, P. (1971). *The American Heritage Word Frequency Book*. Boston: Houghton Mifflin.

Carver, R. P. (1974). Reading as reasoning: implications for measurement. In W. MacGinitie (ed.), *Assessment problems in reading*. Delaware: International Reading Association.

Carver, R. P. (1982). Optimal rate of reading prose. *Reading Research Quarterly* XVIII (1), 56–88.

Carver, R. P. (1983). Is reading rate constant or flexible? *Reading Research Quarterly* VXIII (2), 190–215.

Carver, R. P. (1984). Rauding theory predictions of amount comprehended under different purposes and speed reading conditions. *Reading Research Quarterly* XIX (2), 205–218.

Carver, R. P. (1990). *Reading rate: a review of research and theory*. New York: Academic Press.

Carver, R. P. (1992a). Effect of prediction activities, prior knowledge, and text type upon amount comprehended: using rauding theory to critique schema theory research. *Reading Research Quarterly* 27 (2), 165–174.

Carver, R. P. (1992b). What do standardized tests of reading comprehension measure in terms of efficiency, accuracy, and rate? *Reading Research Quarterly* 27 (4), 347–359.

Cavalcanti, M. (1983). *The pragmatics of FL reader–text interaction. Key lexical items as source of potential reading problems*. Unpublished PhD thesis, Lancaster University.

Celani, A., Holmes, J., Ramos, R., and Scott, M. (1988). *The evaluation of the Brazilian ESP project*. São Paulo: CEPRIL.

Chall, J. S. (1958). *Readability – an appraisal of research and application*. Columbus, OH: Bureau of Educational Research, Ohio State University.

Chang, F. R. (1983). Mental processes in reading: A methodological review. *Reading Research Quarterly* XVIII (2), 216–230.

Chapelle, C. A. (1996). Validity issues in computer-assisted strategy assessment for language learners. *Applied Language Learning* 7 (1 and 2), 47–60.

Chihara, T., Sakurai, T., and Oller, J. W. (1989). Background and culture as factors in EFL reading comprehension. *Language Testing* 6 (2), 143–151.

Child, J. R. (1987). Language proficiency levels and the typology of texts. In H. Byrnes and M. Canale (eds.), *Defining and developing proficiency: Guidelines, implementations and concepts*. Lincolnwood, IL: National Textbook Co.

Clapham, C. M. (1996). *The development of IELTS: a study of the effect of background knowledge on reading comprehension.* Cambridge: Cambridge University Press.

Clapham, C. M., and Alderson, J. C. (1997). *IELTS Research Report 3.* Cambridge: UCLES.

Cohen, A. D. (1987). Studying learner strategies: how we get the information. In Wenden, A. and Rubin, J. (eds.).

Cohen, A. D. (1996). Verbal reports as a source of insights into second language learner strategies. *Applied Language Learning* 7 (1 and 2), 5–24.

Cooper, M. (1984). Linguistic competence of practised and unpractised nonnative readers of English. In J. C. Alderson and A. H. Urquhart (eds.), *Reading in a Foreign Language.* London: Longman.

Council of Europe (1996). *Modern languages: learning, teaching, assessment. A Common European framework of reference.* Strasbourg: Council for Cultural Co-operation, Education Committee.

Council of Europe (1990a). *Threshold 1990.* Strasbourg: Council for Cultural Co-operation, Education Committee.

Council of Europe (1990b). *Waystage 1990.* Strasbourg: Council for Cultural Co-operation, Education Committee.

Crocker, L., and Algina, J. (1986). *Introduction to classical and modern test theory.* Orlando, FL: Harcourt Brace Jovanovich.

Culler, J. (1975). *Structuralist poetics: structuralism, linguistics and the study of literature.* London: Routledge and Kegan Paul.

Cummins, J. (1979). Linguistic interdependence and the educational development of bilingual children. *Review of Educational Research* 49, 222–251.

Cummins, J. (1991). Conversational and academic language proficiency in bilingual contexts. In J. Hulstijn and A. Matter (eds.), *AILA Review* Vol. 8, pp. 75–89.

Dale, E. (1965). Vocabulary measurement: techniques and major findings. *Elementary English* 42, 895–901, 948.

Davey, B. (1988). Factors affecting the difficulty of reading comprehension items for successful and unsuccessful readers. *Experimental Education* 56, 67–76.

Davey, B., and Lasasso, C. (1984). The interaction of reader and task factors in the assessment of reading comprehension. *Experimental Education* 52, 199–206.

Davies, A. (1975). Two tests of speeded reading. In R. L. Jones and B. Spolsky (eds.), *Testing language proficiency.* Washington, DC: Center for Applied Linguistics.

Davies, A. (1981). Review of Munby, J., 'Communicative syllabus design'. *TESOL Quarterly* 15 (2), 332–335.

Davies, A. (1984). Simple, simplified and simplification: what is authentic? In

J. C. Alderson and A. H. Urquhart (eds.), *Reading in a Foreign Language*. London: Longman.

Davies, A. (1989). Testing reading speed through text retrieval. In C. N. Candlin and T. F. McNamara (eds.), *Language learning and community*. Sydney, NSW: NCELTR.

Davies, F. (1995). *Introducing reading*. London: Penguin.

Davis, F. B. (1968). Research in comprehension in reading. *Reading Research Quarterly* 3, 499–545.

Deighton, L. (1959). *Vocabulary development in the classroom*. New York: Bureau of Publications, Teachers College, Columbia University.

Denis, M. (1982). Imaging while reading text: A study of individual differences. *Memory and Cognition* 10 (6), 540–545.

de Witt, R. (1997). *How to prepare for IELTS*. London: The British Council.

Dörnyei, Z., and Katona, L. (1992). Validation of the C-test amongst Hungarian EFL learners. *Language Testing*, vol. 9, 2, 187–206.

Douglas, D. (2000). *Assessing languages for specific purposes*. Cambridge: Cambridge University Press.

Drum, P. A., Calfee, R. C., and Cook, L. K. (1981). The effects of surface structure variables on performance in reading comprehension tests. *Reading Research Quarterly* 16, 486–514.

Duffy, G. G., Roehler, L. R., Sivan, E., Rackcliffe, G., Book, C., Meloth, M. S., Vavrus, L. G., Wesselman, R., Putnam, J., and Bassiri, D. (1987). Effects of explaining the reasoning associated with using reading strategies. *Reading Research Quarterly* XXII (3), 347–368.

Eignor, D., Taylor, C., Kirsch, I., and Jamieson, J. (1998). *Development of a scale for assessing the level of computer familiarity of TOEFL examinees*. TOEFL Research Report 60. Princeton, NJ: Educational Testing Service.

Engineer, W. (1977). *Proficiency in reading English as a second language*. Unpublished PhD thesis, University of Edinburgh.

Erickson, M., and Molloy, J. (1983). ESP test development for engineering students. In J. Oller (ed.), *Issues in language testing research*. Rowley, MA: Newbury House.

Eskey, D., and Grabe, W. (1988). Interactive models for second-language reading: perspectives on interaction. In P. Carrell, J. Devine, and D. Eskey (eds.), *Interactive approaches to second-language reading*. Cambridge: Cambridge University Press.

Farr, R. (1971). Measuring reading comprehension: an historical perspective. In F. P. Green (ed.), *Twentieth yearbook of the National Reading Conference*. Milwaukee: National Reading Conference.

Flores d'Arcais, G. (1990). Praising principles and language comprehension during reading. In D. Balota, G. Flores d'Arcais, K. Rayner, *Comprehension processes in reading*. Hillsdale, NJ: Lawrence Erlbaum.

Fordham, P., Holland, D., and Millican, J. (1995). *Adult literacy: a handbook for development workers.* Oxford: Oxfam/Voluntary Service Overseas.

Forrest-Pressley, D. L., and Waller, T. G. (1984). *Cognition, metacognition and reading.* New York: Springer Verlag.

Fransson, A. (1984). Cramming or understanding? Effects of intrinsic and extrinsic motivation on approach to learning and test performance. In J. C. Alderson and A. H. Urquhart (eds.), *Reading in a foreign language.* London: Longman.

Freebody, P., and Anderson, R. C. (1983). Effects of vocabulary difficulty, text cohesion, and schema availability on reading comprehension. *Reading Research Quarterly* XVIII (3), 277–294.

Freedle, R., and Kostin, I. (1993). The prediction of TOEFL reading item difficulty: implications for construct validity. *Language Testing* 10, 133–170.

Fuchs, L. S., Fuchs, D., and Deno, S. L. (1982). Reliability and validity of curriculum-based Informal Reading Inventories. *Reading Research Quarterly* XVIII (1), 6–25.

García, G. E., and Pearson, P. D. (1991). The role of assessment in a diverse society. In E. F. Hiebert (ed.), *Literacy for a diverse society.* New York: Teachers College Press.

Garner, R., Wagoner, S., and Smith, T. (1983). Externalizing question-answering strategies of good and poor comprehenders. *Reading Research Quarterly* XVIII (4), 439–447.

Garnham, A. (1985). *Psycholinguistics: central topics.* New York: Methuen.

Goetz, E. T., Sadoski, M., Arturo Olivarez, J., Calero-Breckheimner, A., Garner, P., and Fatemi, Z. (1992). The structure of emotional response in reading a literary text: Quantitative and qualitative analyses. *Reading Research Quarterly* 27 (4), 361–371.

Goodman, K. S. (1969). Analysis of oral reading miscues: Applied psycholinguistics. *Reading Research Quarterly* 5, 9–30.

Goodman, K. S. (1973). *Theoretically based studies of patterns of miscues in oral reading performance* (Final Report Project No. 9–0375). Washington, DC: US Department of Health, Education and Welfare, Office of Education, Bureau of Research.

Goodman, K. S. (1982). *Process, theory, research.* (Vol. 1). London: Routledge and Kegan Paul.

Goodman, K. S., and Gollasch, F. V. (1980). Word omissions: deliberate and non-deliberate. *Reading Research Quarterly* XVI (1), 6–31.

Goodman, Y. M. (1991). Informal methods of evaluation. In J. Flood, J. M. Jensen, D. Lapp, and J. Squire (eds.), *Handbook of research on teaching the English language arts.* New York: Macmillan.

Goodman, Y. M., and Burke, C. L. (1972). *Reading miscue inventory kit.* New York: The MacMillan Company.

Gorman, T. P., Purves, A. C., and Degenhart, R. E. (eds.). (1988). *The IEA study of written composition 1: the international writing tasks and scoring scales*. Oxford: Pergamon Press,

Gottlieb, M. (1995). Nurturing student learning through portfolios. *TESOL Journal* 5 (1), 12–14.

Gough, P., Ehri, L., and Treiman, R. (eds.). (1992a). *Reading Acquisition*. Hillsdale, NJ: L Erlbaum.

Gough, P., Juel, C., and Griffith, P. (1992b). Reading, speaking and the orthographic cipher. In P. Gough, L. Ehri, and R. Treiman (eds.), *Reading acquisition*. Hillsdale, NJ: L. Erlbaum.

Grabe, W. (1991). Current developments in second-language reading research. *TESOL Quarterly* 25 (3), 375–406.

Grabe, W. (2000). Developments in reading research and their implications for computer-adaptive reading assessment. In M. Chalhoub-Deville (ed.), *Issues in computer-adaptive tests of reading*. Cambridge: Cambridge University Press.

Gray, W. S. (1960). The major aspects of reading. In H. Robinson (ed.), *Sequential development of reading abilities* (Vol. 90, pp. 8–24). Chicago: Chicago University Press.

Grellet, F. (1981). *Developing reading skills*. Cambridge: Cambridge University Press.

Griffin, P., Smith, P. G., and Burrill, L. E. (1995). *The Literacy Profile Scales: towards effective assessment*. Belconnen, ACT: Australian Curriculum Studies Association, Inc.

Guthrie, J. T., Seifert, M., and Kirsch, I. S. (1986). Effects of education, occupation, and setting on reading practices. *American Educational Research Journal* 23, 151–160.

Hagerup-Neilsen, A. R. (1977). *Role of macrostructures and linguistic connectives in comprehending familiar and unfamiliar written discourse*. Unpublished PhD thesis, University of Minnesota.

Halasz, L. (1991). Emotional effect and reminding in literary processing. *Poetics* 20, 247–272.

Hale, G. A. (1988). Student major field and text content: interactive effects on reading comprehension in the Test of English as a Foreign Language. *Language Testing* 5 (1), 49–61.

Halliday, M. A. K. (1979). *Language as social semiotic*. London: Edward Arnold.

Hamilton, M., Barton, D., and Ivanic, R. (eds.). (1994). *Worlds of literacy*. Clevedon: Multilingual Matters.

Haquebord, H. (1989) Reading comprehension of Turkish and Dutch students attending secondary schools. Unpublished PhD thesis, University of Gronigen.

Harri-Augstein, S., and Thomas, L. (1984). Conversational investigations of reading: the self-organized learner and the text. In J. C. Alderson and A. H. Urquhart (eds.), *Reading in a foreign language*. London: Longman.

Harrison, C. (1979). Assessing the readability of school texts. In E. Lunzer and K. Gardner (eds.), *The effective use of reading*. London: Heinemann.

Heaton, J. B. (1988). *Writing English language tests*. (Second ed.). Harlow: Longman.

Hill, C., and Parry, K. (1992). The Test at the gate: models of literacy in reading assessment. *TESOL Quarterly* 26 (3), 433–461.

Hirsh, D. and Nation, P. (1992). What vocabulary size is needed to read unsimplified texts for pleasure? *Reading in a Foreign Language* 8 (2), 689–696.

Hock, T. S. (1990). The role of prior knowledge and language proficiency as predictors of reading comprehension among undergraduates. In J. H. A. L. d. Jong and D. K. Stevenson (eds.), *Individualizing the assessment of language abilities*. Clevedon, PA: Multilingual Matters.

Holland, D. (1990). *The Progress Profile*. London: Adult Literacy and Basic Skills Unit (ALBSU).

Holland, P. W., and Rubin, D. B. (eds.). (1982). *Test Equating*. New York: Academic Press.

Holt, D. (1994). *Assessing success in family literacy projects: alternative approaches to assessment and evaluation*. Washington, DC: Center for Applied Linguistics.

Hosenfeld, C. (1977). A preliminary investigation of the reading strategies of successful and nonsuccessful second language learners. *System* 5 (2), 110–123.

Hosenfeld, C. (1979). Cindy: a learner in today's foreign language classroom. In W. C. Born (ed.), *The learner in today's environment*. Montpelier, VT: NE Conference in the Teaching of Foreign Languages.

Hosenfeld, C. (1984). Case studies of ninth grade readers. In J. C. Alderson and A. H. Urquhart (eds.), *Reading in a foreign language*. London: Longman.

Hudson, T. (1982). The effects of induced schemata on the 'short-circuit' in L2 reading: non-decoding factors in L2 reading performance. *Language Learning* 32 (1), 1–31.

Huerta-Macías, A. (1995). Alternative assessment: responses to commonly asked questions. *TESOL Journal* 5 (1), 8–11.

Hughes, A. (1989). *Testing for language teachers*. Cambridge: Cambridge University Press.

Hunt, K. W. (1965). *Grammatical structures written at 3 grade levels*. Champaign, IL: National Council of Teachers of English.

Ivanic, R., and Hamilton, M. (1989). Literacy beyond schooling. In D. Wray, *Emerging partnerships in language and literacy*. Clevedon: Multilingual Matters.

Jakobson, R. (1960). Linguistics and poetics. In T. A. Sebeok (ed.), *Style in language*. New York: Wiley.

Jamieson, J., and Chapelle, C. (1987). Working styles on computers as evidence of second language learning strategies. *Language Learning* 37 (523–544).

Johnston, P. (1984). Prior knowledge and reading comprehension test bias. *Reading Research Quarterly* XIX (2), 219–239.

Jonz, J. (1991). Cloze item types and second language comprehension. *Language Testing*, vol. 8, 1, 1–22.

Kinneavy, J. L. (1971). *A theory of discourse*. Englewood Cliffs, NJ: Prentice Hall.

Kintsch, W., and van Dijk, T. A. (1978). Toward a model of text comprehension and production. *Psychological Review* 85, 363–394.

Kintsch, W., and Yarbrough, J. C. (1982). Role of rhetorical structure in text comprehension. *Educational Psychology* 74 (6), 828–834.

Kirsch, I., Jamieson, J., Taylor, C., and Eignor, D. (1998). *Familiarity among TOEFL examinees* (TOEFL Research Report 59). Princeton, NJ: Educational Testing Service.

Kirsch, I. S., and Jungblut, A. (1986). *Literacy: profiles of America's young adults* (NAEP Report 16–PL-01). Princeton, NJ: Educational Testing Service.

Kirsch, I. S., and Mosenthal, P. B. (1990). Exploring document literacy: Variables underlying the performance of young adults. *Reading Research Quarterly* XXV (1), 5–30.

Klein-Braley, C. (1985). A cloze-up on the C-test: a study in the construct validation of authentic tests. *Language Testing*, vol. 2, 1, 76–104.

Klein-Braley, C., and Raatz, U. (1984). A survey of research on the C-test. *Language Testing*, vol. 1, 2, 134–146.

Koda, K. (1987). Cognitive strategy transfer in second-language reading. In J. Devine, P. Carrell, and D. E. Eskey (eds.), *Research in reading in a second language*. Washington, DC: TESOL.

Koda, K. (1996). L2 word recognition research: a critical review. *The Modern Language Journal* 80 (iv), 450–460.

Koh, M. Y. (1985). The role of prior knowledge in reading comprehension. *Journal of Reading in a Foreign Language*, vol. 3, 1, 375–380.

Kundera, M. (1996). *The Book of Laughter and Forgetting*. Faber and Faber. Translation by A. Asher.

Laufer, B. (1989). What percentage of text-lexis is essential for comprehension? In C. Lauren and M. Nordman (eds.), *Special language: from humans thinking to thinking machines*. Philadelphia: Multilingual Matters.

Lee, J. F. (1986). On the use of the recall task to measure L2 reading comprehension. *Studies in Second Language Acquisition* 8 (1), 83–93.

Lee, J. F., and Musumeci, D. (1988). On hierarchies of reading skills and text types. *Modern Language Journal* 72, 173–187.

Lennon, R. T. (1962). What can be measured? *Reading Teacher* 15, 326–337.

Lewkowicz, J. A. (1997). *Investigating authenticity in language testing*. Unpublished PhD thesis, Lancaster University.

Li, W. (1992). *What is a test testing? An investigation of the agreement between students' test-taking processes and test constructors' presumptions.* Unpublished MA thesis, Lancaster University.

Liu, N., and Nation, I. S. P. (1985). Factors affecting guessing vocabulary in context. *RELC Journal* 16 (1), 33–42.

Lumley, T. (1993). The notion of subskills in reading comprehension tests: an EAP example. *Language Testing* 10 (3), 211–234.

Lunzer, E., and Gardner, K. (eds.) (1979). *The effective use of reading.* London: Heinemann Educational Books.

Lunzer, E., Waite, M., and Dolan, T. (1979). Comprehension and comprehension tests. In E. Lunzer and K. Garner (eds.), *The effective use of reading.* London: Heinemann Educational Books.

Lytle, S., Belzer, A., Schultz, K., and Vannozzi, M. (1989). Learner-centred literacy assessment: An evolving process. In A. Fingeret and P. Jurmo (eds.), *Participatory literacy education.* San Francisco: Jossey-Bass.

Mandler, J. M. (1978). A code in the node: the use of a story schema in retrieval. *Discourse Processes* 1 (114–35).

Manning, W. H. (1987). *Development of cloze-elide tests of English as a second language* (TOEFL Research Report 23). Princeton, NJ: Educational Testing Service.

Martinez, J. G. R., and Johnson, P. J. (1982). An analysis of reading proficiency and its relationship to complete and partial report performance. *Reading Research Quarterly* XVIII (1), 105–122.

Matthews, M. (1990). Skill taxonomies and problems for the testing of reading. *Reading in a Foreign Language* 7 (1), 511–517.

McKeon, J., and Thorogood, J. (1998). *How it's done: language portfolios for students of language NVQ units. Tutor's Guide.* London: Centre for Information on Language Teaching and Research.

McKeown, M. G., Beck, I. L., Sinatra, G. M., and Loxterman, J. A. (1992). The contribution of prior knowledge and coherent text to comprehension. *Reading Research Quarterly* 27 (1), 79–93.

McNamara, M. J., and Deane, D. (1995). Self-assessment activities: toward autonomy in language learning. *TESOL Journal* 5 (1), 17–21.

Mead, R. (1982). Review of Munby, J. 'Communicative syllabus design'. *Applied Linguistics* 3 (1), 70–77.

Messick, S. (1996). Validity and washback in language testing. *Language Testing* 13 (3), 241–256.

Meyer, B. (1975). *The organisation of prose and its effects on memory.* New York, NY: North Holland.

Miall, D. S. (1989). Beyond the schema given: Affective comprehension of literary narratives. *Cognition and Emotion* 3, 55–78.

Mislevy, R. J., and Verhelst, N. (1990). Modelling item responses when different subjects employ different solution strategies. *Psychometrika* 55 (2), 195–215.

Mitchell, D., Cuetos, F., and Zagar, D. (1990). Reading in different languages: is there a universal mechanism for parsing sentences? In D. Balota, G. F. d'Arcais, and K. Rayner (eds.), *Comprehension processes in reading*. Hillsdale, NJ: Lawrence Erlbaum.

Moffet, J. (1968). *Teaching the universe of discourse*. Boston, MA: Houghton Mifflin.

Mountford, A. (1975). *Discourse analysis and the simplification of reading materials for ESP*. Unpublished MLitt thesis, University of Edinburgh.

Moy, R. H. (1975). *The effect of vocabulary clues, content familiarity and English proficiency on cloze scores*. Unpublished Master's thesis, UCLA, Los Angeles.

Munby, J. (1968). *Read and think*. Harlow: Longman.

Munby, J. (1978). *Communicative syllabus design*. Cambridge: Cambridge University Press.

Nesi, H., and Meara, P. (1991). How using dictionaries affects performance in multiple-choice EFL tests. *Reading in a Foreign Language* 8 (1), 631–645.

Nevo, N. (1989). Test-taking strategies on a multiple-choice test of reading comprehension. *Language Testing* 6 (2), 199–215.

Newman, C., and Smolen, L. (1993). Portfolio assessment in our schools: implementation, advantages and concerns. *Mid-Western Educational Researcher* 6, 28–32.

North, B., and Schneider, G. (1998). Scaling descriptors for language proficiency scales. *Language Testing* 15 (2), 217–262.

Nuttall, C. (1982). *Teaching reading skills in a foreign language*. (First ed.). London: Heinemann.

Nuttall, C. (1996). *Teaching reading skills in a foreign language*. (Second ed.). Oxford: Heinemann English Language Teaching.

Oller, J. W. (1973). Cloze tests of second language proficiency and what they measure. *Language Learning* 23 (1).

Oller, J. W. (1979). *Language tests at school: a pragmatic approach*. London: Longman.

Oltman, P. K. (1990). *User interface design: Review of some recent literature* (Unpublished research report). Princeton, NJ: Educational Testing Service.

Patton, M. Q. (1987). *Creative evaluation*. Newbury Park, CA: Sage.

Pearson, P. D., and Johnson, D. D. (1978). *Teaching reading comprehension*. New York, NJ: Holt, Rinehart and Winston.

Peretz, A. S., and Shoham, M. (1990). Testing reading comprehension in LSP. *Reading in a Foreign Language* 7 (1), 447–455.

Perfetti, C. (1989). There are generalized abilities and one of them is reading. In L. Resnick (ed.), *Knowing, learning and instruction*. Hillsdale, NJ: Lawrence Erlbaum.

Perkins, K. (1987). The relationship between nonverbal schematic concept formation and story comprehension. In J. Devine, P. L. Carrell and D. E. Eskey (eds.), *Research in Reading in English as a Second Language*. Washington, DC: TESOL.

Pollitt, A., Hutchinson, C., Entwistle, N., and DeLuca, C. (1985). *What makes exam questions difficult? An analysis of 'O' grade questions and answers*. Edinburgh: Scottish Academic Press.

Porter, D. (1988). Book review of Manning: 'Development of cloze-elide tests of English as a second language'. *Language Testing* 5 (2), 250–252.

Pressley, M., Snyder, B. L., Levin, J. R., Murray, H. G., and Ghatala, E. S. (1987). Perceived readiness for examination performance (PREP) produced by initial reading of text and text containing adjunct questions. *Reading Research Quarterly* XXII (2), 219–236.

Purpura, J. (1997). An analysis of the relationships between test takers' cognitive and metacognitive strategy use and second language test performance. *Language Learning* 42 (2) 289–325.

Rankin, E. F., and Culhane, J. W. (1969). Comparable cloze and multiple-choice comprehension scores. *Journal of Reading* 13, 193–198.

Rayner, K. (1990). Comprehension process: an introduction. In D. A. Balota *et al.* (eds.) (1990).

Rayner, K., and Pollatsek, A. (1989). *The psychology of reading*. Englewood Cliffs, NJ: Prentice Hall.

Read, J. (2000). *Assessing vocabulary*. Cambridge: Cambridge University Press.

Rigg, P. (1977). *The miscue–ESL project*. Paper presented at TESOL, 1977: Teaching and learning ESL.

Riley, G. L., and Lee, J. F. (1996). A comparison of recall and summary protocols as measures of second-language reading comprehension. *Language Testing* 13 (2), 173–189.

Ross, S. (1998). Self-assessment in second language testing: a meta-analysis and analysis of experiential factors. *Language Testing* 15 (1), 1–20.

Rost, D. (1993). Assessing the different components of reading comprehension: fact or fiction? *Language Testing* 10 (1), 79–92.

Rubin, J. (1987). Learner strategies: theoretical assumption, research history. In Wenden and Rubin (eds.).

Rumelhart, D. E. (1977). *Introduction to Human Information Processing*. New York: Wiley.

Rumelhart, D. E. (1977). Toward an interactive model of reading. In S. Domic (ed.). *Attention and Performance UL*. New York: Academic Press.

Rumelhart, D. E. (1980). Schemata: the building blocks of cognition. In R. J. Spiro *et al.* (eds.), pp. 123–156.

Rumelhart, D. E. (1985). Towards an interactive model of reading. In H. Singer and R. B. Ruddell (eds.), *Theoretical models and processes of reading*. Newark, Delaware: International Reading Association.

Salager-Meyer, F. (1991). Reading expository prose at the post-secondary level: the influence of textual variables on L2 reading comprehension (a genre-based approach). *Reading in a Foreign Language* 8 (1), 645–662.

Samuels, S. J., and Kamil, M. J. (1988). Models of the reading process. In P. Carrell, J. Devine, and D. Eskey (eds.), *Interactive approaches to second-language reading.* Cambridge: Cambridge University Press.

Schank, R. C. (1978). Predictive understanding. In R. N. Campbell and P. T. Smith (eds.), *Recent advances in the psychology of language – formal and experimental approaches.* New York, NJ: Plenum Press.

Schlesinger, I. M. (1968). *Sentence structure and the reading process.* The Hague: Mouton (Janua Linguarum 69).

Schmidt, H. H., and Vann, R. (1992). *Classroom format and student reading strategies: a case study.* Paper presented at the 26th Annual TESOL Convention, Vancouver, BC.

Seddon, G. M. (1978). The properties of Bloom's Taxonomy of Educational Objectives for the Cognitive Domain. *Review of Educational Research* 48 (2), 303–323.

Segalowitz, N., Poulsen, C., and Komoda, M. (1991). Lower level components or reading skill in higher level bilinguals: Implications for reading instruction. In J. H. Hulstijn and J. F. Matter (eds.), *Reading in two languages,* AILA Review, vol. 8, pp. 15–30. Amsterdam: Free University Press.

Shohamy, E. (1984). Does the testing method make a difference? The case of reading comprehension. *Language Testing* 1 (2), 147–170.

Silberstein, S. (1994). *Techniques and resources in teaching reading.* Oxford: Oxford University Press.

Skehan, P. (1984). Issues in the testing of English for specific purposes. *Language Testing* 1 (2), 202–220.

Smith, F. (1971). *Understanding reading.* New York, NY: Holt, Rinehart and Winston.

Spearitt, D. (1972). Identification of subskills of reading comprehension by maximum likelihood factor analysis. *Reading Research Quarterly* 8, 92–111.

Spiro, R. J., Bruce, B. C. and Brewer, W. F. (eds.) (1980) *Theoretical issues in reading comprehension.* Hillsdale, NJ: Erlbaum.

Stanovich, K. E. (1980). Towards an interactive compensatory model of individual differences in the development of reading fluency. *Reading Research Quarterly* 16 (1), 32–71.

Steen, G. (1994). *Understanding metaphor in literature.* London and New York: Longman.

Steffensen, M. S. Joag-Dev, C., and Anderson, R. C. (1979). A Cross-cultural Perspective on Reading Comprehension. *Reading Research Quarterly* 15, 10–29.

Storey, P. (1994). *Investigating construct validity through test-taker introspection.* Unpublished PhD thesis, University of Reading.

Storey, P. (1997). Examining the test-taking process: a cognitive perspective on the discourse cloze test. *Language Testing* 14 (2), 214–231.

Street, B. V. (1984). *Literacy in theory and practice.* Cambridge: Cambridge University Press.

Strother, J. B., and Ulijn, J. M. (1987). Does syntactic rewriting affect English for science and technology (EST) text comprehension? In J. Devine, P. L. Carrell, and D. E. Eskey (eds.), *Research in reading in English as a second language.* Washington, DC: TESOL.

Suarez, A., and Meara, P. (1989). The effects of irregular orthography on the processing of words in a foreign language. *Reading in a Foreign Language* 6 (1), 349–356.

Swain, M. (1985). Large-scale communicative testing: A case study. In Y. P. Lee, C. Y. Y. Fox, R. Lord and G. Low (eds.), *New Directions in Language Testing.* Hong Kong: Pergamon Press.

Swales, J. M. (1990). *Genre analysis: English in academic and research settings.* Cambridge: Cambridge University Press.

Taylor, C., Jamieson, J., Eignor, D., and Kirsch, I. (1998). *The relationship between computer familiarity and performance on computer-based TOEFL tasks* (TOEFL Research Report 61). Princeton, NJ: Educational Testing Service.

Taylor, W. L. (1953). Cloze procedure: a new tool for measuring readability. *Journalism Quarterly* 30, 415–453.

Thompson, I. (1987). Memory in language learning. In A. Wenden and J. Rubin (eds.) (pp. 43–56).

Thorndike, R. L. (1917). *Reading as reasoning.* Paper presented at the American Psychological Association, Washington, DC.

Thorndike, R. L. (1974). Reading as reasoning. *Reading Research Quarterly* 9, 135–147.

Thorndike, E. L. and Lorge, I. (1944). *The Teacher's word book of 30,000 words.* New York, NY: Teachers College, Columbia University.

Tomlinson, B., and Ellis, R. (1988). *Reading. Advanced.* Oxford: Oxford University Press.

UCLES (1997a). *First Certificate in English: a handbook.* Cambridge: UCLES.

UCLES (1997b). *Preliminary English Test Handbook.* Cambridge: UCLES.

UCLES (1998a). *Certificate of Advanced English handbook.* Cambridge: UCLES.

UCLES (1998b). *Certificate of Proficiency in English handbook.* Cambridge: UCLES.

UCLES (1998c). *Cambridge Examinations in English for Language Teachers handbook.* Cambridge: UCLES.

UCLES (1998d). *Key English Test handbook.* Cambridge: UCLES.

UCLES (1999a). *Certificate in Communicative Skills in English handbook.* Cambridge: UCLES.

UCLES (1999b). *International English Language Testing System handbook and specimen materials.* Cambridge: UCLES, The British Council, IDP Education, Australia.

Urquhart, A. H. (1984). The effect of rhetorical ordering on readability. In J. C. Alderson and A. H. Urquhart (eds.), *Reading in a foreign language.* London: Longman.

Urquhart, A. H. (1992). *Draft band descriptors for reading* (Report to the IELTS Research Committee ). Plymouth: College of St Mark and St John.

Vähäpassi, A. (1988). The domain of school writing and development of the writing tasks. In T. P. Gorman, A. C. Purves and R. E. Degenhart (eds.), *The IEA study of written composition I: The international writing tasks and scoring scales.* Oxford: Pergamon Press.

Valencia, S. W. (1990). A portfolio approach to classroom reading assessment: the whys, whats and hows. *The Reading Teacher* 43, 60–61.

Valencia, S. W., and Stallman, A. C. (1989). Multiple measures of prior knowledge. Comparative predictive validity. *Yearbook of the National Reading Conference, 38,* 427–436.

van Dijk, T. A. (1977). *Text and Context: Explorations in the Semantics of Text.* London: Longman.

van Dijk, T. A., and Kintsch, W. (1983). *Strategies of discourse comprehension.* New York: Academic Press.

van Peer, W. (1986). *Stylistics and Psychology: Investigations of Foregrounding.* London: Croom Helm.

Vellutino, F. R., and Scanlon, D. M. (1987). Linguistic coding and reading ability. In D. S. Rosenberg (ed.), *Reading, writing and language learning* (vol. 2, pp. 1–69). Cambridge: Cambridge University Press.

Wallace, C. (1992). *Reading.* Oxford: Oxford University Press.

Weir, C. J. (1990). *Communicative language testing.* London: Prentice Hall International (UK) Ltd.

Weir, C. J. (1993). *Understanding and developing language tests.* Hemel Hempstead: Prentice Hall International (UK) Ltd.

Weir, C. J. (1983). Identifying the language problems of overseas students in tertiary education in the UK. Unpublished PhD thesis, Institute of Education, University of London.

Weir, C. J. (1994). *Reading as multi-divisible or unitary: between Scylla and Charybdis.* Paper presented at the RELC, SEAMEO Regional Language Centre, Singapore.

Wenden, A. (1987). Conceptual background and utility. In A. Wenden and J. Rubin (eds.), *Learner strategies in language learning.* London: Prentice Hall International.

Wenden, A., and Rubin, J. (eds.) (1987). *Learner strategies in language learning.* London: Prentice Hall International.

Werlich, E. (1976). *A text grammar of English.* Heidelberg: Quelle and Meyer.

Werlich, E. (1988). *A student's guide to text production.* Berlin: Cornelsen Verlag.

West, M. (1953). *A general service list of English words.* London: Longman.

Widdowson, H. G. (1978). *Teaching language as communication.* Oxford: Oxford University Press.

Widdowson, H. G. (1979). *Explorations in applied linguistics.* Oxford: Oxford University Press.

Williams, R., and Dallas, D. (1984). Aspects of vocabulary in the readability of content area L2 educational textbooks: a case study. In J. C. Alderson and A. H. Urquhart (eds.), *Reading in a foreign language.* London: Longman.

Wood, C. T. (1974). *Processing units in reading.* Unpublished doctoral dissertation, Stanford University.

Yamashita, J. (1992). *The relationship between foreign language reading, native language reading, and foreign language ability: interaction between cognitive processing and language processing.* Unpublished MA thesis, Lancaster University.

Zwaan, R. A. (1993). *Aspects of literary comprehension: a cognitive approach.* Amsterdam, PA: John Benjamins Publishing Company.

# Index

Abdullah, K. B. 21
ability
    general cognitive problem-solving 48
    synthesising 114
    *see also* communicative language
        ability; general reading ability;
        reading ability
abstracts, article 64
academic purposes
    reading for *see* academic reading
    testing for 109, 154, 292
academic reading 104, 130–1, 180
    and grammar test 98
access, lexical 76
accuracy criteria 268
achievement, measures of 350–1
acquisition, hierarchy of 8
ACTFL *see* American Council for the
    Teaching of Foreign Languages
    (ACTFL)
Adams, M. J. 20
adaptive tests 162, 198
adjunct questions 42, 51
administration of test 168, 198
admissions decisions, example 178–85,
    292
adult literacy 257, 269
    informal assessment of 257, 258

Adult Literacy Basic Skills Unit
    (ALBSU), UK 260
Advanced Reading, examples 322–30
advertisements 77
affect 4, 54–6, 83, 123, 165–6, 202
ALBSU *see* Adult Literacy Basic Skills
    Unit (ALBSU)
Allan, A. I. C. G. 304, 331, 333, 334
Allen, E. D. 279–80
ALTE *see* Association of Language
    Testers in Europe (ALTE)
Alvarez, G. 346
American Council for the Teaching of
    Foreign Languages (ACTFL),
    proficiency guidelines 104, 278–81
amount of reading 283
analytic approaches *see* discrete-point
    methods
Anderson, N. 87, 88–9, 97
Anderson, R. C. 68, 69
anonymity 144
answers *see* responses
Anthony, R. 269
antonymy, gradable 346
anxiety 54–5, 56, 83, 123
    *see also* state anxiety; trait anxiety
applied linguistics 61, 77
appreciation 95, 115, 123, 133

questions (ctd.)
  with or without presence of text
    106–8, 114
  *see also* multiple-choice questions;
    textually explicit; textually implicit

Raatz, U. 225
raters
  inter-rater correlation 231–2
  reliability 151
  training 96, 151, 170, 304
rating instruments 89–90, 96–7, 304
rauding (Carver), 12, 52, 57–8, 106
rauding rate 47, 57–8
Rayner, K. 35, 56, 57, 75
re-reading 133
reactivity 162–3
  adaptivity 163, 184
  non-reciprocal 163, 196
  reciprocal 162–3
Read, J. 35, 99
readability 5, 71–4, 83–4, 205
  and cohesion 67–8
  formulae 71–2, 280
  measures of 71–2
  and vocabulary difficulty 99
reader intent *see* purpose of reading
reader variables 32, 33–60, 80
readers
  active 19
  defining the construct of reading
    ability 116–37
  distinguishing types of 5
  as passive decoders 17
  personal characteristics of 165
  practised and unpractised 37–8
  stable characteristics 33, 56–60
  *see also* bilingual readers; good
    readers; poor readers
reading
  and cognition 21–2
  constructs of 120–4
  contamination with writing 236
  Gough's two-component theory of 35
  integration into other language use
    tasks 147–8
  and intelligence 101–2

as meaning construction 6, 25
multi-divisibility view of 305–6
the nature of 1–31, 84
and other literacy skills 12, 25–6,
  147–8
passive 7, 17
'pure' measures of 26
and reasoning 21, 22, 101–2
in relation to its uses 167–201
as socio-cultural practice 25–8
task characteristics 13–16
and thinking 21–2
reading ability
  components of 94–5
  construct of 1–2, 116–37
  defining 49, 355
  descriptors of 132–4
  and levels of understanding 7–8,
    9–13
  predictions of 18
  and thinking ability 22
  transfer across languages 23–4
  *see also* reading skills; reading
    subskills
reading aloud 4, 186–7, 257, 259
  omissions of words from text 340
reading assessment
  future procedures 112–13
  guidelines for 29–30
  nature of 110–13
  research into 85–115
reading comprehension exercises,
  classification of 312–13
reading comprehension tests 21, 47
Reading Diets 258, 259
reading with intrinsic motivation *see*
  extensive reading
reading knowledge, and language
  knowledge 23–4
reading for pleasure *see* extensive
  reading
reading process 13–16, 356
  text-based factors and knowledge-
    based factors 338
reading processes, Carver's basic 52
reading rate/speed *see* speed,
  reading